Digital Asset Valuation and Cyber Risk
Measurement

Digital Asset Valuation and Cyber Risk Measurement
Principles of Cybernomics

Keyun Ruan

ACADEMIC PRESS
An imprint of Elsevier

Academic Press is an imprint of Elsevier
125 London Wall, London EC2Y 5AS, United Kingdom
525 B Street, Suite 1650, San Diego, CA 92101, United States
50 Hampshire Street, 5th Floor, Cambridge, MA 02139, United States
The Boulevard, Langford Lane, Kidlington, Oxford OX5 1GB, United Kingdom

Notices
Knowledge and best practice in this field are constantly changing. As new research and experience broaden our understanding,
changes in research methods, professional practices, or medical treatment may become necessary.

Practitioners and researchers must always rely on their own experience and knowledge in evaluating and using any information,
methods, compounds, or experiments described herein. In using such information or methods they should be mindful of their
own safety and the safety of others, including parties for whom they have a professional responsibility.

To the fullest extent of the law, neither the Publisher nor the authors, contributors, or editors, assume any liability for any injury
and/or damage to persons or property as a matter of products liability, negligence or otherwise, or from any use or operation of
any methods, products, instructions, or ideas contained in the material herein.

British Library Cataloguing-in-Publication Data
A catalogue record for this book is available from the British Library

Library of Congress Cataloging-in-Publication Data
A catalog record for this book is available from the Library of Congress

ISBN: 978-0-12-812158-0

For Information on all Academic Press publications
visit our website at https://www.elsevier.com/books-and-journals

Publisher: Candice Janco
Acquisition Editor: J. Scott Bentley
Editorial Project Manager: Susan Ikeda
Production Project Manager: Kiruthika Govindaraju
Cover Designer: Victoria Pearson

Typeset by MPS Limited, Chennai, India

To Grandpa

Contents

Preface   xv
Introduction   xvii

1. Digital Assets as Economic Goods   1

1.1 Origins and Philosophical Concepts of Value   2
   1.1.1 Subjective View Versus Objective View   2
   1.1.2 Intrinsic Value Versus Extrinsic Value   4
1.2 What Is an Economic Good?   4
1.3 What Is an Asset?   5
   1.3.1 Definition of Asset   5
   1.3.2 Current Asset Valuation Methods   5
1.4 What Are Digital Assets?   6
   1.4.1 Categorization of Digital Assets   7
     1.4.1.1 *(Networked) System Assets*   7
     1.4.1.2 *Software Assets*   7
     1.4.1.3 *Hardware Assets*   7
     1.4.1.4 *Service Assets*   7
     1.4.1.5 *Robotic Assets*   8
     1.4.1.6 *Data Assets*   8
     1.4.1.7 *Metadata Assets*   8
     1.4.1.8 *Digitally Enabled Devices*   8
   1.4.2 Managing Digital Assets in an Organization   8
     1.4.2.1 *Information Resource Management*   8
     1.4.2.2 *Digital Assets Management*   9
1.5 Unique Attributes of Digital Assets   9
   1.5.1 Characteristic 1: Digital Value Creation Does Not Decrease but Increases Through Usage   10
   1.5.2 Characteristic 2: Duplication Does Not Increase Digital Value   10
   1.5.3 Characteristic 3: Digital Value Production and Distribution Entails Higher Fixed Costs and Lower Variable Costs   10
   1.5.4 Characteristic 4: Digital Value Can Be Distributed via Multi-Sided Markets   10

   1.5.5 Characteristic 5: Digital Value Is Limitless   11
     1.5.5.1 *Characteristic 5a: Digital Value Has Limitless Utility to the Owner*   11
     1.5.5.2 *Characteristic 5b: There Are Limitless Opportunities to Distribute and Consume Digital Value*   11
1.6 Digital Value Matrix: Categorization of Digital Assets Based on Their Economic Functions   11
   1.6.1 Digital Asset on an Individual Level   13
   1.6.2 Digital Asset on an Organizational Level   13
   1.6.3 Digital Asset on a National Level   14
   1.6.4 Digital Asset on the Global Level   14
1.7 Valuation of Digital Assets as Economic Goods   14
   1.7.1 Attributes of Digital Assets Contribute to Intrinsic Digital Value Creation   14
     1.7.1.1 *Data Quality*   14
     1.7.1.2 *Risk Exposure*   15
     1.7.1.3 *Age*   15
     1.7.1.4 *Data Volume*   18
     1.7.1.5 *System Quality*   19
     1.7.1.6 *Production Cost*   19
   1.7.2 Attributes of Digital Assets Contribute to Extrinsic Digital Value Creation   19
     1.7.2.1 *Exclusivity*   19
     1.7.2.2 *Network Connectivity*   20
     1.7.2.3 *Accessibility*   20
     1.7.2.4 *Reproduction Cost*   21
     1.7.2.5 *Economies of Scale*   21
     1.7.2.6 *Data Format*   21
     1.7.2.7 *Level of Structure*   22
     1.7.2.8 *Delivery Cadence*   22
     1.7.2.9 *Power Supplies*   22
1.8 Existing Challenges for Digital Asset Valuation   23
   1.8.1 Inherent Challenges   23
   1.8.2 Market Challenges   23

1.8.3   Taxation Challenges   23
1.8.4   Regulatory and Standardization
         Challenges   23
**1.9   Current Methods for Digital Asset
        Valuation**   **23**
1.9.1   Intrinsic Value   24
1.9.2   Direct Conversion of Financial
         Value   24
1.9.3   Business and Performance
         Value   24
1.9.4   Cost-Based Models   25
1.9.5   Market-Based Models   26
1.9.6   Income-Based Models   27
1.9.7   Option Models   27

2.   Digital Theory of Value   29

**2.1   The Search for a Value Theory
        Supporting the Fourth Industrial
        Revolution**   **30**
2.1.1   Digitization of Everything   30
2.1.2   The Fourth Industrial Revolution   31
         2.1.2.1   Characteristic 1: Velocity   *32*
         *2.1.2.2   Characteristic 2: Cross-
                    Jurisdictional Economies
                    of Scale Without Mass*   *32*
         *2.1.2.3   Characteristic 3: Heavy
                    Reliance on Intangible
                    Assets, Especially
                    Intellectual Property*   *32*
         *2.1.2.4   Characteristic 4: The
                    Importance of Data, User
                    Participation, and Their
                    Synergies With Intellectual
                    Property*   *32*
         *2.1.2.5   Characteristic 5: Fusion of
                    Technologies*   *32*
         *2.1.2.6   Characteristic 6:
                    Consumption Externality*   *32*
         *2.1.2.7   Characteristic 7: Indirect
                    Network Effects*   *33*
         *2.1.2.8   Characteristic 8: Lock-In
                    Effects and Competition*   *33*
2.2   Models for Digital Asset Valuation   **33**
2.2.1   Method 1: Intrinsic Value   33
         *2.2.1.1   1a: Intrinsic Cost of
                    Production*   *33*
         *2.2.1.2   1b: Direct Financial
                    Conversion*   *33*
2.2.2   Method 2: Extrinsic Value   34
         2.2.2.1   2a: Market Value   *34*
         2.2.2.2   2b: Usage Value   *34*
2.2.3   Method 3: Subjective Value   35
2.2.4   Method 4: Opportunity Value   35

2.3   Measuring the Digital Economy   **35**
2.3.1   Measuring Rate of Digitalization of
         Traditional Industries: The Enabler
         and Multiplier   35
2.3.2   Measuring Digital-Native Industries:
         The "Smarter," More Intelligent
         Disrupter   38
Example: platform Revolution   *38*
2.3.3   Measuring the Invisible Economy:
         The Opportunity Value   40
2.4   Digital Theory of Value   **40**
2.4.1   Law of Machine Time   40
         *2.4.1.1   Phenomenon 1a: The
                    Underlying Exponential
                    Function*   *40*
         *2.4.1.2   Phenomenon 1b: The Future
                    Cannot Be Projected From
                    the Past using Current
                    Statistical Methods*   *42*
         *2.4.1.3   Principle 1a: Progress of
                    Digital Economy Should Be
                    Measured Against Machine
                    Time*   *42*
         *2.4.1.4   Principle 1b: Sensemaking
                    Is a Universal Challenge
                    and a Value Driver*   *42*
         *2.4.1.5   Principle 1c: Risk Management
                    Is an Island of Stability in
                    the Sea of Change*   *42*
2.4.2   Law of Recombination   43
         *2.4.2.1   Phenomenon 2a: Quality
                    Data Is the New Oil*   *43*
         *2.4.2.2   Phenomenon 2b: The Fusion
                    of Technologies Is the Fuel
                    for Innovative Breakthroughs*   *43*
         *2.4.2.3   Principle 2: Recombination
                    Is an Engine for Growth*   *43*
2.4.3   Law of Hyperconnectivity   43
         *2.4.3.1   Phenomenon 3a: New Era
                    of Globalized Societies*   *43*
         *2.4.3.2   Phenomenon 3b: New Era
                    of Complexity Economics*   *44*
         *2.4.3.3   Principle 3a: Hyperconnectivity
                    Is an Engine for Growth*   *45*
         *2.4.3.4   Principle 3b: The Gravity of
                    Value Creation will be
                    Increasingly in the Virtual
                    Space where Value Creation
                    is Location Independent*   *45*
         *2.4.3.5   Principle 3c: Nontechnical
                    Barriers Such As Geopolitical,
                    Regulations, and Legal
                    Frameworks Are Limiting
                    Factors*   *45*

2.4.4 Law of Subjectivity   45
    2.4.4.1 Phenomenon 4a: The
    Need to Be Entertained   45
    2.4.4.2 Phenomenon 4b: The
    Demand for Customization   46
    2.4.4.3 Principle 4: A Greater
    Component of Value Is
    Increasingly Subjective,
    Reflecting Only in an
    Entity's Willingness-to-Pay 46
2.4.5 Law of Abundance   46
    2.4.5.1 Phenomenon 5: Once
    Intrinsic Digital Value is
    Created, There are Limitless
    Ways to Multiply it with
    Extrinsic Digital Value   46
    2.4.5.2 Principle 5a: The Digitally
    Empowered Entity has
    Limitless Economic Potential 46
    2.4.5.3 Principle 5b: Consumer
    Reception and Power
    Supply Are Limiting Factors 46
    2.4.5.4 Principle 5c: The Attention
    of a Consumer Is the
    New Scarce Resource   46
2.4.6 Law of New Division of Labor   47
    2.4.6.1 Phenomenon 6a: Labor Is
    Increasingly a Less Important
    Factor in Value Production   47
    2.4.6.2 Phenomenon 6b: New
    Necessities and the Barrier to
    Entry in a Digitized Society 47
    2.4.6.3 Phenomenon 6c: Deep Learning
    and Machine Intelligence
    Are Still Inherently Limited 47
    2.4.6.4 Phenomenon 6d: Accuracy
    Is Not the Truth   48
    2.4.6.5 Principle 6a: The Digital
    Economy Is Creating a New
    Social Divide Based on the
    New Labor Value Chain   48
    2.4.6.6 Principle 6b: The Optimal
    Path to Intrinsic Value
    Creation Is a Combination
    of Human and Machine
    Intelligence   48

**3. Cyber Risk Management: A New
Era of Enterprise Risk Management   49**

3.1 History and Definitions of Risk   49
3.1.1 History of Risk   49
3.1.2 Definitions of Risk as a
    Multidimensional Concept   50

3.1.3 Risk in Computer
    Science and Engineering   50
3.1.4 Risk Can Only Be Relatively Objective 51
3.1.5 Decision Theory and Acceptable
    Risk   51
3.2 Enterprise Risk Management   52
3.2.1 The Discipline of Enterprise Risk
    Management   52
3.2.2 Cyber Risk Management: A New
    Era of Enterprise Risk Management 53
3.3 Risk Analysis   55
3.4 Risk Management   57
3.4.1 Risk Assessment   57
    3.4.1.1 Define the Risk Assessment
    Process   57
    3.4.1.2 System Characterization 57
    3.4.1.3 Risk Classification 57
    3.4.1.4 Threat Identification 57
    3.4.1.5 Vulnerability Assessment 63
    3.4.1.6 Likelihood Determination 66
    3.4.1.7 Impact Analysis   67
    3.4.1.8 Risk Determination   67
3.4.2 Risk Mitigation   68
3.4.3 Effectiveness Assessment   70
3.4.4 Continuous Monitoring   70
3.5 Risk Models   70
3.5.1 Qualitative and Quantitative Models   70
3.5.2 Quantitative Assessment   70
3.5.3 Qualitative Assessment   71
3.5.4 Other Models   71
    3.5.4.1 Perspective: Asset-driven,
    Service-driven, or Business
    driven   72
    3.5.4.2 Resource Valuation:
    Vertical or Horizontal   72
    3.5.4.3 Risk Measurement: Propagated
    or Nonpropagated   72

**4. Cyber Risk Measurement in the
Hyperconnected World   75**

4.1 Cyber Risk as a Critical Business Risk   75
4.2 The Uniqueness of Cyber Risk   76
**4.3 The Need for Cyber Risk Measurement
and Current Challenges   77**
4.4 Cost Models for Incidents and Losses   78
4.4.1 Cost of Cybercrime   78
4.4.2 Cyber incident loss Categories   79
4.4.3 Models for Measuring Expected Loss   79
    4.4.3.1 Expected Loss   79
    4.4.3.2 Expected Severe Loss 79
    4.4.3.3 Standard Deviation of Loss 79
    4.4.3.4 Perceived Composite Risk 80
    4.4.3.5 Loss in Market Value 82

4.5 Methods for Cyber Risk Measurement   82
    4.5.1 Stochastic Modeling   82
    4.5.2 Monte Carlo Simulation   83
    4.5.3 Cyber Value at Risk   83
    4.5.4 The CORAS Method   83
    4.5.5 Common Vulnerability Scoring System   83
    4.5.6 Factor Analysis of Information Risk   84
4.6 Introducing Cyber Risk Quadrant: Applying Medical Risk Measurement to Cyber   84
    4.6.1 Applying Medical Risk Model for Measuring Cyber Risk   84
    4.6.2 Using Scenario Analysis for Control Assessment and Loss Quantification   85

5. Economic Modeling and the Implementation of Effective Mitigating Controls   87
5.1 Definition of Control and Types of Controls   87
    5.1.1 Definition of Control   87
    5.1.2 Types of Control   88
        5.1.2.1 Control Objectives for Information and Related Technology   89
        5.1.2.2 NIST SP 800-53   90
        5.1.2.3 Committee of Sponsoring Organizations of the Treadway Commission   91
        5.1.2.4 ISO/IEC 27002   91
        5.1.2.5 Information Technology Infrastructure Library   91
    5.1.3 Control Selection and Implementation   92
        5.1.3.1 CIS Critical Security Controls   92
        5.1.3.2 National Institute of Standards and Technologies   92
        5.1.3.3 Information Security Management System   93
5.2 Prioritizing Cost-Effective Controls   93
5.3 Measuring Cost of Controls   94
    5.3.1 The Balance Sheet-Oriented Approach   94
    5.3.2 The Security Measure Life-Cycle Approach   94
    5.3.3 IT Security Process-Oriented Approach   95
    5.3.4 Cost to Break   95
5.4 Measuring Benefits of Controls   95
    5.4.1 Security Performance Metrics   96
    5.4.2 Vulnerability Assessments   97
    5.4.3 Penetration Testing   97
    5.4.4 Internal Audit   97

6. The Point of Diminishing Return on Cyber Risk Investment   99
6.1 Economics of Information Security   99
6.2 Current Information Security/Risk Management Budget   102
6.3 Challenges for Cyber Risk Management Cost Optimization   104
    6.3.1 The Challenges in Quantifying Security Costs   104
        6.3.1.1 Cyber Security and Risk Management Is a Cross-Functional Task   104
        6.3.1.2 Divergent Goals Exist for Cost Quantification   104
        6.3.1.3 Lack of Transparency on Hidden Costs   104
        6.3.1.4 Difficulties in Finding the Right Scope and Baseline   105
        6.3.1.5 Lack of Resources and Clear Ownership to Implement Controls   105
    6.3.2 Challenges in Determining the Optimal Level of Investment in Security and Risk   105
    6.3.3 General Limitations of Approaches: Game Theory in Security Investment   106
6.4 Current Models for Cyber Risk Cost Optimization   106
    6.4.1 Cost Models for Determining how much to Investment in Security and Risk   106
        6.4.1.1 Benchmarking   106
        6.4.1.2 Cost-Benefit Analysis   107
        6.4.1.3 Quantitative Risk Assessment   107
        6.4.1.4 Return on Security Investment   107
        6.4.1.5 Net Present Value   108
        6.4.1.6 Internal Rate of Return   109
        6.4.1.7 Comparisons of Return on Investment, Net Present Value and Internal Rate of Return   109
        6.4.1.8 Gordon and Loeb Model   110
        6.4.1.9 Full Cost Accounting Model   111
    6.4.2 Cost Models for Projection   112
    6.4.3 Risk Management Options and Associated Cost   113
        6.4.3.1 Defense-in-Depth and Holistic Thinking   113
6.5 Cost of Security Configurations   113
6.6 Decision Model for Optimal Risk Management Strategies   115

7. Kilogram of Cyber Risk: Introducing Bitmort and Hekla **117**

7.1 **Risk Metrology** **117**
    7.1.1 History of Metrology 117
    7.1.2 Traceability and Calibration 119
    7.1.3 Uncertainty 119
    7.1.4 Metrology and Cyber Risk 120
7.2 **Micromort** **120**
    7.2.1 Willingness-to-Pay and Value of a Micromort 120
    7.2.2 Value of a Statistical Life 121
    7.2.3 Microlife 121
7.3 **Value-at-Risk** **122**
7.4 **Introducing Bitmort and Hekla** **123**
7.5 **Risk Calculations** **125**
    7.5.1 Measuring Strength of Controls for Digital Assets Using Bitmort 125
    7.5.2 Measuring Cost-Effectiveness of Controls for Digital Assets Using Bitmort 125
    7.5.3 Articulating an Entity's "Willingness-to-Pay" for Risk Reduction for Digital Assets Using Bitmort 125
    7.5.4 Articulating an Entity's Cyber Risk Limit Using *Hekla* 125
    7.5.5 Articulating an Entity's Cyber Risk Appetite Using *Hekla* 125
    7.5.6 Measuring an Entity's Cyber Risk Pricing Using *Hekla* 125
    7.5.7 Measuring an Entity's Cost of Risk Reduction Using *Hekla* 125
    7.5.8 Measuring an Entity's Cyber Risk Return on Investment Using *Hekla* 126
    7.5.9 Using Bitmort and *Hekla* on a Portfolio of Entities 126

8. Three Views of Cybernomics: Entity View, Portfolio View, and Global View **127**

8.1 **Cybernomics** **127**
8.2 **Portfolio Level** **128**
    8.2.1 Supplier Risk 128
    8.2.2 Systemic Risk 129
        8.2.2.1 *Systemic Cyber Risk in Financial Services Sector* 129
        8.2.2.2 *Systemic Cyber Risk in Transportation Sector* 130
        8.2.2.3 *Systemic Cyber Risks in the Healthcare Sector* 131
    8.2.3 National Digital Strategies and Policies 132

    8.2.4 Cyber Regulations 132
        8.2.4.1 *General Data Protection Regulation* 132
        8.2.4.2 *NIS Directive* 133
        8.2.4.3 *Cybersecurity Act of 2015* 133
        8.2.4.4 *FISMA Reform* 133
        8.2.4.5 *Gramm—Leach—Bliley Act* 134
        8.2.4.6 *Health Insurance Portability and Accountability Act* 134
8.3 **Global Level** **134**
    8.3.1 Major Infrastructural Cyber Threats 134
        8.3.1.1 *Major Worms* 134
        8.3.1.2 *Cyber Terrorism* 136
        8.3.1.3 *Mega Data Breaches* 136
        8.3.1.4 *Privacy Concerns of Technology Giants* 137
    8.3.2 Risk Data Schemes and Data Sharing: Barriers and Solutions 137
    8.3.3 Cyber Infrastructure as a Public Good and the Privatization of the Internet 138
8.4 **Three Views of Cybernomics** **138**
    8.4.1 Entity Level 138
    8.4.2 Portfolio Level 139
    8.4.3 Global Level 140

9. Principles of Cybernomics **141**

9.1 **Unique Attributes of Digital Assets** **142**
    9.1.1 Characteristic 1: Digital Value Creation Does Not Decrease, but Increases, Through Usage 142
    9.1.2 Characteristic 2: Duplication Does Not Increase Digital Value 142
    9.1.3 Characteristic 3: Digital Value Production and Distribution Entails Higher Fixed Costs and Lower Variable Costs 142
    9.1.4 Characteristic 4: Digital Value Can Be Distributed Via Multi-Sided Markets 143
    9.1.5 Characteristic 5: Digital Value Is Limitless 143
        9.1.5.1 *Characteristic 5a: Digital Value Has Limitless Utility to the Owner* 143
        9.1.5.2 *Characteristic 5b: There Are Limitless Opportunities to Distribute and Consume Digital Value* 144
9.2 **Digital Value Matrix: Categorization of Digital Assets Based on Their Economic Functions** **144**
9.3 **Characteristics of the Fourth Industrial Revolution** **145**
    9.3.1 Characteristic 1: Velocity 145

9.3.2   Characteristic 2: Cross-Jurisdictional
    Economies of Scale Without Mass   145
9.3.3   Characteristic 3: Heavy Reliance
    on Intangible Assets, Especially
    Intellectual Property   145
9.3.4   Characteristic 4: The Importance
    of Data, User Participation, and
    Their Synergies With Intellectual
    Property   145
9.3.5   Characteristic 5: Fusion of
    Technologies   146
9.3.6   Characteristic 6: Consumption
    Externality   146
9.3.7   Characteristic 7: Indirect Network
    Effects   146
9.3.8   Characteristic 8: Lock-In Effects
    and Competition   146
9.4   Models for Digital Asset Valuation   146
9.4.1   Method 1: Intrinsic Value   146
    *9.4.1.1   1a: Intrinsic Cost of
    Production   147*
    *9.4.1.2   1b: Direct Financial
    Conversion   147*
9.4.2   Method 2: Extrinsic Value   147
    9.4.2.1   2a: Market Value   147
    9.4.2.2   2b: Usage Value   147
9.4.3   Method 3: Subjective Value   147
9.4.4   Method 4: Opportunity Value   147
9.5   Measuring the Digital Economy   148
9.6   Digital Theory of Value   148
9.6.1   Law of Machine Time   149
    *9.6.1.1   Principle 1a: Progress of
    Digital Economy Should
    Be Measured Against
    Machine Time   149*
    *9.6.1.2   Principle 1b: Sensemaking
    Is a Universal Challenge
    and a Value Driver   149*
    *9.6.1.3   Principle 1c: Risk
    Management Is an Island
    of Stability in the Sea
    of Change   149*
9.6.2   Law of Recombination   149
    *9.6.2.1   Principle 2: Recombination Is
    an Engine for Growth   149*
9.6.3   Law of Hyperconnectivity   150
    *9.6.3.1   Principle 3a:
    Hyperconnectivity Is an
    Engine for Growth   150*
    *9.6.3.2   Principle 3b: The Gravity of
    Value Creation will be
    Increasingly in the Virtual
    Space Where Value Creation
    is Location Independent   150*

    *9.6.3.3   Principle 3c: Nontechnical
    Barriers, Such As Geopolitical,
    Regulations, Legal
    Frameworks, Are Limiting
    Factors   150*
9.6.4   Law of Subjectivity   150
    *9.6.4.1   Principle 4: A Greater
    Component of Value Is
    Increasingly Subjective,
    Reflecting Only in an
    Entity's Willingness-to-Pay   150*
9.6.5   Law of Abundance   150
    *9.6.5.1   Principle 5a: The Digitally
    Empowered Entity has
    Limitless Economic
    Potential   150*
    *9.6.5.2   Principle 5b: Consumer
    Reception and Power
    Supply are Limiting Factors   150*
    *9.6.5.3   Principle 5c: The Attention
    of a Consumer Is the New
    Scarce Resource   151*
9.6.6   Law of the New Division of Labor   151
    *9.6.6.1   Principle 6a: The Digital
    Economy Is Creating a New
    Social Divide Based on the
    New Labor Value Chain   151*
    *9.6.6.2   Principle 6b: The Optimal
    Path to Intrinsic Value
    Creation Is a Combination
    of Human and Machine
    Intelligence   151*
**9.7   Cyber Risk Quadrant: Applying Medical
Risk Measurement to Cyber   151**
9.7.1   Applying Medical Risk Model for
    Measuring Cyber Risk   151
9.7.2   Using Scenario Analysis for Control
    Assessment and Loss Quantification   152
9.8   Introducing Bitmort and Hekla   153
9.9   Risk Calculations   155
9.9.1   Measuring Strength of Controls
    for Digital Assets Using Bitmort   155
9.9.2   Measuring Cost-Effectiveness of
    Controls for Digital Assets Using
    Bitmort   155
9.9.3   Articulating an Entity's "Willingness-to-
    Pay" for Risk Reduction for
    Digital Assets Using Bitmort   155
9.9.4   Articulating an Entity's Cyber Risk Limit
    Using Hekla   155
9.9.5   Articulating an Entity's Cyber Risk
    Appetite Using Hekla   155
9.9.6   Measuring an Entity's Cyber Risk
    Pricing Using Hekla   155

9.9.7 Measuring an Entity's Cost of Risk
        Reduction Using Hekla   155
9.9.8 Measuring an Entity's Cyber Risk
        Return on Investment Using Hekla   156
9.9.9 Using Bitmort and Hekla on
        a Portfolio of Entities   156
9.10 **Three Views of Cybernomics**   **156**
        9.10.1 Entity View   157
        9.10.2 Portfolio View   157
        9.10.3 Global View   157
9.11 **Discussions and Limitations**   **157**
        9.11.1 Accuracy   157
        9.11.2 Analytical Capabilities   158
        9.11.3 Testing and Validation   158
        9.11.4 Economic Lifespan of Digital
                 Assets   158
        9.11.5 Fundamental Inherent Differences
                 of Digital Assets   158

**10. Case Study: Insuring the Future of
     Everything**   **159**

10.1 History and Context of Cyber Insurance 159
10.2 Current Offerings, Coverage, and
       Policy Limits   161

10.2.1 Current Policy Coverage   161
10.2.2 Types of Breaches That Lead
         to Claims   162
10.2.3 Reputation Loss as Part of
         First-Party Loss   163
10.2.4 Policy Limits   163
10.3 **Underwriting and Assessment Process** **164**
        10.3.1 Conducting a Thorough
                 Information Security Risk Audit 164
        10.3.2 Assessing Current Coverage   164
        10.3.3 Evaluating Available Policies 164
        10.3.4 Selecting Appropriate Policies 164
10.4 **Claim Study**   **165**
10.5 **Current Challenges in the Cyber
       Insurance Market**   **165**
        10.5.1 Lack of Sufficient Quality
                 Actuarial Data   166
        10.5.2 Asymmetric Information   167
10.6 **Cybernomics and the Future Growth
       of the Cyber Insurance Market**   **167**

References   169
Index   179

Preface

This book builds on my 10 years of prior work in cloud forensics, security, and risk management under the context of international standards and enterprise cloud transformation. The more I worked in security and risk management, the more I realized the root problem lies with value, until the theories of cybernomics became inevitable. The way ideas developed for cybernomics has further validated my belief that a more general issue exists; we are solving rapidly evolving new problems from the lenses of fragmented old solutions. I realized how systematically breaking such fragmentation can accelerate transdisciplinary innovation. This is an exciting problem to have. It is also a topic for another theme of work and perhaps another book.

Most of the theories of cybernomics came together organically over the period of about 5 years. I came up with the risk units in 2014. The name Hekla was a serendipitous discovery during a trip to Iceland in 2015. The curve of a volcano resembles a distribution. Volcanos also symbolize uncertainty and potential catastrophe. Sometimes it takes a very long time for ideas to reach pages, if they eventually do. Sometimes the stillness required to hear the stream of thought gets interrupted by the ups and downs in life, hence I could barely write a word in 2017.

The different philosophical approaches from subjective versus objective perspectives toward risk measurement discussed here is apparent in the process of writing it, in that this process is part of the unpredictable and often irrational realities in real life, which is not at all as mechanical as its content. For example, this preface was drafted during a flight when I was cornered by two screaming babies for 3 hours who managed in the end, at least, to synchronize their symphonies. I will always remember the joyful summer nights in Milltown full of laughter while I was on a month-long, 14-hour writing days and felt closest to my calling. I also did not plan to finish the first complete draft of my manuscript at sea, nor click the send button near the island of Dugi Otok, nor finish writing this preface during the earthquake aftershocks in Bali. When I finally got to finish the last line of this book in my new home in London after relocating after 10 years of life in Dublin, a new chapter in my life also began.

This was a marathon side project as I also had a day job. Now that I am at the destination, I can see my personal journey differently. I was so fortunate to be able to continue to work on the questions I am living. If I apply the theories on risk, value, growth, and opportunity value to my own life, I find that there is opportunity cost behind each daily choice I make whether or not to strive for my best life. This entirely subjective risk is perhaps the greatest risk of all because I am only given one shot at each moment I live. The determination and resilience required for me to make better choices can only be inspired by love and gratitude.

Special thanks to my friend Dr. Fred English for introducing medical risk measurement concepts to me, Conor Twomey for brainstorming with me on the comparisons between cyber risk and financial risk, and my research assistant Lauren Forte for supporting me in preparing the material for this book.

I hope the theories introduced in this book can serve discussions in a new area that is fundamental to our understanding of the future of risk and the future of value.

Keyun Ruan
Milltown Hill, Dublin, Ireland
Summer 2018

Introduction

This is a book about the future of value and the future of risk.

The trading of innovative digital goods and services has become so critical to economic competitiveness that it is the reason why over half of the companies on the Fortune 500 have disappeared since the year 2000 (World Economic Forum, 2016). While advancements such as cloud computing and Internet of Things are reshaping the backbone of infrastructure and supply chains, breakthroughs in artificial intelligence (AI), 3D printing, crypto-currency, and virtual reality are transforming information technology from a supportive operational role into the business-critical role of core value creation. In the meantime, cyber risk has also become one of the top three global risks (Allianz, 2016) with significant economic implications for businesses. Companies' cyber security ratings are now being considered in investment assessments (BitSight cyber security rating; Bloomberg, 2014). Since the General Data Protection Regulation (GDPR) came into effect in 2018 in the European Union, companies can be fined a maximum 20 million euros or 4% of global turnover for data breaches. As cyber security enters boardroom discussions worldwide and fills senior executives with fear, billions of investment dollars have been allocated to strengthening security controls (Forbes, 2016) with limited measurement on returns. The economic implications of cyber risk have to be quantified into monetary value for cyber risk management to transform from a compartmentalized technical issue into a business issue, formally integrating it into enterprise risk management (ERM) frameworks such as the Committee of Sponsoring Organizations of the Treadway Commission (COSO).

Data is one of the cornerstones of any risk measurement methodology. The current lack of quantification and consistent measurement of cyber risk is a direct result of insufficient quality data points and data sharing. Cyber risk is the likelihood of economic loss from cyber incidents, but data about such losses has not been adequately collected statistically. There are a wide range of incidents that can cause economic loss, but data breach is the only incident that has been tracked for more than a decade. The availability of breach loss data in different jurisdictions is correlated to when mandatory breach reporting schemes were introduced. More data breaches have been recorded in the United States than in the European Union (Privacyrights.org; Reported data breaches in Europe 2005−15). California has seen the largest amount of data breaches according to publicly available sources, because it was the first state in the United States that introduced mandatory breach reporting. Nevertheless, regulatory support is not the only reason why public access to quality incident and loss data sources is still limited. Security and monitoring companies hold incident and loss data as proprietary competitive advantage. Companies suffering losses prefer to cover them up, while forensic investigators are forbidden from sharing details of incidents.

A robust cyber risk databank not only requires adequate data points, but also significant improvement of data quality. Despite a large number of cyber risk management frameworks, risk assessment methodologies, quantitative risk models, industry surveys, and security analytics tools in the market, little has been done to standardize the measurement unit for cyber risk. While more established fields such as mortality risk management and financial risk management measure risk against defined risk units, the absence of a common point of reference for cyber risk make it difficult to compare different approaches in reducing exposure, assess cost-effectiveness of countermeasures, optimize return on cyber risk spending, and most importantly, structure the risk databank in a consistent and statistically robust manner.

Adequate data collection should occur on the entity level, portfolio level, and global level. This is evident from the challenges faced by the cyber insurance industry today. Although cyber insurance premiums are estimated to triple to US $7.5 billion in annual premiums by 2020 (Insurance Business, 2015), 98% of businesses in the United Kingdom are still "under-insured" (Marsh, 2015). The lack of quality risk data is a key challenge (World Economic Forum, 2015) and a key reason why this market opportunity is still under-exploited. For the insureds, there is a need to articulate entity-level cyber risk appetite into monetary value in order to determine how much residual risk should be transferred to insurers. For insurers and reinsurers, firstly, there is a need to profile risk exposure of entities. Secondly, there is a need to quantify accumulated risk on a portfolio of entities caused by use of a shared technology platform (such as cloud computing) and hyperconnectivity in the digital supply chain (Center for Risk Studies and Risk Modelling Solutions, 2016).

By integrating cyber risk management and economics into cybernomics, this book aims to conceptualize a unifying economic framework to better address data challenges in cyber risk measurement discussed above. It also introduces measurement units for cyber risk first proposed in Ruan (2017). The related work to this book includes the financial valuation of digital assets, cyber risk management, the economics of information security, risk units and risk measurement. Cross-disciplinary methods are used to develop this book, including applying economic theory of value to digital assets, applying medical risk factor categorization scheme to holistic modeling of cyber risk, using scenario analysis for control assessment and loss quantification, and applying value at risk (VaR) and micromort to define cyber risk units hekla and bitmort.

The remainder of this book is organized as follows.

CHAPTER 1: DIGITAL ASSETS AS ECONOMIC GOODS

Chapter 1 first looks at the origins and philosophical concept of value, the different schools of thoughts from the subjective and objective views of value, the differences between intrinsic and extrinsic value, the definition of traditional assets, the definition of economic goods, and current valuation asset valuation methods. This chapter then compares digital assets to traditional assets and outlines the unique characteristics of digital assets that make them different from traditional assets. For example, economic value theories to date are based on scarcity of resources. It is the most fundamental assumptions of the discipline of economics that: (1) the amount of resources available for a society is limited; and (2) the market exists as a measure of substitutability of those limited resources. To find an optimal distribution of resources by means of free competition under these assumptions has always been thought to be the fundamental purpose of economics. Today, some argue "limitless" computing has arrived, making digital value theory inherently unique from past theories.

Chapter 1 then defines intrinsic digital value, extrinsic digital value, and a digital value matrix for categorizing digital assets according to their economic functions, i.e., core value versus supporting value, digitized versus digital native, rather than technical functions—e.g., software, hardware, etc. A list of sample attributes of digital assets that contribute to intrinsic and extrinsic value creation are discussed along with measurement methods. Chapter 1 closes with a review of current methods used for digital asset valuation.

CHAPTER 2: DIGITAL THEORY OF VALUE

Chapter 2 starts with an introduction on the fourth industrial revolution and its characteristics, followed by a discussion on the definition of "digital economy" and its measurement models. This chapter then introduces four models for digital asset valuation: intrinsic, extrinsic, subjective, and opportunity value. Using these models, the digital economy is measured in three ways: (1) digitization of traditional industries; (2) digital native industries; and (3) the "invisible" economy, i.e., the opportunity value created by digital technologies.

The digital theory of value is introduced in Chapter 2 with its six laws: (1) law of machine time; (2) law of recombination; (3) law of hyperconnectivity; (4) law of subjectivity; (5) law of abundance; (6) and law of new division of labor.

CHAPTER 3: CYBER RISK MANAGEMENT: A NEW ERA OF ENTERPRISE RISK MANAGEMENT

Chapter 3 first discusses risk as a multi-dimensional concept and its different interpretations in natural science and social science, the "relatively objective" nature of risk, decision theory and acceptable risk, the microeconomic and macroeconomic risks within ERM, and how cyber risk is spilling over into all areas of enterprise risk. This chapter then provides a review on current methods in use for cyber risk management, including risk assessment, risk classification, threat modeling, vulnerability assessment, impact analysis, risk mitigation, effectiveness assessment, and continuous monitoring. Current quantitative and qualitative risk models are also discussed.

CHAPTER 4: CYBER RISK MEASUREMENT IN THE HYPERCONNECTED WORLD

Chapter 4 introduces cyber risk as a critical business risk spilling over into strategic risk, credit risk and regulatory risk on the entity level, as well as market risk and systemic risk on the portfolio level. It then analyses the uniqueness of cyber risk, the need for cyber risk measurement, and current challenges for cyber risk quantification, followed by a review on cost models for incidents and losses, cost of cybercrime, cyber incident loss categories, models for measuring expected loss from cyber incidents—i.e., annual loss expectancy, standard deviation of loss, perceived composite risk—and methods for cyber risk measurement, including stochastic modeling, Monte Carlo simulation, Cyber Value at Risk, Common Vulnerability Scoring System (CVSS), Factor Analysis for Information Risk (FAIR), among others.

The Cyber Risk Quadrant is introduced in this chapter, applying medical risk measurement to cyber. It categorizes risk factors into technological, nontechnological, inherent (nonmodifiable), and control (modifiable) factors. Examples of scenario analysis for control assessment and loss quantification are also included.

CHAPTER 5: ECONOMIC MODELING AND THE IMPLEMENTATION OF EFFECTIVE MITIGATING CONTROLS

Chapter 5 presents different types of security and risk controls, control frameworks, models in use for measuring cost and benefits of controls, and methods for developing security performance metrics.

CHAPTER 6: THE POINT OF DIMINISHING RETURN ON CYBER RISK INVESTMENT

Chapter 6 begins with a literature review on the field of economics of information security, challenges for cyber risk management cost optimization, challenges in quantifying security costs, challenges in determining the optimal level of investment in security and risk, and game theory in security investment. It then presents current models for cyber risk cost optimization, cost models for projection, and cost models for investment—i.e., determining how much should be spent on cyber risk, including Return on Security Investment (ROSI), Net Present Value (NPV), Internal Rate of Return (IRR). Chapter 6 also discusses decision models of optimal risk management strategies—i.e., when the point of diminishing return on cyber risk investment is reached.

CHAPTER 7: KILOGRAM OF CYBER RISK: INTRODUCING BITMORT AND HEKLA

Chapter 7 discusses metrology and introduces novel risk units for cyber risk measurement. It covers history and applications of micromort, history and applications of VaR. It then discusses how concepts behind micromort and VaR can be applied to the cyber context. Chapter 7 defines bitmort and hekla to measure both objective (e.g., exposure) and subjective (e.g., willingness-to-pay) aspects of cyber risk. Risk calculation examples using bitmort and hekla are also included.

CHAPTER 8: THREE VIEWS OF CYBERNOMICS: ENTITY VIEW, PORTFOLIO VIEW, AND GLOBAL VIEW

Chapter 8 formally introduces cybernomics. Cybernomics is the integration of cyber risk management and economics to study the requirements of a databank in order to improve risk analytics solutions for: (1) the valuation of digital assets; (2) the measurement of risk exposure of digital assets; and (3) the capital optimization for managing residual cyber risk. Establishing adequate, holistic, and statistically robust data points on the entity, portfolio, and global levels for the development of a cybernomics databank is essential for the resilience of our shared digital future.

Chapter 8 also covers the state-of-the-art on portfolio and global levels, including supplier risk, systemic risk (in financial services, transport and healthcare sectors), cyber risk accumulation and aggregation, national digital strategies and policies, cyber regulations including GDPR, major infrastructural cyber threats (cyber terrorism, major worms, major data breaches), privacy concerns of big tech firms, barriers and solutions for risk data schemes and data sharing, cyber infrastructure as a public good, and the privatization of the Internet.

Finally, Chapter 8 introduces the various components of the three views of cybernomics, and how they interact.

CHAPTER 9: PRINCIPLES OF CYBERNOMICS

Chapter 9 brings together all the novel concepts introduced in this book.

CHAPTER 10: CASE STUDY: INSURING THE FUTURE OF EVERYTHING

Chapter 10 is a case study on cyber insurance. It begins with the history and context of cyber insurance, current offerings, coverage, policy limits, underwriting and assessment process, claim study, and current market challenges—e.g., risk correlation, asymmetric information, pricing. It also discusses how principles of cybernomics can contribute to the future growth of the cyber insurance market.

The content introduced in this book should also be used together with resources and examples available at cybernomics.ruankeyun.com.

Chapter 1

Digital Assets as Economic Goods

Chapter Outline

1.1 **Origins and Philosophical Concepts of Value**   **2**
   1.1.1 Subjective View Versus Objective View   2
   1.1.2 Intrinsic Value Versus Extrinsic Value   4
1.2 **What Is an Economic Good?**   **4**
1.3 **What Is an Asset?**   **5**
   1.3.1 Definition of Asset   5
   1.3.2 Current Asset Valuation Methods   5
1.4 **What Are Digital Assets?**   **6**
   1.4.1 Categorization of Digital Assets   7
      1.4.1.1 (Networked) System Assets   7
      1.4.1.2 Software Assets   7
      1.4.1.3 Hardware Assets   7
      1.4.1.4 Service Assets   7
      1.4.1.5 Robotic Assets   8
      1.4.1.6 Data Assets   8
      1.4.1.7 Metadata Assets   8
      1.4.1.8 Digitally Enabled Devices   8
   1.4.2 Managing Digital Assets in an Organization   8
      1.4.2.1 Information Resource Management   9
      1.4.2.2 Digital Assets Management   9
1.5 **Unique Attributes of Digital Assets**   **9**
   1.5.1 Characteristic 1: Digital Value Creation Does Not Decrease but Increases Through Usage   10
   1.5.2 Characteristic 2: Duplication Does Not Increase Digital Value   10
   1.5.3 Characteristic 3: Digital Value Production and Distribution Entails Higher Fixed Costs and Lower Variable Costs   10
   1.5.4 Characteristic 4: Digital Value Can Be Distributed via Multi-Sided Markets   10
   1.5.5 Characteristic 5: Digital Value Is Limitless   11
      1.5.5.1 Characteristic 5a: Digital Value Has Limitless Utility to the Owner   11
      1.5.5.2 Characteristic 5b: There Are Limitless Opportunities to Distribute and Consume Digital Value   11
1.6 **Digital Value Matrix: Categorization of Digital Assets Based on Their Economic Functions**   **11**
   1.6.1 Digital Asset on an Individual Level   13

   1.6.2 Digital Asset on an Organizational Level   13
   1.6.3 Digital Asset on a National Level   14
   1.6.4 Digital Asset on the Global Level   14
1.7 **Valuation of Digital Assets as Economic Goods**   **14**
   1.7.1 Attributes of Digital Assets Contributing to Intrinsic Digital Value Creation   14
      1.7.1.1 Data Quality   14
      1.7.1.2 Risk Exposure   15
      1.7.1.3 Age   15
      1.7.1.4 Data Volume   18
      1.7.1.5 System Quality   19
      1.7.1.6 Production Cost   19
   1.7.2 Attributes of Digital Assets Contributing to Extrinsic Digital Value Creation   19
      1.7.2.1 Exclusivity   19
      1.7.2.2 Network Connectivity   20
      1.7.2.3 Accessibility   20
      1.7.2.4 Reproduction Cost   21
      1.7.2.5 Economies of Scale   21
      1.7.2.6 Data Format   21
      1.7.2.7 Level of Structure   22
      1.7.2.8 Delivery Cadence   22
      1.7.2.9 Power Supplies   22
1.8 **Existing Challenges for Digital Asset Valuation**   **23**
   1.8.1 Inherent Challenges   23
   1.8.2 Market Challenges   23
   1.8.3 Taxation Challenges   23
   1.8.4 Regulatory and Standardization Challenges   23
1.9 **Current Methods for Digital Asset Valuation**   **23**
   1.9.1 Intrinsic Value   24
   1.9.2 Direct Conversion of Financial Value   24
   1.9.3 Business and Performance Value   24
   1.9.4 Cost-Based Models   25
   1.9.5 Market-Based Models   26
   1.9.6 Income-Based Models   27
   1.9.7 Option Models   27

What you risk reveals what you value.

Jeanette Winterson

Digital Asset Valuation and Cyber Risk Measurement. DOI: https://doi.org/10.1016/B978-0-12-812158-0.00001-6

1.1   ORIGINS AND PHILOSOPHICAL CONCEPTS OF VALUE

The concept of value lies at the core of the economic adjustment process, which organized the economic life of society as the basis for deciding what to produce, how to produce, and who gets it. The debate of how value itself was formed has lasted for millennia, dating back to pre-Christian times, when Aristotle (384 BC−322 BC) famously argued that value is based on the need of exchange (Aristotle, 350 BC). It is a fundamental subject of study in philosophy, economics, finance, and risk management (Fogarty, 1996). Theory of value is a generic term that encompasses all the theories within economics that attempt to explain the exchange value or price of goods and services. Key questions in economic theory include why goods and services are priced as they are, how the value of goods and services are determined, and how to calculate the correct prices of goods and services. Value theory is the major intersection between economics and philosophy. The search for a theory of value is really a search for a consistent foundation for economic theory (Taylor, 1996).

1.1.1   Subjective View Versus Objective View

The historical evolution of the value debate has been locked into centuries of old dialectical conflict between objective and subjective approaches, which focus, respectively, on the conditions of production and on the preferences of consumers.

The objective approach is taken primarily in classical political economy, the labor theory of value and the Sraffian revival of classical value theory in the 20th century. Intrinsic theories hold that the price of goods and services is objectively determined by labor, cost of production, etc., and is not a function of subjective judgment (Smith, 1776; Marx, 1867). The cost of production theory of value is the theory that the price of an object or condition is determined by the sum of the cost of the resources that went into making it. The cost can comprise any of the factors of production (including labor, capital, and land) or taxation. Historically, the best-known proponent of this theory is Adam Smith (1723−90), who also developed the Water−Diamond Paradox:

> *The things which have the greatest value in use have frequently little or no value in exchange; and on the contrary, those which have the greatest value in exchange have frequently little or no value in use. Nothing is more useful than water: but it will purchase scarce anything; scarce anything can be had in exchange for it. A diamond, on the contrary, has scarce any value in use; but a very great quantity of other goods may frequently be had in exchange for it.*
>
> Smith (1776)

The labor theory of value argues that the economic value of a good or service is determined by the total amount of "socially necessary labor" required to produce it. It is central to Marxist theory, Karl Marx (1818−83) took the labor theory developed by David Ricardo (1772−1823) and constructed it in a societal manner. Marxist theory holds that the working class is exploited under capitalism, and dissociates price and value (Marx, 1867). Ricardo was also searching for a measure of value, which he found to be truly impossible as the technology of production of a good or service changes or advances, so does its value. The forces that determine the distribution of income also varies with technological change (Ricardo, 1817).

The subjective approach is taken primarily in neoclassical economics, with an emphasis on marginal utility, productivity, equilibrium, and enhancements to utility analysis developed in the late-19th and early 20th centuries. Subjective theories hold that an item's value depends on the consumer, and it must be useful in satisfying human wants and must be in limited supply (Stigler, 1950). The utility theory of value was the belief that price and value were solely based on how much "use" an individual received from a commodity. Pioneered by William Stanley Jevons (1835−82), Carl Menger (1840−1921) (Menger, 1871), and Marie-Esprit-Léon Walra (1834−1910) (Walras, 1874), and then further developed by Alfred Marshall (1842−1924), marginal theory of value focuses on the determination of goods, outputs, and income distributions in markets through supply and demand. This determination is often mediated through a hypothesized maximization of utility by income-constrained individuals and of profits by firms facing production costs and employing available information and factors of production, in accordance with rational choice theory (Marshall, 1890). Today neoclassical economics is usually used to refer to mainstream economics, which rests on three assumptions (Fogarty, 1996; King and McLure, 2014):

1. People have rational preferences between outcomes that can be identified and associated with values.
2. Individuals maximize utility and firms maximize profits.
3. People act independently on the basis of full and relevant information.

From these three assumptions, neoclassical economists have built a structure to understand the allocation of scarce resources among alternative ends. The problem of economics was presented by William Stanley Jevons as:

Given, a certain population, with various needs and powers of production, in possession of certain lands and other sources of material: required, the mode of employing their labour which will maximize the utility of their product.

Jevons (1871)

Below are some fundamental definitions central to economics and the concept of value:

- *Cost*: the amount incurred in the production of goods and services.
- *Price*: the financial reward for providing a good or service including the cost and profit margin, charged by the seller.
- *Money*: a current medium of exchange in the form of coins and banknotes. Money is used to pay the price of a good or service.
- *Trading*: trading is the action or activity of buying and selling goods and services.
- *Supply and demand*: Supply and demand is the backbone of a market economy. Demand refers to how much (quantity) of a product or service is desired by buyers. The quantity demanded is the amount of a product people are willing to buy at a certain price; the relationship between price and quantity demanded is known as the demand relationship. Supply represents how much the market can offer. The quantity supplied refers to the amount of a certain good producers are willing to supply when receiving a certain price. The correlation between price and how much of a good or service is supplied to the market is known as the supply relationship. Price, therefore, is a reflection of supply and demand. The relationship between demand and supply underlie the forces behind the allocation of resources. In market economy theories, demand and supply theory will allocate resources in the most efficient way possible.
- *Marginal benefit*: the additional satisfaction or utility that a person receives from consuming an additional unit of a good or service. A person's marginal benefit is the maximum amount they are willing to pay to consume that additional unit of a good or service.
- *Marginal cost*: the cost added by producing one additional unit of a product or service.
- *Opportunity cost*: the benefits an individual, investor, or business misses out on when choosing one alternative over another.
- *Principle of diminishing marginal utility* states that as an individual consumes more of a good, the marginal benefit of each additional unit of that good decreases.
- *Equilibrium*: a state in which opposing forces or influences are balanced.
- *Macroeconomics*: the branch of economics concerned with large-scale or general economic factors, such as interest rates and national productivity.
- *Microeconomics*: the part of economics concerned with single factors and the effects of individual decisions.

It is also important to note the differences between core concepts related to value, as shown in Table 1.1.

TABLE 1.1 Differences Between Core Concepts Related to Value

Similar Concepts	Distinction
Value and cost	The cost of building something can be high but result in little value.
Cost and price	The price of something has to be higher than the cost to make a profit.
Value and price	Value existed long before price. Price isn't determined by value, it is determined by the intersection of supply and demand. It only exists in the context of trading (Masnick, 2008). Just because people aren't willing to directly pay cash for something doesn't mean they don't find value in an item. We value oxygen as a vital part of life because we need it to exist, for example, but we do not pay to breathe it. It is very important to differentiate product itself from the benefit (value) provided to customers. The makers of horse carriages believed to be in the horse carriage business even though they were actually in the transpiration market. That is why carriage making became a dying industry when railways were built (Masnick, 2008).
Trading and pricing	Trading provides mankind's most significant meeting place, the market. Pricing activities in a market aren't ahistorical or fixed, rather they are historically determined and dynamic. The way a particular market operates is not a snapshot, it's a frame in a picture. The processes, organization, technologies, and techniques that are used to manage prices can either enable or hinder the ability to adapt to a changing market and its conditions.

1.1.2 Intrinsic Value Versus Extrinsic Value

Another perspective to look at value theory is intrinsic and extrinsic value. Intrinsic value has traditionally been thought to lie at the heart of ethics. The intrinsic value of something is said to be the value that that thing has "in itself," "for its own sake," "as such," or "in its own right." For example, cost of production is a type of intrinsic value. In finance, intrinsic value refers to the value of a company, stock, currency, or product determined through fundamental analysis without reference to its market value. Extrinsic value is value that is not intrinsic. As intrinsic value is characterized as a nonderivative value of a certain kind, extrinsic value is a derivative value of that same kind. What is extrinsically good is good not for its own sake, but for the sake of something else to which it is related in some way. Market value, for example, is a type of extrinsic value (Stanford Encyclopedia of Philosophy, 2014).

Ruskin argues that the production of value always involves two aspects: (1) the production of a thing essentially useful; and (2) the production of the capacity to use it—that is, the effectual value of a given quantity of any commodity existing in the world at any moment is, therefore, a mathematical function of the capacity existing in the human race to enjoy it (Ruskin, 1871). Where the intrinsic value and acceptant capacity (extrinsic value) come together there is effectual value or wealth; where there is either no intrinsic value or no acceptant capacity, there is no effectual value; that is to say, no wealth. A horse is no wealth to use if we cannot ride, nor is a picture if we cannot see, nor can any noble thing be wealth, except to a noble person. As the number of consumers with ever higher and diversifying capability of acceptance continues to increase, their behavior will result in a common social stock which, in turn, will be passed on to next generation as a cultural heritage (Ikegami, 1992).

Taking into consideration various perspectives toward traditional value theories discussed so far, this book adopts a holistic view that value is determined by a combination of objective, subjective, intrinsic, and extrinsic factors. As Alfred Marshall puts it:

> We might as reasonably dispute whether it is the upper or under blade of a pair of scissors that cuts a piece of paper, as whether value is governed by utility or costs of production.
>
> Marshall (1890).

1.2 WHAT IS AN ECONOMIC GOOD?

An economic good (often referred to as a commodity in a market) is a good or service that has a benefit (utility) to society with a degree of scarcity and, therefore, has an opportunity cost. A good must have these three characteristics to be considered an economic good:

1. *Source of utility or satisfaction.* Anything which is a nuisance or irritant does not give utility or satisfaction and, so, would not be considered an economic good, for example, cars and beauty treatments are economic goods, whereas swine flu is not an economic good.
2. *Scarcity in relation to demand.* People would need to be willing to pay for it. If something is scarce, it can command a price. People would not be prepared to pay for something if there is plenty of it freely available, for example, sand on a beach is not an economic good.
3. *Transferability.* If the good is not transferable, it would not be possible for one person to sell the good to another person, for example, a person's good health is not an economic good (but has economic value to that person).

Attributes of economic goods:

1. *Excludable* implies that there are barriers in acquiring the good, making it possible that the consumer may be prevented from obtaining the good or service. The most frequent exclusion is price. Other exclusions can be age (alcohol, tobacco, driving), height (amusement park rides), body size (airlines), and weight (weight bearing rides), to name a few.
2. *Nonexcludable* implies that there are no barriers to obtain the product or use the service, for example, sidewalks, water fountains, public schools, public parks, and national defense are nonexcludable.
3. A *rival* good or service is one in which the user is the only consumer.
4. The opposite of a rival good is a *nonrival* good. These goods and services can be consumed by more than one person at the same time, for example, an economics class, a movie, a concert, a bus or plane ride, a park, a baseball game.

Pure private goods are excludable and rival. Goods and services that are either nonrival and excludable (e.g., movies, economics class) or rival and nonexcludable (a library book) are referred to as *semi-private* goods. *Public* goods or service (street lights, law and order) are both nonexcludable and nonrival and are paid indirectly from taxes. Things that are useful, but not scarce enough to have monetary value, are referred to as *"free goods"* (e.g., the Earth's atmosphere).

1.3 WHAT IS AN ASSET?

1.3.1 Definition of Asset

An asset is an economic source of value. The International Accounting Standards Board[1] defines an asset as:

> *An asset is a resource controlled by the enterprise as a result of past events and from which future economic benefits are expected to flow to the enterprise.*

Based on this definition, the essential characteristics of an asset are (Godfrey et al., 1997; Henderson and Peirson, 1998)

1. *An asset has service potential or future economic benefits*. Something is only an asset from an accounting viewpoint if it is expected to provide future services or economic benefits. The benefits may arise from either the use or sale of the asset.
2. *An asset is controlled by the organization*. Control in this sense means the capability of the organization to benefit from the asset and to deny or regulate the access of others to that benefit.
3. *An asset is the result of past transactions*. This means that control over the asset has already been obtained as a result of past transactions, such as purchases, internal development, or discovery.

Under the context of businesses, for example, assets are recorded on companies' balance sheets based on the concept of historical cost (also called "book value"). Historical cost represents the original cost of the asset, adjusted for any improvements or aging. Assets are bought or created to increase the value of a company or to benefit the company's operations, such as generate cash flow, reduce expenses, and improve sales, regardless of whether it's a company's manufacturing equipment or a patent on a particular technology.

An asset represents a present economic resource of a company to which it has a right or other type of access that other individuals or companies do not have. A right or other access is legally enforceable, which means that a company can use the economic resource at its discretion, and its use can be precluded or limited by the owners. For an asset to be present, a company must possess a right to it as of the date of the financial statement.

The management of an asset throughout its lifecycle includes planning and support for the investment decision, acquisition, access, and ongoing maintenance through to replacement or retirement planning. The objective of asset lifecycle management is to optimize asset acquisition, maximize the use of the asset, and reduce associated service and operational costs resulting in increased asset performance and a lower total cost of ownership.

1.3.2 Current Asset Valuation Methods

Current asset valuation methods can be broadly categorized under cost-based, market-based, and utility-based models, as shown in Tables 1.2−1.4 (Moody and Walsh, 1999).

TABLE 1.2 Cost-Based Valuation

Valuation Method	Cost (or Historical Cost)
Description	An asset is valued based on how much was originally paid to acquire the asset, for example, purchase price or development cost. The assumption is that a firm, behaving rationally, will only spend money to acquire an asset if it believes it will receive at least an equivalent amount in the future in service potential or economic benefits.
Pros	Easy to collect, and arguably the most reliable and objective.
Cons	It may not reflect the current value of an asset. For example, a property may have been purchased at a given price, but its value may have increased or decreased dramatically since then.

1. https://www.ifrs.org/.

TABLE 1.3 Market-Based Valuation

Valuation Method	Market (or Current Cash Equivalent)
Description	An asset is valued based on how much other people or organizations are prepared to pay for it, such as: 1. The cost of replacing the asset with a new one, that is, replacement cost. 2. The cost of replacing the asset with a similarly used one, that is, current cost. 3. The amount the asset could be sold for, also called net realization value. This equates to value in exchange. For example, property can be valued based on its estimated selling price.
Pros	It gives a good indication of the current value of the asset.
Cons	It is more time-consuming and expensive than measuring historical cost (Henderson and Peirson, 1998).

TABLE 1.4 Utility-Based Valuation

Valuation Method	Utility (or Present Value)
Description	The asset is valued based on the present value of expected future economic benefits. This equates to value in use. For example, property may be valued based on the discounted value of expected future rents.
Pros	There is wide agreement that, conceptually, this is the best approximation to the true economic value of an asset (Godfrey et al., 1997). In practice, this method is primarily used for long-term monetary assets (e.g., bonds, leases), where the future cash flows are specified by contract and can, therefore, be determined objectively.
Cons	The major weakness of this method is the difficulty of determining the specific future cash flows related to the asset, which is often quite subjective and, therefore, of doubtful value to statement users. For most assets, there is great difficulty estimating future economic benefits; difficulties in converting these economic benefits to monetary equivalents which can be discounted; and there is the technical problem of choosing a discount rate (Henderson and Peirson, 1998). For nonmonetary assets, it is virtually impossible to determine their future cash flows (Godfrey et al., 1997).

1.4   WHAT ARE DIGITAL ASSETS?

In this book, digital assets are defined as:

Asset in digital form the compromise of which will cause economic loss to its owning entity.

Similar to traditional assets, digital assets typically have lifecycles, covering phases of creation, management, distribution, and preservation. Digital assets can be both tangible and intangible.

Intangible digital assets are information assets expressed in discrete numerical form for use by a computing device, that is, intangible digital assets are a subset of information assets. In this book the terms digital assets and information assets are not interchangeable because information assets also include analog information, as shown in Fig. 1.1. For example, a company's reputation is an information asset and is intangible, but is not a digital asset, whereas a company's online reviews and ratings are digital assets. According to Shannon (1948), what can reduce the uncertainty in a given case is called information, and information content is the amount by which the degree of uncertainty can be reduced. More recent definitions of information assets describe it as an umbrella category which includes data, information, and explicit knowledge that is managed as a single unit so it can be understood, shared, protected, and efficiently exploited (Oppenheim et al., 2001). In the context of information risk, an information asset is a resource that is required to be protected by a countermeasure covered in an information system's security policy.

The rapid development of information technology (IT) has given rise to new means of producing intrinsic values in the current economic environment (Ikegami, 1992). Digital assets have been widely recognized as an important, sometimes vital, part of organizational resource. Digital assets provide the capability to deliver services, make better decisions, improve performance, and achieve competitive advantage and can also be sold directly as a product in its own right (Moody and Walsh, 1999).

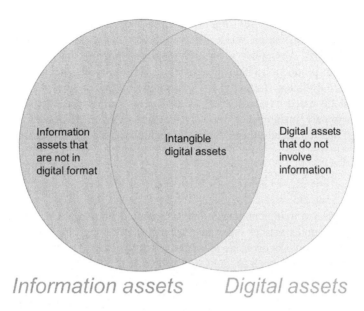

FIGURE 1.1   Information asset and digital asset.

1.4.1   Categorization of Digital Assets

There are many existing ways to categorize digital assets. The categories listed here are not mutually exclusive and may not be exhaustive:

1.4.1.1   (Networked) System Assets

Any software, hardware, data, administrative, or communications resources within a digital system, such as a major application, customer-facing website, general support system, mission critical program, virtual reality system, augmented reality system, digital equipment, or a logically related group of digital systems.

1.4.1.2   Software Assets

Software is a general term for the various kinds of programs used to operate computers and related devices, in contrast to the term hardware which describes the physical aspects of computers and related devices. Examples of software assets include electronic health record applications, laboratory and/or medical specialty applications, medical billing/claims processing applications, email applications, company intranet sites, HR management applications, network file sharing applications, fax applications, payment processing applications, and financial management/reporting applications, etc.

1.4.1.3   Hardware Assets

Computer hardware includes the manufactured physical parts or components of a computer system, such as central processing unit, monitors, keyboards, data storage, graphic cards, sound cards, motherboards, smartphones, smart devices, wearables, connected devices, servers, desktops, laptops, tablets, mobile phones, multifunction printers, and laboratory equipment, etc.

1.4.1.4   Service Assets

OASIS[2] defines a service as a mechanism to enable access to one or more capabilities, where the access is provided using a prescribed interface and is exercised consistently with constraints and policies as specified by the service description. A service asset can involve hardware and robotics. In the context of software architecture, service-orientation, and service-oriented architecture, the term service refers to a software functionality or a set of software functionalities (such as the retrieval of specified information or the execution of a set of operations) with the aim that

2. https://www.oasis-open.org.

different clients can reuse it for different purposes, together with the policies that should control its usage, for example, based on the identity of the client requesting the service. Service assets can also be outsourced and delivered by a third-party supplier (also called a vendor). A supplier is an individual or company that provides goods and/or services to other companies in the economic production chain. Examples of service assets include point-of-sale devices, ATMs, service robots such as Amazon Robotics (formerly Kiva Systems), digital media platforms, search engines, global positioning system (GPS), cloud-based services such as Software-as-a-Service, Platform-as-a-Service (PaaS) and Infrastructure-as-a-Service, hardware maintenance services, backup services, HR/benefits services, payroll services, medical transcription services, and hired consultants/contractors who have regular access to company-sensitive information for process support.

1.4.1.5 Robotic Assets

A robot is a machine that resembles a living creature in being capable of moving independently (as by walking or rolling on wheels) and performing complex actions (such as grasping and moving objects), or a device that automatically performs complicated, often repetitive tasks (as in an industrial assembly line). There are as many types of robots as the types of activities that can be automated, such as industrial robots (e.g., industrial articulated arms), transport robots (e.g., self-driving cars), domestic robots (e.g., robotic vacuum cleaners, robot chef Moley), medical robots (e.g., surgery robots), military robots (e.g., bomb disposal robots), entertainment robots (e.g., toy robots), space robots (e.g., NASA's Mars rovers), competition robots (e.g., Google's AlphaGo), and personal robots (e.g., Apple Siri personal assist), etc. Artificial intelligence (AI), also called machine intelligence, is intelligence demonstrated by machines in contrast to the natural intelligence displayed by humans and other animals. In computer science, AI research is defined as the study of "intelligent agents", which are devices that perceive its environment and takes actions that maximize its chance of successfully achieving its goals. Intelligence agents are also a type of robotic asset.

1.4.1.6 Data Assets

Data assets are information assets in digital form. A data asset may be know-how stored in digital format, Intellectual Property (IP), a system or application output file, database, document, a web page, or a service that may be provided to access data from an application. For example, a service that returns individual records from a database, a website that returns data in response to specific queries (Kissel, 2013), or any business application, system, or solution that creates, receives, maintains, or transmits sensitive information, including protected health information, personally identifiable information, big data analytics programs, access credentials, encryption keys, payment card data, company proprietary business plans, or financial data, etc. Data assets are commonly classified into categories such as: highly restricted, restricted, internal, public, regulated, nonregulated, high risk, medium risk, and low risk, etc. Currently, 70% of European Patent Office (EPO) patents are filed electronically.

1.4.1.7 Metadata Assets

Metadata is often referred to as "data about data." Metadata is descriptive information applied to data assets to support a task or activity. Metadata is widely used in data analytics (e.g., Big Data) applications. Another example is to help users to locate data assets in searches. To help find suitable media, data assets will generally have short descriptions, keywords, or titles added to them as a basic minimum. Workflow and business process information may also be added to determine what procedures are followed when users want to access, download, or process data assets.

1.4.1.8 Digitally Enabled Devices

Appliances, machinery, and cars with embedded hardware allowing them to process information, communicate with each other or connect to the Internet, including the internet of things devices and microchip implants.

1.4.2 Managing Digital Assets in an Organization

Currently, managing digital assets is a daunting task in most organizations. Few organizations have full visibility of their assets or a digital asset register. Listed are selected theory and products that are relevant to digital asset management.

1.4.2.1 Information Resource Management

Information resource management (IRM) is a theoretical approach to manage information assets as a shared organizational resource which contributes directly to its strategic goals and objectives. Core concepts of IRM include (Bergeron, 1996):

1. Recognition of information assets as a resource.
   - Identification of information, including: (1) the broad range of information resources, for example, printed materials, electronic information, and microforms; (2) the various technologies and equipment that manipulate these resources; and (3) the people who generate, organize, and disseminate those resources. This approach helps integrate the management of information and the management of IT.
   - Categorization of information.
   - Valuation of information.
2. An integrative view for managing information lifecycle.

1.4.2.2 Digital Assets Management

Digital asset management (DAM) is a type of software product that allows organizations to manage all of its information assets from one place. A good DAM needs to have a very sophisticated metadata model for asset classification, with options to customize keywords and vocabulary for search queries based on the organization's needs. In this way, a DAM can support asset queries and searches that cannot be done through a file system.

1.5 UNIQUE ATTRIBUTES OF DIGITAL ASSETS

Similar to value creation of traditional assets, digital assets that are not used have a cost, but no value (value-in-use) (McCumber, 2005; Moody and Walsh, 1999). The utility of many digital assets in the information and data categories require both the quality of information and the capability of the user (e.g., decision makers) to appreciate and comprehend (including knowing where it is located and having access to it). The quality of decision-making does not automatically improve when information is provided. This is often called information literacy. On an organizational level, few organizations have an information asset register for cataloging and locating their information assets. Such a situation would be intolerable for physical or financial assets. On a global level, Google's search engine is built on the value it creates for organizing and searching information. Google is currently valued at US$132.1 billion (Badenhausen, 2018).

Digital assets also exhibit attributes of traditional economic goods, as elaborated in Section 1.2 (Table 1.5). As a type of digital asset, data assets also satisfy all of the three attributes set out in Section 1.2 for traditional assets (Moody and Walsh, 1999):

1. Data assets provide the capability to deliver services and to make effective decisions.
2. If an organization owns data assets, it alone has access to it unless it sells or gives access to another party.
3. Data assets are usually collected as the by-product of transactions which have occurred (internal development), or may be the result of a purchase (e.g., a proprietary mailing database) or discovery (e.g., through analysis of data).

TABLE 1.5 Digital Asset Examples as Economic Goods

Attributes of Economic Goods and Services	Digital Asset Examples
Excludable goods and services	Wi-Fi connection; most digital goods and services accessible by the general public are excludable because they require basic computer literacy and ownership of computers or mobile phones.
Nonexcludable goods and services	Community (freely accessible by everyone) computers with free access to the Internet.
Rival goods and services	Personal computing devices; licensed software; Apple music subscription; Cloud-storage subscription; Kindle books.
Nonrival goods and services	Online whitepapers; public-facing websites; AWS infrastructure.
Pure private goods and services	Patented software; computing infrastructure; Amazon Web Services subscription.
Semi-private goods and services	Peer-to-peer based sharing of access to goods and services.
Public goods and services	Broadband connectivity; national ICT infrastructure.
Free goods and services	Digital archives of classics publicly available online.

However, some digital assets also exhibit unique attributes; one of the fundamental distinct attributes of digital assets comparing to traditional asset is that they are not necessarily "scarce" as many types of digital assets are instantly scalable and nonrival. Listed next are characteristics exhibited by some digital assets that are considered unique from traditional assets.

1.5.1   Characteristic 1: Digital Value Creation Does Not Decrease but Increases Through Usage

To the contrary of many traditional physical assets, sharing of intangible digital assets tends to increase its value. The more people use it, the more economic benefits can be extracted from it (Moody and Walsh, 1999; Ikegami, 1992), for example, Wikipedia, Instagram.

1.5.2   Characteristic 2: Duplication Does Not Increase Digital Value

Two copies of data assets have the same value as a single copy because no "new" information is created. Duplication of information does not add new value, but does add additional cost (Moody and Walsh, 1999). Too many copies of the same corporate data, for example, can cause significant additional management overheads. It is important, however, to differentiate duplication from reproduction, elaborated in Characteristic 3.

1.5.3   Characteristic 3: Digital Value Production and Distribution Entails Higher Fixed Costs and Lower Variable Costs

In many cases the production of digital goods and services entails relatively higher fixed costs and lower variable costs.[3] Software development, for instance, requires considerable investments in infrastructure and human labor; however, once the final program has been developed it can be maintained, sold, or distributed at very low marginal costs. While in many cases marginal costs will remain nonnegligible, there are also a range of nonrival consumption goods, such as software, e-books, or music, which can be reproduced at an effective marginal cost of zero (OECD, 2018). For example, WhatsApp has only 50 employees, but was attracting more than 1 million new users per day at the time when it was acquired by Facebook for $19 billion.

1.5.4   Characteristic 4: Digital Value Can Be Distributed via Multi-Sided Markets

The digital economy has given rise to "platform economy" rooted in multi-sided markets (OECD, 2018). In a traditional, single-sided market, sellers engage with only one specific set of customers, for example, a reader buying a book in a book shop. In multi-sided markets, there are more than one set of customers acquiring different products and services from a company, for example, Amazon retail and Uber. Multi-sided markets are defined by the joint presence of two characteristics:

1. *Indirect network externalities.* Indirect network effects occur when an increase in end-users on one side of the market increases the utility of end-users on another market side, for example, Airbnb (OECD, 2018). The prevalence of positive indirect externalities of positive indirect externalities implies that the firm operating the platform can reap benefits over and above the marginal utility of end-users, allowing them to increase the number of users (for transactions) by charging more on one side of the market while reducing the price for end-users on other sides.
2. *Nonneutral pricing strategies.* As a consequence of indirect network externalities, pricing structures are nonneutral in the sense that optimal prices can be below the marginal cost of provision on one market side while being above on the other side(s); end-users with lower price elasticities will typically be overcharged and vice versa. The result also implies that it may be optimal for platform operators, depending on the magnitude of the indirect network externalities as well as on price elasticities, to provide goods or services free of charge to the end-user on one (or potentially more) market sides. As a consequence, so-called barter transactions may arise, implying that goods or services are effectively traded, without monetary compensation, against other valuable inputs such as for example, user engagement, user data or user-generated content. Such as strategy is, for instance, adopted by many social networking platforms, email or media service provides. In these cases, end-users often benefit from "free" access to a specific service. However, platform operators typically compensate for this by extracting data from users and transactions and then selling services based on that data to the other side of the market. A primary example is the sale of

---

3. Variable cost changes in proportion with production volume.

customers-targeted advertisements to advertisers on the other side of the market (OECD, 2018). Many argue that Facebook did not "purchase" user registrations, but user data and user-generated data are the company's core asset, which led to the largest technology Initial Public Offering (IPO) in history.

1.5.5 Characteristic 5: Digital Value Is Limitless

Economic value theories to date are based on scarcity of resources. It is one of the most fundamental assumptions of the discipline of economics. Today, some argue "limitless" computing has arrived,[4] making digital value theory inherently unique from past theories. Of course, nothing is limitless in absolute terms. In this book, "limitless" means that limitation of the resources no longer plays as a constraint in value creation and distribution. The limitless nature of digital value is twofold:

1.5.5.1 Characteristic 5a: Digital Value Has Limitless Utility to the Owner

Referring to Characteristic 1, intangible digital assets cannot be consumed by use, and its utility is maintained regardless of change of ownership. Because intangible digital assets do not only disappear, but increases value through transfer and consumption, it represents a limitless utility to the owner. Thus, this contradicts with the basic premise of conventional theory which says that utility of a resource is limited for the owner (Ikegami, 1992). As to the value of credibility, it shows that utility value of a piece of information depends upon social credibility of the owner. The social credibility arises from the owner's capability to transmit useful information and to coordinate transfer. It presupposes that the owner has some kind of competence to create value (Ikegami, 1992).

1.5.5.2 Characteristic 5b: There Are Limitless Opportunities to Distribute and Consume Digital Value

In the traditional study of economics, it is usual to set up a short run as well as a pair of assumptions that: (1) the amount of resources available for a society is limited; and (2) the market exists as a measure of substitutability of those limited resources. To find an optimal distribution of resources by means of free competition under these assumptions has always been thought to be the fundamental purpose of economics (Andress, 2004). However, with the growth of cloud computing, especially in its third wave of "cloud native" services, both information storage and processing are reaching a state of "limitless." Prospects of quantum computing developments will further unleash the limitless nature of computing. There are limitless ways to distribute and consume digital value. Characteristic 4 is a mere use case of this attribute of digital value. This changes the fundamental assumptions of economics.

Considering the unique attributes of digital value, in this book intrinsic digital value and extrinsic digital value are defined as:

> ***Intrinsic digital value*** *is the critical elements that make it possible for the digital asset to exist in the first place.* ***Extrinsic digital value*** *describes the limitless opportunities to distribute and consume the digital asset so that it is more useful to prospective users.*

1.6 DIGITAL VALUE MATRIX: CATEGORIZATION OF DIGITAL ASSETS BASED ON THEIR ECONOMIC FUNCTIONS

In this book an entity on "micro" level can be an enterprise, an establishment, an organization, a worker, a household, or an individual. An entity's Digital Value Composition (DVC) is like its digital DNA. It is also the underlying attribute that determines the entity's inherent exposure to risk. Existing methods of categorization of digital assets introduced in Section 1.4.1 focuses on technology aspects rather than economic functions of digital assets, this is one of the fundamental reasons why digital asset valuation remains a subject of obscurity. Unlike traditional economic goods and services which are classified by internationally recognized standards such as the Nice Classification,[5] there is no universally accepted taxonomy for digital goods and services that can be used to monitor their production cost and market value. The categorization of digital assets has to reflect their economic functions first before their value can be properly assigned. Moody and Walsh (1999) were the first to propose an economic view towards digital assets. They argued that data is a raw material, information systems (hardware and software) are the manufacturer, and information is the

---

4. Eric Brewer (VP Infrastructure, Google) spoke about the Future of the Cloud at UC Berkeley on May 12, 2016.
5. Nice Classification is an international classification of goods and services: http://www.wipo.int/classifications/nice/en/.

end product that requires valuation. To reflect on the economic functions of digital assets, this categorization method is used in this book:

First dimension: Core value assets (CVs) versus supportive assets. As a strategic resource, digital assets can be the sole value created by the business, serve as a basis for making critical decisions, or keeping and supporting business processes.

Category 1: CAs ("What is"). When digital assets are, or are tied to products and services that define the nature of the entity, what the entity profits from or is about, that is, what the entity "is" digitally. Under the business context, core value creation activities can include product and service development, research and development, marketing, sales, and contract management, etc.

Category 2: Supportive value assets (SAs)[6] ("How it is run"). When digital assets support secondary activities, human needs, technology, organization, and technical infrastructure necessary for the creation, consumption and distribution of goods and services, that is, how the entity is "run" digitally. Under the business context, supportive activities can include procurement, logistics, human resource management, infrastructure, and operations, etc.

Second dimension: Digitized assets (DAs) versus digital-native assets (NAs). As a driver for economic growth, there is a difference between value digitized from traditional economics versus value created from intrinsic digital innovation.

Category 1: DAs. Conversion of traditional assets into digital form, for example, email, electronic patent applications, digital storage, and e-commerce. Digitization helps traditional assets to benefit from leveraging limitless extrinsic digital value.

Category 2: NAs.[7] Intrinsically digital assets that do not have an equivalent or alternative in the physical, analog world, for example, software, blockchain, and multi-sided digital platforms.

Similar to the Nice Classification, an International Digital Asset Classification (IDAC) should be developed on the global level, using more categories that can reflect the economic functions of digital assets.

An entity E's DVC can be, thus, described by the ratio of its CAs to SAs:

$$\text{CA:SA} = \{c_i, p_i\} : \{s_j, q_j\} \quad i = 1, 2, \ldots, N_c, \quad j = 1, 2, \ldots, N_s \tag{1.1}$$

TABLE 1.6 Digital Value Matrix Based on Economic Categories of Digital Assets

	Digitized Assets (DA)	Digital-Native Assets (NA)
Core value (CA)	System assets	System assets
	Software assets	Software assets
	Hardware assets	Hardware assets
	Service assets	Service assets
	Robotic assets	Robotic assets
	Data assets	Data assets
	Metadata assets	Metadata assets
	Intellectual property	Intellectual property
Supportive value (SA)	System assets	System assets
	Software assets	Software assets
	Hardware assets	Hardware assets
	Service assets	Service assets
	Robotic assets	Robotic assets
	Data assets	Data assets
	Metadata assets	Metadata assets
	Intellectual property	Intellectual property

---

6. Previously referred to as "operational assets" in Ruan (2017). The term supportive value is used instead because it encompasses a broader range of activities including operations.

7. Previously referred to as "Assets born digital" in Ruan (2017). The term digital-native is used instead because it is a better phrase which means the same.

where CA—E's core value assets in bytes; SA—E's supportive value assets in bytes; c—a type of asset listed in International Digital Asset Classification (IDAC) which is of core value to E; p—E's core digital asset c in bytes; s—a type of asset listed in IDAC which is of supportive value to E; q—E's supportive value asset s in bytes; N_c—the number of core value assets in entity E; N_o—the number of supportive value assets in entity E.

Similarly, entity E's DAs (in bytes) to NAs (in bytes) ratio can also be calculated. An entity's DVC describes its nature of innovation. For example, a global retail company selling traditional goods will have a low CA:SA ratio and a low NA:DA ratio in its DVC, while a software development company will have a high CA:SA ratio and a high NA:DA ratio in its DVC. A digital value matrix is created using the two dimensions of value categories, as shown in Table 1.6. After assigning economic categories to digital assets, it is easy to see why traditional categorization of digital assets does not fit for the purpose of a better understanding of digital value: all of the traditional categories can fall under all of the economic categories.

Using the economic categorization of digital assets, below are some examples[8] on individual, organizational, national, and global levels.

1.6.1   Digital Asset on an Individual Level

See Table 1.7.

TABLE 1.7 Examples of Digital Assets on an Individual Level

	Digitized	Digital-Native
Core value	Personal digital storage, digital photos, videos, documents, personal data (e.g., payment card number with CVV2, health data), digital diary, emails, personal online accounts, and identities	Social media profile (e.g., Facebook, Twitter, YouTube, Instagram)
Supportive value	Digital documents (e.g., presentations), cloud-storage subscription	Internet connectivity, digital devices (e.g., smartphones, wearables)

1.6.2   Digital Asset on an Organizational Level

See Table 1.8.

TABLE 1.8 Examples of Digital Assets on an Organizational Level

	Digitized	Digital-Native
Core value	Customers' information, payment application of a bank, sharing economy (digital platforms), online sales portal, digital payment systems, digital marketing, IP documented in digital format, design files, corporate emails, licenses, contracts	Digital payment application of a fintech company, digital IP such as software, cloud services of a cloud provider, 3D printing design files, cyber-physical systems (e.g., drones) of a producer, patented navigation software in self-driving cars of a producer, data warehouse of an analytics company
Supportive value	Employees' information, suppliers' information, survey data, automated operational procedures, online press release, live streams, customer reviews, critical operational business application (e.g., office productivity tools)	Infrastructural hardware (e.g., server, desktop, switch, computer equipment, computer network, router, connectors, hub), databases, robots for process automation, encryption key, login credentials, cloud services of a cloud consumer used for supportive purposes, cyber-physical systems (e.g., drones) of a consumer used for supportive purposes, navigation software in self-driving cars of a consumer, data warehouse used for supportive purposes

---

8. The purpose of these examples is to ground digital value matrix into everyday life, so some examples are highly generalized and broadly categorized.

1.6.3   Digital Asset on a National Level

See Table 1.9.

TABLE 1.9 Examples of Digital Assets on a National Level

	Digitized	Digital-Native
Core value	E-commerce, E-governance platforms	ICT industries
Supportive value	Critical infrastructure supported by computing (e.g., nuclear plants, air traffic control, smart grid)	National ICT infrastructure

1.6.4   Digital Asset on the Global Level

See Table 1.10.

TABLE 1.10 Examples of Digital Assets on the Global Level

	Digitized	Digital-Native
Core value	Internet of Things (IoT), Wikipedia, scientific research data	Social media, blockchain, bitcoin, quantum computing
Supportive value	Google maps	Global Positioning System (GPS), Cloud infrastructure, Internet backbone, data centers

1.7   VALUATION OF DIGITAL ASSETS AS ECONOMIC GOODS

In this section, a nonexhaustive list of characteristics of digital assets that contribute to intrinsic and extrinsic digital value creation given as examples and are analyzed, before discussing current methods of digital asset valuation.

1.7.1   Attributes of Digital Assets Contributing to Intrinsic Digital Value Creation

1.7.1.1   Data Quality

See Table 1.11.

TABLE 1.11 Data Quality Attributes and Measurements

Attributes	How to Measure
Accuracy. The degree to which data correctly describes the "real world" object or even being described (Moody and Walsh, 1999). In general, the more accurate information is, the more useful and therefore valuable it is. There is a point of diminishing marginal returns, where increasing the accuracy further provides little additional benefit; 100% accurate information is rarely required in a business context. On the contrary, once the accuracy of information falls below a certain level, it becomes a liability rather than an asset. At this point, it becomes "misinformation" and people will stop using it. For decision-making purposes, often just knowing the accuracy of information is as important as having accurate information.	The percentage of data entries that pass the accuracy rules, that is, the degree to which the data mirrors the characteristics of the real-world object or objects it represents.
Data integrity. Data integrity is the maintenance of, and the assurance of the accuracy and consistency of, data over its entire lifecycle, and is a critical aspect to the design, implementation and usage of any system which stores, processes, or retrieves data. Integrity breach contaminates data assets and causes economic loss, often leaving data assets with zero economic value.	The percentage of data entries that pass the integrity check, There are many tools available for continuous data integrity verification, such as using MD5 hash function as a checksum.

(Continued)

TABLE 1.11 (Continued)

Attributes	How to Measure
Completeness. The proportion of stored data against the potential of "100% complete" according to defined business rules.	The percentage of absence of blank (null or empty string) values or the presence of nonblank values of 0%–100% of critical data to be measured in any data item, dataset or database.
Consistency. The absence of difference, when comparing two or more representations of a data entry against a definition, measured against the data entry itself or its counterpart in another dataset or database.	The percentage of data entries that pass the consistency check, that is, assessment of data entries across multiple datasets and/or assessment of values or formats across data items, records, datasets and databases.
Uniqueness. No data entry will be recorded more than once based on how that data entry is recorded, measured against the data entry itself, or its counterpart in another dataset or database. Uniqueness is the inverse of an assessment of the level of duplication.	The number of things as assessed in the "real world" compared to the number of records of entries in the dataset, measured against all records within a single dataset. The real-world number of things could be either determined from a different and perhaps more reliable dataset or a relevant external comparator.
Timeliness of data. the degree to which data represent reality from the required point in time referring to the time the real-world event being recorded occurred. Each dataset will have a different proportion of volatile and nonvolatile data as time acts differently on static and dynamic records.	Time difference of any data item, record, dataset or database.
Validity. Data are valid if it conforms to the syntax (format, type, range) according to database, metadata or documentation rules as to the allowable types (string, integer, floating point, etc.), the format (length, number of digits, etc.) and range (minimum, maximum or contained within a set of allowable values).	Percentage of data deemed valid to invalid, based on comparison between the data and the metadata or documentation for the data item.
Credibility of data source. Usually, a buyer of goods or services is able to evaluate what he/she is going to buy,. In contrast, it is often difficult for buyers to determine the value of informationhe/she propose to acquire, because it is dependent on the content of information offered to him/her. For this reason, a piece of informationcan be often valued on the basis of credibility of the owner. Transaction of knowledge, for example, requires first of all judgment as to standing and credibility of owner of the knowledge, rather than evaluation of the knowledge itself (BSI, 1999). For this reason, and unlike ordinary commodities, credible information is hardly substitutable. Information referred to as "classics," "invention," "discovery," "scientific knowledge," "knowhow" is information that has intrinsic value and unlimited utility to the owner, and at the same time, is based on common language, experience, and perception, making it acceptable and comprehensible to other people at large. Such information cannot be substituted by other information, as distinguished from all other information (Ikegami, 1992).	Number of scholarly citations for scientific data source, credibility score, industry ranking, customer rating or reputation of business, credit scores of businesses, or individuals.

1.7.1.2 Risk Exposure

Risk exposure is a quantified loss potential of business. Risk exposure is usually calculated by multiplying the probability of an incident occurring by its potential losses. Attributes that can affect risk exposure include asset classification and regulatory requirement (Table 1.12). More on risk management and measurement is covered in Chapter 3, Cyber Risk Management: A New Era of Enterprise Risk Management, and Chapter 4, Cyber Risk Measurement in the Hyperconnected World.

1.7.1.3 Age

All digital assets have an economic lifecycle. In this book, digital death is defined as:

A binary condition when a digital asset loses all of its economic value.

TABLE 1.12 Risk Exposure Attributes and Measurements

Attributes	How to Measure
Asset classification. A risk-based categorization that classifies assets according to loss impact when compromised, for example, high-moderate-low risk, high-moderate-low impact.	Economic loss from past incidents (of the asset or similar assets), or projected loss from simulations or other risk measurement methods.
Regulatory requirement. Compliance constraints of assets according to applicable standards, law, policies and regulations.	Financial consequences of regulatory fines and penalties.

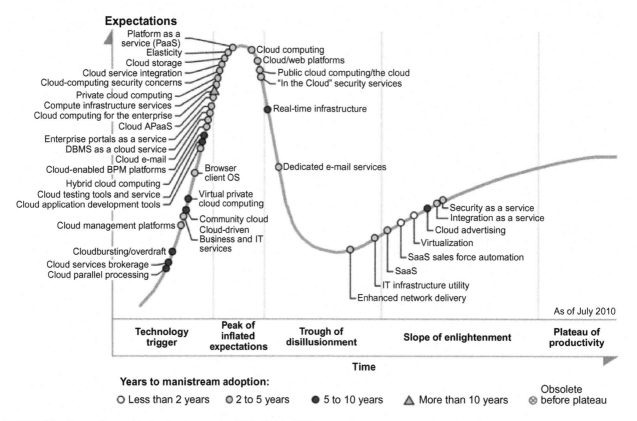

FIGURE 1.2   Gartner hype cycle for cloud computing 2010 (Smith, 2010).

Age of data and value decay are proportional to its shelf-life. Data degradation is the gradual corruption of computer data due to an accumulation of noncritical failures in a data storage device. The phenomenon is also known as data decay, data rot, or bit rot. Most data assets lose their economic value long before degradation. Effectively, data has three "lives": an operational shelf-life, a decision support shelf life, and a statutory/archival shelf life.

Today, the retirement of systems and devices is rarely the result of them being worn-out, but that they have become outdated and incompatible with new tools. Hence, the aging of a system is proportional to technological growth. Growth and lifecycle of specific technologies can be described using the five phases of Gartner's Hype Cycle[9]:

- *Technology trigger.* A potential technology breakthrough that kicks things off. Early proof-of-concept stories and media interest trigger significant publicity. Often no usable products exist, and commercial viability is unproven.

---

9. Gartner Hype Cycle: https://www.gartner.com/technology/research/methodologies/hype-cycle.jsp.

- *Peak of inflated expectations.* Early publicity produces a number of success stories—often accompanied by scores of failures. Some companies act; most don't.
- *Trough of disillusionment.* Interest wanes as experiments and implementations fail to deliver. Producers of the technology shake out or fail. Investment continues only if the surviving providers improve their products to the satisfaction of early adopters.
- *Slope of enlightenment.* More instances of how the technology can benefit the enterprise start to crystallize and become more widely understood. Second- and third-generation products appear from technology providers. More enterprises fund pilots; conservative companies remain cautious.
- *Plateau of productivity.* Mainstream adoption starts to take off. Criteria for assessing provider viability are more clearly defined. The technology's broad market applicability and relevance are clearly paying off. If the technology has more than a niche market then it will continue to grow. Fig. 1.2 shows the Gartner hype cycle for cloud computing.

An example of a hype cycle is Amara's law, coined by Roy Amara (1925−2007):

We tend to overestimate the effect of a technology in the short run and underestimate the effect in the long run.

Growth rate of technology can also be measured using Moore's Law discovered by Gordon Moore (1929−). Moore's law is the observation that the number of transistors in a dense integrated circuit doubles about every 2 years, as shown in Fig. 1.3. The period is often quoted as 18 months after some adjustments over time (Table 1.13).

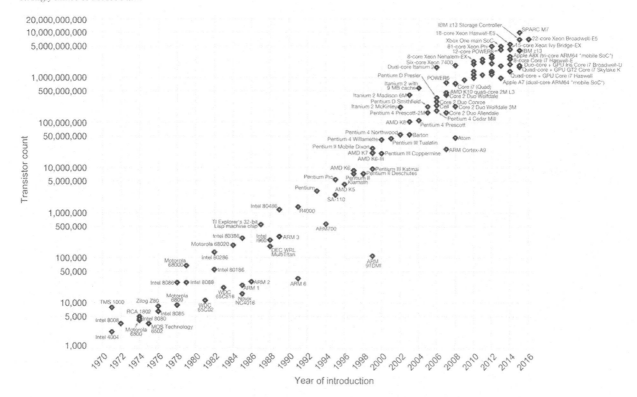

FIGURE 1.3 Moore's law.

TABLE 1.13 Aging Attributes and Measurements

Attributes	How to Measure
Operational shelf life of data. The duration of time that data is useful for operational purposes. For example, airline tickets must be kept for a year because tickets are valid for one year after purchase. Data has a relatively short useful lifetime at the operational level. Usually, the only data of relevance is very recent information—a customer's current address or their last bill. It has a much longer lifetime for decision support purposes. In practice, operational systems often discard data once it has exceeded its operational shelf life, making it unavailable for subsequent decision-making purposes. Data warehousing provides a mechanism for storing historical data which has exceeded its operational life, and making it available for decision support and analysis (Inmon, 1992).	Duration of validity based on defined purpose of data.
Decision support shelf life of data. The duration of time that data is useful for decision support. For example, ticket sales for the past five years may be relevant to help spot trends and patterns.	According to system design considerations, organizational policies, etc.
Statutory/archival shelf life of data. Beyond operational and decision support purposes, there are sometimes legal or preservation requirements to keep records for a defined number of years.	According to relevant data archiving and retention requirements.
Aging of systems	Based on year of manufacturing and in proportion to technological growth, measured using models such as Gartner Hype Cycle and Moore's Law.

1.7.1.4 Data Volume

See Table 1.14.

TABLE 1.14 Data Volume Attributes and Measurements

Attributes	How to Measure
Storage volume. The amount of data stored in a file or database.	Below is a list of all the standard units of measurement used for data storage, from the smallest to the largest:
	Bit (b): $\frac{1}{8}$ of a byte
	Byte (B): 1 byte
	Kilobyte (kb): 1000 bytes
	Megabyte (MB): 1000^2 bytes
	Gigabyte (GB): 1000^3 bytes
	Terabyte (TB): 1000^4 bytes
	Petabyte (PB): 1000^5 bytes
	Exabyte (EB): 1000^6 bytes
	Zettabyte (ZB): 1000^7 bytes
	Yottabyte (YB): 1000^8 bytes
	In 2010, it was estimated that storing a yottabyte on terabyte-size disk drives would require one billion city block-size data-centers.
Bandwidth. Bandwidth is the amount of data that can be transmitted in a fixed amount of time.	Measured in bits per second(bps) or bytes per second.

TABLE 1.15 System Quality Attributes and Measurements

Attributes	How to Measure
Storage capability. Specific amount of data storage that a system can accommodate.	Refer to data volume.
Processing power. The ability of a system to manipulate data.	Measured by clock speed and calculated in megahertz (MHz) and gigahertz (GHz).
Security. A composite of confidentiality, integrity and availability.	Measured by economic loss and frequencies from past incidents.
Resilience. The ability of a server, network, storage system, or an entire data center, to recover quickly and continue operating even when there has been an equipment failure, power outage or other disruption.	As defined in service level agreements for a service asset or measured by system monitoring tools for a system asset.
Reliability. Ability of a product to "not fail" in a given time-frame.	Measured by mean time to first failure, reflected in service level agreements (SLA) or system specs.
Availability. In computer systems and networking, availability is a general term that is used to describe the amount of time over a 1-year period that the system resources are available in the wake of component failures in the system.	Availability (%) = (AST − downtime)/AST × 100.
	Agreed service time (AST) is the amount of time a system or service should be available over a given period of time,
	Reflected in service level agreements or system specs.

1.7.1.5 System Quality

Within system engineering, quality attributes are realized nonfunctional requirements used to evaluate the performance of a system. They are usually architecturally significant requirements[10] that require architects' and designers' attention. Some of them can be measured by evaluations against standards such as ISO/IEC 25010:2011.[11] There are hundreds of such attributes. Some of the common subsets include:

- RASUI: Reliability, availability, serviceability, usability, and installability.
- FURPS: Functionality, usability, reliability, performance, and supportability.
- Agility: An aggregate of debuggability, extensibility, portability, scalability, securability, testability, and understandability.
- RASR: Reliability, availability, scalability, and recoverability.
- ACID: Atomicity, consistency, isolation, and durability.
- RAMS: Reliability, availability, maintainability, and safety.
- Dependability: An aggregate of availability, reliability, safety, integrity, and maintainability.

  A few examples are listed in Table 1.15.

1.7.1.6 Production Cost

Production cost refers to the cost incurred when producing a digital asset. It has no direct relation to the value of the asset, that is, it can be costly to develop a software product that has no value. Production cost includes a variety of expenses, such as cost of labor, cost of equipment, and tools. For intangible digital asset, production cost can include, for example, cost of data collection and analysis.

1.7.2 Attributes of Digital Assets Contributing to Extrinsic Digital Value Creation

1.7.2.1 Exclusivity

See Table 1.16.

---

10. Architecturally significant requirements (ASRs) are those requirements that have a measurable effect on a software system's architecture.
11. ISO/IEC 25010:2011: Systems and software engineering—systems and software quality requirements and evaluation (SQuaRE)—system and software quality models.

TABLE 1.16 Exclusivity Attributes and Measurements

Attributes	How to Measure
Exclusive. The right to ownership of the asset and the permit to deny others the right to have access to the asset. Exclusive rights can be established by law or by contractual obligation, but the scope of enforceability will depend on the extent to which others are bound by the instrument establishing the exclusive right. Many scholars argue that such rights form the basis for the concepts of property and ownership. Exclusive rights also often come with a defined duration. Types of ownership include: *Buying*. Transfer of ownership. *Leasing*. Allowing use for a fixed time. *Licensing*. Allowing limited use for a specific purpose (Shen et al., 2016).	Cost of purchase for exclusivity.
Nonexclusive. The absence of exclusive rights, including free and open access via initiatives such as open source[a] and creative commons (CC).[b]	Free

[a]*The open source definition is a document published by the open source initiative: https://opensource.org/.*
[b]*Creative commons (CC) is an American nonprofit organization devoted to expanding the range of creative works available for others to build upon legally and to share: https://creativecommons.org/.*

1.7.2.2   Network Connectivity

See Table 1.17.

TABLE 1.17 Network Connectivity Attributes and Measurements

Attributes	How to Measure
Speed. The number of bytes per second that data travels from user's device to a network (upload) and from the network (download).	Refer to bandwidth.
Coverage. The geographical area in which a network is serviced to its users.	Measured by signal strength for wireless connections, or areas covered by wired networks.
Spread. The geographical diversification of the network.	Measured by the physical distance in varied geographical areas and regions where the users have access to the network. For example, the Internet has a global spread.

1.7.2.3   Accessibility

See Table 1.18.

TABLE 1.18 Accessibility Attributes and Measurements

Attributes	How to Measure
Number of users. Unused data should be considered to have zero value, this can be determined via data usage statistics. The number of users and number of accesses to the data should be used to multiply the value of information. When information is used for the first time, it will be valued at cost of collection. Each subsequent use will add to this value. This allows the historical cost of the information to be modified in the light of its use in practice and reflects the cumulative nature of its value across different users.	Data usage statistics.
Demographics of users.	Statistical analysis based on user profiles.
Specialized accessibility. In human−computer interaction, accessibility refers to specialized hardware or software, or a combination of both, designed to enable use of a computer by a person with a disability or impairment, including the demographics of aged population.	Scored assessment can be conducted against international standards ISO 9241-171.[a]

[a]*ISO 9241-171: Ergonomics of human−system interaction−guidance on software accessibility.*

1.7.2.4   Reproduction Cost

Reproduction cost refers to the costs involved with identically reproducing an asset using the same method and input based on current prices (Table 1.19).

TABLE 1.19 Reproduction Cost Attributes and Measurements

Attributes	How to Measure
Reproduction cost of intangible digital assets. The cost of a cloning process that involves bit stream copy (or referred to as mirroring or imaging) that exactly replicates the data asset ensuring data integrity.	Minimal or zero cost
Reproduction cost of tangible digital assets.	Cost of reproducing the physical component of the asset (i.e., manufacturing cost, 3D printing cost) combined with any cost incurred for reproducing any intangible element involved in the asset (refer to above).

1.7.2.5   Economies of Scale

See Table 1.20.

TABLE 1.20 Economies of Scale Attributes and Measurements

Attributes	How to Measure
In microeconomics, economies of scale are the cost advantages that enterprises obtain due to their scale of operation, with cost per unit of output decreasing with increasing scale. Due to low marginal cost of reproduction, digital assets frequently bring advantages of economies of scale. For example, the economic benefit of cloud computing is often associated with the economies of scale that it brings by increasing the utilization ratio of a pool of configurable computing resources.	Typically measured by amount of economic output produced.

1.7.2.6   Data Format

Data format enables the processing device to logically determine what is to be done with the data and how to go about doing it (Table 1.21).

TABLE 1.21 Data Format Attributes and Measurements

Attributes	How to Measure
Data type. Constraint placed upon the interpretation of data in a type of system. Some defined data types include String, Integer, Float, Boolean, Array, Object, qualitative, quantitative, etc.	Cost of system required to interpret the data.
File format. A format for encoding data for storage in a computer file. A comprehensive dynamic collection of existing and archived file formats can be found on Wikipedia.[14]	Cost of application required to read the file.
Content format. A format for representing media content as data, for example, audio format is for encoded sound data, video format is for encoded video data. Some common content formats include: • Document file • Audio data recording • Visual data recording (including 3D displays) • Motion graphics (e.g., computer animation) • Instruction encoding (e.g., musical notation) • Natural languages (e.g., writing systems) • Expert languages (e.g., statistical model, DNA sequence, biometric data) • Code • Communication signaling	Cost of application required to consume the content.

---

14. https://en.wikipedia.org/wiki/List_of_file_formats

1.7.2.7   Level of Structure

The level of structure of data determines how the dataset can be consumed. See Table 1.22.

TABLE 1.22 Level of Structure Attributes and Measurements

Attributes	How to Measure
Structured. Structured data refers to information with a high degree of organization such that inclusion in a relational database is seamless and readily searchable by simple, straightforward search engine algorithms or other search operations. There are four types of structural database management systems: hierarchical, network, relational, and object-oriented.	Cost to search and find desired results.
Unstructured. Unstructured data cannot be processed and analyzed using conventional tools. It has no predefined structure that makes it easy to classify in a relational database. Examples of unstructured data include text files, video files, audio files, mobile activity, social media activity, sensor activity, geolocation activity, satellite imagery, etc.	
Graph database. A graph database is a database that uses graph structures for semantic queries with nodes, edges and properties to represent and store data. A key concept of the system is the graph (or edge or relationship), which directly relates to data items in the store. In some regards, graph database can be considered the next generation of relational databases, because each node (entity or attribute) in the graph database model directly and physically contains a list of relationship-records that represent its relationships to other nodes.	

1.7.2.8   Delivery Cadence

See Table 1.23.

TABLE 1.23 Delivery Cadence Attributes and Measurements

Attributes	How to Measure
One-time-purchase. The purchase of the product generates one charge to the customer, and that's all.	Purchase cost.
Batch. The purchase of the product generates a number of charges to the customer that occurs over given time period at defined intervals.	Total charge from all batches.
Continuous, for example, subscription-based. The subscription business model is a business model where a customer must pay a subscription price to have access to a product or service. The model was initially pioneered by magazines and newspapers.	Subscription fee × duration of subscription.

1.7.2.9   Power Supplies

See Table 1.24.

TABLE 1.24 Power Supplies Attributes and Measurements

Attributes	How to Measure
A power supply provides computing components with electric power.	Common battery capacity of electronics is measured in Ah (lead acid battery amp hours). To make a practical measurement, apply a fixed, constant and measured current load of X amperes and start a clock. When the voltage reaches the end of discharge voltage, stop the clock at measured time T. The measured capacity is $X \times T$ Ah.

1.8 EXISTING CHALLENGES FOR DIGITAL ASSET VALUATION

Digital assets currently consume huge but unreported amounts of resources in the economy (Sajko et al., 2006), but there is no generally accepted approach to measuring the value of digital assets. It typically receives no financial recognition on the balance sheet and has largely resisted quantitative measurement (Moody and Walsh, 1999). The major barrier being a lack of understanding of the nature of them as an economic good. The challenges to digital asset valuation are summarized below.

1.8.1 Inherent Challenges

Rapid pace of change of technology. Digital technologies are changing at an exponential rate, which means digital assets devalue much faster and it is much harder to estimate future earnings due to unpredictable disruptive changes in the ecosystem. Historical data also can become entirely irrelevant when new technologies replace the old.

Unpredictability of future return. There are too many variables to consider when modeling future return of digital assets, including factor of pace of technology as described above. For example, traditional valuation models such as discounted cash flow valuation often do no work for fast growing technology companies.

1.8.2 Market Challenges

Impacted by inherent challenges above, the market today for digital asset is far from mature. Taking data assets as an example, little transparency exists between buyers and sellers regarding how data has been collected and manipulated prior to sale, and how it will be used post-sale. This is in part a competitive strategy for companies, but it can hinder the market. This lack of transparency leads parties involved in the transaction to be misinformed and results in asymmetric information (Shen et al., 2017). In a mature data trading market, a standard pricing model should consider various value-creating attributes as described in Section 1.7 and facilitate transparent transactions in the data trading ecosystem. Sellers should be able to price optimally in the market and buyers should be able to make appropriate comparisons across data service providers to get a fair price.

1.8.3 Taxation Challenges

Corporate taxation aims to tax profits where value is created, but the current international tax framework was designed for the traditional economy. It is unable to take account of new modes of value creation in the digital economy, which require less physical presence and where user contributions and intangible assets play significant roles. As a result, public budgets, and social fairness are affected (European Commission, 2018).

1.8.4 Regulatory and Standardization Challenges

Currently there is a lack of asset standards or commonly agreed taxonomy for digital goods and services (such as Nice[12] or Asset Standards set by International Valuation Standards Council), which can be used as a common language for accounting purposes. As discussed in this chapter, current categorization of digital assets only reflects their technical functions instead of economic functions. Financial regulations and reporting standards also need to catch-up to ensure fair value of digital assets are captured.

1.9 CURRENT METHODS FOR DIGITAL ASSET VALUATION

Any valuation method must first fulfill these requirements:

1. *It must produce a no-arbitrage value*: A value that cannot be improved upon to yield a "better" valuation. Only then can the calculated value be a basis for challenging a market price which may not be a no-arbitrage ("efficient") price. The no-arbitrage value is firmly established in the theory of finance. The value of an investment is given by the future consumption that it is expected to yield, discounted for both the time value of money (the risk-free interest rate) and the risk that the expectation may not be realized (Penman, 2016).

---

12. Nice Classification: http://www.wipo.int/classifications/nice/nclpub/en/fr/.

2. *It must be practical*: There must be clear models for calculation that is feasible and repeatable in real circumstances.
3. *It is a matter of accounting*: A valuation model is only as good as the accounting that it involves. Currently, IFRS (International Financial Reporting Standards) is a global standard providing common language for business affairs so that company accounts are understandable and comparable across international boundaries.

Different quantitative valuation methods reveal different aspects of digital value. Within each of the basic valuation models, there are different variations that can be applied. The choice of model significantly influences the valuation estimate that is ultimately derived. At least in part, it also reflects the goals and concerns regarding the development and use of the asset (Matsuura, 2004). However, we are still far away from a simple and easy-to-understand calculation methods unveiling the complete and true value of digital assets. A new valuation model based on Digital Value Matrix (DVM) will be proposed in Chapter 2, Digital Theory of Value.

1.9.1   Intrinsic Value

Valuation models based on intrinsic value does not consider the business value at all, but focuses instead on the digital asset's intrinsic value (Laney, 2017). The model quantifies digital value by breaking it into characteristics such as accuracy, accessibility and completeness, as outlined in Section 1.7.

1.9.2   Direct Conversion of Financial Value

For digital assets whose value are directly proportional to their financial value (e.g., licenses, patents, original designs, projects, and prescriptions), the valuation can be written as:

$$V_{\text{direct}} \approx F_{\text{value}} \ (F_{\text{value}} = \text{financial value})$$

1.9.3   Business and Performance Value

Business value is a type of utility value. Valuation models based on business value measures characteristics of digital assets in relation to one or more business processes. This method focuses business functions, processes and decisions in which information appears as a critical driver (Laney, 2017; Laskowski, 2014). Performance value is a type of business value that measures impact of the digital asset on one or more Key Performance Indicators (KPIs) over time.

KPI is a type of performance measurement for evaluating the success of an organization or of a particular activity (such as projects, programs, products, and other initiatives) in which it engages. Examples of KPIs include profit, cost, cost of goods sold, revenue versus target, expenses versus budget. Choosing the right KPIs relies upon a good understanding of what is important to the organization. Under the business context, business processes should serve defined KPIs, so there are overlaps between business value and performance value (Laney, 2017; Laskowski, 2014). A sample list of value drivers of intangible assets is shown in Table 1.25.

TABLE 1.25 Value Drivers of Intangible Assets

Value Driver	Definition
Customer	The economic value that results from the associations (e.g., loyalty, satisfaction, longevity) and enterprise has built with consumers of its goods and services.
Competitor	The economic value that results from the position (e.g., reputation, market share, name recognition, and image) and enterprise built into the business market price.
Employee	The economic value that results from the collective capabilities (e.g., knowledge, skill, competence, know-how) of an enterprise's employees.
Information	The economic value that results from an enterprise's ability to collect and disseminate its information and knowledge in the right form and content to the right people at the right time.

(Continued)

TABLE 1.25 (Continued)

Value Driver	Definition
Partner	The economic value that results from associations (financial, strategic, authority, and power) and enterprise has established with external individuals and organizations (e.g., consultants, customers, suppliers, allies, and competitors) in pursuit of advantageous outcomes.
Process	The economic value that results from an enterprise's ability (e.g., policies, procedures, methodologies, and techniques) to leverage the ways in which the enterprise operates and creates value for its employees and customers.
Product/service	The economic value that results from an enterprise's ability to develop and deliver its offerings (i.e., products and services) that reflects an understanding of market and customer/s requirements, expectations and desires.
Technology	The economic value that results from the hardware and software an enterprise has invested in to support its operations, management, and future renewal.

TABLE 1.26 IT Value Grid

		Four sources of value			
		Efficiency	Effectiveness	Innovation	Flexibility
Four dimensions of competition	*Price*		Enable for price differentiation		
	Product		Enable for customization	Enable build to order	
	Promotion	Enable one-to-one marketing		Create new promotion channels	
	Placement		Enable when/where you want delivery		
Four groups of business processes	*Value adding*	Increase use of production resources	Allow for outsourcing	Create new channels	Allow for deferral of investments
	Innovating	Allow for interactive marketing		Allow for collaboration	
	Directing		Speed-up decision making		Be informed anytime, anywhere
	Controlling resources	Automate supportive tasks			Increase scalability of resources

One proposed approach to assess the value of information technology (IT) for an organization's business process and performance is using an IT value grid (IDG Research and Getronics, 2002). The IT value grid shown in Table 1.26 is based on 4 × 4 source of value representing external impact and internal impact:

1. Both internal business processes and external positioning of the organization: efficiency, effectiveness, innovation and flexibility.
2. External positioning for marketing and competitiveness: price, product, placement and promotion.

1.9.4 Cost-Based Models

Cost-based models measure the cost of acquiring or replacing lost digital assets including the cost incurred to produce, buy, reconstruct, change or compensate them, as well as the maintenance cost considering any regulatory obligations. Cost-based models do not generally address the potential future benefits that can be derived from the asset (e.g., licensing revenue), but are generally backward looking and often includes some form of adjustment for depreciation of the asset over time. The utility of cost-based models is limited due to the historical perspective. They do not present a complete picture of the potential applications for the assets, and are often applied in response to specific regulatory requirements, for example, for accounting, tax, and audit purposes. Cost-based models also do not capture the full impact of legal aspects of intangible asset management. Although cost-based models account for legal costs associated with obtaining and maintaining intellectual property rights (e.g., costs of patent protections and maintenance), they do not evaluate the future enforceability of patent or other intellectual property rights. Different companies will likely choose to incorporate different costs into their model. For this reason, cost-based models commonly vary from industry to industry and from company to company (Matsuura, 2004; Laney, 2017; Laskowski, 2014).

Example: Total Cost of Ownership (TCO)

Total cost of ownership is a financial estimate popularized by Gartner in 1987[13] to help buyers and owners determine the direct and indirect costs of a product or system. It is a cost-based model. The roots of this concept date at least back to the first quarter of the 21st century. It is a comprehensive assessment of IT or other costs across enterprise boundaries over time. For IT, TCO includes hardware and software acquisition, management and support, communications, end-user expenses and the opportunity cost of downtime, training and other productivity losses, for example:

- Computer hardware and programs: network hardware and software, server hardware and software, workstation hardware and software, installation and integration of hardware and software, purchasing research, warranties and licenses, license tracing, migration expenses, and risk management (patches, availability upgrades, etc.).
- Operation expenses: infrastructure, electricity, testing costs, downtime, outage and failure expenses, and diminished performance.
- Long-term expenses: replacement, future upgrade or scalability expenses, and decommissioning.

Some cost categories of IT include:

1. Hardware costs, for example, equipment costs, hardware maintenance, taxes, and upgrades.
2. Software costs, for example, OS/hypervisor licenses, software development, infrastructure management tools (servers, storage, and network), application management tools (change, service, and perf.), software maintenance, application software, and security software.
3. IT administration staff costs, for example, system administration, storage administration, network administration, security administration, and application administration.
4. Facility costs, for example, lease/loan payments, building security, facilities staff, building maintenance, taxes, upgrades, and power/cooling.

TCO has been used in evaluating cost of cloud adoption, for example, in comparing on-premise data center and public cloud Infrastructure-as-a-Service (IaaS) costs. Cost reduction was a key driver for cloud adoption in its early days. However, today organizations may not save money by migrating to IaaS deployments. Organizations must consider the Total Value of Ownership (TVO), including factors such as resiliency, availability and value-added services, and the use cases that yield the greatest advantages. TVO is a valuation model based on business and performance value (Gartner, 2017).

1.9.5 Market-Based Models

Market-based models estimate the value of digital assets by looking into the marketplace. Assets comparable to those in questions are identified, and the revenue actually derived from those comparable assets in the marketplace is used as an estimate of the value of the new assets. When comparable intangible assets can be readily identified, market-based valuation models are relatively easy to apply and can yield accurate projections. A significant problem associated with market-based valuation models is appropriate choice of comparable intangible assets. The accuracy of a market-based estimate is largely driven by selection of a model asset that provides an appropriate point of comparison. For this reason, market-based models work well when there is an established marketplace for

---

13. Garnter glossary: https://www.gartner.com/it-glossary/total-cost-of-ownership-tco.

the asset in question, and they are ineffective when there is no clearly defined marketplace relevant to the asset. Market-based models also fail to account for the full range of legal activities that affect intangible asset value. To the extent that the comparable assets that form the basis for the valuation model have legal characteristics comparable to those of the company applying the model, the legal attributes included in the model are more likely to be valid (Matsuura, 2004).

Different companies choose different markets as the basis for the valuation; there is substantial variety from company to company even when they each apply a market-based valuation approach (Laney 2017; Laskowski, 2014).

Example: Market for Personal Data

Personal data is said to be the "energy" or "new money" of digital world. Personal data refers to characteristic individual behavior data generally considered private, which is produced in personal life activities or work, and can be owned or controlled by an individual, including basic personal information, personal income, personal property, personal friends, personal health, personal education, personal diaries, personal memories, personal documents, personal views, and personal perception information. Its value is often highly subjective and tend to be underestimated by the owning individual. Technology giants (such as all of leading social media platforms) have profited from personal data collected from its users, creating a market for trading personal data. The digital platforms are often based on a "freemium" business model, where its users become the "product" of the platform (Ng and Ho, 2014).

1.9.6 Income-Based Models

Income-based models measure how a digital asset contributes to the revenue of an organization. What happens if the rival has it? Income-based valuation models make use of forecast future revenues to develop a current estimate of asset value. An intellectual asset's value is primarily established by the royalty revenue it can generate in a licensing structure. These models adopt a forward-looking perspective, estimating future earnings that can be derived from commercial use of intangible assets. Different companies apply different definitions and projections regarding revenue forecasting. As a consequence of this diversity, the income-based valuation models differ, in practice, from company to company (Laney, 2017; Laskowski, 2014).

Income-based models are commonly built on future cash flow estimates associated with a particular asset. These models project future earnings and expenditures attached to the asset. Those estimates are also discounted to account for the time value of money and the uncertainty as to the accuracy of the projected cash flow. The net present value of the future earnings is calculated so that the estimated potential value of the asset can be compared with similar estimates for other potential projects, and current resource allocation decisions can be made based on comparative future value of different projects.

As is the case with market-based models, income-based models function best when there is accurate information to support the future income and cash flow projections. Such information is more likely to be available when the asset in question is very similar to one already in the commercial marketplace or when the asset will reach a clearly defined and well-established market. Income-based models are less effective when market information is sketchy or speculative.

Selection of an appropriate discount rate also poses a major challenge, particularly with regard to the estimate of risk. The accuracy of the overall forecast hinges significantly on the accuracy of the selected discount rate. The discount rates should address both the time value of money and the risk that the estimated income flow will be inaccurate.

Income-based models can effectively capture the costs associated with obtaining and maintain intellectual property rights (e.g., the cost of patent prosecution and maintenance), but they do not assess the costs associated with enforcement of the legal rights that are tied to the asset including risks associated with enforceability of the patent.

1.9.7 Option Models

Another approach to estimating value of digital assets (e.g., intellectual property) makes use of the concept of options. An option is a choice that can be exercised at a specific time, but need not be exercised. Owners of digital assets have a variety of choices about the development and commercial use of their property. Those options include: what form of rights to invoke, whether to license the asset, how to price the asset, and when to apply legal means to enforce rights associated with an asset. Option models attempt to estimate economic values for each of those choices. The estimated economic values of the different options can be combined and compared, thus providing an analytical framework for selecting a commercialization strategy. Companies commonly define and identify options differently; thus, the versions of the option model applied by any two different organizations may be quite varied in structure and result (Matsuura, 2004).

Option models are most effective when the various options can be readily identified and valued. The models are more effective when the values for the options are stable, and not subject to dramatic shifts in value. Option models also perform more effectively when the options have set terms and cannot be exercised before they mature. Unfortunately, in the realm of intangible assets, these factors are difficult to satisfy. For example, the risks associated with the various options associated with commercialization of the asset change continuously over time. It is not feasible to adjust the discount factor continuously; thus, that factor will never be able to reflect precisely the true character of the risks associated with the options. It is also difficult to structure an option valuation model so that it effectively accounts for the actual future cash flow associated with commercialization of the asset. Advanced forms of option models could capture many of the costs associated with legal rights affecting intangible assets. Integration of those legal activities into the already complex option models is, however, another difficult challenge.

Chapter 2

Digital Theory of Value

Chapter Outline

2.1 The Search for a Value Theory Supporting the Fourth Industrial Revolution 30
  2.1.1 Digitization of Everything 30
  2.1.2 The Fourth Industrial Revolution 31
    2.1.2.1 Characteristic 1: Velocity 32
    2.1.2.2 Characteristic 2: Cross-Jurisdictional Economies of Scale Without Mass 32
    2.1.2.3 Characteristic 3: Heavy Reliance on Intangible Assets, Especially Intellectual Property 32
    2.1.2.4 Characteristic 4: The Importance of Data, User Participation, and Their Synergies With Intellectual Property 32
    2.1.2.5 Characteristic 5: Fusion of Technologies 32
    2.1.2.6 Characteristic 6: Consumption Externality 32
    2.1.2.7 Characteristic 7: Indirect Network Effects 33
    2.1.2.8 Characteristic 8: Lock-In Effects and Competition 33
2.2 Models for Digital Asset Valuation 33
  2.2.1 Method 1: Intrinsic Value 33
    2.2.1.1 1a: Intrinsic Cost of Production 33
    2.2.1.2 1b: Direct Financial Conversion 33
  2.2.2 Method 2: Extrinsic Value 34
    2.2.2.1 2a: Market Value 34
    2.2.2.2 2b: Usage Value 34
  2.2.3 Method 3: Subjective Value 35
  2.2.4 Method 4: Opportunity Value 35
2.3 Measuring the Digital Economy 35
  2.3.1 Measuring Rate of Digitalization of Traditional Industries: The Enabler and Multiplier 35
  2.3.2 Measuring Digital-Native Industries: The "Smarter," More Intelligent Disrupter 38
  2.3.3 Measuring the Invisible Economy: The Opportunity Value 40
2.4 Digital Theory of Value 40
  2.4.1 Law of Machine Time 40
    2.4.1.1 Phenomenon 1a: The Underlying Exponential Function 40
    2.4.1.2 Phenomenon 1b: The Future Cannot Be Projected From the Past using Current Statistical Methods 42

    2.4.1.3 Principle 1a: Progress of Digital Economy Should Be Measured Against Machine Time 42
    2.4.1.4 Principle 1b: Sensemaking Is a Universal Challenge and a Value Driver 42
    2.4.1.5 Principle 1c: Risk Management Is an Island of Stability in the Sea of Change 42
  2.4.2 Law of Recombination 43
    2.4.2.1 Phenomenon 2a: Quality Data Is the New Oil 43
    2.4.2.2 Phenomenon 2b: The Fusion of Technologies Is the Fuel for Innovative Breakthroughs 43
    2.4.2.3 Principle 2: Recombination Is an Engine for Growth 43
  2.4.3 Law of Hyperconnectivity 43
    2.4.3.1 Phenomenon 3a: New Era of Globalized Societies 43
    2.4.3.2 Phenomenon 3b: New Era of Complexity Economics 44
    2.4.3.3 Principle 3a: Hyperconnectivity Is an Engine for Growth 45
    2.4.3.4 Principle 3b: The Gravity of Value Creation will be Increasingly in the Virtual Space where Value Creation is Location Independent 45
    2.4.3.5 Principle 3c: Nontechnical Barriers Such As Geopolitical, Regulations, and Legal Frameworks Are Limiting Factors 45
  2.4.4 Law of Subjectivity 45
    2.4.4.1 Phenomenon 4a: The Need to Be Entertained 45
    2.4.4.2 Phenomenon 4b: The Demand for Customization 46
    2.4.4.3 Principle 4: A Greater Component of Value Is Increasingly Subjective, Reflecting Only in an Entity's Willingness-to-Pay 46
  2.4.5 Law of Abundance 46
    2.4.5.1 Phenomenon 5: Once Intrinsic Digital Value is Created, There are Limitless Ways to Multiply it with Extrinsic Digital Value 46
    2.4.5.2 Principle 5a: The Digitally Empowered Entity has Limitless Economic Potential 46

Digital Asset Valuation and Cyber Risk Measurement. DOI: https://doi.org/10.1016/B978-0-12-812158-0.00002-8

2.4.5.3 Principle 5b: Consumer Reception and
Power Supply Are Limiting Factors 46

2.4.5.4 Principle 5c: The Attention of a
Consumer Is the New Scarce Resource 46

2.4.6 Law of New Division of Labor 47

2.4.6.1 Phenomenon 6a: Labor Is Increasingly
a Less Important Factor in Value Production 47

2.4.6.2 Phenomenon 6b: New Necessities and the
Barrier to Entry in a Digitized Society 47

2.4.6.3 Phenomenon 6c: Deep Learning and
Machine Intelligence Are Still Inherently
Limited 47

2.4.6.4 Phenomenon 6d: Accuracy Is Not the Truth 48

2.4.6.5 Principle 6a: The Digital Economy Is
Creating a New Social Divide Based on
the New Labor Value Chain 48

2.4.6.6 Principle 6b: The Optimal Path to Intrinsic
Value Creation Is a Combination of Human
and Machine Intelligence 48

The search for a theory of value is really a search for a consistent foundation for economic theory.

—Kit Sims Taylor.

2.1 THE SEARCH FOR A VALUE THEORY SUPPORTING THE FOURTH INDUSTRIAL REVOLUTION

2.1.1 Digitization of Everything

Digitalization is an enabler, multiplier, and a disruptor.

The economic impact of digitalization has been the subject of an increasing amount of theoretical and empirical research since at least the early 2000s. The term "digital economy" was coined in Don Tapscott's 1995 best-seller *The Digital Economy: Promise and Peril in the Age of Networked Intelligence* (Tapscott, 1994), one of the first books to show how the Internet would change the way we did business. Today, digitization is ubiquitous, penetrating every aspect of work and life, from watching World Cup 2018 in a virtual reality (VR) lounge to embedding microchips under the skin to replace identity cards. As of 2018, the top five most valuable brands in business are all digital technology businesses: Apple, Google, Microsoft, Facebook, and Amazon. To start off, it is necessary to first clarify the differences between a few commonly used terms of digital economy:

Digitization: (1) Creating a digital (bits and bytes) version of analogue/physical things such as paper documents, microfilm images, photographs, sounds, and more. It is simply converting and/or representing something into a digital format that can be processed by a computing system. (2) Creating an automated process or workflow (often to replace manual ones) in business.

Digitalization: (1) In business, digitalization most often refers to enabling, improving, and transforming business operations, functions, models, processes, or activities by leveraging digital technologies and a broader context of digital data turned into actionable knowledge with a specific benefit in mind. Digitalizing is seen as the road of moving toward digital business and digital transformation, as well as the creation of new, digital revenue streams and offerings while doing so. (2) Digitalization can be used for a specific environment or area of business, for example, a digital workplace means a workforce that uses digital tools such as mobile devices, social collaboration, and unified communication platforms. (3) The adoption of digital technologies across all possible societal and human activities.

Digital sector is defined by IMF (2018) as core activities of digitalization, including Information and Communication Technologies (ICT) goods and services, online platforms, and platform-enabled activities, such as the sharing economy. One view is that the digital sector and ICT sector largely overlap (Barefoot et al., 2018). *Digital markets* are defined as the infrastructure on which digitized businesses develop (OECD, 2018). OECD[1] and BEA define *digital economy* as:

- *The digital-enabling infrastructure.* Digital-enabling infrastructure is comprised of the basic physical materials and organizational arrangements that support the existence and use of computer networks and the digital economy, including computer hardware, software, telecommunication equipment and services, Internet of things (IoT), as well as support structures and services necessary for the function of digital infrastructure such as construction of data centers, semiconductor fabrication plants, the installations of fiber optic cables, switches, repeaters, digital consulting services, and computer repair services.
- *E-commerce.* E-commerce describes all digital transactions that take place over computer networks, including digitally ordered, digitally delivered, or platform-enabled transactions, including business-to-business (B2B),

---

1. OECD Digital Economy: http://www.oecd.org/sti/ieconomy/.

business-to-consumer, and peer-to-peer (P2P) e-commerce. The "sharing" economy, also known as platform-enabled e-commerce, involves the exchange of goods and services between consumers facilitated through a digital application. These include, but are not limited to, ride dispatching, accommodation rentals, delivery and courier services, landscaping, food preparation, consumer goods rentals, laundry services, and janitorial services.

- *Digital media.* The content that people create, access, store, or view on digital devices, including direct sale and free digital media. The BEA definition of digital media also includes big data (OECD, 2014; Barefoot et al., 2018).

The view in this book is that currently the definition of digital economy for the purpose of economic measurements is narrow and siloed, preventing the real economic output from digitization to be fully captured:

- *The definitions are based on technological categories.* Instead of viewing from an economic lens, the current definition of digital economy is centered around technologies that have created significant economic impact, such as digital media. As technologies change and new digital game changers emerge, these definitions will have to be amended. This puts our economic understanding of digitization always one step behind the curve, playing catching-up.
- *The lack of definition of digital assets.* This is the root cause of the previous point. Without understanding digital assets as economic goods as discussed in detail in Chapter 1, Digital Assets as Economic Goods, it is not possible to gain a full picture of the economic implication of digitization.
- *Not counting the "invisible" opportunity cost of not having digital tools.* The current definition of digital economy underestimates the economic output from digitization because it does not count the cost savings, increased productivity, and reduced labor from using digital tools, many of which are "free" for the end users (e.g., Google maps, Google search). However, if such digital tools did not exist in the first place, the traditional alternative would have costed a lot more to produce the same result.

One of the main objectives of this book is to introduce models for measuring the wider "digital economy" that is rapidly transforming societies and businesses, bringing structural changes to value creation. In this book, digital economy is defined as the aggregated value created from digital-native goods, services, and the digitization of traditional industries.

2.1.2 The Fourth Industrial Revolution

Every major advancement in economic theories coincide with the introduction of new technologies that revolutionized industries.

The First Industrial Revolution (1760−1840) used water and steam power to transition from hand production to mechanize production, when classical economic theories of labor and cost of production were developed. The Second Industrial Revolution (1870−World War I) used electric power to create mass production. Electrification and automobiles created giant industrial corporations and stock markets. With a better understanding of the forces behind profit generation and capitalism, marginal theories were developed, followed by postdepression economics. The Third Industrial Revolution, often called the "digital revolution" (The Economist, 2012), can be dated to the invention of the first computer in 1946. Electronics, information technology (IT), and the Internet not only automated production, but also brought the world closer than ever before. In the meantime, the modern monetary system was created in 1944,[2] enabling economic structures allowing global corporations, global trade, and commerce. Now a Fourth Industrial Revolution is building on the Third. It is characterized by a fusion of technologies that is blurring the lines between the physical, digital, and biological spheres (WEF, 2016). The speed of current breakthroughs has no historical precedent. When compared with previous industrial revolutions, the Fourth is evolving at an exponential rather than a linear pace. It is disrupting almost every industry in every country, and the breadth and depth of these changes herald the transformation of entire systems of production, management, and governance.

The possibilities of billions of people connected by mobile devices, with unprecedented processing power, storage capacity, and access to knowledge. And these possibilities will be multiplied by emerging technology breakthroughs in fields such as artificial intelligence (AI), robotics, the IoT, autonomous vehicles, 3D printing, nanotechnology, biotechnology, materials science, energy storage, and quantum computing. Already, AI is all around us, from self-driving cars and drones to virtual assistants and software that translate or invest. Impressive progress has been made in AI in recent years, driven by exponential increases in computing power and by the availability of vast amounts of data, from software used to discover new drugs to algorithms used to predict our cultural interests. Digital fabrication

---

2. Two institutions were created as an outcome of the Bretton Woods Conference in 1944 attended by representatives from 44 nations: The International Monetary Fund (IMF) and the International Bank for Reconstruction and Development (IBRD), now known as the World Bank Group.

technologies, meanwhile, are interacting with the biological world on a daily basis. Engineers, designers, and architects are combining computational design, additive manufacturing, materials engineering, and synthetic biology to pioneer a symbiosis between microorganisms, our bodies, the products we consume, and even the buildings we inhabit (WEF, 2016).

Phenomena and characteristics of the Fourth Industrial Revolution are summarized next.

2.1.2.1 Characteristic 1: Velocity

Digitization has led to an acceleration of economic activities. In the digital space, transactions between end users in different jurisdictions can be concluded without loss of time and digital content can be accessed immediately from any device connected to the Internet. As a result, digital products and services disseminate faster, markets clear faster, ideas circulate faster, and it becomes much easier for businesses to identify, engage, and develop their customer bases. These increases in the speed of economic activity imply that businesses can gain significant competitive advantages by being the first to move into, and potentially dominate, a new market.

2.1.2.2 Characteristic 2: Cross-Jurisdictional Economies of Scale Without Mass

The digital market provides any digital products and services the potential to reach a global spread. Production of digital value has much lower barrier to entry and can happen from anyone who has access to a device connected to the Internet (Ross, 2016). Economic activities occur in digital markets by breaking traditional jurisdictional boundaries and creating multifaceted challenges to global regulatory and legal frameworks. For example, a user contributes to value creation by sharing his/her preferences (e.g., liking a page) on a social media forum. This data will later be used and monetized for targeted advertising. The profits are not necessarily taxed in the country of the user (and viewer of the advert), but rather in the country where the advertising algorithms have been developed. This means that the user contribution to the profits is not taken into account when the company is taxed (European Commission, 2018; OECD, 2018).

2.1.2.3 Characteristic 3: Heavy Reliance on Intangible Assets, Especially Intellectual Property

Digitized enterprises are characterized by the growing importance of investment in intangible assets, especially intellectual property (IP) assets which could either be owned by the business or leased from a third party. For many digitalized enterprises, the intense use of IP assets such as software and algorithms supporting their platforms, websites, and many other crucial functions are central to their business models (OECD, 2018).

2.1.2.4 Characteristic 4: The Importance of Data, User Participation, and Their Synergies With Intellectual Property

Data, user participation, network effects and the provision of user-generated content are commonly observed in the business models of more highly digitalized businesses. The benefits from data analysis are also likely to increase with the amount of collected information linked to a specific user or customer. The important role that user participation can play is seen in the case of social networks, where without data, network effects, and user-generated content, the businesses would not exist as we know them today. In addition, the degree of user participation can be broadly divided into two categories: active and passive user participation. However, the degree of user participation does not necessarily correlate with the degree of digitalization: for example, cloud computing can be considered as a more highly digitalized business that involves only limited user participation (OECD, 2018).

2.1.2.5 Characteristic 5: Fusion of Technologies

The Fourth Industrial Revolution is characterized by its fusion of technologies that blurs the boundaries between digital, physical, and biological worlds; and this fusion is not limited to these three spheres. The majority of MIT Breakthrough Technologies from 2010 involve innovations spanning multiple disciplines. The majority of today's top issues require multidisciplinary inputs. The fusion is everywhere, and it is a main driver for economic growth.

2.1.2.6 Characteristic 6: Consumption Externality

In digital markets, utility from the consumption of a specific good or service is often dependent on the number of other end users consuming the same good or service. This effect is called a direct network externality, sometimes also referred to as a direct network effect or consumption externality; it is a positive externality in that the larger the network, the larger the end-user utility. Consumption externality is a prevalent force behind the rise of the platforms. The most obvious examples are social media and online messaging services. Both applications are practically useless to the user if he or she is the only person using them, however, their value increases as the number of other users increases. The effect is apparent, for instance, in the case of online gaming (OECD, 2018).

2.1.2.7 Characteristic 7: Indirect Network Effects

In contrast to direct network effects, indirect network effects arise in the context of multisided markets, which occur when a specific group of end users (e.g., users of a social network) benefit from interacting with another group of end users (e.g., advertisers on a social network) via an online platform. Digitization has allowed the emergence of online platforms and networks, and we have seen an increasing number of platform-based businesses in many different sectors such as accommodation rental, transportation, or P2P e-commerce (OECD, 2018).

2.1.2.8 Characteristic 8: Lock-In Effects and Competition

Digital transactions can be carried out on different electronic devices; however, end-user devices often rely on different operating systems. As a result, customers may be locked-in to a particular operating system once they have acquired a specific device. This effect is due to psychological as well as monetary switching costs which end users have to incur in order to switch from one system to another, for example, a change from a specific smartphone (including operating system) to another, implies loss in access to previously accumulated applications and data (OECD, 2018). For a global corporation, a change from a primary cloud provider to another could imply significant costs in re-architecting applications. Due to the ubiquitous and pervasive nature of many digital technologies and devices that people are exposed to on a daily basis, for example, iOS versus Android, how these systems dictate our everyday choices and options can be comparable to political systems.

In terms of competition, it may be more difficult for new firms to gain significant market shares if an incumbent firm already dominates the market (OECD, 2018). Once a critical mass of end users has switched to the new product, it becomes possible for the formerly dominant firm to lose its entire market share within a short time space. This has been the case, for instance, with search engines, web browsers, and social media platforms (OECD, 2018). As Alstyne et al. (2016) puts it, scale now trumps differentiation.

Classic value theories cannot support the unique characteristics of digital assets discussed in Chapter 1, Digital Assets as Economic Goods, which are fundamental to wealth generation in the Fourth Industrial Revolution. The theory discussed in this book is aimed to search for a value theory that can support the Fourth Industrial Revolution.

2.2 MODELS FOR DIGITAL ASSET VALUATION

Built on digital value matrix introduced in Chapter 1, Digital Assets as Economic Goods, four methods are outlined below for digital asset valuation.

2.2.1 Method 1: Intrinsic Value

Intrinsic digital value is the critical elements that make it possible for the digital asset to exist in the first place. The intrinsic value of the digital asset is determined through fundamental analysis without reference to its market value. Intrinsic value can be measured using:

2.2.1.1 1a: Intrinsic Cost of Production

Replacement cost or cost to produce the critical elements that make it possible for the digital asset to exist, including labor, capital, infrastructure, and taxation, etc. For example, the value of a piece of software is the amount of man-days, technology cost, IP, and other costs that were put into the development of it.

2.2.1.2 1b: Direct Financial Conversion

Direct conversion of the financial value of the nondigital equivalent of the asset.

2.2.2   Method 2: Extrinsic Value

Extrinsic digital value describes the limitless opportunities to distribute and consume the digital asset so that it is more useful to prospective users. The extrinsic value of a digital asset is determined using its market price, or its usage value (Fig. 2.1).

As discussed in Chapter 1, Digital Assets as Economic Goods, digital assets can be categorized into core value assets and supportive assets. Table 2.1 shows core value activities and supportive value activities based on a generic business model. Digitization can automate, increase cost efficiency, productivity, extend shelf-life, or end-user empowerment of all the activities listed in Table 2.1.

2.2.2.1   2a: Market Value

The extrinsic market value of the digital asset is the price at which the digital valuable would trade in a competitive market. For example, according to a 2015 study, payment card numbers with CVV2 and date of birth are sold at US$15 per record in the United States and at US$30 per record in the United Kingdom. Payment card numbers with full personal information are sold at $30 per record in the United States and at $35 per record in the United Kingdom (Intel Security, 2015). Extrinsic market value can be measured using market-based, income-based, and options models.

2.2.2.2   2b: Usage Value

Usage value is a different concept from value-in-use. Extrinsic consumption from usage value considers the characteristics of digital assets that their value increases through usage. Digitization always makes it easier to share, reproduce, reuse, and increase the shelf-life of an asset, hence usage value is a multiplying factor. The valuation of mobile application start-ups, for example, is directly correlated with the size of its user base. The more a photo or a story is shared on a free social media platform such as Facebook, the more "valuable" it becomes, and this cannot be explained by classical economics.

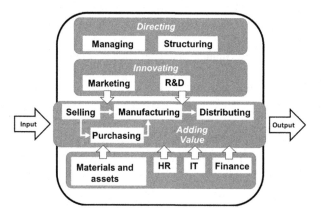

FIGURE 2.1   Generic business model based on traditional value chain (Porter, 1985).

TABLE 2.1 Core Value Activities and Supportive Value Activities

Core Value Activities	Supportive Value Activities
Creation of a product or service	Procurement
Marking and sales	Human resources
Execution	Firm infrastructure (including technical infrastructure)
Distribution/transfer to the customer	Inbound and outbound logistics
Research and development (including problem-finding and acquisition, problem-solving, choice)	Operations

2.2.3 Method 3: Subjective Value

The subjective value of the digital asset is determined by the importance the entity places on it; it is measured by how much an entity is willing to pay.

2.2.4 Method 4: Opportunity Value

Opportunity value is a concept originated from opportunity cost. Opportunity cost is the value of the choice in terms of the best alternative while making a decision, for example, firm A chooses to digitize part of its business while firm B does not. Opportunity value of the digital asset is defined in this book as:

> The **opportunity value of digitized asset** *is the value of using it comparing to using the non-digital alternative; the* **opportunity value of digital-native asset** *is the value of using it comparing to the nonexistent alternative, that is, the alternative that such asset did not exist at all.*

Business Impact Analysis (BIA) can be used to calculate OV when the digital option is unavailable, and the resulting nondigital or nonexistent alternative becoming the only option. Business Consequences (BC) can include financial, legal, reputation, and regulatory impact (ISF, 2000). For example, Amazon's 2013 service down time cost Amazon as a cloud service provider $66,240 per minute (Clay, 2013). Business impact can be measured using scenario analysis combined with defined loss categories.

Through BIA, the time and effort saved from having the digital option can be revealed from the difference between cost of the alternative and cost of the digital option required to produce the same result. For example, a study in 2010 has concluded that the average search time is 22 minutes offline comparing to 7 minutes online (Chen et al., 2010).

Based on the 4 methods introduced above, digital assets in economic categories introduced in Chapter 1, Digital Assets as Economic Goods, can be valued using the Digital Valuation Model in Table 2.2.

Here, selected digital asset examples introduced in Chapter 1, Digital Assets as Economic Goods, are reused to broadly demonstrate the valuation methods (Table 2.3).

2.3 MEASURING THE DIGITAL ECONOMY

Based on this analysis, the total output of digital economy should be measured from three components:

- Value created from digitalization of traditional industries, where digitization serves as the enabler and multiplier.
- Value created from digital-native industries, where digitization servers as the disrupter.
- Value created from the digital option. Opportunity value created from the mere existence of digital technologies comparing to two scenarios: (1) the nondigital alternative, or (2) the nonexistent alternative.

2.3.1 Measuring Rate of Digitalization of Traditional Industries: The Enabler and Multiplier

The current "measured" digital economy has been growing at triple the pace of the United States' GDP (Bloomberg, 2018). In the European Union, digital firms are growing at 14%, IT and telecoms are growing at 3%, while other multinationals are growing at 0.2% (Moscovici, 2018). These statistics mostly cover industries that are digitizing their core value. This is where digitalization serves as the enabler and multiplier, through increased extrinsic consumption. According to McKinsey Global Institute's Sector Digitization Index in Fig. 2.2, the pace of digitalization of industries from high to low is categorized into (McKinsey Global Institute, 2015):

1. Knowledge-intensive sectors, highly digitized.
2. Capital-intensive, potential to further digitize their assets.

TABLE 2.2 Digital Valuation Model

	Digitized	Digital-Native
Core value	Direct financial conversion × extrinsic (usage)	*f* (intrinsic, extrinsic (market, usage), subjective)
Supportive value	Opportunity value	

TABLE 2.3 Examples of Digital Asset Valuation

Category	Asset	Valuation Method
Digitized core value (individual)	Digital photos, videos, documents	Direct financial conversion of value of the asset × extrinsic (usage) The value of the photos, videos, and documents is directly converted from their physical equivalents, then multiplied by the usage value from increased accessibility, audience reached, and extended shelf life
	Personal data (e.g., payment card number with CVV2, health data)	Direct financial conversion of value of the asset × extrinsic (usage) The value of digitized personal data comes from direct conversion from their physical equivalent multiplied by the usage value from increased accessibility and extended shelf life
Digitized core value (organizational)	IP in digital format	Direct financial conversion of value of the asset × extrinsic (usage) The value of digitized personal data comes from direct conversion from their physical equivalent multiplied by the usage value from increased accessibility and extended shelf life
	Customer information	Direct financial conversion of value of the asset × extrinsic (usage) The value of digitized customer information comes from direct conversion from their physical equivalent multiplied by the usage value from increased accessibility, widened distribution channels, and extended shelf life
Digitized core value (national)	E-governance services	Direct financial conversion of value of the asset × extrinsic (usage) The value of e-governance services comes from direct conversion from their physical equivalent multiplied by the usage value from increased accessibility, widened outreach, and extended shelf life
Digitized core value (global)	Wikipedia	Direct financial conversion of value of the asset × extrinsic (usage) The value of Wikipedia comes from direct conversion from physical encyclopedia multiplied by the usage value from increased accessibility, widened outreach, and extended shelf life
Digitized supportive value (individual)	Digital documents (e.g., presentations)	OV Cost savings and increased productivity comparing to using paper-based documents
Digitized supportive value (organizational)	Critical operational business applications (e.g., office productivity tools, emails)	OV Cost savings and increased productivity comparing to using non-digital processes (e.g., paper-based office productivity, postal services)
Digitized supportive value (national)	National ICT infrastructure	OV Economic loss incurs when ICT infrastructure becomes unavailable
Digitized supportive value (global)	Google maps	OV Cost savings and increased productivity comparing to using manual maps
Digital-native supportive value (individual)	Cloud-storage subscription	OV Economic loss from not having access to cloud-based data and services
Digital-native supportive value (organizational)	Encryption keys	OV Economic loss from not having access to encrypted data. If the encryption keys provide access to business critical data, then the value of the keys can be equivalent to the value of the business

(Continued)

TABLE 2.3 (Continued)

Category	Asset	Valuation Method
Digital-native supportive value (national)	Critical infrastructure supported by computing (e.g., Nuclear plants, air traffic control, smart grids)	OV Economic loss from dysfunctional or disrupted critical infrastructure
Digital-native supportive value (global)	Cloud infrastructure	OV Economic loss from not having cloud computing
Digital-native core value (individual)	Personal online accounts (e.g., Facebook, Twitter, YouTube, Instagram)	*f* [intrinsic, extrinsic (market, usage), subjective] The value of personal online accounts can come from market data in trading, reflected in how much they are consumed (e.g., social influence score). The value of personal online accounts can also be subjective to each individual. As these accounts often provide access to large volume of personal data created through day-to-day activities, there is an intrinsic value to the production of such profiles.
Digital-native core value (organizational)	Digital IP such as software	*f* [intrinsic, extrinsic (market, usage)] The value of digital-native IP can be first of all intrinsic calculated from cost of production. Once the IP is in the market and being used, both extrinsic market and usage value can also contribute as components of its valuation
	Cloud services of a cloud provider	Extrinsic (market, usage) The value of cloud services is calculated directly using the market price of the service and user base
	3D printing design files	*f* [intrinsic, extrinsic (market, usage)] The value of 3D printing design files can be first of all intrinsic calculated from cost of production. Once the design is in the market and being used, both extrinsic market and usage value can also contribute as components of its valuation
	Metadata used for analytics	Extrinsic (market, usage) The value of metadata is calculated from its market pricing in trade or usage value while being used as data input
	Cyber-physical systems (e.g., drones) of a producer	*f* [intrinsic, extrinsic (market, usage)] The value of cyber-physical systems can be first of all intrinsic calculated from cost of production. Once the product is in the market and being sold, its value should come from pricing of the product and user base
Digital-native core value (national)	ICT industries	Intrinsic The value of ICT industries should come from its total cost of production
Digital-native core value (global)	Bitcoin	Extrinsic (market) Valuation of bitcoin is based on its market price

3. Service sectors with long tail of small firms having room to digitize customer transactions.
4. Business to Business (B2B) sectors with the potential to digitally engage and interact with their customers and users.
5. Labor-intensive sectors with the potential to provide digital tools and skills to their workforce; and
6. Large, localized, low productivity could transform for productivity and delivery of services.

Adapted from EU digital tax proposal (European Commission, 2018), below factors are proposed for measuring economic value from digitalization of industries over a taxable year, They reflect the direct conversion of physical value creation, extrinsic market, and usage value of digital assets:

- *Digital revenue*. Revenue generated by digital services over a taxable year.

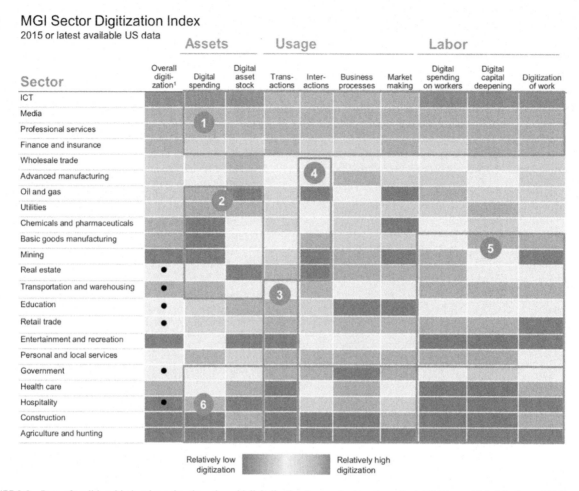

FIGURE 2.2   Pace of traditional industries going through rapid digitalization (core value transformation) (McKinsey Global Institute, 2015).

- *Digital contracts.* Number of business contracts for digital services between the business provider and business consumers including business consumers, end users, service users, P2P users.
- *Digital access.* Amount of access from consumers to its digital services without a business contract, e.g., free service, including social media feeds.

2.3.2   Measuring Digital-Native Industries: The "Smarter," More Intelligent Disrupter

Digital-native is the real driver of the Fourth Industrial Revolution. Digital-native value creation models disrupt traditional models such as business models built on cloud computing, 3D printing, virtual reality , and AI. The valuation of digital native industries should use a combination of intrinsic and extrinsic models on a case-to-case basis. On the supply side, many industries are seeing the introduction of new technologies that create entirely new ways of serving existing needs and significantly disrupt existing industry value chains. Disruption is also flowing from agile, innovative competitors who, thanks to access to global digital platforms for research, development, marketing, sales, and distribution, can oust well-established incumbents faster than ever by improving the quality, speed, or price at which value is delivered. Major shifts on the demand side are also occurring, as growing transparency, consumer engagement, and new patterns of consumer behavior (increasingly built upon access to mobile networks and data) force companies to adapt the way they design, market, and deliver products and services (WEF, 2016). In fact, the start-ups with highest valuation today are *all* digital-natives (Table 2.4).

Example: Platform Revolution

The technology-enabled platform revolution is a creation of digital-native. Back in 2007, the five major mobile phone manufacturers—Nokia, Samsung, Motorola, Sony Ericsson, and LG—collectively controlled 90% of the industry's

TABLE 2.4 Most Valued Start-Ups in 2018

Company	Last Valuation (US$ Billion)	Last Valuation Date	Description
Ant financial	150	May 2018	Formerly known as Alipay, Ant Financial is an affiliate company of the Chinese Alibaba Group and the highest valued fintech company in the world
Uber	68	June 2016	A peer-to-peer ride-sharing, taxi cab, food delivery, and transportation network company
Didi Chuxing	50	April 2017	A major Chinese ride-sharing, AI and autonomous technology company
Xiaomi	46	December 2014	A Chinese electronics company that makes and invests in smartphones, mobile apps, laptops, and related consumer electronics
Airbnb	31	March 2017	An online marketplace and hospitality service for short-term lodging, holiday cottages, apartments, homestays, hostel beds, or hotel rooms
Alibaba Cloud	30	January 2018	A cloud computing company
Palantir	20	October 2015	An American software company that specializes in big data analytics
WeWork	20	July 2017	An American company that provides shared workspace, technology start-up subculture communities, and services for entrepreneurs, freelancers, start-ups, small business, and large enterprises

TABLE 2.5 Platform Revolution in Hospitality Industry (Hagiu and Rothman, 2016)

Company	Number of Rooms	Founded	Market Cap	Time to 1M Rooms	Real Estate Assets
Airbnb	1M +	2008	$25B	7 years	$0
Marriott	1.1M	1957	$16B	58 years	$985M
Hilton	745K	1919	$19B	N/A	$9.1B
Intercontinental Hotel Group	727K	1988	$9B	N/A	$741M

global profits. That year, Apple's iPhone burst onto the scene and began gobbling up the market share. By 2015, the iPhone singlehandedly generated 92% of global profits, while all but one of the former incumbents made no profit at all. In 2016, private equity markets gave Uber (founded in 2009) a valuation higher than GMs (founded in 1908). It took Airbnb (founded in 2008) 7 years to reach one million rooms compared to 58 years for Marriott. Today, Airbnb is more profitable than all of the incumbents, as shown in Table 2.5, with zero ownership in real estate assets. Alstyne et al. (2016) argues that when a platform enters the market of a pure pipeline business, the platform virtually always wins.

Conventional "pipeline" businesses have dominated industry for decades; they create value by controlling a linear series of activities—the classic value-chain model with inputs at one end and an output that is worth more: the finished product. The technology-enabled platform economy comprises a distinctly new set of economic relations that depend on the Internet, computation, and data. The ecosystem created by each platform is a source of value and sets the terms by which users can participate (Kenny and Zysman, 2016). Platforms combine both demand and supply to disrupt existing industry structures, such as those we see within the "sharing" or "on demand" economy. These technology platforms, rendered easy-to-use by the smartphone, convene people, assets, and data—thus, creating entirely new ways of consuming goods and services in the process. In addition, they lower the barriers for businesses and individuals to create wealth and altering the personal and professional environments of workers. These new platform businesses are rapidly multiplying into many new services, ranging from laundry to shopping, from chores to parking, from massages to travel (WEF, 2016).

The move from pipeline to platform is inherently disruptive, which involves three key shifts (Alstyne et al., 2016):

- *From resource control to resource orchestration.* The resource-based view of competition holds that firms gain advantage by controlling scarce and valuable—ideally, inimitable—assets. With platforms, the assets that are hard to copy are the community and the resources its members own and contribute, be they rooms or cars or ideas and information. In other words, the network of products and consumers is the chief asset.
- *From internal optimization to external interaction.* The emphasis shifts from dictating processes in pipeline to persuading participants in platforms, and ecosystem governance becomes an essential skill. Platforms create value by facilitating interactions between external producers and consumers. They often shed even variable cost of production because of this external orientation.
- *From a focus on customer value to a focus on ecosystem value.* Pipelines seek to maximize the lifetime value of individual customers of products and services, who in effect sit at the end of a linear process. By contrast, platforms seek to maximize the total value of an expanding ecosystem in a circular, iterative, feedback-driven process.

2.3.3 Measuring the Invisible Economy: The Opportunity Value

In a 2015 McKinsey report in an attempt to measure the digital economy, it demonstrated that ICT sector counts as 5% of GDP in official statistics, 10% as a share of GDP taking into account price effects (McKinsey Global Institute, 2015). However, if the impact of the digital economy is evaluated based on percentage of population that have access to high-speed wireless Internet which can be taken away, it is 98%. This revealed the unmeasured "invisible economy." If access to high-speed Internet is taken away, how much of American economy will be halted? The opportunity cost of not having access to digitally enabled economic resources, has not been properly measured.

As of June 2017, 51% of the world's population has internet access. In 2015, the International Telecommunication Union estimated that about 3.2 billion people, or almost half of the world's population, would be online by the end of that year. In 2017, phone connections have reached 7.7 billion globally, which has exceeded the total population on Earth. Access to digital tools has become a core value generator of the modern economy. An experimental study was carried out to study the impact on productivity in a day without a search engine. A more accurate valuation of the invisible economy should be based on such experiments on all digital options supporting our economy today.

2.4 DIGITAL THEORY OF VALUE

To conclude what have been discussed in Chapter 1, Digital Assets as Economic Goods, and this chapter, this section introduces digital theory of value in an attempt to summarize unique phenomena that cannot be explained by any traditional theories of values, and principles that can help us understand various forces behind the formation of the future of value.

In this book, the digital value of an entity is defined as:

The sum of the aggregated value from its core value assets and the aggregated value from its supportive value assets.

Entity E's total digital value can be calculated as:

$$V = \sum_{i=1}^{N_c} cv_i + \sum_{j=1}^{N_s} sv_j \qquad (2.1)$$

where V is the total digital value of entity E; cv the value of core value asset c of entity E; sv the value of supportive value asset o of entity E; N_c the number of core value assets in entity E; and N_s the number of supportive value assets in entity E.

2.4.1 Law of Machine Time

2.4.1.1 Phenomenon 1a: The Underlying Exponential Function

Fig. 2.3 shows long-term history of world GDP. Plotted on a linear scale, the history of the world economy looks like a flat line hugging the X-axis, until it suddenly spikes vertically upward. Even when the figure is zoomed in on the most recent 10,000 years, the pattern remains essentially one of a single 90-degree angle. Only within the past 200 years or so does the curve lift perceptibly above the zero level (Bostrom, 2014). The diagram basically numerically says that most of human history is boring. For many thousands of years, humanity entertained a very gradual upward trajectory.

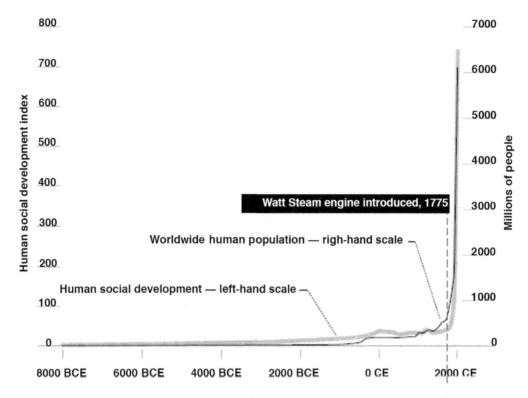

FIGURE 2.3   What bent the curve of human history? The Industrial Revolution (Bostrom, 2014; Brynjolfsson and McAfee, 2014).

Progress was achingly slow, almost invisible. Animals and farms, wars and empires, philosophies and religions all failed to exert much influence, but just over 200 years ago, something sudden and profound arrived and bent the curve of human history—of population and social development. The sudden change in the graph in the late-18th century corresponds to the Industrial Revolution, which was the sum of several nearly simultaneous developments in mechanical engineering, chemistry, metallurgy, and other disciplines. This led to factories and mass production, to railways and mass transportation. It led, in other words, to modern life (Brynjolfsson and McAfee, 2014). The ability to generate massive amounts of mechanical power was so important that in James Morris's words, it "made mockery of all the drama of the world's earlier history."

The most current curve since a few decades ago is, however, bent at almost 90 degrees. This time, the exponential growth corresponds to Moore's law, which describes the growth trajectory of computing power. This validates Martin Weitzman's view that the long-term growth of an advanced economy is dominated by the behavior of technical progress (Weitzman, 1998). When progress is at such an exponential rate it becomes incomprehensible, simply because the standard linear spacing is not great for showing exponential growth. If the vertical axis is changed to logarithmic spacing, where each of the segments of the vertical axis represents a 10-fold increase, the exponential growth becomes a perfectly straight line (Fig. 2.4).

It has become common sense that digital luxuries are being "crammed" into necessities at an exponential rate, as a result of Moore's law. The computing power used to land people on the moon has long been surpassed by the computing power in everybody's average smartphone. The ASCI Red, the first product of the US Government's Accelerated Strategic Computing Initiative designed for calculation intense tasks like simulating nuclear tests, was the world's fastest supercomputer when it was introduced in 1996. It cost $55 million to develop and its one hundred cabinets occupied nearly 148 m^2 of floor space. Nine years later, the same computing power was "crammed" into a Sony PlayStation 3 console (Brynjolfsson and McAfee, 2014). To help put the underlying exponential growth function into a perspective that everyone can easily grasp:

If we change our biological time into machine time, the year 2018 is not the same length as the year 2000, but 4096 times of it, i.e., we have lived 4096 years of progress in 2018 relative to year 2000.

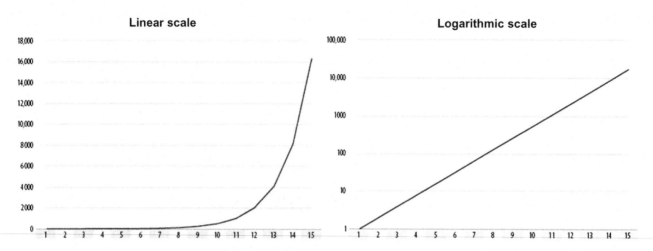

FIGURE 2.4   Exponential growth represented in a logarithmic graph.

2.4.1.2   Phenomenon 1b: The Future Cannot Be Projected From the Past using Current Statistical Methods

The exponential nature of machine time will rapidly change and challenge our perception of pretty much everything that we are used to throughout human evolution. Sea changes and paradigm shifts are arriving faster and more frequent with greater impact. Under the technological context, the historical perspective is rapidly becoming completely irrelevant. It is increasingly challenging to statistically project the future using historical data. What exponential growth brings are richer data points in a shorter time frame which make our current data collection methods inadequate.

2.4.1.3   Principle 1a: Progress of Digital Economy Should Be Measured Against Machine Time

Currently, all of our economy measures are still based on traditional metrics against "human time" that we are most familiar with. The fact that machine time is different from human perception of time due to its exponential nature means progress of the digital economy is measured using the wrong yardstick.

In digital theory of value, the relative machine time is calculated as:

$$\text{Number of years} = \frac{2^{\frac{2(\text{Current year}-1965)}{3}} - 2^{\frac{2(\text{Current year}-1966)}{3}}}{2^{\frac{2(\text{Base year}-1965)}{3}} - 2^{\frac{2(\text{Base year}-1966)}{3}}}$$

where current year is the year of calculation, base year is the relative year that the current year is compared to. For example, using this equation, the progress we experienced in 2018 is equivalent to 4096 years using the base year of 2000.

2.4.1.4   Principle 1b: Sensemaking Is a Universal Challenge and a Value Driver

Exponential progress makes it increasingly challenging to force old perceptions, old solutions, and old mindsets into the new problems that arise. For example, in problem-solving, almost all problems require a multidisciplinary approach. This is because the old disciplinary boundaries cannot accommodate the complexity of today's problems as they span multiple disciplines. The rising instability of global systems as a result of the pace of change can cause significant fear, division, isolation, and instability (Guillen, 2015). The rapid disappearance of history and a familiar frame of references means revolutionary mega-structures are required to address the constant challenge of sensemaking, which will be an important driver for the future of value. This book is all about starting such efforts to build such new structures.

2.4.1.5   Principle 1c: Risk Management Is an Island of Stability in the Sea of Change

Exponential progress toward a future that is harder to predict makes risk management an island of stability in the sea of change. With value comes risk. Risk management around the future of value require highly adaptive models that can respond to more "Black Swan" events.[3] As Charles Darwin puts it, "it is not the strongest of the species that survives,

---

3. The black swan theory or theory of black swan events is a metaphor that describes an event that comes as a surprise, has a major effect, and is often inappropriately rationalized after that fact with the benefit of hindsight.

nor the most intelligent. It is the one that is the most adaptive to change." Chapter 3, Cyber Risk Management: A New Era of Enterprise Risk Management, and Chapter 4, Cyber Risk Measurement in the Hyperconnected World, are dedicated to risk management and measurement to address this need.

2.4.2 Law of Recombination

2.4.2.1 Phenomenon 2a: Quality Data Is the New Oil

Quality data is the new oil and the new "raw material" for value creation. Being a data scientist is called "the sexist job of the 21st century" (Davenport and Patil, 2012). Data science is an interdisciplinary field that uses scientific methods, processes, algorithms, and systems to extract knowledge and insights from data in various forms, both structured and unstructured, in order to understand and analyze actual phenomena with data. It employs techniques and theories drawn from many fields within the context of mathematics, statistics, information science, and computer science. A key measure differentiating good data science from bad is how its defined algorithms help bring divergent data sources and facts together and generate useful correlations and insights. As discussed in Chapter 1, Digital Assets as Economic Goods, more data do not automatically generate more value, and can incur cost instead. A large volume of low-quality data can be seen as a type of "data pollution."

2.4.2.2 Phenomenon 2b: The Fusion of Technologies Is the Fuel for Innovative Breakthroughs

The Fourth Industrial Revolution is characterized by "a fusion of technologies that is blurring the lines between physical, digital, and biological worlds" (WEF, 2016). Almost all of the innovations listed in MIT Breakthrough Technologies from 2010[4] combine expertise and tools from multiple disciplines and domains. The average researcher today has access to more scientific research resources and powerful open-platform processing tools than ever before, which leads to more cross-disciplinary collaborations and innovations.

2.4.2.3 Principle 2: Recombination Is an Engine for Growth

Transdisciplinarity connotes a research strategy that crosses many disciplinary boundaries to create a holistic approach; such as research on effective information systems for biomedical research, that is, bioinformatics, as well as concepts or methods that were originally developed by one discipline, but are now used by several others, such as ethnography, a field research method originally developed in anthropology, but now widely used by other disciplines. Steve Jobs famously said that "the musicians play their instruments. I play the orchestra," and acknowledged that the skill for "connecting the dots" will be high on the value chain.

In genetics, recombination is defined as the formation by the process of crossing-over and independent assortment of new combinations of genes in progeny that did not occur in the parents. Weitzman (1998) borrowed the term to describe an idea-based growth model, which shows that knowledge can build upon itself in a combinatoric feedback process that may have significant implication for economic growth. Referring to Characteristics 2 of digital assets in Chapter 1, Digital Assets as Economic Goods, digitization has made collaboration of ideas faster and easier than ever. Meaningful and divergent aggregation of quality data can fuel the recombinant growth of ideas which can lead to powerful and innovative breakthroughs. Recombination is the growth mindset and a multiplying factor in the digital economy.

2.4.3 Law of Hyperconnectivity

2.4.3.1 Phenomenon 3a: New Era of Globalized Societies

It is very interesting how new means of transportation is always central to any industrial revolution. From the building of canals, invention of the steam engine, to railways, automobiles, and airplanes, connecting societies more efficiently has always been an engine for accelerating economic activities. The essence of economic opportunities, though, lies in having access to economic information that describes desires and demands from the markets.

The Third and Fourth Industrial Revolution, however, has brought globalization to a whole new level, that is, through allowing instant exchange of economic information without any requirement of physical movement and transport, anytime from anywhere that has an Internet connection. This means an explosion of economic opportunities. For example, social media has connected the global population to an extent that the wants and needs of

---

4. Breakthrough technologies is an annual list composed by MIT Technology Review since 2001, retrieved from https://www.technologyreview.com/lists/technologies/2018/.

people on one side of the world are instantly transmitted to the other side. The IoT continue to spread this level of connectivity to the world of machines.

We now live in a new era of globalized societies where communities are brought together faster and closer through virtual networks. More and more young people grow up as "digital nomads." Before global citizenship becomes a reality, our "digital-selves," that is, the aggregated digital footprint of our online identities, have already become global citizens. Hyperconnectivity beyond geographical and physical borders, value creation, exchange and distribution beyond existing trading systems of physical goods have rendered nation states paralyzed as structures of wealth creation and economic analysis in the digital economy. Today, large multinational technology companies have more influence on everyday decision-making of the networked population than any governments. When it comes to digital infrastructure under the highly sophisticated context of digital sovereignty, the top cloud computing providers are either Americans or Chinese.

This new era of globalization also reflects in whether the virtual or physical world is the main driver of value creation. In the earlier phases of digitization, the virtual world is often seen as a reflection of the physical, largely represented by the digitization of industries. In contrast, now the gravity of productivity is gradually moving into the virtual space and digital-native has become a primary growth driver in value creation. The physical world, in turn, is becoming the part that needs to adapt and accommodate the virtual space.

2.4.3.2 Phenomenon 3b: New Era of Complexity Economics

Hyperconnected societies and the multilayered interdependencies among multisided economic agents are giving rise to an explosion of complexity. Complexity economics[5] is the application of complexity science to the problems of economics. It sees the economy not as a system in equilibrium, but as one in motion, perpetually constructing itself anew (Arthur, 2015; Beinhocker, 2006). It uses computational rather than mathematical analysis to explore how economic structure is formed and reformed, in continuous interaction with the adaptive behavior of the agents in the economy. Barkley (1999) describes several features of complex systems that deserve greater attention in economics:

- *Dispersed interaction.* The economy has interaction between many dispersed, heterogenous agents. The action of any given agent depends upon the anticipated actions of other agents and on the aggregate state of the economy.
- *No global controller.* Controls are provided by mechanisms of competition and coordination between agents. No global entity controls interactions.
- *Cross-cutting hierarchical organization.* The economy has many levels of organization and interaction. The overall organization is more than hierarchical, with many sorts of tangling interactions (associations, channels of communications) across levels.
- *Ongoing adaptation.* Behaviors, actions, strategies, and products are revised frequently as the individual agents accumulate experience.
- *Novelty niches.* Such niches are associated with new markets, new technologies, new behaviors, and new institutions. The very act of filling a niche may provide new niches. The result is ongoing novelty.
- *Out-of-equilibrium dynamics.* Because new niches, new potentials, new possibilities, are continually created, the economy functions without attaining any optimum or global equilibrium.

The behavior and computability of complexity economic models may in turn be classified according to corresponding levels of complexity which are associated with the same hierarchies of linguistic complexity:

- Systems which have a "point attractor," that is, there exists a single equilibrium state of the system to which the system will "gravitate" in time. In general, this equilibrium state is computable by neoclassical means of economic theory.
- Systems which exhibit cyclical behavior such as is seen in business cycles, the parameters if which can be computed by the methods of structural economic theory.
- Chaos (also known as "strange attractor"), the quasi-equilibrium of the system is chaotic behavior in which there is no stable equilibrium state and no detectable periodic behavior.
- Complex behavior in which the system moves sharply and unpredictably toward different equilibrium states, periodic behavior, or chaos, but the outcome is indefinitely sensitive to initial conditions and formally unpredictable, like the notorious butterfly which "causes" a tornado.

---

5. Complexity economics at Santa Fe Institute. Retrieved from: http://tuvalu.santafe.edu/~wbarthur/complexityeconomics.htm.

2.4.3.3   Principle 3a: Hyperconnectivity Is an Engine for Growth

The world is now "flat." As a main feature of the new era of globalization, hyperconnectivity has given rise to multi-sided markets where consumers are also participants of the creation of new products and services. It provides an instant global reach to any digitally empowered entity. In highly interdependent, hyperconnected societies, access to information is no longer the barrier; the challenge is to capture insight that generates economic value, and this is the new battlefield of innovation and IP creation. This requires new mega global structures that can adapt to the explosion of complex economic information created from connecting the world population to a new level.

2.4.3.4   Principle 3b: The Gravity of Value Creation will be Increasingly in the Virtual Space where Value Creation is Location Independent

Digitization will continue to change our way of work, bringing greater flexibility. The future of work is mobile and location independent. With nearly 50% of millennial workers already freelancing, freelancers are predicted to become the US workforce majority within a decade. Its growth has outpaced overall US workforce growth by three times since 2014 (Upwork, 2017). This means, the traditional major city hubs for value creation in various sectors and industries—for example, San Francisco for start-ups, London for finance—may gradually be replaced by virtual communities made of global nomads who are not bound to a fixed location of work (Ross, 2016). This is also the driver behind the emergence of coworking and coliving spaces around the world for millennials who combine work, travel, and play, without compromising overall productivity.

2.4.3.5   Principle 3c: Nontechnical Barriers Such As Geopolitical, Regulations, and Legal Frameworks Are Limiting Factors

While digital growth accelerates, the real limiting factors are nontechnical constraints systems developed for problem-solving in the "old world" which are failing to adapt and catch up. This includes legal and regulatory frameworks currently used to govern digital issues such as cyber security, privacy, and financial reporting, which are by default pan-jurisdictional.

2.4.4   Law of Subjectivity

2.4.4.1   Phenomenon 4a: The Need to Be Entertained

Reduced labor and automation bring more free time and, hence, the need to be entertained. Some 400 hours of videos are uploaded to YouTube every minute. The world watches over 1 billion hours of YouTube videos and generates over 1 billion mobile video views in a day.[6] Netflix users streamed 42.5 billion hours of content in 2015 (McAlone, 2016). Instagram users "like" over 4.2 billion posts per day.

Virtual reality (VR) is an artificial, computer-generated simulation or recreation of a real-life environment or situation. It immerses the user by making them feel like they are experiencing the simulated reality firsthand, primarily by simulating their vision and hearing. VR is typically achieved by wearing a headset like Facebook's Oculus. Augmented reality (AR) is a technology that layers computer-generated enhancements atop an existing reality in order to make it more meaningful through the ability to interact with it. AR is developed into apps and used on mobile devices to blend digital components into the real world in such a way that they enhance one another, but can also be separated easily. Both AR and VR provide complete immersion and will play major roles in shaping the future of entertainment. While in the past they seemed merely a figment of science fiction imagination, new artificial worlds come to life under the user's control, and deeper layers of interaction with the real world are also achievable (Augment, 2015). For creators, the new field represents near-limitless boundaries for creativity and valuable user experiences.

Powered by AI and machine learning, media and entertainment is changing from a "watch only" medium to being fully interactive. Digitalization is extending entertainment from the theaters into day-to-day lives. Today, content creation is all about deepening interactive possibilities with its consumers. Currently, algorithms not only influence what audiences see on different platforms, but also the content that is being created in the first place (Towards Data Science, 2018). This value creation process for the consumer is highly personalized, subjective, and engaging.

---

6. Source: https://www.brandwatch.com/blog/39-youtube-stats/.

2.4.4.2 Phenomenon 4b: The Demand for Customization

If the industrial age and mass production created standard consumer products, digitization is bringing back the highly tailored, personalized products that are high on subjective value. In 2018, a Facebook "like" means outreach and customer engagement for brands. AI and machine learning algorithms are constantly analyzing and discovering what each of the consumers are interested in, that is, "likes," so products and contents can be shipped to their screens. The number of social media followers creates a value of emotional fulfillment for the average user that is very hard to quantify. There is also a growing industry in experience design that can be digitized using AR and VR technologies.

2.4.4.3 Principle 4: A Greater Component of Value Is Increasingly Subjective, Reflecting Only in an Entity's Willingness-to-Pay

Phenomena described here both contribute to the conclusion that a much greater component of value in digital economy will be subjective. It is up to the consumers how much attention, time, and money they are willing to spend on a product or service. There will also be a greater influence from the herd mentality, that is, people can be influenced by their peers to adopt certain behaviors on a largely emotional, rather than rational, basis. It requires new systems of regulation and new tools for prediction.

2.4.5 Law of Abundance

2.4.5.1 Phenomenon 5: Once Intrinsic Digital Value is Created, There are Limitless Ways to Multiply it with Extrinsic Digital Value

The characteristics of digital economy determine that as long as competitive intrinsic value is created, there are limitless ways to scale its value. Global computing and storage capacity is reaching a state of being limitless, hence it can theoretically support the distribution of any idea as long as it is a good idea.

2.4.5.2 Principle 5a: The Digitally Empowered Entity has Limitless Economic Potential

Comparing to traditional means of value creation where the business owner must employ thousands of people or spend a fortune upfront in its infrastructure (factory, computing infrastructures, manufacturing equipment, etc.), digital value creation and distribution often incur much lower reproduction cost. Digitization gives the digitally empowered entity access to more economic potential than ever before. Because digital value has unlimited utility to the owner with low marginal cost, and there is limitless ways to scale its value, the digitally empowered entity has limitless economic potential. The most important competitive edge then becomes creating intrinsic value in the first place

2.4.5.3 Principle 5b: Consumer Reception and Power Supply Are Limiting Factors

Given limitless potential for value creation, the only limiting factors are two:

1. Battery power. Our digital life today is still constrained by battery life.
2. Human cognitive capability to consume as long as humans are targeted as consumers. As discussed in Chapter 1, Digital Assets as Economic Goods, value creation requires the capability to comprehend from the user. Studies show that humans are slow to comprehend exponential growth, and growth of digitization is constrained by how fast human consumers can adapt to it.

2.4.5.4 Principle 5c: The Attention of a Consumer Is the New Scarce Resource

The explosion of digital content, services and products have led to the billion-dollar wellness industry, developing tools, trainings, meditative habits, and a culture for balance between the online and offline world. "Digital-detox," has become the latest trend for people who are constantly exposed to a hyperconnected world of distraction. In the digital economy where consumers are also participants of value creation, their contribution is often paid by "paying attention," for example, by following a brand on social media, and every economic decision requires attention. A successful app often employs the smartest people, uses the smartest algorithms in order to monetize from how much attention and time its users are spending on it, even if it is a free app. As long as humans are still targeted as consumers of the digital economy, the competing demand for human attention makes this the new scarce resource in the economy of abundance.

2.4.6   Law of New Division of Labor

2.4.6.1   *Phenomenon 6a: Labor Is Increasingly a Less Important Factor in Value Production*

More and more traditional jobs and professions will become redundant as a result of automation which has significant lower marginal cost, from manufacturing, transport, to knowledge-intensive professions such as law and consulting (Susskind and Susskind, 2016).

As labor becomes a less important factor in production compared to owning intellectual capital, a majority of citizens may find the value of their labor insufficient to afford a socially acceptable standard of living (Stanford, 2016). In the longer term, AI may be thought of as a radically different mechanism for wealth creation in which everyone should be entitled to a portion of the world's AI-produced treasures (Stanford, 2016).

Collaborative intelligence, crowdsourcing, and crowdfunding are all activities that also demonstrate the power of the crowd as a means for distributed value creation. Similar to how mass production model revolutionized factory manufacturing lines and multiplied efficiency and productivity, the power of the crowd has disrupted traditional linear value chains and made the users participants of the value creation process, taking advantage of the hyper-connectivity of digital platforms. The number of participants is not restricted by any physically bounded areas or geo-regions. Any "cause" or "initiative" has the potential of a global reach. The power of the crowd has made previously challenging goals (e.g., funding a product, crowd-sourcing knowledge, supporting a cause) much more achievable as long as it appeals to the desires of the crowd.

2.4.6.2   *Phenomenon 6b: New Necessities and the Barrier to Entry in a Digitized Society*

Digital necessity is defined in this book as:

> *The minimum enabling technological entry that allows a person to have a socially acceptable standard of living.*

The majority of digital goods and services are excludable, simply because a person needs to have a computing device and often an Internet connection in order to benefit from them. The cost of devices and connectivity along with the skills to use them create the barrier to entry into the digitalized society.

2.4.6.3   *Phenomenon 6c: Deep Learning and Machine Intelligence Are Still Inherently Limited*

Deep learning is part of a broader family of machine learning methods. Learning can be supervised, semisupervised, or unsupervised. Deep learning architectures such as deep neural networks, deep belief networks, and recurrent neural networks have been applied to fields including computer vision, speech recognition, natural language processing, audio recognition, social network filtering, machine translation, bioinformatics, and gaming; where they have produced results comparable to and in some cases superior to human experts. Deep learning is essentially a statistical technique for classifying patterns based on sample data, using neural networks with multiple layers. In principle, given infinite data, deep learning systems are powerful enough to represent any finite deterministic "mapping" between any given set of inputs and a set of corresponding outputs, though in practice whether they can learn such a mapping depends on many factors. One common concern is getting caught in *local minima*, in which a system gets stuck on a suboptimal solution, with no better solution nearby in the space of solutions being searched. Experts use a variety of techniques to avoid such problems, to reasonably good effect. Inherently, deep learning still has limitations (Marcus, 2017), such as:

1. Data hungry.
2. Shallow and has limited capacity for transfer.
3. No natural way to deal with hierarchical structure.
4. Struggles with open-ended inference.
5. Not sufficiently transparent.
6. Not well integrated with prior knowledge.
7. Cannot inherently distinguish causation from correlation.
8. Presumes a largely stable world in ways that may be problematic.
9. Works well as approximation, but cannot be fully trusted.
10. Difficult to engineer with.

2.4.6.4   Phenomenon 6d: Accuracy Is Not the Truth

The recent exponential demand of technically skilled workforce has resulted in the unpopularity of social sciences in universities (Dean, 2015). The rise of Big Data has also made data scientist one of the most in demand professions. However, accuracy is not the truth. Many see software development as the construction process of virtual infrastructure. While this process is maturing, there will be increasing needs in humanities, social sciences, philosophy, justice, and ethics. Hence, humanities will make its return to high on the value chain.

2.4.6.5   Principle 6a: The Digital Economy Is Creating a New Social Divide Based on the New Labor Value Chain

Taking into consideration the power and limitations of automation, the new labor value chain will create a greater social divide based on skillsets that are important for the future of value creation (in the order from high value to low value):

1. Human labor that participate in job creation in the new economy
2. Conventional human labor that is difficult to be replaced by automation
3. Human labor that supports the operations of digital systems (the new blue-collar workers)
4. People who will not be able to keep up or are below the barrier to entry

   Skills that will remain high on the labor value chain (referring to point 2):

1. Cognitive skills that require high adaptivity, spontaneity without prior knowledge (out-of-the box thinking), for example, from creative work, scientific research, to performance arts and stand-up comedy
2. Relationship skills used for intensive human interaction and communications in complex situations
3. Physical skills that require high adaptivity

2.4.6.6   Principle 6b: The Optimal Path to Intrinsic Value Creation Is a Combination of Human and Machine Intelligence

Given the limitations and constraints of both machine and human intelligence, the optimal path forward in intrinsic value creation, e.g., through building high performing teams, is to combine them. Such teams should leverage the processing speed, storage capacity, and analytical power from machines combined with the adaptivity, intuition, ability to imagine, and build trusting relationships from billions of years of natural evolution. The labor force of the crowd is also a form of human participation in intrinsic value creation, which is inherently a highly efficient global labor force that is not limited by any geographical boundaries.

Chapter 3

Cyber Risk Management: A New Era of Enterprise Risk Management

Chapter Outline

3.1 History and Definitions of Risk — 49
  3.1.1 History of Risk — 49
  3.1.2 Definitions of Risk as a Multidimensional Concept — 50
  3.1.3 Risk in Computer Science and Engineering — 50
  3.1.4 Risk Can Only Be Relatively Objective — 51
  3.1.5 Decision Theory and Acceptable Risk — 51
3.2 Enterprise Risk Management — 52
  3.2.1 The Discipline of Enterprise Risk Management — 52
  3.2.2 Cyber Risk Management: A New Era of Enterprise Risk Management — 53
3.3 Risk Analysis — 55
3.4 Risk Management — 57
  3.4.1 Risk Assessment — 57
    3.4.1.1 Define the Risk Assessment Process — 57
    3.4.1.2 System Characterization — 57
    3.4.1.3 Risk Classification — 57
    3.4.1.4 Threat Identification — 57

    3.4.1.5 Vulnerability Assessment — 63
    3.4.1.6 Likelihood Determination — 66
    3.4.1.7 Impact Analysis — 67
    3.4.1.8 Risk Determination — 67
  3.4.2 Risk Mitigation — 68
  3.4.3 Effectiveness Assessment — 70
  3.4.4 Continuous Monitoring — 70
3.5 Risk Models — 70
  3.5.1 Qualitative and Quantitative Models — 70
  3.5.2 Quantitative Assessment — 70
  3.5.3 Qualitative Assessment — 71
  3.5.4 Other Models — 71
    3.5.4.1 Perspective: Asset-driven, Service-driven, or Business driven — 72
    3.5.4.2 Resource Valuation: Vertical or Horizontal — 72
    3.5.4.3 Risk Measurement: Propagated or Nonpropagated — 72

We are not able in life to avoid risk but only to choose between risks. Rational decision-making requires, therefore, a clear and quantitative way of expressing risk so that it can be properly weighed, along with all other costs and benefits, in the decision process.

—Stanley Kaplan and B. John Garric

3.1 HISTORY AND DEFINITIONS OF RISK

3.1.1 History of Risk

The concept of risk originated in the seventeenth century with the mathematics associated with gambling. Risk referred to a combination between probability and magnitude of potential gains and losses. During the eighteenth-century, risk, seen as a neutral concept, still considered both gains and losses and was employed in the marine insurance business. Risk in the study of economics emerged in the 19th century. The concept of risk, by now seen more negatively, caused entrepreneurs to call for special incentives to take the risk involved in investment. By the 20th century, a complete negative connotation was made when referring to outcomes of risk in engineering and science, with particular reference to the hazards posed by modern technological developments such as in the petrol-chemical and nuclear industries (The Royal Society, 1992).

Digital Asset Valuation and Cyber Risk Measurement. DOI: https://doi.org/10.1016/B978-0-12-812158-0.00003-X

TABLE 3.1 Definition of Risk

Scenario	Likelihood	Consequences
S_1	p_1	x_1
S_2	p_2	x_2
$\vdots$	$\vdots$	$\vdots$
S_N	p_N	x_N

3.1.2   Definitions of Risk as a Multidimensional Concept

Based on the British Standard 4778,[1] risk is defined by the Royal Society as "a combination of the probability or frequency of occurrence of a defined hazard and the magnitude of the consequences of the occurrence" (The Royal Society, 1992).

All risks can be calculated as:

$$\text{Risk} = \text{Likelihood} \times \text{Consequences}$$

And cyber risk is a function of:

$$R = \{s_i, p_i, x_i\}, \quad i = 1, 2, \ldots, N$$

where R is the risk; s the description of a scenario (undesirable event); p the probability of a scenario; x the measure of consequences or damage caused by a scenario; and N the number of possible scenarios that may cause damage to a system (Kaplan and Garrick, 1981) (Table 3.1).

There are serious difficulties in attempting to view risk as a one-dimensional concept when a particular risk or hazard means different things to different people in different contexts, hence risk is socially constructed (The Royal Society, 1992). Various contexts in which risk is discussed include business risk, social risk, economic risk, safety risk, investment risk, military risk, political risk, etc. The literature of the subject of risk has grown very large (Kaplan and Garrick, 1981) because the concept of risk is so complex and can often cause ambiguity between natural and social scientists (Frosdick, 1997).

The most obvious difference between the natural sciences and the social sciences is that the natural sciences deal more with objectively measurable phenomena, whereas the social sciences are more involved with human behavior and social activity.

The term "science" is usually considered to be a synonym of natural science (Suojanen, 2000). Natural science develops through the use of a systematic approach, known as the scientific method, which is based on objective analysis rather than personal belief (Burnie, 2003). The engineering paradigm is one based on quantification and focuses more on technology than on people since its techniques employ quantified comparisons and is technically inclined. Social science provides information that helps us understand the different ways in which individuals interact, make decisions, exercise power, and respond to change.[2] Thus, the way in which social scientists evaluate risk is by subjective public perception based on values, belief, and opinion, which are, in turn, influenced by factors such as history, culture, politics, law, and religion. Kirkwood (1994) describes a subjective or perceived risk as one arrived at without a scientific assessment.

In the natural sciences, risk is seen as objective and nonjudgmental (evaluated risk), because the scientific assessment methods used to evaluate risk follow precise calculations, formulae, and exact experiments (Kirkwood, 1994). In the social sciences, however, risk is seen as subjective and heuristic (perceived risk), because it is a decision arrived at without a "scientific" assessment, often based on rule-of-thumb guidelines following experiences, judgment, and ingenuity rather than mathematics (Kirkwood, 1994). Table 3.2 shows a comparison between risks in the natural sciences and social sciences.

3.1.3   Risk in Computer Science and Engineering

Originated from mathematics and engineering, computer science is a combination of theory, engineering, and experimentation (Bob, 2003; Gerber and von Solms, 2005). It is believed to be positioned on common ground between the

---

1. BS 4778-3.1:1991 Quality vocabulary. Availability, reliability, and maintainability terms. Guide to concepts and related definitions
2. US Department of Labor (2002–03), Bureau of labor statistics: occupational handbook. Retrieved from www.bls.gov/home.htm.

TABLE 3.2 Risk in Natural Sciences and Social Sciences

Risk in Natural Sciences and Engineering	Risk in Social Sciences
• Risk analysis is more concerned about the identification of technical failures than it is about social issues • Risk management is a field of objective, scientific analysis that can be divorced from political values (Mayo and Hollander, 1991) • Risk assessment employs quantified comparisons and is technically inclined, which mainly involves putting numbers on risk, based firstly on calculations of probabilities and secondly, on the use of databank information on failures and reliability, to determine consequences in terms of fatalities	• Risk is socially constructed (Royal Society, 1992) • Risk perception depends very much on beliefs, cultural bias, human communication failures, feelings and judgments and has major influence on the tolerability or acceptance of risk (Strutt, 1993) • Risk is highly subjective; a particular risk or hazard means different things to different people in different contexts

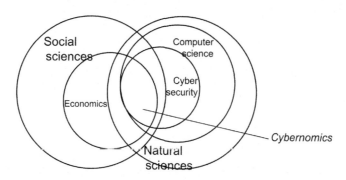

FIGURE 3.1   Risk in cybernomics

natural science paradigm and the theoretical (abstract) science paradigm. Its approaches are highly mathematical and logical. In computer science, risk is called "information security risk," or more recently, "cyber risk." The difference between the two terms is that cyber risk emphasizes the threats from external networks. The term cyber risk will be used in this book for the purpose of consistency. As a part of an entity's total risk, cyber risk is defined as:

Risks that arise from the loss of confidentiality, integrity, or availability of information or information systems and reflect the potential adverse impacts to organizational operations (i.e., mission, functions, image, or reputation), organizational assets, individuals, other organizations, and the Nation (NIST, 2012).

Key cyber risk components include (NIST, 2012):

- *Threats*: A threat is any circumstance or event with the potential to adversely impact organizational operations and assets, individuals, other organizations, or the nation through an information system via unauthorized access, destruction, disclosure, or modification of information, and/or denial of service (DoS).
- *Vulnerabilities*: A vulnerability is a weakness in an information system, system security procedures, internal controls, or implementation that could be exploited by a threat source.
- *Likelihood*: The likelihood of occurrence is a weighted risk factor based on an analysis of the probability that a given threat is capable of exploiting a given vulnerability (or set of vulnerabilities).

3.1.4   Risk Can Only Be Relatively Objective

Economics is a part of social science. Computing is a part of natural science. Hence, the theories discussed in this book sit in the intersection of the two paradigms and requires both subjective and objective measures, as shown in Fig. 3.1.

In this book, risk is seen as a combination of the two dimensions, it can only be relatively objective. Information should be the linking factor between the two defined paradigms for risk management and they should move closer together (Gerber and von Solms, 2005), because separating tools from culture can lead to half-truths and disillusionment.

3.1.5   Decision Theory and Acceptable Risk

The subjective element of risk perception leads to the conclusion that risk must be always considered within a decision theory context (Kaplan and Garrick, 1981). Considered in isolation, no risk is acceptable. A rational person would not accept any risk at all except possibly in return for any benefits that come along with it. Hence the purpose of risk analysis is always to provide input to an underlying decision problem which involves not just risk, but also costs and benefits. One needs to adopt a decision theory point-of-view, and ask: "What are my options, what are the costs, benefits, and risks of each?" The option with the optimum mix of cost, benefit, and risk is selected. The risk associated with that option is acceptable. All others are unacceptable.

The "optimum" option, however, is subjectively based on the rational person's risk appetite. Broadly speaking, there are three types of risk appetite:

- *Risk neutral*: A term used to describe the mental framework of a person when deciding where to allocate money. A risk-neutral investor is only concerned about the expected return of his investment. When faced with a choice between receiving either US$100 with 100% certainty or US$200 with 50% certainty, the risk-neutral investor has no preference either way, since the expected value of US$100 is the same for both outcomes. In contrast, the risk-averse investor generally settles for the "sure thing" or 100% certain US$100, while the risk-seeking investor opts for the 50% chance of getting US$200.
- *Risk averse*: The description of an investor who, when faced with two investments with a similar expected return, prefers the one with the lower risk.
- *Risk seeking*: An acceptance of greater volatility and uncertainty in investments or trading in exchange for anticipated higher returns. Risk seekers are more interested in capital gains from speculative assets than capital preservation from lower risk assets.

Finally, distinctions between key concepts related to risk are clarified in Table 3.3.

3.2 ENTERPRISE RISK MANAGEMENT

3.2.1 The Discipline of Enterprise Risk Management

Enterprise risk management (ERM) is the discipline by which an organization of any industry assesses, controls, exploits, finances, and monitors risks from all sources for the purpose of increasing the organization's short-term and

TABLE 3.3 Differences Between Risk Concepts

Risk-Related Concepts	Distinction
Risk versus uncertainty	Risk involves both uncertainty and loss. Hence, risk = uncertainty + loss
Risk versus hazard	Hazard is a source of danger. Risk involves the likelihood of converting that source into actual loss. Hence, risk = hazard/safeguards. This equation also mean that risk can never be zero, but it can be extremely small
Probability versus frequency	Frequency and probability both describe degree of uncertainty (Kaplan and Garrick, 1981). People have been arguing about the meaning of probability for at least 200 years, since the time of Laplace and Bayes. The major polarization of the argument is between the "objectivist" or "frequentist" school who view probability as something external, the result of repetitive experiments, and the "subjectivists" who view probability as an expression of an internal state; a state of knowledge or state of confidence, Table 3.4 shows a more detailed comparison
Probability versus statistics	Statistics is the study of frequency type information. It is the science of handling data. On the other hand, probability is the science of handling the lack of data (Kaplan and Garrick, 1981)

TABLE 3.4 Difference Between Frequency and Probability

Frequency	Probability
• Frequency is a "hard" measurable number. It is well defined and objective • Frequency refers to the outcome of an experiment of some kind involving repeated trials	• Probability is a "soft" measure. It is changeable and subjective • Probability communicates a state of mind of imperfect knowledge, a degree of belief or a state of confidence

TABLE 3.5 Enterprise Risk Management

Type of Risk		Description
Microeconomic risks	Strategic risk	Both internal and external risks that could impede the achievement of strategy and strategic objectives, impacting shareholder and stakeholder value
	Credit risk	Credit risk is one of the most fundamental types of risk; for it represents the chance an investor will lose their investment. Factors affecting credit risk are many and they can influence an issuer's credit risk in varying degrees, such as poor or falling cash flow from operations, rising interest rates, adverse changes in the nature of the marketplace, changes that affect the issuer, as in changes in technology, experiencing an increase in competition, as well as regulatory changes. Crucial changes in nature of risk exposure may not be obvious
	Operational risk	Operational risk is the risk of loss that results from inadequate or failed internal process, people and systems, or from external events.[a] This includes legal risks, but excludes reputational and strategic risks
	Regulatory and compliance risk	Regulatory risk is generally defined as the risk of having the "license to operate" withdrawn by a regulator, or having conditions applied (retrospectively or prospectively) that adversely impact the economic value of an enterprise
Macroeconomic risks	Market risk	Market risk is the risk mark to market value portfolio, instrument or investment increasing or decreasing as a result of volatility and unpredicted movement in mark valuations. Market risk management involves analyzing and quantifying market risk, developing a strategy to manage market risk, setting risk appetite, developing appropriate policies, process and organization structures for market risk management
	Systemic risk	Systemic risk is the possibility that an event at the company level could trigger instability or collapse an entire industry or economy. Systemic risk was a major contributor to the financial crisis of 2008. Companies considered to be a systemic risk are called "too big to fail." These institutions are large relative to their respective industries or make up a significant part of the overall economy. A company highly interconnected with others is also a source of systemic risk. Systemic risk should not be confused with systematic risk; systematic risk relates to the entire financial system.

[a]*Basel II. Retrieved from: https://www.bis.org/publ/bcbsca.htm.*

long-term value to its stakeholders. First, ERM is a discipline. This is meant to convey that ERM is an orderly or pre-scribed conduct or pattern of behavior for an enterprise, that it has the full support and commitment of the management of the enterprise, that it influences corporate decision-making, and that it ultimately becomes part of the culture of that enterprise. Second, ERM, applies to all industries. Third, the specific mention of exploiting risk as a part of the risk management process (along with the stated objective of increasing short-term and long-term value) demonstrates that the intention of ERM is to be value creating as well as risk mitigating. Fourth, all sources of risk are considered, not only the hazard risk with which casualty actuaries are particularly familiar, or those traditionally managed within an enterprise (such as financial risk). Lastly, ERM considers all stakeholders of the enterprise, which include shareholders and debtholders, management and officers, employees, customers, and the community within which the enterprise resides. Implicit in this definition is the recognition of ERM as a strategic decision support framework for management. It improves decision-making at all levels of the organization. Risks considered as part of ERM can be both microeco-nomic and macroeconomic, as shown in Table 3.5.

COSO is a formal framework for ERM. A model for brainstorming to brainstorm risks at organizational (and supply chain) tiers is shown in Fig. 3.2.

3.2.2 Cyber Risk Management: A New Era of Enterprise Risk Management

Cyber risk has become a business imperative for every other part of ERM. Businesses need to think about cyber risk not as its own independent entity, but as part of the many portions of the enterprise risk model. The ultimate goal of cyber risk management is to maximize the organization's output (products or services), while at the same time

FIGURE 3.2   COSO framework.

minimizing the unexpected negative outcomes generated by potential cyber risks (Liu et al., 2009; Wheeler, 2011). It is important that risks be managed in a way that gives confidence to all stakeholders[3] and provides an appropriate level of security for the digital systems that support the organization's ongoing operations (Jones, 2007; Ross, 2007). Cyber risk management activities might include:

- *Threat and vulnerability models* help in identifying and categorizing the threats, as well as in analyzing their impacts, and subsequently prioritizing them.
- *Maturity models/frameworks* enable the integration of strategies, capabilities and governance structures to improving an organization's capabilities, with specific reference to effectively managing cyber risks, making risk-based decisions, and increasing value derived over time.
- *Cyber-insurance* transfers risk and absorbs losses caused by cyber breaches as well as supplementing the existing set of security tools to manage residual cyber risk after investments are made.
- *Regulatory requirements* set requirements for cyber risk, as they demand the implementation of an internal control structure, its correct documentation and the monitoring of the internal control system, thereby ensuring the integrity and correctness of regulated assets (e.g., financial data).
- *Formal standards*, such as the ISO/IEC 27000 series, which consists of standards on information security and provides guidance on Information Security Management System (ISMS) (Kosub, 2015).

Currently, cyber risk typically falls under operational risk as part of ERM framework. This is problematic and is a result of the same reasons discussed in Chapter 1, Digital Assets as Economic Goods, and Chapter 2, Digital Theory of Value, that the current categorization of digital assets is heavily technology-centric. For businesses that generate core value from digital assets, cyber risk should be a critical component of all aspects of ERM. The current narrow understanding of cyber risk can lead to significant underestimation of potential economic losses from cyber incident. Given the size of digital economy today, cyber risk means a new era of ERM, the measurement of which will be covered in Chapter 4, Cyber Risk Measurement in the Hyperconnected World, while the remainder of this chapter focuses on a comprehensive review on the methods and models available today.

Fig. 3.3 shows commonly accepted main steps and components of the management of risk. It should be noted that there is no universal agreement on these processes (Microsoft, 2004; Hoo, 2000).

It is also necessary to clarify the difference between "risk management" from "the management of risk." The Royal Society (1992) considers that risk management is the making of decisions concerning risks and their subsequent

---

3. ISO/IEC 27000:2012 Information technology—security techniques—Information security management systems—overview and vocabulary. Retrieved from: www.iso.org/standard/56891.html.

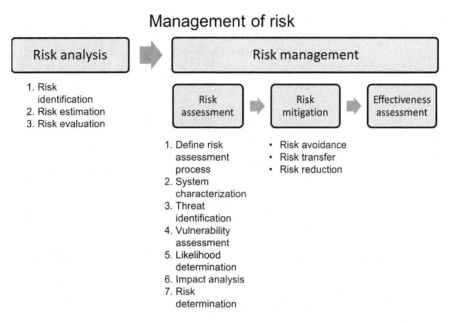

FIGURE 3.3 Management of risk.

implementation and flows from risk estimation and risk evaluation, whereas the management of risk is described as the "overall process by which risks are analyzed and managed" (Scarff et al., 1993). The management of risk should be a continuous process in order to adapt to changes of both internal and external environments. The three components of the management of risk are risk analysis, risk management and risk monitoring.

3.3   RISK ANALYSIS

Risk analysis is the first step of overall management of risk, followed by risk management (Gerber and van Solms, 2005; Bandyopad-hyay et al., 1999; Owens, 1998; Moses, 1992). It is defined as a systematic process to examine the threats facing the digital assets and the vulnerabilities of these assets and to show the likelihood that these threats will be realized. Frosdick (1997) suggests that risk analysis is the sum of risk identification, estimation and evaluation. The results of risk analysis techniques ensure the decision-making processes of risk management are scientifically informed.

The techniques of risk identification include facilitative tools, intended to maximize the opportunity of identifying all the risks associated with digital assets within an established boundary, as well as threats and vulnerabilities associated with these assets, that is, "what can go wrong" (Jung et al., 1999; Frosdick, 1997). Fig. 3.4 demonstrates an example of a "what-if" analysis.

Risk identification tools may be broadly categorized as intuitive, inductive and deductive. The intuitive approach replies on intuitive decisions, often referred to as "expert judgement" or "mere guesses," which may be just as effective in decision-making and sometimes more efficient and effective depending on the decision-maker's level of expertise on the subject matter. The inductive approach moves from specific instances into a generalized conclusion. It works from the perspective that a risk is present then try to evaluate how it would manifest itself. The deductive approach moves from generalized principles that are known to be true to a true and specific conclusion. It assumes that a risk has already been observed and worked backward to find the root cause of the risk. The "guessing" involved in risk analysis techniques contributes to the subjective nature of risk analysis (Gerber and van Solms, 2005).

Risk estimation attempts to put ballpark estimates on risk. Identified risks are estimated in two dimensions: (1) the probability of risk occurring and (2) how severe the consequences should it occur. Component reliability, that is, the probability that a component will perform a required specified function (The Royal Society, 1992), is a key element within the first dimension. Techniques for the first dimension include fault and event trees as shown in Fig. 3.5, reliability block diagrams, mathematical network analysis, etc. Techniques for the second dimension include computer modeling, testing or expert value judgments (Frosdick, 1997). Risk estimation requires deep knowledge and intensive domain experience (Jung et al., 1999).

What-if	Because of an error on the magnetic disc some accounting data disappear	An employee illicitly discredit some data about salaries
Condition of evidence	Technical error, sabotage, bad maintenance, or lack of knowledge	Employee is not satisfied with conditions, employee wants to profit from leaked data
Consequences	Service unavailable for 24 h, support required from employees for reconstruction of data	Revealing business secret, dissatisfaction of other employees, unauthorized change of salaries, theft of financial assets
Security measures	Data reconstruction from additional backup	Cryptography, identity, and access management
Potential loss	2 man-days, credibility with customers and suppliers	Credibility damage, bad working culture, reputational damage, fluctuation of employees
Character of loss	Direct (financial), indirect	Indirect
Size of losses	< $10,000	> $50,000
Risk rating	Green (low)	Red (high)

FIGURE 3.4   Example of "What-if" analysis.

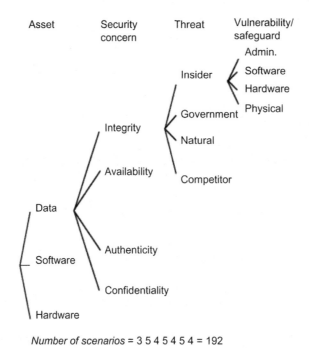

Number of scenarios = 3 5 4 5 4 5 4 = 192

FIGURE 3.5   Event tree example.

Risk evaluation aims to comprehensively assess identified risks and is also referred to as risk assessment in many literatures. Risk assessment is the first step of risk management following risk analysis. In this book risk evaluation and risk assessment are interchangeable terms; the detailed steps of risk evaluation will be covered in Section 3.4.1 (risk assessment).

3.4   RISK MANAGEMENT

Risk management can be divided into the three processes risk assessment, risk mitigation, and effectiveness assessment (NIST, 2002; Farahmand et al., 2003; Alberts and Dorofee, 2003; Vorster and Labuschagne, 2005; Stoneburner et al., 2002; Chen, 2008). Both proactive and reactive approaches can be adopted in risk management.

3.4.1   Risk Assessment

Modern risk assessment traces its roots to the nuclear power industry, where carefully constructed risk assessment methodologies were developed to analyze the operations of the very new and potentially dangerous nuclear power facilities (Ramona and Cristina, 2011). Risk assessment is the first process in the risk management methodology. Its objective is to determine the extent of risks and the countermeasures that could be implemented. The outcome of risk assessment can be used to indicate the tolerability or acceptability of the risks (Gerber and van Solms, 2005).

In cyber risk, risk assessment is defined as:

The process of identifying, estimating, and prioritizing information security risks. Assessing risk requires the careful analysis of threat and vulnerability information to determine the extent to which circumstances or events could adversely impact an organization and the likelihood that such circumstances or events will occur (NIST, 2012).

Main steps of risk assessment generally include (Ramona and Cristina, 2011; NIST, 2012; Chen, 2008):

3.4.1.1   Define the Risk Assessment Process

This step establishes the working procedure of the assessment, covering:

- An explicit model, defining key terms and assessable risk factors and the relationships among the factors.
- An assessment approach (e.g., quantitative, qualitative), specifying the range of values those risk factors can assume during the risk assessment and how combinations of risk factors are identified/analyzed so that values of those factors can be functionally combined to evaluate risk.
- An analysis approach (e.g., threat-oriented, asset/impact-oriented, or vulnerability-oriented), describing how combinations of risk factors are identified/analyzed to ensure adequate coverage of the problem space at a consistent level of detail.
- Compliance with applicable regulations ensuring the effectiveness of risk assessment activities.

3.4.1.2   System Characterization

This step provides information about the resources, data and boundaries of the computing system. It is very important to define the specific field of interest, links and dependencies between the resources that are being analyzed. The responsible person has to collect information about hardware, software, data and information, system interfaces, system mission, persons who support and use the information technology (IT) system, system security architecture, system security policies, technical, operational and management controls, using questionnaires, on-site interviews, documents review, and automated scanning tools. This activity can be conducted throughout the risk assessment process.

3.4.1.3   Risk Classification

One approach to system categorization is using risk-based categories. Common risk classification categories include restricted—confidential—unrestricted, low—moderate—high, very low—low—moderate—high—very high, regulated—nonregulated. An example is shown in Table 3.6 using FIPS 199 impact levels (FIPS, 2004).

3.4.1.4   Threat Identification

This step identifies threat sources to threat events. A threat source is characterized as: (1) the intent and method targeted at the exploitation of a vulnerability; or (2) a situation and method that may accidentally exploit a vulnerability. An example lists of threats and consequences are shown in Table 3.7.

In general, types of threat sources include:

- Hostile cyber or physical attacks
- Human errors of ommission or commission

TABLE 3.6 Risk Classification Based on Impact Levels (FIPS, 2004)

Impact Level	Definition	Application
Low	The loss of confidentiality, integrity, or availability could be expected to have a limited adverse effect on organizational operations, organizational assets, or individuals	A limited adverse effect means that, for example, the loss of confidentiality, integrity, or availability might: (1) cause a degradation in mission capability to an extent and duration that the organization is able to perform its primary functions, but the effectiveness of the functions is noticeably reduced; (2) result in minor damage to organizational assets; (3) result in minor financial loss; or (4) result in minor harm to individuals
Moderate	The loss of confidentiality, integrity, or availability could be expected to have a serious adverse effect on organizational operations, organizational assets, or individuals	A serious adverse effect means that, for example, the loss of confidentiality, integrity, or availability might: (1) cause a significant degradation in mission capability to an extent and duration that the organization is able to perform its primary functions, but the effectiveness of the functions is significantly reduced; (2) result in significant damage to organizational assets; (3) result in significant financial loss; or (4) result in significant harm to individuals that does not involve loss of life or serious life threatening injuries
High	The loss of confidentiality, integrity, or availability could be expected to have a severe or catastrophic adverse effect on organizational operations, organizational assets, or individuals	A severe or catastrophic adverse effect means that, for example, the loss of confidentiality, integrity, or availability might: (1) cause a severe degradation in or loss of mission capability to an extent and duration that the organization is not able to perform one or more of its primary functions; (2) result in major damage to organizational assets; (3) result in major financial loss; or (4) result in severe or catastrophic harm to individuals involving loss of life or serious life threatening injuries

TABLE 3.7 Examples of Information Technology Threats and Their Consequences

Threat	Consequence
Human Malicious	
Accessing public material	Alteration of data, data destruction, theft of proprietary data
Blackhat hackers (lightweight to heavyweight)	Backup and recovery costs
Bombing	Bankruptcy
Career criminals	Building collapse
Computer viruses (stealth, polymorphic, macro)	Business interruption
Corporate espionage	Covert takeover of someone's computer
Crackers/script kiddies (amateurs, novices; considerably less skilled than hackers)	Crime (noncomputer, computer)
Cybercrime/fraud	Decreased productivity
Data diddling	Equipment replacement costs
Denial-of-service attacks	Financial loss
Dumpster diving	Fraud, theft, larceny, bribery
Employees, management (greed, vices, financial pressure, extravagant lifestyle, real or imagined grievances, workplace pressure/stress)	Frustration
	Ill will
	Injury

(Continued)

TABLE 3.7 (Continued)

Threat	Consequence
High-energy radio frequency attacks (laser-like device aimed at buildings, housing, computers)	Inaccurate data
	Eavesdropping, password theft
Impersonation/spoofing (email spoofs, anonymous remailers, use of someone's login and password)	Location of modems to exploit
	Loss of competitive edge
Intelligence agencies	Loss of data
Looping IP address (always-on Internet connections vulnerable)	Loss of life
	Loss of time
Password crackers (such as L0phtCrack software)	Lost productivity
Physical attacks	Meltdown of computer chips
Remote access control software (examples include PCAnywhere, Timbuktu, NetBus, Back Orifice)	Pick-up electromagnetic force fields emitted by hardware devices
Sabotage	Property damage
Social engineering (attacks against persons, using fake badges, blackmail, threat, harassment, bribery and impersonation)	Processing delays, reruns
	Reconstruction of shredded documents
	Search of the Internet for vulnerable websites
Surveillance (shoulder surfing, high-powered photography)	Shutdown of networks or websites using software such as Nuke, Nuke II, Bluebomb, Teardrop, or Bonk
Terrorists	Location of holes in the networks
War dialing	Inability to process critical applications
Web crawlers	Unauthorized access or break-ins to network, other systems (crawl under a raised computer floor, pick locks, duplicate keys, circumvent alarm systems)
Human Nonmalicious (Often Caused by Ignorant Employees)	
Computer operator errors	Business interruptions
Data entry (input) errors	Cost overruns
Fire	Employee turnover
Inadequate access controls	Frustration
Inadequate training	Ill will
Inadequate human resource policies	Inaccurate reports
Inadequate program testing/controls incorporated into computer programs	Lack of management confidence in IS department
Inadequate risk analysis undertaken	Loss of management time
Inadequate supervision	Loss of life
Lack of ethics	Lost deadlines
Mislaid disk files	Lost productivity
Physical damage to disk	Processing delays
Poor management philosophy/attitude	Rerun costs
Unlocked trash containers	
Update of wrong file	
Weak internal controls	

(Continued)

TABLE 3.7 (Continued)

Threat	Consequence
Accidents	
Air conditioning failure	Business interruption
Building collapse	Data destruction
Destruction of data, disks, documents, reports	Financial loss
Destruction of water mains, sewer lines	Inaccurate information, reports
Failure of hardware	Injuries, loss of life
	Lost customer goodwill
Failure of computer programs	Lost data
Fire	Processing delays
	Replacing costs (software, hardware, other)
Gas line explosions	Reprocessing, reconstruction costs
Power outages (brownouts, blackouts, transients, spikes, sags and power surges)	
Product failure	
Software failure (operating system, database software)	
Natural Disasters and Other Unexpected Disruptions	
Global warming	Bankruptcy
Ice and snow	Damage
Floods	Injury
Hurricanes	Financial loss
Lighting	Long-term business interruption
Tornadoes, wind damage	Loss of life
Tsunamis	
Epidemic	

- Structural failures of organization-controlled resources, e.g., hardware, software, environmental controls
- Natural and human-made disaster, accidents, and failures beyond the control of the organization (NIST, 2012)

Confidentiality, integrity, and availability, also known as the Central Intelligence Agency (CIA) triad, is a security objective model that can be used as common taxonomy for threat identification. The definitions of the components of CIA and threat factors that can be considered during this phase are shown in Table 3.8. An example of threat analysis using CIA is shown in Table 3.9.

Deliberate human threat events for cyber or physical attacks can be characterized by the tactics, techniques, and procedures employed by adversaries. Understanding adversary-based threat events gives organizations insights into the capabilities associated with certain threat sources. In addition, having greater knowledge about who is carrying out the attacks gives organizations a better understanding of what adversaries desire to gain by the attacks. Knowing the intent and targeting aspects of a potential attack helps organizations narrow the set of threat events that are most relevant to consider (NIST, 2012). Threat modeling is a tool that provides defenders with a systematic analysis of the probable attacker's profile, the most likely attack vectors, and the assets most desired by an attacker. Generally accepted IT threat modeling processes include:

- *Data flow diagram (DFD)*: A tool for system engineers to communicate on a high level how an application caused data to flow, be stored, and manipulated by the infrastructure upon which the application runs.

TABLE 3.8 Threat Analysis Using CIA (NIST, 2008)

Security Objectives	FIPS 199 Definition (FIPS, 2004)	Threat Factors (NIST, 2008)
Confidentiality	A loss of confidentiality is the unauthorized disclosure of information	• How can a malicious adversary use the unauthorized disclosure of information to do limited/serious/severe harm to agency operations, agency assets, or individuals? • How can a malicious adversary use the unauthorized disclosure of information to gain control of agency assets that might result in unauthorized modification of information, destruction of information, or denial of system services that would result in limited/serious/severe harm to agency operations, agency assets, or individuals? • Would unauthorized disclosure/dissemination of elements of the information type violate laws, executive orders, or agency regulations?
Integrity	A loss of integrity is the unauthorized modification or destruction of information	• How can a malicious adversary use the unauthorized modification or destruction of information to do limited/serious/severe harm to agency operations, agency assets, or individuals? • Would unauthorized modification/destruction of elements of the information type violate laws, executive orders, or agency regulations?
Availability	A loss of availability is the disruption of access to or use of information or an information system	• How can a malicious adversary use the disruption of access to or use of information to do limited/serious/severe harm to agency operations, agency assets, or individuals? • Would disruption of access to or use of elements of the information type violate laws, executive orders, or agency regulations?

TABLE 3.9 Threat Analysis Based on CIA

Threats	C	I	A
1. *Human*			
1.1. *Deliberate human threats*			
Interception and espionage	X		
Placing destructive codes	X	X	X
Destruction with intention of date and facilitates		X	X
Unauthorized access to data	X	X	
Use of pirated software			X
Falsifying identify	X	X	
1.2. *Unintentional human threats*			
Personnel operating errors		X	X
Programming errors	X	X	X
Technical failure		X	X
2. *Nonhuman*			
2.1. *External operating environment*			
Fire		X	X
Earthquakes		X	X

(Continued)

TABLE 3.9 (Continued)			
Threats	**C**	**I**	**A**
Floods		X	X
2.2. *Internal operating environment*			
Supply voltage drops			X
Voltage fluctuations	X		X

- *Process flow diagram (PFD)*: A tool to allow Agile software development teams to create threat models based on the application design process.

  Focalizations of threat modeling include:

- *Software/architecture-centric*: Concentrates on the security of software for an evaluated web application, starting with a model of the system/application/software.
- *Asset-centric*: Concentrates on more risk-based approach to application threat modeling, starting with the data/assets classifications/values.
- *Attacker-centric*: Concentrates on the attacker's goals/targets and how they can be achieved, starting with a model of the threat agents and the attack vectors.
- *Security-centric*: Addresses security and technical risks to threats revealed by application threat model, starting with business objectives, security, and compliance requirements.

  Following are some of the popular threat modeling methods.

3.4.1.4.1 STRIDE

STRIDE is a threat classification model developed by Microsoft to help reason and find threats to a computer system. It is used in conjunction with a model of the target system that can be constructed in parallel, including a full breakdown of processes, data stores, data flows, and trust boundaries. It provides a mnemonic for security threats in six categories:

1. *Spoofing*: When a person or program successfully masquerades as another by falsifying data to gain an illegitimate advantage.
2. *Tampering*: The act of deliberately modifying data through unauthorized channels.
3. *Repudiation*: When an application or system do not adopt controls to properly track and log user actions, thus permitting malicious manipulation or forging the identification of new actions.
4. *Information disclosure*: An attack, such as a privacy breach or data leak, that results in an information system revealing sensitive information that should not be disclosed.
5. *Denial of service*: A cyberattack in which the perpetrator seeks to make a machine or network resource unavailable to its intended users by temporarily or indefinitely disrupting services of a host connected to the Internet.
6. *Elevation of privilege (EoP)*: Giving an attacker authorization permission beyond those initially granted.

3.4.1.4.2 Process for Attack Simulation and Threat Analysis

The process for attack simulation and threat analysis (PASTA) provides a seven-step model for threat identification, enumeration, scoring. This methodology uses DFD visualization and is intended to provide an attacker-centric view of the application and infrastructure from which defenders can develop an asset-centric mitigation strategy. The seven steps of PASTA are:

1. Define business context of application: considers the inherent application risk profile and address other business impact considerations early in the software development life cycle.
2. Technology enumeration: decomposes the technology stack that supports the application components that realize the business objectives identified.
3. Application decomposition: focuses on understanding the data flows among application components and services in the application threat model.

4. Threat analysis: reviews threat assertions from data within the environment as well as industry threat intelligence that is relevant to service, data, and deployment model.
5. Vulnerability identification: identifies the vulnerabilities and weaknesses within the application design and code to see if it supports the threat assertions.
6. Attack simulation: emulates attacks that could exploit identified vulnerabilities and determines the threat viability via attack patterns.
7. Residual risk analysis: remediates vulnerabilities or weaknesses in code or design that can facilitate threats and underlying attack patterns (Ucedavélez and Marco, 2015).

3.4.1.4.3 Trike

The Trike model uses a DFD visualization and is often used to satisfy the security auditing process. Trike threat models are based on requirements model which establishes the stakeholder-defined acceptable level of risk assigned to each asset class. Analysis of the requirements model yields a threat model form which threats are enumerated and assigned risk values. The completed threat model is used to construct a risk model based on asset, roles, actions, and calculated risk exposure (Eddington et al., 2005).

3.4.1.4.4 Visual, Agile, and Simple Threat (VAST) Modelling

The underlying principle of the VAST methodology is the necessity of scaling the threat modeling process across the infarstructure and entire Software Development Life Cycle (SDLC), and integrating it seamlessly into an Agile software development methodology. The methodology seeks to provide actionable outputs for the unique needs of various stakeholders: application architects and developers, cybersecurity personnel, and senior executives. Using PFD, the methodology provides a unique application and infrastructure visualization scheme such that the creation and use of threat models do not require specific security subject matter expertise.

3.4.1.5 Vulnerability Assessment

Most information system vulnerabilities can be associated with security controls that either has not been applied (either intentionally or unintentionally) or have been applied, but retain some weakness. It is also important to allow for the possibility of emergent vulnerabilities that can arise naturally over time as organizational missions/business functions evolve, environments of operation change, new technologies proliferate, and new threats emerge. Vulnerabilities are not identified only within information systems. They can also be found in:

- *Organizational governance structures*, for example, the lack of effective risk management strategies and adequate risk framing, poor intraagency communications, inconsistent decisions about relative priorities of missions/business functions, or misalignment of enterprise architecture to support mission/business activities.
- *External relationships*, for example, dependencies on particular energy sources, supply chains, IT, and telecommunications providers.
- *Mission/business processes*, for example, poorly defined processes or processes that are not risk-aware.
- *Enterprise/information security architectures*, for example, poor architectural decisions resulting in lack of diversity or resiliency in organizational information systems.

In general, risks materialize as a result of a series of threat events, each of which takes advantage of one or more vulnerabilities. Organizations can define threat scenarios to describe how the events caused by a threat source can contribute to or cause harm, as shown in Table 3.10. Development of threat scenarios is analytically useful, since some vulnerabilities may not be exposed to exploitation unless and until other vulnerabilities have been exploited. Analysis that illuminates how a set of vulnerabilities, taken together, could be exploited by one or more threat events is therefore more useful than the analysis of individual vulnerabilities. In addition, a threat scenario tells a story, and hence is useful for risk communication as well as for analysis (NIST, 2012).

3.4.1.5.1 The Common Vulnerability Scoring System

Common Vulnerability Scoring System (CVSS)[4] is a rating system designed to provide open and universally standard severity ratings of software vulnerabilities. It was created as a global framework for disclosing information about security vulnerabilities and help IT managers convert mountain of vulnerability data into actionable priorities. CVSS has

---

4. Common Vulnerability Scoring System SIG. (n.d.). Retrieved June 15, 2017, from www.first.org/cvss/.

TABLE 3.10 Vulnerability Assessment Example

Vulnerability	Threat Scenarios	Affected Assets
No backup	Fire	Data
	Earthquakes	
	Floods	
	Supply voltage drops	
	Voltage fluctuations	
	Use of pirated software	
	Unauthorized access of data	
	Placing destructive codes	
Inadequate configuration	Technical malfunction	Data
Unauthorized changes of the attributions of programmers with operational staff	Technical malfunction	Data
	Error programming	Software
Inadequate training of staff responsible for data communications	Routing rerouting wrong messages	Data
Security measures implemented in a wrong way	Denial of service	Data
	Unauthorized access of data	Software
Nonregularly updating antivirus software	Malicious code	Data
		Software
Lack of business continuity plans or procedures for data recover	Fire	Data
	Earthquakes	Software
	Floods	Hardware
	Supply voltage drops	Ancillary facilities
	Voltage fluctuations	
	Use of pirated software	
	Unauthorized access of data	
	Placing destructive codes	

been adopted globally, and used by vulnerability bulletin providers, software application vendors, user organizations, vulnerability scanning and management companies, security and risk management firms, as well as research institutes. CVSS is composed of three metric groups, each consisting of a set of metrics (Fig. 3.6).

- *Base*: represents the intrinsic and fundamental characteristics of a vulnerability that are constant over time and user environments.
- *Temporal*: represents the characteristics of a vulnerability that change over time, but not among user environments.
- *Environmental*: represents the characteristics of a vulnerability that are relevant and unique to a particular user's environment.

3.4.1.5.2 The Open Web Application Security Project Top 10

The Open Web Application Security Project (OWASP) is an open community dedicated to enabling organizations to develop, purchase, and maintain applications and Application Programing Interfaces (APIs) that can be trusted. The OWASP Top 10[5] is a powerful awareness project for web application security to educate developers, designers,

---

5. OWASP Top 10: www.owasp.org/index.php/Top_10-2017_Top_10.

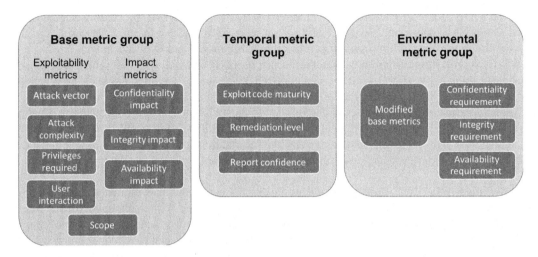

FIGURE 3.6 CVSS metric groups.

TABLE 3.11 OWASP Evolution of Vulnerabilities From 2013 to 2017

OWASP Top 10—2013	OWASP Top 10—2017
A1:2013—Injection	A1:2017—Injection
A2:2013—Broken Authentication and Session Management	A2:2017—Broken Authentication
A3:2013—Cross-Site Scripting	A3:2017—Sensitive Data Exposure
A4:2013—Insecure Direct Object References	A4:2017—XML External Entities
A5:2013—Security Misconfiguration	A5:2017—Broken Access Control
A6:2013—Sensitive Data Exposure	A6:2017—Security Misconfiguration
A7:2013—Missing Function Level Access Control	A7:2017—Cross-Site Scripting
A8:2013—Cross-Site Request Forgery (CSRF)	A8:2017—Insecure Deserialization
A9:2013—Using Components with Known Vulnerability	A9:2017—Using Components with Known Vulnerability
A10:2013—Unvalidated Redirects and Forwards	A10:2017—Insufficient Logging and Monitoring

architects, managers, and organizations about the consequences of the most common and most important web application security weaknesses. It represents a broad consensus about the most critical security risks to web applications. Project members include a variety of security experts from around the world who have shared their expertise to produce this list (Table 3.11).

3.4.1.5.3 The Open Web Application Security Project 2017

1. *Injection*: Injection flaws, such as Structured Query Language (SQL), Not Only SQL (NoSQL), Operating System (OS), and Lightweight Directory Access Protocol (LDAP) injection, occur when untrusted data is sent to an interpreter as part of a command or query. The attacker's hostile data can trick the interpreter into executing unintended commands or accessing data without proper authorization.
2. *Broken authentication*: Application functions related to authentication and session management are often implemented incorrectly, allowing attackers to compromise passwords, keys, or session tokens, or to exploit other implementation flaws to assume other users' identities temporarily or permanently.
3. *Sensitive data exposure*: Many web applications and APIs do not properly protect sensitive data, such as financial, healthcare, and PII. Attackers may steal or modify such weakly protected data to conduct credit card fraud, identity theft, or other crimes. Sensitive data may be compromised without extra protection, such as encryption at rest or in transit, and requires special precautions when exchanged with the browser.

4. *XML External Entity (XXE) Processing*: Many older or poorly configured XML processors evaluate external entity references within XML documents. External entities can be used to disclose internal files using the file URI handler, internal file shares, internal port scanning, remote code execution, and DoS attacks.

5. *Broken access control*: Restrictions on what authenticated users are allowed to do are often not properly enforced. Attackers can exploit these flaws to access unauthorized functionality and/or data, such as access other users' accounts, view sensitive files, modify other users' data, change access rights, etc.

6. *Security misconfiguration*: Security misconfiguration is the most commonly seen issue. This is commonly a result of insecure default configurations, incomplete or ad hoc configurations, open cloud storage, misconfigured HTTP headers, and verbose error messages containing sensitive information. Not only must all operating systems, frameworks, libraries, and applications be securely configured, but they must be patched and upgraded in a timely fashion.

7. *Cross-site Scripting (XSS)*: XSS flaws occur whenever an application includes untrusted data in a new web page without proper validation or escaping, or updates an existing web page with user-supplied data using a browser API that can create HTML or JavaScript. XSS allows attackers to execute scripts in the victim's browser which can hijack user sessions, deface websites, or redirect the user to malicious sites.

8. *Insecure deserialization*: Insecure deserialization often leads to remote code execution. Even if deserialization flaws do not result in remote code execution, they can be used to perform attacks, including replay attacks, injection attacks, and privilege escalation attacks.

9. *Using components with known vulnerability*: Components, such as libraries, frameworks, and other software modules, run with the same privileges as the application. If a vulnerable component is exploited, such an attack can facilitate serious data loss or server takeover. Applications and APIs using components with known vulnerabilities may undermine application defenses and enable various attacks and impacts.

10. *Insufficient logging and monitoring*: Insufficient logging and monitoring, coupled with missing or ineffective integration with incident response, allows attackers to further attack systems, maintain persistence, pivot to more systems, and tamper, extract, or destroy data. Most breach studies show time to detect a breach is over 200 days, typically detected by external parties rather than internal processes or monitoring.

3.4.1.6 *Likelihood Determination*

The likelihood risk factor combines an estimate of the likelihood that the threat event will be initiated with an estimate of the likelihood of impact, that is, the likelihood that the threat event results in adverse impacts. For adversarial threats, an assessment of likelihood of occurrence is typically based on: (1) adversary intent; (2) adversary capability; and (3) adversary targeting. For other than adversarial threat events, the likelihood of occurrence is estimated using historical evidence, empirical data, or other factors. Note that the likelihood that a threat event will be initiated or will occur is assessed with respect to a specific time frame a specific time frame, e.g., the next 6 months, the next year, or the period until a specified milestone is reached. If a threat event is almost certain to be initiated or occur in the (specified or implicit) time frame, the risk assessment may take into consideration the estimated frequency of the event. The likelihood of threat occurrence can also be based on the state of the organization, including, for example, its core mission/business processes, enterprise architecture, information security architecture, information systems, and environments in which those systems operate. It should also take into consideration predisposing conditions and the presence and effectiveness of deployed security controls to protect against unauthorized/undesirable behavior, detect and limit damage, and/or maintain or restore mission/business capabilities. The likelihood of impact addresses the probability (or possibility) that the threat event will result in an adverse impact, regardless of the magnitude of harm that can be expected.

Organizations typically employ a three-step process to determine the overall likelihood of threat events:

1. Assess the likelihood that threat events will be initiated for adversarial threat events or will occur for nonadversarial threat events.

2. Assess the likelihood that the threat events once initiated or occurring, will result in adverse impacts or harm to organizational operations and assets, individuals, other organizations, or the nation.

3. Assess the overall likelihood as a combination of likelihood of initiation/occurrence and likelihood of resulting in adverse impact.

Threat-vulnerability pairing, i.e., establishing a one-to-one relationship between threats and vulnerabilities may be undesirable when assessing likelihood at the mission/business function level, and in many cases, can be problematic even at the information system level due to the potentially large number of threats and vulnerabilities. This approach typically drives the level of detail in identifying threat events and vulnerabilities, rather than allowing organizations to make effective use of threat information and/or to identify threats at a level of detail that is meaningful. Depending on the level of detail in threat specification, a given threat event could exploit multiple vulnerabilities. In assessing likelihoods, organizations examine vulnerabilities that threat events could exploit and also the mission/business function susceptibility to events for which no security controls or viable implementations of security control exist, e.g., due to functional dependencies, particularly external dependencies. In certain situations, the most effective way to reduce mission/business risk attributable to information security risk is to redesign the mission/business processes so there are viable work-arounds when information systems are compromised. The concept of threat scenarios described above may help organizations overcome some of the limitations of threat-vulnearbility pairing.

In addition, organizations may also consider predisposing conditions. A predisposing condition is a condition that exists within an organization, a mission or business process, enterprise architecture, information system, or environment of operation. It increases or decreases the likelihood that threat events, once initiated, result in adverse impact to organizational operations and assets, individuals, other organizations, or the nation. Predisposing conditions include, for example, the location of a facility in a hurricane-prone or flood-prone region (increasing the likelihood of exposure to hurricanes or floods) or a stand-alone information system with no external network connectivity (decreasing the likelihood of exposure to a network-based cyberattack). Vulnerabilities resulting from predisposing conditions that cannot be easily corrected could include, for example, gaps in contingency plans, use of outdated technologies, or weaknesses/deficiencies in information system backup and failover mechanisms. In all cases, these types of vulnerabilities create a predisposition toward threat events having adverse impacts on organizations (NIST, 2012).

3.4.1.7 Impact Analysis

The level of impact from a threat event is the magnitude of harm that can be expected to result from the consequences of unauthorized disclosure of information, unauthorized modification of information, unauthorized destruction of information, loss of information, or information system availability. Such harm can be experienced by a variety of organizational and nonorganizational stakeholders including, for example, heads of agencies, mission and business owners, information owners/stewards, mission/business process owners, information system owners, or individuals/groups in the public or private sectors relying on the organization. In essence, anyone with a vested interest in the organization's operations, assets, or individuals, including other organizations in partnership with the organization.

Organizations should make explicit:

- The Process used to conduct impact determinations
- Assumptions related to impact determinations
- Sources and methods for obtaining impact information
- The rationale for conclusions reached with regard to impact determination

Organizations may explicitly define how established priorities and values guide the identification of high-value assets and the potential adverse impacts to organizational stakeholders. If such information is not defined, priorities and values related to identifying targets of threat sources and associated organizational impacts can typically be derived from strategic planning and policies. For example, security categorization levels indicate the organizational impacts of compromising different types of information. Privacy Impact Assessments (PIA) and criticality levels (when defined as part of contingency planning or mission/business impact analysis) indicate the adverse impacts of destruction, corruption, or loss of accountability for information resources to organizations.

Strategic plans and policies also assert or imply the relative priorities of immediate or near-term mission/business function accomplishment and long-term organizational viability, which can be undermined by the loss of reputation or by sanctions resulting from the compromise of sensitive information. Organizations can also consider the range of effects of threat events including the relative size of the set of resources affected, when making final impact determinations. Risk tolerance assumptions may state that threat events with an impact below a specific value do not warrant further analysis (NIST, 2012). An example of impact level definitions is shown in Table 3.6.

3.4.1.8 Risk Determination

The role of this step is to determine the type of the risk, especially the acceptability of risk, in preparation of existing or planned security controls to be implemented in order to reduce or eliminate risk. As shown in Table 3.12, a risk scale can be used to differentiate different levels of risks.

TABLE 3.12 Risk Scale Example

Consequence	Value	Criteria
Catastrophic	5	1. Generates loss of confidentiality of information that can be useful for individuals, competitors or other internal or external parties, with nonrecoverable effect for the company 2. Generates loss of integrity of information internally or externally with nonrecoverable effect for the company 3. Generate loss of availability of information with nonrecoverable effect for the company
High	4	1. Generate loss of confidentiality of information that can be useful for individuals, competitors or other internal or external parties, with mitigated or recoverable effects in the long term 2. Generates loss of integrity of information internally or externally with mitigated or recoverable effects in the long term 3. Generates loss of availability of information with mitigated or recoverable effects in the long term
Moderate	3	1. Generates loss of confidentiality of information that can be useful for individuals, competitors or other internal or external parties, with mitigated or recoverable effects in the medium term 2. Generates loss of integrity of information internally or externally with mitigated or recoverable effects in the medium term 3. Generates loss of availability of information with mitigated or recoverable effects in the medium term
Minor	2	1. Generate loss of confidentiality of information that can be useful for individuals, competitors, or other internal or external parties, with mitigated or recoverable effects in the short term 2. Generates loss of integrity of information internally or externally with mitigated or recoverable effects in the short term 3. Generates loss of availability of information with mitigated or recoverable effects in the short term
Insignificant	1	1. Generates loss of confidentiality of information that is not useful for individuals, competitors or other internal or external parties 2. Generates loss of integrity of information internally or externally with no effects for the company 3. Generates loss of availability of information with no effects for the company

Risks can also be categorized into negligible, acceptable, or unacceptable:

1. The *negligible risk* does not need any countermeasure to be implemented as long as it is monitored periodically.
2. The *acceptable risk* does not need any countermeasure to be implemented until its monitored potential impact reaches an unacceptable level that can affect the objective of the organization.
3. The *unacceptable risk* needs to be treated, and the management team must identify and implement the right countermeasure to reduce or eliminate the risk to a level that is acceptable or negligible.

Another way to visualize risk is to create a risk map, often called a heat map. These are usually two-dimensional representations of impact plotted against likelihood. They can also depict other relationships such as impact versus vulnerability.

3.4.2 Risk Mitigation

Risk mitigation is about taking steps to reduce adverse effects. It often involves developing a strategic plan to prioritize the risks identified in risk assessment and take steps to selectively reduce the highest priority risks under the constraints of an organization's limited resources. It is infeasible to defend against all possible threats, and a certain level of risk may be acceptable (Chen, 2008). Hence, the process of risk mitigation is always around economic decision-making to strategically investment limited resources to change unacceptable risks into acceptable ones. Acceptable risks are generally the low risks, but a careful cost–benefit analysis should be done to decide which risks to accept.

Risk mitigation under the context of cyber risk can involve both technical and nontechnical changes:

- *Technical mitigation* changes can involve security equipment, e.g., access controls, cryptography, firewalls, intrusion detection systems, physical security, antivirus software, audit trails, backups, and management of the equipment.
- *Nontechnical mitigation* changes could include policy changes, user training, and security awareness.

Broadly speaking, there are four types of risk mitigation strategies (Gerber and van Solms, 2005; Ramona and Cristina, 2011; Herrera, 2017):

1. *Risk avoidance*. Taking steps to end the exposure to certain risks by removing the cause of risk or giving up potential chances to take such risks by engaging in different activities. For example, by abandoning the use of USB flash drives or CDs on computer systems connected with the business network, hence avoiding risks of malware infection from external data sources.
2. *Risk transfer*. Handing risk off to a willing third party. For example, numerous companies outsource/subcontract certain operations such as customer service and payroll services, etc. This can be beneficial for a company if a transferred risk is not a core competency of that company (Herrera, 2017). The most common form of risk transference is "insurance," which allows an organization to avoid the risk of potentially catastrophic loss in exchange for a fixed loss (payment of insurance premiums). Chapter 10, Case Study: Insuring the Future of Everything, provides a detailed case study on cyber-insurance.
3. *Risk limitation/reduction*. Risk limitation means taking some actions to reduce the risk to an acceptable level by implementing controls to reduce the impact or expected frequency. For example, firewalls and access controls can be hardened to make it more difficult for external attackers to gain access to an organization's private network. Corrective controls reduce the effect of an attack. Detective controls discover attacks and trigger corrective controls. Chapter 5, Economic Modeling and the Implementation of Effective Mitigating Controls, covers various aspects of implementing countermeasures more in detail.
4. *Risk acceptance*. Risk acceptance is to make an informed decision to accept the likelihood and impact of a particular risk. Risk acceptance depends on risk criteria and the risk appetite of top management therefore it concerns the communication of residual risks to the decision makers (ENISA, 2016). The management needs to be informed about any resulting risks and has to explicitly accept them.[6] Risks that are accepted on an involuntary basis need to be explicitly specified.

The choice of risk mitigation depends on the specific business environment and circumstances in which the organization conducts its business. Even after all security controls are in place, there will still be some form of risk remaining. The remaining risk is called residual risk, and it is defined as:

The amount of risk left over after natural or inherent risks have been reduced by risk controls.

Gregory (2008)

The residual risk might be the result of some assets being intentionally left unprotected either because of low risk being assessed or because of high cost of the suggested control. Residual risks need to be classified as either being "acceptable" or "unacceptable." Unacceptable risks should not be tolerated, and decisions should be taken to apply additional controls or more stringent controls, which will further reduce risk (Humphreys et al., 1998). Below are the general steps of risk mitigation:

1. *Prioritize actions*. The risks with their corresponding levels identified through the risk assessment process will suggest what actions should be taken. Obviously, the risks with unacceptably high levels should be addressed with the greatest urgency. This step should identify a ranked list of actions needed to address the identified risks.
2. *Identify possible controls*. This step examines all possible actions to mitigate risks. Some controls will be more feasible or cost effective than others, but that determination is left for later. The result from this step is a list of control options for further study.
3. *Cost—benefit analysis*. The heart of risk mitigation is an examination of trade-offs between costs and benefits related to every control option (Gordon and Loeb, 2002; Mercuri, 2003). This step recognizes that an organization's resources are limited and should be spent in the most cost-effective manner to reduce risks. A control is worthwhile only if its cost can be justified by the reduction in the level of risk. Cost of controls is often challenging to quantify, in addition to hardware and software costs, there may be costs for personnel training, time, additional human resources, policy implementation as well as impact on the efficiency of systems. More on cost of controls are covered in Chapter 5, Economic Modeling and the Implementation of Effective Mitigating Controls.
4. *Select controls for implementation*. Based on outcome of cost—benefit analysis, decisions on which controls to implement is made. Presumably, the recommended controls will require a budget, and the budget must be balanced

---

6. ISO/IEC 27000 family — Information security management systems.
Retrieved from: www.iso.org/isoiec-27001-information-security.html.

against the organization's other budget demands. That is, the final selection of controls to implement depends not only on the action priorities (from step 1) but also on all competing priorities of the organization (Geer et al., 2003).

5. *Assign responsibilities.* Ultimately, implementation will depend on personnel with the appropriate skills. The personnel might be available within an organization, but for any number of reasons, an organization might decide to delegate responsibilities to a third party.

6. *Implementation.* In the final step, the selected controls must be implemented by the responsible personnel (Chen, 2008).

3.4.3   Effectiveness Assessment

The goal of effectiveness assessment is to measure and verify that the objectives of risk mitigation have been met (Chen, 2008). If not, the steps in risk assessment and risk mitigation may have to be updated. Essentially, effectiveness assessment gives feedback to the first two processes to ensure correctness. Effective assessment is necessary because firstly, risk assessment is not an exact science. There are uncertainties related to the real range of threats, likelihood of threats, impacts, and expected frequency. Similarly, in the risk mitigation process, there are uncertainties in the estimation of costs and benefits for each control option. The uncertainties may result in misjudgments in the risk mitigation plan. Hence, an assessment of the success or failure of the risk mitigation plan is necessary. It provides useful feedback into the process to ensure correctness. Secondly, an organization's environment cannot be expected to remain static. Over time, an organization's network, computers, software, personnel, policies, and priorities will all change. Continuous monitoring is needed to ensure that risk assessment and mitigation are repeated and updated periodically to keep current.

3.4.4   Continuous Monitoring

An organization's environment is not static. There should be a continual evaluation process to update the risk mitigation strategy with new information. In the context of constant technological and nontechnological changes that occur both internally and externally, existing security controls may become inadequate and may need to be reassessed for effectiveness. The tendency for security controls to potentially degrade in effectiveness over time reinforces the need to maintain risk assessments during the entire system development life cycle and also the importance of continuous monitoring programs to obtain ongoing situational awareness of the organizational security posture (NIST, 2012).

3.5   RISK MODELS

3.5.1   Qualitative and Quantitative Models

There are many approaches to risk models. The most important differentiator is quantitative versus qualitative approaches. The primary difference between the quantitative and qualitative models is the subjectivity of determining the likelihood of threats. Quantitative models use a numerical scale, while qualitative models use a relative or descriptive scale. Hybrid models use a combination of the two. A comparison of the two approaches is shown in Table 3.13.

3.5.2   Quantitative Assessment

Quantitative risk assessment is the use of measurable, objective data to determine asset value, probability of loss, and associated risk(s). Quantitative techniques range from risk rankings, risk maps (or called heat map), risk correlations, benchmarking, and scenario analysis to generating forward-looking point estimates (deterministic models) and then to generating forward-looking distributions (probabilistic models). Generally, quantitative approaches follow a basic formula that identifies assets, threats to those assets, assigns a probability to a threat's occurrence and then multiplies this probability by an asset valuation. The sum of this formula provides a basic calculation which factors in the likelihood of a loss and the value of the loss if it occurs. Many modern-day quantitative approaches have become sophisticated actuarial models with the application of historical occurrence data to determine the likelihood of an event occurring (Harris, 2005).

TABLE 3.13 Comparison Between Qualitative and Quantitative Approaches to Risk Model (Staff, 2006)

Technique	Advantages	Disadvantages
Qualitative	• Is relatively quick and easy • Provides rich information beyond financial impact and likelihood such as vulnerability, speed of onset, and nonfinancial impact such as health, safety, and reputation • Is easily understood by a large number of employees who may not be trained in sophisticated quantification techniques	• Gives limited differentiation between levels of risk (i.e., very high, high, medium, and low) • Is imprecise. Risk events that plot within the same risk level can represent substantially different amounts of risk • Cannot numerically aggregate or address risk interactions and correlations • Provides limited ability to perform cost–benefit analysis
Quantitative	• Allows numerical aggregation considering risk interactions when using an "at-risk" measure such as cash flow at risk • Permits cost–benefit analysis of risk response options • Enable risk-based capital allocation to business activities with optimal return • Helps compute capital requirements to maintain solvency under extreme conditions	• Can be time-consuming and costly, especially at first during model development • Must choose units of measure such as dollars and annual frequency which may result in qualitative impact being overlooked • Use of number may imply greater precision than the uncertainty of input warrants • Assumptions may not be apparent

TABLE 3.14 Qualitative and Quantitative Risk Management Methodologies

Qualitative Methods	Quantitative Methods
• The IT Infrastructure Library (ITIL) • Control Objectives for Information and Related Technology (COBIT) • ISO/IEC 27005:2011 • Information Security Forum (ISF) Simplified Process for Risk Identification (SPRINT) and Simple to Apply Risk Analysis (SARA) • Operational Critical Threat and Vulnerability Evaluation (OCTAVE) • NIST Special Publication 800-53 • NIST Special Publication 800-37 • ISO/IEC 31000:2009 • Consultative, Objective and Bi-functional Risk Analysis (COBRA) • Construct a platform for Risk Analysis of Security Critical Systems (CORAS). • Business Process: Information Risk Management (BPIRM)	• Information Security Risk Analysis Method (ISRAM) • Central computer and Telecommunication Agency Risk Analysis and Management Method (CRAMM) • BSI Guide-RuSecure-Based on BS7799 Standard • Cost-of-Risk Analysis (CORA)

3.5.3   Qualitative Assessment

The most commonly used assessment techniques are interviews, cross-functional workshops, surveys, benchmarking, scenario analysis, fault trees, and event trees. Qualitative approaches to risk tend to be applied to those risks that are difficult to quantify. Qualitative approaches replace the quantitative values by assigning a subjectively determined value such as high, medium, or low. Note that theoretically, even qualitative models apply the basic formula to risk: determine the risk, determine its likelihood of occurrence, and determine the potential loss (Harris, 2005).

Qualitative and quantitative risk models currently in use are summarized in Table 3.14.

3.5.4   Other Models

A comprehensive study (Shameli-Sendi et al., 2016) on all existing risk models introduced the three new categories below in additional to qualitative versus quantitative models.

3.5.4.1   Perspective: Asset-driven, Service-driven, or Business driven

There are three perspectives to analyze risks: asset-driven, service-driven, and business-driven. The main focus of this category is to choose a level of the organization's resources, i.e., asset, service, or business process, to identify their corresponding risks. The asset-driven perspective identifies the assets and their associated risks in asset level, whereas the business-driven identifies risks to the business processes directly. The service-driven perspective, on the other hand, uses services as input of risk assessment and considers risks to services rather than assets or business processes.

3.5.4.2   Resource Valuation: Vertical or Horizontal

An important stage in risk analysis is to identify the value of resources, i.e., assets, services, business processes. No matter which perspective is chosen, resource valuation cannot be completely isolated from each other and may have horizontal and/or vertical connections. As a result, resource valuation can be obtained from two views: (1) vertical view and (2) horizontal view. The vertical view is a bottom–up view and it considers the resources' contribution degree of a level in the upper level, while the horizontal view refers the dependencies between resources at the same level (Shameli-Sendi et al., 2016).

3.5.4.3   Risk Measurement: Propagated or Nonpropagated

The third new category refers to the risk measurement: propagated or nonpropagated. In a nonpropagated model, risk is measured regardless of its impact propagation to other resources. For example, if risk assessment is business-driven, risk measurement can be evaluated by multiplying three parameters: business process value, vulnerability effect, and threat effect. Risk is measured regardless of its impact propagation from the compromised business process to other business process. In propagated model, the impact of the attack on the compromised resource is considered to propagate to other resources (Jahnke et al., 2007; Kheir et al., 2010; Mahmoud et al., 2011). A resource dependency graph can be used to measure the propagated risk. A summary of advantages and disadvantages of risk models are shown in Table 3.15.

TABLE 3.15 Summary of Advantages and Disadvantages of Risk Models (Shameli-Sendi et al., 2016)

	Advantages	Disadvantages
Quantitative	• Risks levels may be identified in monetary terms • Results can be expressed in management-specific language • Great effort is put into resource value definition and risk mitigation • Cost–benefit assessment effort is possible	• Estimation of damage probability of each resource is imprecise • The numerical/monetary results may be difficult for nontechnical people to interpret • Calculation can be challenging, expensive, and time consuming
Qualitative	• It is not necessary to quantify threat likelihood • Prioritizes the risks and identifies areas for immediate action and improvement • Save time, effort, and expenses • Easier to involve people who are not experts on security or computers	• Does not provide monetary values and probabilities • Making a cost–benefit analysis of recommended controls is more difficult • Very subjective and prone to errors and imprecision
Hybrid	• It has the flexibility to change quantitative inputs to qualitative outputs and vice versa	
Asset-driven	• The majority of tools available on the market are designed based on this perspective • It needs less expertise and is easy to understand	• Makes the calculation error-prone for the large number of resources in a medium to large organization • It makes risk reduction inefficient

(Continued)

TABLE 3.15 (Continued)

	Advantages	Disadvantages
Service-driven	• Services are easier to evaluate • Services are better understood and easier to identify and grasp than assets • Save time and effort in large organizations	• May be too challenging for small organizations • It is more suitable for organizations with, a service-based approach in delivering their business processes
Business-driven	• Those risks that have high impact in organization are well reflected in risk assessment • Financial impact of risks is better evaluated • Easier to present to and gain support from top management • It leads to efficient risk reduction	• Maybe be too challenging for small organizations • It requires insight into the business and its processes
Vertical	• It produces realistic estimates of resource value	• It is difficult to consider all the dependencies for determining the resource value
Horizontal	• It produces more realistic estimates of resource value • It facilitates the separation of critical from noncritical resources	• It needs to keep track of the different kinds of dependencies between resources
Nonpropagated	• It makes the risk measurement easy for the large number of risks and resources	• Imprecise • It may lead to selecting inappropriate security safeguards • It cannot be used to estimate the potential damage cost in subsequent steps of an attack in the future if they were to occur
Propagated	• Risks are calculated more accurately • It indicates exactly what part of the network will be affected from an attack • It can predict the potential damage cost which may be done by the attacker in the next step	• It requires accurate knowledge about the type of attack, the dependency severity between resources in terms of confidentiality, integrity, and availability, and the type of predefined access permission between resources • Thorough change management is needed to update dependencies

Chapter 4

Cyber Risk Measurement in the Hyperconnected World

Chapter Outline

4.1 Cyber Risk as a Critical Business Risk	75	
4.2 The Uniqueness of Cyber Risk	76	
4.3 The Need for Cyber Risk Measurement and Current Challenges	77	
4.4 Cost Models for Incidents and Losses	78	
4.4.1 Cost of Cybercrime	78	
4.4.2 Cyber incident loss Categories	79	
4.4.3 Models for Measuring Expected Loss	79	
4.4.3.1 Expected Loss	79	
4.4.3.2 Expected Severe Loss	79	
4.4.3.3 Standard Deviation of Loss	79	
4.4.3.4 Perceived Composite Risk	80	
4.4.3.5 Loss in Market Value	82	

4.5 Methods for Cyber Risk Measurement	82
4.5.1 Stochastic Modeling	82
4.5.2 Monte Carlo Simulation	83
4.5.3 Cyber Value at Risk	83
4.5.4 The CORAS Method	83
4.5.5 Common Vulnerability Scoring System	83
4.5.6 Factor Analysis of Information Risk	84
4.6 Introducing Cyber Risk Quadrant: Applying Medical Risk Measurement to Cyber	84
4.6.1 Applying Medical Risk Model for Measuring Cyber Risk	84
4.6.2 Using Scenario Analysis for Control Assessment and Loss Quantification	85

The revolutionary idea that defines the boundary between modern times and the past is the mastery of risk: the notion that the future is more than a whim of the gods and that men and women are not passive before nature. Until human beings discovered a way across that boundary, the future was the mirror of the past or the murky domain of oracles and soothsayers who held a monopoly over knowledge of anticipated events.

— Peter Bernstein

4.1 CYBER RISK AS A CRITICAL BUSINESS RISK

Cyber risk has traditionally fallen under operational risk in enterprise risk management. This historical view of seeing cyber as only an operational asset is limiting because it neglects the economic role digital assets are playing in the core value generation processes of businesses. Under today's business context, it is increasingly evident that cyber risk is spilling over into all parts of critical business risk.

Cyber risks have become more worrisome to large organizations than traditional natural catastrophe risks. 41% of large business with more than 500 employees believe that cyber risks are greater than other insurable business risks such as natural disasters, business interruption, and fires (Wells, 2013). According to the Aon and Ponemon Institute (2017), nearly 65% of organizations expect their cyber risk exposure to increase in the next 2 years. When comparing to property, plant, and equipment (PP&E) assets:

- The impact of business disruption to cyber assets is 72% greater than to PP&E assets.
- Organizations valued cyber assets 14% more than PP&E assets.
- Quantification of probable maximum loss from cyber assets is 27% higher than from PP&E assets.
- Organizations insure on average 59% of PP&E losses, compared to an average of 15% of cyber exposures.

On the microeconomic level, cyber risk has already become an important component of enterprise strategic risk, credit risk, as well as regulatory risk. An organization's strategy can be impacted by a cyber-attack. This

Digital Asset Valuation and Cyber Risk Measurement. DOI: https://doi.org/10.1016/B978-0-12-812158-0.00004-1

has resulted in cyber security and risk discussions entering boardrooms worldwide. Reports have estimated that 60% of small and medium size business go out of business within as quickly as a 6-month period due to a successful attack (Symantec, 2018). Competitive advantages or trade secrets are often primary targets of cyber-attacks. Study shows that one in five businesses hit by ransomware are forced to close (Malwarebytes, 2016). Cyberattacks on the private sector are an increasingly important risk in corporate credit analysis (Volz 2015). Companies' cyber security ratings[1] are now being considered in investment assessments (Bloomberg, 2014). As news of more data breaches from third-party cyber-attacks and threats emerge, business and regulators are sharpening their focus on how to report and alleviate these risks. After the General Data Protection Regulation (GDPR) came into effect in 2018 in the EU, companies can be fined a maximum of 20 million euros or 4% of global turnover for data breaches.[2]

On the macroeconomic level, cyber risk can clearly impact markets and pose systemic risk. Cyber risks have been kept at the forefront of practitioners' minds, thanks to a robust focus from financial regulators and levels of media attention. The Federal Reserve Bank of New York has went as far as identifying cyber as one of its top risk priorities and that it could trigger the next financial crisis.

In finance, systemic risk is the risk of collapse of an entire financial system or entire market, as opposed to risk associated with any one individual entity, group or component of a system, that can be contained therein without harming the entire system.

Ninety percent of respondents from an American International Group (AIG) survey believe that cyber risk is systemic. Respondents also ranked a mass distributed a Distributed Denial of Service (DDoS) attack on a major cloud provider as the most likely cross-sector mega event (AIG, 2016). In fact, this has already happened in reality. Outages caused by a typo from Amazon Cloud (Newton, 2017) has grounded the Internet to a halt. Firms have to understand that many IT systems (hardware and software) are mainly mass products and thus a particularly high correlation of risks is possible, leading to potential accumulation risks (Kosub, 2015). In short, there is a lack of technological diversification in our system design, which may lead to cascading consequences where attackers exploit the right vulnerabilities.

A single cyber-attack can affect tens, hundreds, or even thousands of institutions at the same time. In late-2016 and early-2017, hackers launched an extortion campaign on customers of a widely used open-source database platform, MongoDB. The hackers targeted older versions with default security settings that made it easier to access, view, edit, or delete data. Security researchers suggest that between 50,000 and 100,000 databases were exposed globally across many sectors including healthcare, financial services, education, and travel. Flashpoint, a cyber security firm, estimates that at least 20,000 databases were permanently deleted. One prominent healthcare institution is reported to have lost 3 years of research data when its database was deleted in the attack. The type of cyber-attack that could have a systemic impact include:

- Mass business interruption from mass DDoS on a large cloud provider.
- Mass data theft from a flaw in commonly used electronic medical record software.
- Mass data theft from a flaw in widely used payment processing software/hardware.
- Mass data theft from a flaw in commonly used software.
- Mass business interruption from mass DDoS coordinated against financial institutions.
- Mass business interruption from a flaw in commonly used industrial control systems.
- Mass physical property damage, bodily injury, and business interruption from a flaw in commonly used industrial control systems.

Systemic cyber risk will be covered more in detail in Chapter 8, Three Views of Cybernomics: Entity View, Portfolio View and Global View.

4.2   THE UNIQUENESS OF CYBER RISK

The rapid pace of increasing complexity and the increasingly crippling impact of cyber-specific threats demand a different degree of prioritization, resources, and tireless attention than any other type of risk corporations face today. In the same way that technology will change the way we do business more in the next 5 years than any other catalyst,

---

1. BitSight cyber security rating: www.bitsighttech.com/.
2. General Data Protection Regulation, European Commission: http://eur-lex.europa.eu/legal-content/EN/TXT/?uri = CELEX%3A32016R0679.

cyber risks will challenge our ability to operate under more than any other threat (Hectus, 2016). Cyber risk is unique comparing to traditional business risks for its velocity, scale, and complexity.

1. **Velocity**

Unlike traditional risk, active cyber adversaries are constantly changing their attack strategy. Technology advancements introduce new cyber-attack surfaces at an ever-increasing pace, from Internet of Things (IoT), cloud computing, cognitive computing, to the use of Artificial Intelligence (AI).

The fast-changing technological evolution demands for a dynamic cyber risk management process, which quickly adapts to a changed cyber environment and thus cyber risk exposures (Kosub, 2015). Knowledge deficits are also a constant challenge, which can reflect in the inaccurate asset valuation/loss estimation, data insufficiencies, the lack of awareness among stakeholders, or the lack of skills in the workforce.

2. **Scale**

While the political, social, and economic implications are not fully clear, gigabit connectivity represents a significant overnight leap forward (ISF, 2017). This enables the IoT and new class of applications to emerge that exploits the combination of big data, position system location, weather, personal health monitoring devices, etc. Low-cost connectivity is available at scale and sensors are embedded just about everywhere. This raises issues about not only privacy and data access, but also expands the reality of threat landscape at global scale.

3. **Transdisciplinarity**

Cyber risk reaches beyond technology. A greater degree of cyber risk factors are socio-economic and human factors, which heavily correlate with attackers' profiles. An essential challenge for effective cyber risk management is also presented by people. The general awareness of cyber risks, its threats and consequences seems lacking among a large share of its users. In the geo-political dimension, state-sponsored attacks and attempts of cyber warfare are bringing inter-state conflicts into a brand-new era. Today's digital giants also have greater political power than nations, given their influences on how people make daily decisions. In the ethical dimension, the future of digitization and its pervasive nature are challenging how societies view privacy, collaboration, identity, and moral baselines. No other business risk today requires collaborative insights from such a diverse and complex combination of disciplines.

4.3 THE NEED FOR CYBER RISK MEASUREMENT AND CURRENT CHALLENGES

What cannot be measured cannot be managed. Currently, qualitative risk models lack granularity, objectivity, and the ability to assist in cost-benefit analyses, while quantitative models lack efficiency, statistical robustness, and reliable asset valuations (Suh and Han, 2003). In general, current cyber risk management models have these limitations.

1. **Current Methods Focus on Technology and Are Limited in Covering People, Processes, and Socio-Economic Risk Factors**

Current methods focus on technology and are limited in covering people, process, and socio-economic risk factors (Spears, 2005). An information system is comprised of technology, people, processes, and data. Therefore, effective risk analysis must examine each of these aspects. As such, traditional risk models are seen as inadequate as they are technology-driven and focuses primarily on known threats to types of computing assets employed by an organization (Halliday et al., 1996; Humphreys et al., 1998; Gerber and von Solms, 2005). This is due, in large part, to the historical origin of widely-used computer security guidelines that were initially developed for securing governmental and military computing infrastructures, and not for information systems within a business environment (Spears, 2005).

The bottom-up nature of the traditional method (i.e., driven from a micro, technology assets perspective) tends to be a time-consuming process, especially in medium to large organizations (Halliday et al., 1996). Significant amounts of time may be spent analyzing assets of low importance to critical business processes. Expected financial losses based on asset value typically do not include the social impact of a potential breach, such as loss of customer confidence (Bennett and Kailay, 1992).

A tech-centric approach to security risk analysis does not involve business users to the extent necessary to identify a comprehensive set of risks, or to promote risk awareness throughout an organization. For example, risk inherent in business processes that could be identifiable by a business user may go undetected by a technical professional.

Finally, the lack of solid business case for risk evaluation means the lack of accountability and prioritization in implementing mitigating actions. In practice, risk assessment and measurement are widely viewed as a barrier to day-to-day business activities yielding no value. Despite a wealth of risk analysis and assessment models, there is reluctance in organizations to adopt robust process for risk data collection, if not under regulatory pressure.

2. **More Accurate Estimates Often Require Access to Data and Knowledge That a Single Entity Does Not Possess**

   The traditional risk analysis method employs calculations based largely on guesswork to estimate probability and financial loss of a security breach. Probability estimates of the likelihood of an identified vulnerability being exploited are commonly considered to be wild guesswork for two reasons. First, likelihood is often determined by past history of security breaches which is largely underreported (Strang, 2001; Yazar, 2002; Keeney et al., 2005). Second, making a more accurate estimate requires a higher level of expertise by the estimator which an organization may not possess (Gerber and von Solms, 2005).

   Risk assessment data do not always reflect reality. Organizations often use qualitative tools, such as questionnaires and surveys, to which the answers are provided to please the assessors. They end up censoring the real area of vulnerability, which affects the purpose of the assessment process.

   Without mandatory incident reporting, public—private data sharing partnerships, and standard data collection schemes, it is challenging to collect quality incident data for robust statistical analysis. Organizing and processing limited available historical data can be difficult due to quality issues and different approaches toward data collection.

3. **Domain-Based Risk Assessment Is Not Effective for Risk Prioritization**

   Predominant risk assessment frameworks, such as ISO/IEC 27002, are structured based on security control domains. These methods comprehensively assess an entity's security posture, but are not effective in assessing an entity's preparedness toward a set of high-risk loss scenarios developed around critical digital assets.

4. **Lack of a Common Point of Reference**

   More fundamentally, the proliferation of risk assessment methodologies in the absence of a common point of reference has caused undesirable inconsistency in measuring cyber risk. This is unlike other risk fields, such as in finance and medicine.

4.4 COST MODELS FOR INCIDENTS AND LOSSES

The foremost requirement for analyzing cyber risk from an economic perspective is estimating the cost of security, or lack thereof. Unfortunately, current practices estimating expected losses from cyber incidents can be widely inaccurate for a variety of reasons. First, as discussed in Chapter 2, Digital Theory of Value, determining the value of intangible digital assets is challenging (Gerber and von Solms, 2005) even though digital assets are the focal points of cyber risk management. Second, estimates for the value of tangible digital assets may be inaccurate due to the lack of formal valuation models. For example, in many cases only replacement costs are considered, which does not include the financial loss due to disruption of operations. In cases where cost of disruption of operations is included in the asset value, the estimate is highly subjective (Suh and Han, 2003). Grossly underestimating cost of incidents and associated losses can lead to poor investment decisions in security and risk management (Jajodia and Miller, 2003).

Current cost models for incident and losses are reviewed in this section.

4.4.1 Cost of Cybercrime

According to Ponemon Institute (2016), on average, organizations have spent US$10 million in response to third-party breaches over a 12-month period. Not only revenue loss is faced, but reputation is impacted, regulatory exposure and lawsuits can cause lasting damage and leads to job losses for executives, directors and others within that organization. Cybercrime has surpassed drug dealing (Dethlefs, 2015) because of its returns. The estimated annual cost to the global economy due to cybercrime ranges from a conservative estimate of US$35 billion to a staggering US$575 billion. Even the smallest estimate can easily surpass the national income of most countries and governments. The cost of cybercrime also affects hundreds of millions of people having their personal information stolen. Incidents in 2013 included more than 40 million in the United States, 54 million in Turkey, 20 million in Korea, 16 million in Germany and more than 20 million in China. However, loss means more than dollar signs. The most critical cost of cybercrime is the damage done to a company's performance—damages in trade, competition, innovation, and global economic growth. The cost of cybercrime will continue to increase as more business functions move online and more companies' customers connect to the Internet. Losses from theft of intellectual property will also increase as countries improve their ability to utilize technology to manufacture competing goods (Intel Security, 2015).

4.4.2   Cyber incident loss Categories

Following is a simple list of questions for estimating loss from cyber incidents (Dittrich, 2002):

1. Who worked on responding to or investigating the incident?
2. How many hours did each of them spend?
3. How many people were prevented from working because of the incident?
4. How much production did each of them lose?
5. How much do you pay each of those people to work for you?
6. How much overhead do you pay for your employees?

More comprehensively, Table 4.1 covers loss categories that can be considered in a more formal loss estimation. These categories are not mutually exclusive.

4.4.3   Models for Measuring Expected Loss

This section provides a summary of the existing four models for measuring expected loss: expected loss, expected severe loss, standard deviation of loss (Bodin, et. al., 2008), and perceived composite risk.

4.4.3.1   Expected Loss

The *expected loss* is derived by taking the sum of the product of each loss with its respective probability. Based on this metric, the larger the expected loss, the larger the risk associated with a cyber incident. *Annual Loss Expectancy* (ALE) measure can be used to measure expected loss:

$$ALE = ARO \times SLE$$

where ARO is annual rate of occurrence and SLE is the single loss expectancy. Suppose that an asset is valued at US $100,000, and the Exposure Factor (EF) for the asset is 25%. The SLE is US$25,000. For an ARO of 3, ALE equals US$75,000.

ALE is a quantitative method introduced in a 1976 FIPS publication (NIST, 1975) by the National Institute of Standards and Technologies (NIST) as appropriate for use by large data centers (Mercuri, 2003). It is one of the earliest-used estimators in the computer industry. The method was criticized because of the lack of empirical data on frequency of occurrence of impacts and the related consequences, thus producing an interpretation of results as having more precision than they actually had.

4.4.3.2   Expected Severe Loss

The *expected severe loss* focuses only on the incidents that put the survivability of the organization at risk. In order to calculate the expected severe loss, one has to first specify the magnitude of loss that, were it to occur, would threaten the very survivability of the organization. The expected severe loss is derived by taking the sum of the product of each severe loss, that is, each loss that is greater or equal to the specified threshold, with its respective probability. Based on this metric, the larger the expected severe loss, the larger the risk associated with a cyber incident.

4.4.3.3   Standard Deviation of Loss

The *standard deviation of loss* (which is the square root of the variance of loss) represents the dispersion around the expected loss. The standard deviation of loss is computed by taking the square root of the product of squares of the deviation of each loss from the expected loss multiplied by the probability of that loss. Based on this metric, the larger the standard deviation, the larger the risk associated with a security breach.

TABLE 4.1 Cyber Incident Cost Categories

Loss Category	Description
Direct cost (or first-party loss)	Losses that directly impact the organization. Common first-party loss scenarios include: • Malicious destruction of data. • Denial of service attack. • Virus, malware, spyware, etc. • Accidental damage of data. • Human error. • Electrical power surges/natural disasters. • IT system failure. • Cyber extortion threats.
Indirect cost (or third-party loss)	Losses that indirectly impact the organization, e.g., from legal liabilities. Common third-party loss scenarios include: • Loss of public image. • Loss of employee confidence, as with employee privacy violations. • Potential legal actions, both civil and criminal. • Loss of proprietary data are examples of loss which tend to produce indirect cost which should be grossly estimated (Courtney, 1982).
Short-term cost (or transitory cost)	Short-term costs incurred only during the period in which the incident occurs, which may include: • Lost business and worker productivity because of breached information resources, labor, and material costs required to detect, contain, repair, and reconstitute the breached resources. • Costs associated with finding, evidence collection, and prosecution of the attacker. • Media-related costs to providing information to customers and the public.
Long-term cost (or permanent cost)	Long-term costs incurred after the immediate effects of the incident are dealt with, which may include: • Those related to loss of customers that switch to competitors. • Inability to attract new customers because of perceived poor security. • Loss of trust of customers and business partners. • Potential future legal liabilities arising out of the breach. • Cost of competitor's access to confidential or proprietary information. • Increased insurance cost or higher capital cost in debt and equity markets because of perceived increase of business risk (Cavusoglu et al., 2004).
Tangible cost	Tangible costs may include: • Lost sales, material, and labor. • Insurance.
Intangible cost	Intangible costs may include: • Reputational damage. • Loss of customer trust.
Cost in anticipation	Security costs made in anticipation of preventing problems. Cost in anticipation can be a fixed cost (Walker, 2012).
Cost in response	Security costs made in response to information security failures that have already occurred (Geer, 2004). Cost in response is a variable (Walker, 2012).

4.4.3.4 Perceived Composite Risk

For a given set of information security activities, perceived composite risk (PCR) is the linear combination of the expected loss, the expected severe loss, and the standard deviation of loss that can be attributable to a breach:

$$\text{PCR} = E[X] + [B/A] \cdot E\,[\text{severe loss}] + [C/A] \cdot \sigma$$

where the weights A, B, and C are determined from analytic hierarchy process (AHP). AHP is a decision support system to deal with multi-criteria decision-making (MCDM) problems developed by Saaty (1990). It aims to quantify relative priorities for a given set of alternatives on a ratio scale, based on decision-maker judgements, by strictly following consistency standard of the pairwise comparison in the decision-making process (Syamsuddin and Hwang, 2010). The weights A, B, and C are positive, sum to one, and measure the emphasis that the decision-maker wants to place on the three risk measures, i.e., the expected loss, the expected severe loss, and the standard deviation.

PCR is equal to the expected loss plus two penalty terms:

- The penalty term, $[B/A] \cdot E[\text{severe loss}]$, measures an additional perceived loss due to a severe loss occurring.
- The penalty term, $[C/A] \cdot \sigma$, measures an additional perceived loss due to variability in predicting the loss.

For a Chief Information Security Officer (CISO) faced with selecting among four equal cost proposals for reducing cyber risk exposure and suppose that the CISO and his staff have estimated the loss probabilities associated with the three proposed sets of information security activities. The estimated loss probabilities associated with each proposal have been broken down into ten discrete amounts as displayed in Table 4.2.

Let X be a variable representing loss from an incident (in millions of dollars). For Proposal 1 aimed at reducing cyber risk exposure, X has the following discrete uniform distribution:

$$P[X = x] = 0.1 \quad \text{for } x = 0, 1, 2, \ldots, 9.$$

The expected loss $E[X]$ under Proposal 1 is given by:

$$E[X] = \sum_{(x=0)}^{9} x \cdot P[X = x] = 0 \cdot [0.1] + 1 \cdot [0.1] + \ldots + 9 \cdot [0.1] = 4.5$$

Suppose the threshold level $T = 8$, the expected severe loss under Proposal 1 is given by:

$$E[\text{severe loss}] = \sum_{(x=0)}^{9} x \cdot P[X = x] = 8 \cdot [0.1] + 9 \cdot [0.1] = 1.7$$

The standard deviation of loss σ under the loss function defined for Proposal 1 is given by:

$$\sigma = \sqrt{\sum_{x=0}^{9} (x - E[X])^2 \cdot P[X = x]} = \sqrt{8.25} \approx 2.872$$

Suppose that the threshold level T of a severe loss is $8 million. Table 4.3 shows the values of the three individual risk measures for each of the four proposals, as well as the value of the PCR for each proposal, assuming that $A = 0.4$, $B = 0.4$, and $C = 0.2$.

TABLE 4.2 Probability of Losses Under Four Cyber Proposals

| | Losses From Cyber Incidents in Millions of Dollars | | | | | | | | | | |
	0	1	2	3	4	5	6	7	8	9	Other
Probability of Loss-Proposal 1	0.1	0.1	0.1	0.1	0.1	0.1	0.1	0.1	0.1	0.1	0
Probability of Loss-Proposal 2	0	0	0.2	0	0	0.5	0	0.1	0.2	0	0
Probability of Loss-Proposal 3	0.3	0.2	0	0	0	0	0.05	0.05	0.1	0.3	0
Probability of Loss-Proposal 4	0.0	0.0	0	0	0	0	0	0.45	0.45	0.1	0

TABLE 4.3 Value of Three Individual Risk Measures of the Four Proposals

	Expected Loss, $E[X]$	Expected Severe Loss	Standard Deviation of Loss, σ	Perceived Composite Risk (PCR)
Proposal 1	4.5	1.7	2.872	7.636
Proposal 2	5.2	1.6	1.990	7.795
Proposal 3	4.35	3.5	4.028	9.864
Proposal 4	7.65	4.5	0.654	12.477

Some of the problems with using the popular metric of expected loss as a sole measure of risk can be easily seen by examining Tables 4.2 and 4.3. According to the expected loss metric, the most preferred proposal is Proposal 3 to be followed in order by Proposal 1, Proposal 2, and Proposal 4. Note that although Proposal 3 minimizes the expected loss it also generates the second highest probability of threatening the survivability of the organization ($\Pr[X > 8] = 0.4$) and generates the highest standard deviation of loss.

From Table 4.3, we also see that based on the expected severe loss criterion, the most preferred proposal is Proposal 2 to be followed in order by Proposal 1, Proposal 3, and Proposal 4. Further, based on the standard deviation criterion, Proposal 4 is the most preferred proposal followed in order by Proposal 2, Proposal 1, and Proposal 3. Thus, a decision-maker interested in minimizing the risk of an incident, could rationally select Proposal 2, Proposal 3, or Proposal 4, depending on the single risk metric being considered. The PCR combines the three risk measures through a procedure that carefully determines the decision maker's relative weighting of the risk criteria. The weights are decision-maker dependent, so that the rankings based on the PCR may vary from person to person. With the values of A, B, and C given by 0.4, 0.4, and 0.2, respectively, Proposal 1 is preferred to Proposal 2, which, in turn, is preferred to Proposal 3, which is preferred to Proposal 4. It is interesting to note that Proposal 1 had the smallest value of the PCR even though Proposal 1 did not dominate any individual metric. However, if the decision maker's weights were $A = 0.1$, $B = 0.2$, and $C = 0.7$, then based on the PCR, Proposal 4 is preferred to Proposal 2, which is preferred to Proposal 1, which in turn is preferred to Proposal 3. Quite simply put, the common approach of using expected loss of a breach as the ranking criterion gives the CISO a narrow analysis of the alternatives and may lead to misleading results. Examining these other risk measures helps the CISO determine the best proposal to select and implement.

4.4.3.5 Loss in Market Value

Another way to estimate cost of incidents, especially the intangible cost, is the loss in market value of the firm due to security breach announcements (Cavusoglu et al., 2004). Security breaches signal to the market a lack of concern for customer privacy and/or poor security practices within the firm. These signals, in turn, lead investors to question the long-term performance of the firm. In efficient markets, investors are believed to revise their expectations based on new information in announcements and reflect those expectations in the market value of the firm (Fama et al., 1969). Using investors' reactions in capital markets as a proxy to estimate cost of incidents, Cavusoglu et al. (2004) found that publicly traded breached firms, on average, lost approximately 2.1% of their market value within 2 days surrounding the security breaches.[3]

This percentage translated into a US\$1.65 billion average loss in market capitalization per breach based on the mean market value of firms in their data set. The magnitude of the loss was the same across different breach types. Also, the average market value loss increased over time, which suggests that investors are becoming more aware of the security issues and are likely to penalize firms more for security breaches. The estimates based on market value may be noisy because of uncertainties. However, even if the estimates are discounted, there is an order of magnitude difference between the firms' reported estimates and the market value loss. This means that the intangible costs of cyber incidents can be much larger than the tangible costs. Hence, firms that ignore the intangible costs are perhaps grossly underestimating the loss from cyber incidents (Cavusoglu et al., 2004).

4.5 METHODS FOR CYBER RISK MEASUREMENT

In conjunction with measurement models for expected loss in Section 4.4 existing methods for cyber risk measurement are summarized in this section.

4.5.1 Stochastic Modeling

In probability theory and related fields, a stochastic or random process is a mathematical object usually defined as a collection of random variables. Historically, the random variables were associated with or indexed by a set of numbers, usually viewed as points in time, giving the interpretation of a stochastic process representing numerical values of some system randomly changing over time. Stochastic process is widely used as mathematical models of systems and phenomena that appear to vary in a random manner.

---

3. This study was based on 66 security incidents occurred between 1996 and 2001. Although both small and large firms were represented in the sample, the data set was skewed towards larger firms. The market value of firms varied from US\$158 million to US\$461 billion with an average of US\$78.3 billion.

4.5.2 Monte Carlo Simulation

Monte Carlo methods are a broad class of computational algorithms that reply on repeated random sampling to obtain numerical results. Their essential idea is using randomness to solve problems that might be deterministic in principle. They are most useful when it is difficult or impossible to use other approaches. In principle, Monte Carlo methods can be used to solve any problem having a probabilistic interpretation. Data at NASA from over 100 space missions showed that Monte Carlo simulations beat other methods for estimating cost, schedule and risks (Hanson and Beard, 2010).

Monte Carlo methods can be used for modeling attack simulations, cyber risks, and cyber security investments. Instead of using point estimates, ranges of loss events and their costs are defined as inputs for the Monte Carlo simulation to identify tens of thousands of possible outcomes. All the outcomes then are put on a graph to show where total loss exposure is likely to fall.

4.5.3 Cyber Value at Risk

The World Economic Forum's Partnering for Cyber Resilience initiative (WEF, 2015) developed a preliminary framework for a statistical model which CIOs and other executives can use to begin quantifying the financial impact of cyber threats. The concept of Cyber VaR is based on the notion of VaR, a statistical technique widely used in the financial services industry to express a bank's level of financial risk (or the financial risk associated with a specific investment portfolio) over a period of time. Similarly, Cyber VaR seeks to use probabilities to estimate likely losses from cyber-attacks during a given time frame. Cyber VaR considers three primary drivers of cyber risk for an organization: (1) vulnerability; (2) assets; and (3) the profile of its potential attackers. The risk units introduced in Chapter 7, Kilogram of Cyber Risk: Introducing BM and Hekla, also leverages from VaR. It took the financial service industry 30 years to refine VaR to the point where it is useful and trustworthy. With a conceptual framework of Cyber VaR established, the next step is applying real-world data to the model for it to evolve and mature. Current limitations of the proposed Cyber VaR model include (Deloitte, 2016):

- The range of possible vulnerabilities an attacker may exploit may not be perfectly quantifiable. For example, software vulnerabilities sometimes remain unidentified for years, dependencies on third-party infrastructure may limit visibility into the status of various assets.
- The degree of complexity and rate of change in many environments will continue to require an emphasis on establishing vigilance to detect the unexpected and resilience programs to support business recovery when a successful attack does occur.
- The lack of standard maturity frameworks also limits Cyber VaR's current effectiveness. The number of incidents an organization is likely to experience depends in parts on its relative cyber maturity.
- Cyber VaR supports only a limited number of risk scenarios at this time. The probability and impact of outlier incidents, like an attacker stealing a waste management company's credentials to a client's systems in order to compromise the client's network, remain difficult to determine using Cyber VaR.

4.5.4 The CORAS Method

Construct a platform for Risk Analysis of Security Critical Systems (CORAS), whish is a method for conducting security risk analysis. CORAS provides a customized language for threat and risk modeling. It comes with detailed guidelines explaining how the language should be used to capture and model relevant information during the various stages of the security analysis. The Unified Modeling Language is typically used to model the target of the analysis.

4.5.5 Common Vulnerability Scoring System

As covered in Chapter 3, Cyber Risk Management: A New Era of Enterprise Risk Management, the Common Vulnerability Scoring System (CVSS) is a published standard developed by NIST. It provides a way to capture the principal characteristics of a vulnerability and produce a numerical score reflecting its severity. The numerical score can then be translated into a qualitative representation, such as low, medium, high and critical, to help organizations properly assess and prioritize their vulnerability management processes.

4.5.6 Factor Analysis of Information Risk

Factor Analysis of Information Risk (FAIR)[4] is a methodology for quantifying and managing risk in organizations. Through a foundation of taxonomy, definitions, and analysis methods, FAIR adds a financial dimension to enterprise risk management framework. It provides a framework for establishing data collection criteria, measurement scales for risk factors and is constructed for analyzing complex risk situations.

RiskLens is a cyber risk management software built on FAIR. Monte Carlo method is used in FAIR and RiskLens platform.

The Open Group has chosen FAIR as its international standard information risk management model. More than 450 organisations are part of the Open Group, including HP, IBM, Oracle, Accenture, Capgemini, and MITRE.

4.6 INTRODUCING CYBER RISK QUADRANT: APPLYING MEDICAL RISK MEASUREMENT TO CYBER

4.6.1 Applying Medical Risk Model for Measuring Cyber Risk

In this book, medical risk measurement models are applied to cyber risk and the development of Cyber Risk Quadrant (CRQ). In order to measure cyber risk, a cyber risk databank is required in order to identify Key Cyber Risk Factors (KCRF) correlated with an entity's risk profile. Cyber risk exposure of an entity is influenced by a wide range of dynamic technological and non-technological profiling factors, internal vulnerabilities, and external threats. Motives of the attackers, in particular, are largely determined by nontechnological factors (Huq and TrendLabs Research, 2015).

In medicine, modifiable risk factors are factors that can be treated or controlled, including lifestyle factors such as cigarette-smoking, physical inactivity, and excessive alcohol use (Derby et al., 2000). Non-modifiable risk factors refer to any risk factor for a particular condition which cannot be modified. Age, for example, is the most important non-modifiable risk factor for stroke (Sacco, 1995). Borrowing this established risk categorization scheme, in this book, cyber risk factors are categorized under the CRQ within four types of factors:

1. *Technological factors.* Attributes that are related to the usage of technology.
2. *Nontechnological factors.* Attributes that are not related to the usage of technology, including people, process, socio-economic, geo-political factors.
3. *Inherent factors.* Intrinsic attributes based on nature of business, industry, core operations, goods and services the entity provides, or macro trends and attributes that have pan-industry impact on entities in certain geo-regions or even global impact. Inherent factors determine an entity's inherent cyber risk exposure and are factors the entity cannot easily change.
4. *Control factors.* Attributes of the entity that are non-intrinsic and can be changed or improved. Control factors reflect an entity's control effectiveness against cyber loss and are the subject of investment when it comes to risk mitigation.

Some examples of various cyber risk factors are shown in Table 4.4.

An entity's residual cyber risk is then calculated as:

$$\text{Residual cyber risk} = \text{inherent risk} \div \text{control effectiveness}$$

So, the cyber risk factor categorization scheme makes the calculation of an entity's residual cyber risk very straightforward. It can also help the entity holistically identify, monitor and benchmark on both technological and nontechnological factors. Traditional threat and vulnerability analyses still apply. Vulnerabilities can fall under both inherent factor (when they are inherent to the business and cannot be mitigated) and control factor (when necessary security measures are not in place).

KCRF can be identified only with consistent monitoring and correlation of risk factors and cyber loss. In order to standardize incident data collection, an International Classification of Cyber Incidents (ICCI) also needs to be developed in conjunction with the International Digital Asset Classification (IDAC), similar to the International Classification of Disease (ICD).[5] The first attempt to classify diseases systematically was made by Sir George Knibbs (Knibbs, 1929), who credited François Boissier de Sauvages de Lacroix (1706−77). At the beginning of the 19th century, the classification of disease in most general use was developed by William Cullen (1710−90) (Cullen, 1780). The

---

4. www.fairinstitute.org/.
5. International Classification of Diseases. Retrieved from: www.who.int/classifications/icd/en/.

TABLE 4.4 Cyber Risk Quadrant

	Technological Factors	Non-Technological Factors
Control factors	Implementation of firewall	Business process design and criticality
	Implementation of anti-virus applications	Cross-function incident response competencies
	Level of application security	Training and awareness
	Deployment of Security Operations Center (SOC)	Location of business
	Percentage of workload in the cloud	Cyber risk team structure
	Design of security architecture	Outsourcing strategy
	Network segregation	Appointment of a Chief Information Security Officer (CISO)
Inherent factors	Digital customer base	Regulatory requirements
	Usage of industry-standard applications (e.g. Bloomberg for banking industry)	Data protection legislations
		Nature of business
	Industry digitization index	Core goods and services
	Pace of digitization (e.g., Moore's law)[a]	Motivation level for inside threat
		Likelihood of human error
	Smartphone penetration rate	Unemployment rate
	Digital economy and society index[b]	Average age of suspected cyber attackers (U.K. National Crime Agency, 2015)
	Cloud adoption rate[c]	Crime rate
	Number of reported vulnerabilities[d]	Cultural perception of privacy
	Depreciation rate of digital devices	Country risk
	Number of companies certified with ISO/IEC 270001 (ISO Survey, 2014)	Political risk
	Total records breached[e,f]	Geo-political climate
	Size of digital universe	Global risks

[a]As of 2016, Moore's Law is no longer valid after half a century of accurate projection. Retrieved from: http://www.telegraph.co.uk/technology/2016/02/25/end-of-moores-law-whats-next-could-be-more-exciting/
[b]Digital economy and society index. Retrieved from: https://digital-agenda-data.eu/datasets/desi/indicators.
[c]Cloud computing statistics on the use by enterprises. Retrieved from: http://ec.europa.eu/eurostat/statistics-explained/index.php/Cloud_computing_-statistics_on_the_use_by_enterprises.
[d]Common Vulnerabilities and Exposures (CVE). Retrieved from: https://cve.mitre.org/.
[e]Dataloss DB. Retrieved from: http://datalossdb.org/.
[f]ID Theft Center. Retrieved from: http://www.idtheftcenter.org/id-theft/data-breaches.html.

statistical study of disease began a century earlier with the work of John Graunt on the London Bills of Mortality[6] in an attempt to estimate the proportion of children who died before reaching the age of six. Therefore, the current scientific robustness in quantifying a person's medical risk is a result of 400 years of standardized risk data collection. The lessons learned should be applied in cyber risk management whenever possible.

4.6.2   Using Scenario Analysis for Control Assessment and Loss Quantification

In order to identify controls that will be the most effective in reducing an entity's cyber risk exposure, scenario analysis[7] is used in this book to assess the entity's controls against its most damaging cyber loss events. Once the entity

---

6. Bills of Mortality were the weekly mortality statistics in London, designed to monitor burials from 1592 to 1595 and then continuously from 1603.
7. Scenario analysis is a process of analyzing possible future events by considering alternative possible outcomes. As a main method of projections, scenario analysis does not try to show one exact picture of the future.

TABLE 4.5 Digital Assets and Associated Cyber Loss Events

Digital Valuables		Cyber Loss Scenarios
Core value assets	IP of a critical product	IP theft, industrial espionage, etc.
	Regulated PII	Data breach, data leakage, etc.
	Sensitive financial data	Cyber fraud, data corruption, malfunction of trading algorithms, ransomware, etc.
Operational assets	Business critical IT services	System downtime due to technical malfunction, human error, etc.
	Payment website	Denial-of-Service (DoS) attack, insider attack, etc.

TABLE 4.6 Microeconomic Loss Quantification Method

Loss Category	Microeconomic Loss Quantification Method
Direct loss (financial loss, physical asset damage, death and bodily injury)	Loss based on valuation of the digital valuable affected, direct losses on expenses, etc.
Incident investigation and response	Cost of paying internal forensic team and external consultants for investigation and response to the incident, including technical tools and applications required for purchase and installation.
Reputational damage (applicable after incident has gone public)	Estimated economic loss correlated to the size of the readership of the media the incident is publicized on, and through reputation rating agencies (e.g., BizRate[a]).
Legal liabilities	Liability (e.g., per record in case of PII breach) as defined in laws, regulations, contracts and agreements.
Regulatory penalties	Regulatory fines, e.g., 5% of revenue.
Impact on share price	From implicit market value (estimates) and explicit market value (observed).

[a]*BizRate.com. (n.d.). Retrieved from: http://www.bizrate.com.*

has identified its most valuable digital assets, a cyber loss scenario inventory can be developed around those assets. These are the loss events the entity's is "genetically" most exposed to. A basic example is shown in Table 4.5.

Then, microeconomic loss can be quantified using the sample loss categories listed in Table 4.6. Monetary loss estimation under each loss category can come from historical incidents, industry reports, forensic reports, expert judgment, external studies, and statistical databases, etc.

With increasing sophistication and interdependency of IT outsourcing, and the usage of cloud computing in particular, quantifying macroeconomic losses in IT supply chains has become a main obstacle for cyber insurers and reinsurers. Cambridge Center of Risk Studies has proposed two stress test scenarios for cyber catastrophes to quantify macroeconomic losses (Ruffel et al., 2014; Centre for Risk Studies, 2014).

Scenario analyses are currently recommended in all cases of cyber loss quantification to compensate for the lack of quality historical loss data. Going forward, both the statistical approach and scenario analysis should be used. The statistical approach involves forecasting an entity's cyber loss using probability and statistical models with the aid of the cyber risk databank. It should be used to monitor risks continuously. Scenario analysis, especially stress scenario analysis, does not necessarily require the use of a probability or statistical model. Instead, the conditions of a cyber incident can be arbitrarily chosen or based on major incidents in crisis situations. Scenario analysis should be used on a case-by-case basis to estimate risk in unique circumstances.

Chapter 5

Economic Modeling and the Implementation of Effective Mitigating Controls

Chapter Outline

5.1 Definition of Control and Types of Controls   **87**
   5.1.1 Definition of Control   87
   5.1.2 Types of Control   88
     5.1.2.1 Control Objectives for Information and Related Technology   89
     5.1.2.2 NIST SP 800-53   90
     5.1.2.3 Committee of Sponsoring Organizations of the Treadway Commission   91
     5.1.2.4 ISO/IEC 27002   91
     5.1.2.5 Information Technology Infrastructure Library   91
   5.1.3 Control Selection and Implementation   92
     5.1.3.1 CIS Critical Security Controls   92

     5.1.3.2 National Institute of Standards and Technologies   92
     5.1.3.3 Information Security Management System   93
5.2 Prioritizing Cost-Effective Controls   **93**
5.3 Measuring Cost of Controls   **94**
   5.3.1 The Balance Sheet-Oriented Approach   94
   5.3.2 The Security Measure Life-Cycle Approach   94
   5.3.3 IT Security Process-Oriented Approach   95
   5.3.4 Cost to Break   95
5.4 Measuring Benefits of Controls   **95**
   5.4.1 Security Performance Metrics   96
   5.4.2 Vulnerability Assessments   97
   5.4.3 Penetration Testing   97
   5.4.4 Internal Audit   97

The cost to break should always be higher than the cost to build.

—Author Unknown

5.1 DEFINITION OF CONTROL AND TYPES OF CONTROLS

5.1.1 Definition of Control

One of the most generic terms in security is controls. The word is used in a variety of ways; the downfall is that its definition becomes blurred. In this book, we will use the following definition for control:

A control is a risk management technique that seeks to reduce the possibility that a loss will occur and/or reduce the severity of those that do occur. More specifically, it is the technique of minimizing the frequency or severity of losses with training, safety, and security measures.

Cyber security controls are safeguards or countermeasures to avoid, detect, counteract, or minimize risks to digital assets, for example, to protect the Confidentiality, Integrity, and/or Availability of data assets, the so-called CIA Triad (Table 5.1).

An organization's control environment is a term of financial audit, internal audit, and Enterprise Risk Management (ERM). It means the overall attitude, awareness, and actions of directors and management regarding the internal control system and its important to the entity. They express it in management style, corporate culture, values, philosophy, and operating style, the organization structure, human resources policies, and procedures. The control environment aligned with enterprise's management philosophy and operating style should include certain elements, such as expectations/requirements regarding delivery of value from investments, appetite for risk, integrity, ethical values, staff competence,

Digital Asset Valuation and Cyber Risk Measurement. DOI: https://doi.org/10.1016/B978-0-12-812158-0.00005-3

TABLE 5.1 Example of Risk Control

Risk Cause	Control	Attribute
Lack of security patches	Patch management process	List of missing security patches that does not affect the performance of the system
		Log of successfully installed security patches for the system

TABLE 5.2 Value and Risk Drivers for Enterprise Control Environment

Value Drivers	Risk Drivers
• Comprehensive IT control environment • Comprehensive set of policies • Increased IT awareness of the organization's mission • Proper use of applications and IT services	• Miscommunications about organizational mission • Management's philosophy misinterpreted • Actions not aligned with the organization's business objectives • Not transparent IT control environment • Compliance and security issues

accountability, and responsibility.[1] The control environment should be based on a culture that supports value delivery while managing significant risks, encourages cross-divisional co-operation and teamwork, promotes compliance and continuous process improvement, and handles process deviations (including failure) well. Value drivers and risk drivers of enterprise control environment are listed in Table 5.2.

A good control practice should:

- Align the IT management and control environment with the organization's general risk and control environment.
- Assign accountability and responsibility, including supervisory roles for creating procedures and practices to operationalize the control framework.
- Ensure that the environment clearly defines the control culture and philosophy of the enterprise, risk appetite, ethical values, code of conduct, accountability, and requirements for management integrity in the IT management and control environment.
- Create an approach for the communication of policies and procedures supported by appropriate awareness training to ensure transparency and understanding of these policies.
- Ensure that the organizational structure for defining and developing the control framework clearly defines key areas of authority and responsibility.
- Ensure that the human resources environment fosters and supports the adherence to policies and procedures.

5.1.2 Types of Control

There are a wide range of controls to select from based on the outcome of risk assessments.

Preventive controls are for reducing risk. *Detective controls* are for identifying violations and incidents. *Corrective controls* are for remedying violations and incidents and improving existing preventive and detective controls. *Deterrent controls* are for discouraging violations. *Recovery controls* are for restoring systems and information. *Compensating controls* are for providing alternative ways of achieving a task.[2] Controls can also be *physical*, *legal*, *technical*, and *nontechnical*. Nontechnical controls include *management*, *operational*, *procedural* controls, focusing on policies, guidelines, and standards for information protection.

Table 5.3 includes some examples of controls broadly placed under preventive, detective, technical, and nontechnical categories.

---

1. ISACA Policy and Control Environment: https://www.isaca.org/Groups/Professional-English/po6-1-it-policy-and-control-environment/Pages/Overview.aspx.
2. CISSP (ISC)2 Certified Information Systems Security Professional Guide.

TABLE 5.3 Examples of Technical, Nontechnical, Preventive, and Detective Controls

	Preventive Controls	Detective Controls
Technical controls	• Identification: identify users, processes, and information resources • Cryptographic keys: key generation, distribution, storage, and maintenance • Security administration: measures that must be configured to meet security system requirements • System protection: the quality of IT system implementation in terms of design and manner in which the implementation was accomplished • Authentication: passwords, PINs, personal identification numbers • Authorization: measures that verify if employees are authorized to make changes to the system • Protected communications: measures that ensure integrity, confidentiality, availability of sensitive data during their transmission • Transaction privacy: measures that protect against loss of privacy of important information • Monitoring controls, security intelligence controls • Intrusion Prevention Systems (IPS) • Antivirus software	• Intrusion detection: measures that ensure the detection of possible events with negative impact in order to avoid them or reduce their impact • Restore secure state: measures capable of bringing the system to last known security state after a security breach occurs • Virus detection and eradication: measures that detect, identify and remove viruses to ensure system and data integrity • CCTV cameras • Intrusion Detection Systems (IDS)
Non-technical controls	• Incident response processes, management oversight, security awareness and training • Development and maintenance of system security plans in order to support the organization's mission • Implementation of personnel security controls, including separation of duties, least privilege, user computer access registration and termination • Provide continuity of support and develop, test, and maintain the operations plans • Establish the system capacity to respond to the incident and return the IT system to operational status • Controlling data access • Limiting external data distribution • Provide emergency power source • Control the humidity and temperature of the computing	• Implementation of personnel security controls, including personnel investigation, rotation of duties • Periodic review of security controls to ensure that they are effective • Periodic system audits • The existence of a continuous management process • Providing physical security (motion detectors, sensors, and alarms) • Ensuring environmental security (smoke and fire detectors, fire sensors and alarms)

Organizations often adopt a control framework to aid in their development of control environment. Some relevant control frameworks include:

- Control Objectives for Information and Related Technology (COBIT)
- National Institute of Standards and Technologies (NIST) Special Publication 800-53
- COSO (Committee of Sponsoring Organizations of the Treadway Commission)
- ISO/IEC 27002
- ITIL (Information Technology Infrastructure Library)

5.1.2.1 Control Objectives for Information and Related Technology

Developed by the Information Systems Audit and Control Association (ISACA) and the IT Governance Institute (ITGI), Control Objectives for Information and Related Technologies (COBIT) consists of several components, including:

- *Framework*. Organizes IT governance objectives and best practices.
- *Process descriptions*. Provides a reference model and common language.
- *Control objectives*. Documents high-level management requirements for control of individual IT processes.
- *Management guidelines*. Tools for assigning responsibility, measuring performance, and illustrating relationships between processes.
- *Maturity models*. Assess organizational maturity/capability and address gaps.

The COBIT framework is popular in organizations that are subject to the Sarbanes-Oxley Act.

5.1.2.2 NIST SP 800-53

NIST SP 800-53: Security and Privacy Controls for Federal Information Systems and Organizations, known as NIST SP 800-53, is a very popular and comprehensive controls framework required by all U.S. government agencies. It also is widely used in private industry. NIST SP 800-53v4 provides over 800 controls for low—moderate—high impact systems as categorized using (FIPS, 2004). Impact levels definitions shown in Table 5.4. The controls are based on control families listed in Table 5.5 (NIST, 2013).

TABLE 5.4 NIST SP800-53 Control Families

ID	Family	ID	Family
AC	Access control	MP	Media protection
AT	Awareness and training	PE	Physical and environment protection
AU	Audit and accountability	PL	Planning
CA	Security assessment and authorization	PS	Personnel security
CM	Configuration management	RA	Risk assessment
CP	Contingency planning	SA	System and services acquisition
IA	Identification and authentication	SC	System and communications protection
IR	Incident response	SI	System and information integrity
MA	Maintenance	PM	Program management

TABLE 5.5 FIPS 199 Impact Levels (FIPS, 2004)

Impact Level	Definition	Application
Low	The loss of confidentiality, integrity, or availability could be expected to have a limited adverse effect on organizational operations, organizational assets, or individuals	A limited adverse effect means that, for example, the loss of confidentiality, integrity, or availability might: (1) cause a degradation in mission capability to an extent and duration that the organization is able to perform its primary functions, but the effectiveness of the functions is noticeably reduced; (2) result in minor damage to organizational assets; (3) result in minor financial loss; or (4) result in minor harm to individuals.
Moderate	The loss of confidentiality, integrity, or availability could be expected to have a serious adverse effect on organizational operations, organizational assets, or individuals	A serious adverse effect means that, for example, the loss of confidentiality, integrity, or availability might: (1) cause a significant degradation in mission capability to an extent and duration that the organization is able to perform its primary functions, but the effectiveness of the functions is significantly reduced; (2) result in significant damage to organizational assets; (3) result in significant financial loss; or (4) result in significant harm to individuals that does not involve loss of life or serious life threatening injuries.
High	The loss of confidentiality, integrity, or availability could be expected to have a severe or catastrophic adverse effect on organizational operations, organizational assets, or individuals	A severe or catastrophic adverse effect means that, for example, the loss of confidentiality, integrity, or availability might: (1) cause a severe degradation in or loss of mission capability to an extent and duration that the organization is not able to perform one or more of its primary functions; (2) result in major damage to organizational assets; (3) result in major financial loss; or (4) result in severe or catastrophic harm to individuals involving loss of life or serious life threatening injuries.

TABLE 5.6 ISO 27002 Control Domains

A.1: Information security policies	A.8: Operations security
A.2: Organization of information security	A.9: Communications security
A.3: Human resources security	A.10: Secure acquisition, development, and maintenance
A.4: Asset management	A.11: Supplier relationships
A.5: Access controls	A.12: Information security incident management
A.6: Cryptography	A.13: Information security aspects of business continuity management
A.7: Physical and environmental security	A.14: Compliance

5.1.2.3 Committee of Sponsoring Organizations of the Treadway Commission

Developed by the Institute of Management Accountants (IMA), the American Accounting Association (AAA), the American Institute of Certified Public Accountants (AICPA), The Institute of Internal Auditors (IIA), and Financial Executives International (FEI), the Committee of Sponsoring Organizations of the Treadway Commission (COSO) framework consists of five components:

- *Control environment.* Provides the foundation for all other internal control components.
- *Risk assessment.* Establishes objectives through identification and analysis of relevant risks and determines whether anything will prevent the organization from meeting its objectives.
- *Control activities.* Policies and procedures that are created to ensure compliance with management directives.
- *Information and communication.* Ensures appropriate information systems and effective communications processes are in place throughout the organization.
- *Monitoring.* Activities that assess performance over time and identify deficiencies and corrective actions.

5.1.2.4 ISO/IEC 27002

ISO/IEC 27002[3] specifies 114 controls in 14 domains listed in (Table 5.6).

5.1.2.5 Information Technology Infrastructure Library

The Information Technology Infrastructure Library (ITIL) is a set of best practices for IT service management consisting of five volumes as follows:

- *Service strategy.* Addresses IT services strategy management, service portfolio management, IT services financial management, demand management, and business relationship management.
- *Service design.* Addresses design coordination, service catalog management, service level management, availability management, capacity management, IT service continuity management, information security management system, and supplier management.
- *Service transition.* Addresses transition planning and support, change management, service asset and configuration management, release and deployment management, service validation and testing, change evaluation, and knowledge management.
- *Service operation.* Addresses event management, incident management, service request fulfillment, problem management, and access management.
- *Continual service improvement.* Defines a seven-step process for improvement initiatives, including identifying the strategy, defining what will be measured, gathering the data, processing the data, analyzing the information and data, presenting and using the information, and implementing the improvement.

---

3. ISO/IEC 27002:2013 Information technology—security techniques—code of practice for information security controls.

TABLE 5.7 CIS Critical Controls

Basic CIS controls	1. Inventory and control of hardware assets 2. Inventory and control of software assets 3. Continuous vulnerability management 4. Controlled use of administrative privileges 5. Secure configuration for hardware and software on mobile devices, laptops, workstations, and servers 6. Maintenance, monitoring and analysis of audit logs
Foundational CIS controls	1. Email and web browser protections 2. Malware defenses 3. Limitation and control of network ports, protocols and services 4. Data recovery capabilities 5. Secure configuration for network devices, such as firewalls, routers and switches 6. Boundary defense 7. Data protection 8. Controlled access based on the need to know 9. Wireless access control 10. Account monitoring and control
Organizational CIS controls	1. Implement a security awareness and training program 2. Application software security 3. Incident response and management 4. Penetration tests and red team exercises

5.1.3   Control Selection and Implementation

5.1.3.1   CIS Critical Security Controls

The Center for Internet Security (CIS) Critical Security Controls[4] are a recommended set of actions for cyber defense that provide specific and actionable ways to stop today's most pervasive and dangerous attacks. A principal benefit of the CIS controls is that they prioritize and focus a smaller number of actions with high pay-off results. They are effective because they are derived from the most common attack patterns highlighted in the leading threat reports and vetted across a very broad community of government and industry practitioners (Table 5.7).

5.1.3.2   National Institute of Standards and Technologies

NIST (2013) recommends a lifecycle approach to control selection and implementation, following six steps as shown in Fig. 5.1.

- *Step 1*: Categorize the information system based on chosen risk classification model.
- *Step 2*: Select the applicable security control baseline based on the results of the security categorization and apply tailoring guidance (including the potential use of overlays). *Baseline controls* are the starting point for the security control selection process are chosen based on the security category.
- *Step 3*: Implement the security controls and document the design, development, and implementation details for the controls.
- *Step 4*: Assess the security controls to determine the extent to which the controls are implemented correctly, operating as intended, and producing the desired outcome with respect to meeting the security requirements for the system.
- *Step 5*: Authorize information system operation based on a determination of risk to organizational operations and assets, individuals, other organizations, and the nation resulting from the operation and use of the information system and the decision that this risk is acceptable.
- *Step 6*: Monitor the security controls in the information system and environment of operation on an ongoing basis to determine control effectiveness, changes to the system/environment, and compliance to legislation, executive orders, directives, policies, regulations, and standards.

---

4. https://www.cisecurity.org/controls/.

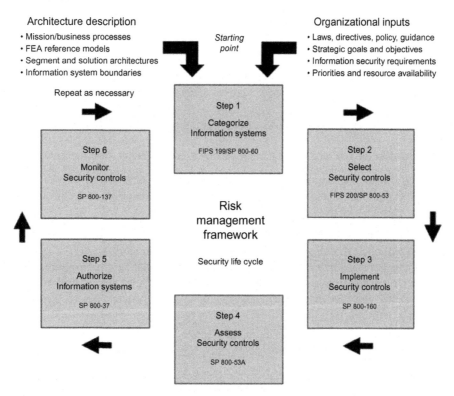

Note: *CNSS instruction* 1253 *provides guidance for RMF steps* 1 *and* 2 *for National Security Systems (NSS).*

FIGURE 5.1   NIST life cycle approach to control selection and implementation (NIST, 2013).

5.1.3.3 *Information Security Management System*

ISO/IEC 27001[5] standard provides a framework for information security risk management within organizations. The purpose of ISMS is to identify and minimize risks when handling information within the company's processes, so the confidentiality, integrity, and availability of the information are preserved, maximizing its value as input to the value chain processes within the corporation. ISMS suggests a Plan, Do, Check, Act (PDCA) cycle. The objectives for each step of the cycle are:

1. *Plan*: to establish information security policy and objectives to manage risk and improve the level of risk exposure.
2. *Do*: implement the security controls planned for the ISMS in accordance with established information policy and security objectives.
3. *Check*: to evaluate and measure process performance and controls against established guidelines.
4. *Act*: take corrective and preventive actions based on the results of verification in order to implement a continuous improvement to the ISMS.

Because many company executives do not understand the need of measure for security control performance, attaining resources can often be a difficult task requiring a significant number of justifications just to determine if information security controls are necessary and good for business. In order to provide convincing arguments to management to initiate an information security program, CISO must identify risks to organizational processes and develop a measurement system capable of determining the effectiveness of controls.

5.2 PRIORITIZING COST-EFFECTIVE CONTROLS

Organizations can help control risks by performing analyses of various mitigation options. For example, one option is to use a commercially available capability instead of a contractor developed one. Once an organization identifies and prioritizes risks and the gaps that exist in current security controls, it is possible to build a prioritized remediation plan that focuses on improving existing security controls or adding security controls to mitigate high-priority risks first, then

---

5. ISO/IEC 27001:2013 Information technology—security techniques—information security management systems—requirements.

medium priority, and then low priority, as appropriate. To avoid losing the focus organizations should develop Key Performance Indicators or other quantifiable measurement that can be used to track the progress in achieving control objectives (Humberto and Peláez, 2010). These rules should be followed when deciding if a measure is implemented or not:

- If the implementation reduces the level of risk more than is necessary, a less expensive alternative should be chosen.
- If the implementation costs more than the benefit that would be obtain after the implementation, another control should be sought.
- If the implementation does not reduce the level of risk enough, more effective controls preferable with a similar cost should be sought.
- If the implementation reduces the risk at an acceptable level and is cost-effective. The measure should be implemented.

Without understanding effectiveness of control implementation, organizations may expose to higher risk exposure because controls are operating at below optimal effectiveness (Institute of Standards and Technology). Some challenges in measuring control effectiveness include:

- Metrics that measure effectiveness can be difficult to define.
- Resulting measurements can be difficult to interpret by nonsecurity professionals.
- Effectiveness metrics cannot be easily compared to allow benchmarking of an organization's performance.
- Security teams often find it easier to measure risk by following a compliance and audit checklist; however, this misconception fails to not only consider the constant nuances of regulations and their requirements of businesses but also the advancements of cyber-threats.
- Employing point technologies without considering the complexity of integrating into existing systems.
- Relying on traditional security controls that are out of date and processes that have not adapted to the changing threat landscape.

Current available approaches to measuring cost and benefits of controls are summarized in Sections 5.3 and 5.4.

5.3 MEASURING COST OF CONTROLS

5.3.1 The Balance Sheet-Oriented Approach

It is common to use structures for classifying costs that are oriented towards the chart of accounts. A typical example for that is the model developed by Gartner for total cost of ownership (TCO). To cover the costs spent on cyber security, Gartner uses a scheme which distinct between the four cost categories:

1. *Personal costs*: includes all personnel costs supporting information security functions.
2. *Hardware*: dedicated security hardware, e.g., security gateways, disaster recovery hardware.
3. *Software*: license costs of software dedicated to managing security systems, e.g., IAM, endpoint security suites.
4. *Outsourcing/managed security services (MSS)*: costs of monitoring/managing security devices, systems and processes or other costs related to MSS.

Gartner found a distribution of the cyber security budget in 21% hardware, 29% software, 40% personnel, and 10% outsourcing for the year 2011 (Gartner, 2011). In general, this approach is a first step towards the classification of cyber security costs. It allows organizations to easily determine their costs in those categories using existing accounting/budgeting processes. At the same time, it is limited because a more granular analysis of the results of this approach is not possible, too much information about the creation of reference data is missing or unclear. Thus, a comparison between several organizations may hardly be possible.

5.3.2 The Security Measure Life-Cycle Approach

This approach not only covers the cost of purchase for a security measure but also other costs within its life cycle, including: (1) cost of purchase; (2) cost of setup; (3) cost of operation; and (4) cost of change. This approach is well-suited for cost-benefit analysis of single measures since it covers all aspects of costs that are connected to the implementation of a security measure. The values can be compared to the potential benefits in risk reduction. It can also be used to sell different security measures. However, it is hardly possible to apply this approach to an organization's cyber risk management as a whole because it lacks a process perspective and is mainly focused on IT. This approach is also not suitable for benchmarking between several organizations because no reference values are calculated or presented.

5.3.3 IT Security Process-Oriented Approach

The approach proposed by Brecht and Nowey (2012) gives a comprehensive picture of costs associated with IT-security activities in four dimensions depicted in Table 5.8. The focus of this approach is on single security measures especially costs for operation. It also covers some high-level aspects such as change of processes. It primarily focuses on IT security. This approach has a few limitations. The fact that the categories are not compatible with standard cost accounting models can complicate the collection of data. Another major limitation is considering cost of managing residual risk part of indirect cost. The purpose of security spending is about managing and reducing risks, hence this categorization creates a recurring loop that is difficult to implement.

5.3.4 Cost to Break

Annual cost to break (CTB) is another useful angle to look at cost of controls. It is defined as the annual CTB into the defense mechanisms or the annual cost to exploit vulnerabilities in a system. Schechter (2002) suggests that organizations employ personnel to attempt to break into the system to obtain a value of this figure.

5.4 MEASURING BENEFITS OF CONTROLS

Determining the effectiveness of controls is a fundamental exercise used to assess risk, but the measurement of efficiency has a number of costs involved, in the end increasing the TCO of infrastructure and therefore affects the cost of goods and services originating in the organization. The measurement scheme chosen should be effective and efficient enough to not blur the use of resources (Humberto and Peláez, 2010). There are three primary ways to implement processes to monitor cybersecurity control performance and effectiveness:

- Establish and regularly review based on security performance metrics.
- Conduct vulnerability assessments and penetration testing to validate security configuration.
- Complete an internal audit (or other objective assessment) to evaluate security control operation.

A simple scoring metrics, such as the example shown in Table 5.9, can also be used for communicating cost-effectiveness of controls.

TABLE 5.8 Cost Associated With IT Security Activities

Direct cost	Costs for tool, e.g., purchase, operation, implementation, depreciation
	Consulting costs, e.g., conception, implementation, rating, management system
Indirect cost	Costs for operation, e.g., management system, losses due to change of processes
	Costs of risk, e.g., residual risk, costs of uncertainty

TABLE 5.9 Control Score Metrics

Control Score Definitions	Score
The outcome rarely or never happens when needed	0
The outcome sometimes happens when needed, but unreliably. Rework is common	3
The outcome happens consistently with some minor flaws from time-to-time. Rework sometimes happens, but is uncommon	5
The outcome happens consistently with great effectiveness and high quality	8
The outcome happens at excessive financial cost. Or, it exceeds the requirements without additional tangible benefit	10

5.4.1 Security Performance Metrics

A *measurement* is something that is quantifiable and observable. A *metric* is something supported by measurements that intends to facilitate decision making, improve performance and accountability. To measure controls, quality metrics with these characteristics need to be developed (Humberto and Peláez, 2010):

- *It must be universal.* A metric is universal if it is composed of a clearly defined set of variables that can be used in any type of Information Security Management System (ISMS) to which you want to apply the measurement. A metric is universal when it can be applied regardless of the architecture, code, interface, or system conditions.
- *It must yield significant results with respect to the issue it seeks to measure.* It is important to define a set of metrics that are useful to the assessment group to get the information required, without elaboration and without the need for further information.
- *It must be accurate and represent what cyber security officers really want and need to know.* A metric should not divert attention to another aspect other than the purpose for which it was intended. Moreover, it should accurately portray the results, avoiding bias, both by the group responsible for the measurement and the decision makers. Obtaining results should be feasible, i.e., it should be possible to obtain the data and variables involved in the measurement, so as to optimize resources and avoid waste of effort, time and money on measurements impossible perform.
- *Must be reproducible.* Different people at different times should be able to make the same measurement. It is vital the metric be consistently repeatable, regardless of who made the measurement or the moment in time that the measurement takes place, provided that the conditions for measurement are preserved.
- *It must be objective.* A metric must not be tied to variable factors such as the knowledge of people, the ability to memorize, and product perception, etc. It should avoid subjective factors that could skew or corrupt the results.
- *It must be impartial.* A metric must be fair and equitable, must have a clearly defined set of values with which one can determine if the result is acceptable or not, and to know the level and/or the trending of attributes of the system.

For example, ISO/IEC 27004[6] defines a measurement for organizations to fulfill the requirements of ISO/IEC 27001:2013. It establishes:

1. The monitoring and measurement of information security performance
2. The monitoring and measurement of the effectiveness of an ISMS including its processes and controls
3. The analysis and evaluation of the results of monitoring and measurement

There are three main categories of security performance measures:

1. *Operational statistics* include the counts of activity within an environment. These don't necessarily reflect action by the organization, but they do help to build a general awareness of security-related activity within an organization.
2. *Performance measures* are derived or calculated metrics that quantify an organization's behavior or performance against a stated objective, such as specific actions taken by employees to help maintain an organization's security posture.
3. *Compliance goals* are a specific type of performance measure focused on demonstrating whether an organization is complying with organizational policy.

Some challenges in developing security performance metrics are:

- *Difficulty in benchmark selection.* As the method for collecting and defining metrics differs across organizations, choosing metrics as benchmarks is difficult. For example, comparing how well the effectiveness of two organizations antivirus is performing does not take into account the importance of the control to the organization. If the organization is operating a standalone network with no onward connections the risk mitigated by antivirus could be smaller than an organization with a connection to the Internet.
- *Misleading metrics.* Without the true context for the measurement the metric could be misleading. This problem increases outside of an organization's security team and the results of the metric could be misunderstood by many.
- *Incomplete output.* Metrics may not always provide the data required to make meaningful conclusions. For example, an antivirus management server may easily provide a metric on the number of clients with an up-to-date installation, but a potentially more important metric is the number of clients without any antivirus installation. This second

---

6. ISO/IEC 27004:2016 Information technology—security techniques—information security management—monitoring, measurement, analysis and evaluation.

metric would be harder to obtain than just using the metric already provided by the management server. However, it may give more meaningful results when determining the effectiveness of the antivirus control.

- *Expensive manual data collection.* The process of collecting metric data can be expensive without automation. Substantial time cost can incur especially when the metric requires manual data collection or inspection, for example, with physical and procedural controls. The tedious manual assessment can also be prone to error.
- *Reliance on subjective judgments.* Some of the current security metrics implemented by organizations are based on a qualitative scale and required an expert to evaluate the control's current implementation. As this measurement is not based on the actual measurement of a tangible characteristic, results can vary depending on who conducted the assessment. This leads to issues in comparing metrics over time as well as skepticism in accepting the results.

5.4.2   Vulnerability Assessments

In order to verify the effectiveness of security configuration, all organizations should conduct vulnerability assessments. The purpose of the vulnerability assessment is to identify system security patches the organization may have missed or any weak security configurations the organization has applied. Security firms use a variety of automated scanning tools to compare system configurations to published lists of known vulnerabilities.

5.4.3   Penetration Testing

Penetration testing (often shortened to pentest) takes vulnerability scanning a step further. A skilled, ethical hacker leverage identified vulnerabilities and simulates real-life attack scenarios to determine whether these vulnerabilities can be exploited and lead to an actual breach. An organization can use the results of vulnerability scanning and penetration testing to identify any security gaps as well as consider the root cause of what permitted these vulnerabilities to get introduced within the organization.

In a pentest, one or more people are authorized to perform automated and manual tests to see whether they can break into an organization's network in a wide variety of ways. Some organizations perform pentests using their own in-house security experts, while others hire outside experts who specialize in conducting these tests. Regardless of who performs the pentests, the cyber security team should be responsible for managing the process and tracking the results. While pentesting is an effective approach, it usually does not reveal as wide a range of vulnerabilities, because it is not as exhaustive as a properly implemented vulnerability assessment. Therefore, it is recommended to supplement any pentests with other methodologies (Microsoft, 2004).

As an evolved version of traditional pentesting, red team—blue team is a simulation and training exercise where members of an organization are divided into teams to compete in combative exercises, in order to identify vulnerabilities and find security holes in an organization's infrastructure. The war games are also used to test and train security staff.

5.4.4   Internal Audit

The three lines of defense model has been widely adopted in regulated organizations for risk governance, as shown in Table 5.10.

Given the current state of information security and the constant evolution of security threats, it is imperative that internal audit departments act as a third LOD and verify cybersecurity control performance to assist in enhancing the overall security posture of the organization. Leveraging the results of a cybersecurity risk assessment, a good

TABLE 5.10 Three Lines of Defense

Line of Defense (LoD)	Functions
1st LoD	Functions that own and manage risk
2nd LoD	Functions that oversee or specialize in risk management and compliance
3rd LoD	Functions that provide independent assurance, above all internal audit

verification process begins with the review of organizational cybersecurity policies, procedures, guides, and standards. A successful cybersecurity internal audit needs sponsorship from executive management to facilitate the process.

An internal audit kicks off the audit process by conducting interviews with key stakeholders to confirm an understanding of the activities taking place with respect to satisfying cybersecurity control objectives. As part of the audit, it would be typical to conduct a gap analysis against either the organization's security policy and standards, or an independent control framework to determine whether cybersecurity controls are suitably designed to meet the security objective, and that they are in place and aligned with the organization's risk assessment. Additionally, it's important to evaluate whether personnel roles and responsibilities for cybersecurity are clearly defined and properly assigned to employees with sufficient skill and authority to perform these controls.

Based on the results of the design evaluation, an organization can provide higher levels of assurance by determining whether cybersecurity controls are operating effectively. The audit team will use the organization's documented security policies and procedures to establish cybersecurity control audit testing procedures. Evidence of control activity performance is then obtained and reviewed for all controls that have a manual component, e.g., user account management, infrastructure and application change management, and systems backup. Lastly, for systems-based controls—e.g., firewall settings, antivirus settings, data encryption settings—an internal audit examines specific systems configurations to determine whether they are set as expected.

In the absence of an in-house internal audit capability, an objective third-party can be leveraged to undertake a similar assessment.

Chapter 6

The Point of Diminishing Return on Cyber Risk Investment

Chapter Outline

6.1 Economics of Information Security 99
6.2 Current Information Security/Risk Management Budget 102
6.3 Challenges for Cyber Risk Management Cost Optimization 104
  6.3.1 The Challenges in Quantifying Security Costs 104
    6.3.1.1 Cyber Security and Risk Management Is a Cross-Functional Task 104
    6.3.1.2 Divergent Goals Exist for Cost Quantification 104
    6.3.1.3 Lack of Transparency on Hidden Costs 104
    6.3.1.4 Difficulties in Finding the Right Scope and Baseline 105
    6.3.1.5 Lack of Resources and Clear Ownership to Implement Controls 105
  6.3.2 Challenges in Determining the Optimal Level of Investment in Security and Risk 105
  6.3.3 General Limitations of Approaches: Game Theory in Security Investment 106
6.4 Current Models for Cyber Risk Cost Optimization 106
  6.4.1 Cost Models for Determining how much to Investment in Security and Risk 106
    6.4.1.1 Benchmarking 106
    6.4.1.2 Cost-Benefit Analysis 107
    6.4.1.3 Quantitative Risk Assessment 107
    6.4.1.4 Return on Security Investment 107
    6.4.1.5 Net Present Value 108
    6.4.1.6 Internal Rate of Return 109
    6.4.1.7 Comparisons of Return on Investment, Net Present Value and Internal Rate of Return 109
    6.4.1.8 Gordon and Loeb Model 110
    6.4.1.9 Full Cost Accounting Model 111
  6.4.2 Cost Models for Projection 112
  6.4.3 Risk Management Options and Associated Cost 113
    6.4.3.1 Defense-in-Depth and Holistic Thinking 113
6.5 Cost of Security Configurations 113
6.6 Decision Model for Optimal Risk Management Strategies 115

The first rule of IT security is that you should never spend more to protect something than a thing is actually worth.

— Jeff Crume

6.1 ECONOMICS OF INFORMATION SECURITY

The importance of information security in a computer-based environment has resulted in a large stream of research that focuses on the technical defenses (e.g., encryption, access control, and firewalls) associated with protecting information (Gordon and Loeb, 2002; Anderson, 1972; Wiseman, 1986; Simmons, 1994; Muradlidhar et al., 1995; Denning and Branstad, 1996; Sandhu et al., 1996; Schneier, 1996; Pfleeger, 1997; Larsen, 1999; Peyravian et al., 1999; Osborn et al., 2000) and intrusion detection systems (Denning, 1987; Daniels and Spafford, 1999; Vigna and Kemmeerer, 1999; Axelsson, 2000; Frincke, 2000). In addition, research has been rapidly developing that focuses on the behavioral aspects of reducing information security breaches (Straub and Welke, 1998; Loch et al.,1992; Straub and Welke, 1998). In contrast, research focusing on the economic aspects of information security is rather sparse. The work that does exist on, or related to economic aspects of information security provides little generic guidance on how to allocate scarce information security dollars in organizations that possess limited resources (Millen, 1992; Luotonen, 1993; McKnight et al., 1997; Finne, 1998; Jones, 1997; Buzzard, 1999; Hoo, 2000; Anderson, 2001; Meadows, 2001; Powers, 2001). For years, the Fear, Uncertainty and Doubt has been used to sell investment in security (Gordon and Loeb, 2002).

The economics of information security is a field that has a decade of literature (Courtney, 1982). The fundamental principle of the economics of information security is that a control should not be implemented if it costs more than tolerating the problem (Courtney, 1982; Cavusoglu et al., 2004). Organizations should manage investment as any other investment by analyzing the cost-benefit tradeoffs. The growing importance of analyzing these tradeoffs is evident from

Digital Asset Valuation and Cyber Risk Measurement. DOI: https://doi.org/10.1016/B978-0-12-812158-0.00006-5

the emphasis and discussion on return on security investment (ROSI) by both academics and practitioners (Cavusoglu et al., 2004). The focus of IT security management should shift from what is technically possible to what is economically efficient (Anderson, 2001; Courtney, 1982) and should shift from a compartmentalized focus with budget managed only by the IT departments to be better aligned with wider business processes (Neubauer et al., 2006).

Economics is the study and social science of human behavior in relation to how scarce resources are allocated and how choices are made between alternative uses (Hackett, 2010). It studies mankind's activities, which are production, distribution, exchange, and consumption of goods and services that are capable of satisfying human wants and desires. The economic perspective of information security means providing maximum protection of assets at the minimum cost (Gordon and Loeb, 2002; Geer, 2004). If the budget is fixed, it then becomes an economic optimization problem (Geer, 2004). To integrate economics and information security, Fig. 6.1 describes the cost relationships that must be considered. As controls are implemented, losses go down and the cost of controls rises. The sum of losses and control costs reaches, at some point, a minimum. Organizations should aim to establish that point, operate near there and avoid operating to the right of that minimum (Courtney, 1982; Bojanc and Jerman-Blažič, 2012). The organization's goal should be the implementation of security measures to the point where the benefits minus the costs have a maximum value, because the net benefits (i.e., benefits minus costs) of implementation of cyber security over maximum point are negative. The implementation of cyber security activities over this point means that the marginal costs of additional security are greater than marginal benefits of additional security. In other words, it is cheaper to live with the situation (Courtney, 1982; Mizzi, 2005; Bojanc and Jerman-Blažič, 2012). A concrete example is given by researchers on a Defense Advanced Research Projects Agency (DARPA)-funded project (Beattie and Butzmann, 2002), who developed a mathematical model of the potential costs involved in patching and not patching at a given time. They observed that the risk of loss of functionality from applying a bad patch decreases in time, while the risk of loss due to penetration while the patch is not applied increases with time, so the optimal time to apply the patch is when these curves cross (Mercuri, 2003).

The current thinking of the role of economics fall into below categories (Walker, 2012):

- Security investment models such as ROSI and net present value (NPV).
- A body of work that captures many of the issues around the economics of security, principally driven by Ross Anderson, such as the issue of network effects (i.e., externalities) are of significance.
- A limited body of work on events contingent on security failures, which is by its nature incomplete without regulatory pressure, as organizations are unwilling to discuss the true scale and impact of security issues.
- Works around the cost of cybercrime, especially data breach. As of 2018, the average cost of a data breach has exceeded $3.8 million (Ponemon Institute, 2018).
- The asymmetry of information problem around information security investments that contributes to "the market of lemons," or more correctly an absence of information problem regarding likely future outcomes of multi-round interactions between "attack" and "defense."

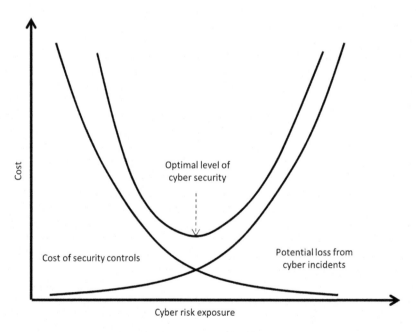

FIGURE 6.1 Optimal level of security investment.

- The cumulative effect of incomplete information and ineffective incentivization of security spending may lead to suboptimal investment decisions. Information security cannot be effectively accounted for without better data. To a certain extent this can be generated within organization, but more robust data sets would come from a sectoral or national view.
- The assessment of cost-effectiveness of security controls. Given a fixed budget, entities should be able to spend in the most cost-effective manner to reduce its information risks (Gordon and Loeb, 2002). The cost-effectiveness justification approach attempts to justify each security controls' costs and benefits to arrive at an optimal mix of security controls (Frosdick, 1997; Cerullo and Cerullo, 2005). This is covered in Chapter 5, Economic Modeling and the Implementation of Effective Mitigating Controls.

Anderson and Moore have flagged a number of key concepts in their work around the economic aspects of information security. Their 2008 paper is a summation of various earlier pieces of their work, and hence forms a useful reference point. There are two fundamental points that underlie much of their work. First of these is that economics and security (Walker, 2012; Anderson and Moore, 2008), historically, have been intimately linked, e.g., wealthy nations could afford larger (or, perhaps more accurately, more effective) armies and navies, and were thus more secure. Secondly, psychology has an immensely important role to play in the economics of information security, as it informs the context in which economic decisions are made, and is pertinent to some observable characteristics of information security.

In their 2006 science article (Anderson and Moore, 2006a), the authors point out that systems are particularly prone to failure when the person guarding them is not the person who bears the entire cost of the failure. This is particularly pertinent in large organizations where there is a clear distinction between the "guard" entity, and the "business" entity. The former is likely to be in the form of a discrete IT or information security function, while the latter is likely to have control over the financial resources required for information security-related investments. This creates misaligned incentives the business stakeholders in an investment will tend to see the investment as a "one off" activity, to be achieved at lowest cost since many benefits accrue to other players.

This underlines the significance of externalities in security investment, as effective protection often depends on the efforts of many actors. At the same time, the benefits of a secure business environment may accrue to many parties. Hence, information security economics displays both positive and negative externalities, and, importantly, network effects (Anderson and Moore, 2006a). A network externality is a network, or a community of software users, that is more valuable to its members the larger it is. This not only helps explain the rise and dominance of operating systems, from System/360 through Windows to Symbian, and of music platforms such as iTunes; it also helps explain the typical pattern of security flaws. Put simply, while platform vendors are building market dominance, they have to appeal to vendors of complementary products as well as to their direct customers; not only does this divert energy that might be spent on securing the platform, but security could get in the way by making life harder for the implementers. So, platform vendors commonly ignore security in the beginning, as they are building their market position; later, once they have captured a lucrative market, they add excessive security in order to lock their customers in tightly (Anderson and Moore, 2006a).

Another instance of externalities can be found when analyzing security investment, as protection often depends on the efforts of many principals. Budgets generally depend on the manner in which individual investment translates to outcomes, but this, in turn, depends not just on the investor's own decisions, but also on the decisions of others.

System reliability can depend on the sum of individual efforts, the minimum effort anyone makes, or the maximum effort any makes. Program correctness can depend on the weakest-link (the most careless programmer introducing a vulnerability) while software validation and vulnerability testing might depend on the sum of everyone's efforts. There can also be cases where the security depends on the best effort—the effort of an individual champion. A simple model by Varian provides interesting results when players choose their effort levels independently. For the total-effort case, system reliability depends on the agent with the highest benefit-cost ratio, and all other agents free-ride. In the weakest-link case, the agent with the lowest benefit-cost ratio dominates. As more agents are added, systems become increasingly reliable in the total-effort case but increasingly unreliable in the weakest-link case. One of the implications is that software companies should hire more software testers and fewer (but more competent) programmers.

Work such as this has inspired other researchers to consider *interdependent risk*. An influential model by Kunreuther and Heal (2003) notes that the security investments can be strategic complements: an individual taking protective measures creates positive externalities for others that in turn may discourage their own investment. This result has implications far beyond cyber security. The decision by one apartment owner to install a sprinkler system that minimizes the risk of fire damage will affect the decisions of his neighbors; airlines may decide not to screen luggage transferred from other carriers who are believed to be careful with security; and people thinking of vaccinating their children against a contagious disease may choose to free-ride off the herd immunity instead. In each case, several widely varying Nash equilibrium outcomes are possible, from complete adoption to total refusal, depending on the levels of coordination between principals.

Katz and Shapiro (1985) famously noted how network externalities affected the adoption of technology. Network effects can also influence the deployment of security technology. The benefit a protection technology provides may depend on the number of users that adopt it. The cost may be greater than the benefit until a minimum number of players adopt. So each decision-maker might wait for others to go first, and the technology never gets deployed. Ozment and Schechter (2006) have analyzed different approaches for overcoming bootstrapping problems faced by those who would deploy security technologies. This challenge is particularly topical. A number of core internet protocols, such as domain name system (DNS) and routing, are considered insecure. More secure protocols exist; the challenge is to get them adopted. Two security protocols that have already been widely deployed, secure shell (SSH) and IPsec, both overcame the bootstrapping problem by providing significant intra-organizational benefits. In the successful cases, adoption could be done one organization at a time, rather than needing most organizations to move at once. The deployment of fax machines also occurred through this mechanism: companies initially bought fax machines to connect their own offices (Anderson and Moore, 2006a).

Taking these factors into account, as Nagaraja and Anderson (2006) point out, this may mean that, in scenarios where there are continual multi-round interactions between attack and defense, e.g., in the case of the protection of an organization's information assets against outside infiltration and attack, there are implications for defensive structures. Localized cliques are better able to align their incentives than larger structures based on concentric rings of defense. They point to examples of this in the real world where political revolutionary organizations set up "cell" structures as a defensive measure, and, in the IT world, the relative fragility of ring-architecture based peer-to-peer architectures (Walker, 2012).

Citing Akerlof's Nobel prize-winning work on the "market for lemons" (Akerlof, 1970), Anderson and Moore point out the significance of information asymmetry, or rather the absence of information, i.e., security investment are designed to an extent to protect against future events about which there exists limited information. This would tend to suggest that there will be investment decisions made on observable characteristics, e.g., price, rather than less readily observable characteristics, such as effectiveness. As a consequence, cheaper, less effective security measures may drive out more expensive, but more effective, ones.

Gordon and Loeb (2002) presented an economic model to determine the optimal amount for an enterprise investment towards protecting a digital asset. This model is such that, for a given potential loss, the optimum amount to spend to protect an information asset does not always increase with an increase in an information set's vulnerability. It indicates that, even within the range of justifiable investments in information security, the maximum amount a risk-neutral firm should spend is only a fraction of the expected loss due to security breaches. For two broad classes of security breach probability functions, this fraction never exceeds 37% of the expected loss. For most cases, however, this fraction is substantially below the 37% level (Gordon and Loeb, 2002). It is shown that for a given potential loss, a firm should not necessarily focus its investments on information sets with the highest vulnerability. Since extremely vulnerable information sets may be inordinately expensive to protect, a firm may be better off concentrating its efforts on information sets with midrange vulnerabilities.

6.2 CURRENT INFORMATION SECURITY/RISK MANAGEMENT BUDGET

According to a 2016 survey, about 40% of financial services in North America alone with more than $1 billion in revenue had budgeted $10 million or more for information security (Office of Financial Research, 2017). During a February 2017 survey, 14% of C-level respondents stated that cyber security accounted for more than 10% of their annual IT budget.[1] Tables 6.1 and 6.2 show more detailed figures on security spending. Table 6.3 shows the drivers and focus areas of money spent.

---

1. https://www.statista.com/statistics/811116/us-consumer-business-cyber-security-budget-percentage/.

TABLE 6.1 Median Budget and Percentage Allocated to Security by Year by Organization Size (SANS, 2016)

Classification	IT Budget		
	2014	2015	2016
Large	$1M–$10M	$1M–$10M	$10M–$50M
Medium	$500K–$1M	$1M	$1M–$10M
Small	$100K–$500K	$100K–$500K	$100K–$500K
Classification	%Budget for Security		
	2014	2015	2016
Large	4%–6%	4%–6%	7%–9%
Medium	4%–6%	4%–6%	7%–9%
Small	3%–4%	4%–6%	6%–7%

TABLE 6.2 Median Budget and Percentage Allocated to Security by Year by Industry (SANS, 2016)

Industry	IT Budget		
	2014	2015	2016
Financial services	$1M	$500K–$1M	$500K–$1M
Technology/IT services	$100K	$100K–$500K	$100K–$500K
Government	$500K–$1M	$500K–$1M	$1M–$10M
Education	$1M–$10M	$1M–$10M	$1M–$10M
Health care	$1M–$10M	$1M–$10M	$1M–$10M
Industry	Budget for Security		
	2014	2015	2016
Financial services	7%–9%	7%–9%	10%–12%
Technology/IT services	1%–3%	4%–6%	4%–6%
Government	4%–6%	4%–6%	7%–9%
Education	1%–3%	3%–4%	1%–3%
Health care	4%–6%	4%–6%	4%–6%

TABLE 6.3 Drivers and Focus Areas of Cyber Security Spending (SANS, 2016)

Drivers Behind Spending on Cyber Security (From High to Low)	Operational Areas That Account for Security Spending (From High to Low)
1. Protection of sensitive data	1. Protection and prevention
2. Regulatory compliance	2. Detection and response
3. Reducing incidents and breaches	3. Compliance and audit (including legal)
4. Protection of intellectual property	4. Risk reduction
5. Alignment with organizational and IT strategic planning	5. End user training and awareness
6. Protecting brand reputation	6. Governance/policies
7. Reducing attack surface	7. Staff training and certification
8. Improving visibility into security operations	8. Security program or project management
9. New, advanced threats and techniques	9. Design/development
10. End user education and awareness	10. Discovery and forensics
11. Improving incident response	11. Other

6.3 CHALLENGES FOR CYBER RISK MANAGEMENT COST OPTIMIZATION

Currently, most organizations do not have any models in place to measure the return of their investment in cyber risk management. Challenges lie in a few areas discussed below.

6.3.1 The Challenges in Quantifying Security Costs

Firstly, challenges remain in quantifying security costs.

6.3.1.1 Cyber Security and Risk Management Is a Cross-Functional Task

Information security is a cross-divisional task that encompasses technical and organizational aspects. With information security awareness becoming more and more important virtually every employee in a company can do his/her bit to provide information security. The cross-divisional nature is a huge challenge for categorizing and analyzing information security costs. On the one hand, information security costs cannot be easily mapped to one single category of traditional cost accounting. On the other hand, it is not easily possible to define what part of the costs of a measure are directly accountable to information security. It is also hard to determine which part of the investment is accounted to information security. For example, programming guidelines are used to improve the security of a company's products, but in a case where employees write hundreds or thousands of lines of code a day, no one can tell what amount of time is really invested into security.

6.3.1.2 Divergent Goals Exist for Cost Quantification

Organizations have different reasons and goals for quantifying costs in general and information security costs in particular. Each of the information needs may require a different perspective on information security costs to appropriately answer the questions. A flexible cost model is required that can satisfy different demands by enabling different perspectives on information security costs in the enterprise (Table 6.4).

6.3.1.3 Lack of Transparency on Hidden Costs

A major challenge in analyzing security costs are hidden costs that are not directly related to a security risk management decision but inherently caused by it, such as outsourcing and management security services. There are four types of outsourcing that are often incur hidden costs:

- Costs that occur during the search for a suitable vendor during the contracting phase.
- Switching the in-house delivery of a service to another company during the transition phase.
- Switching from the outsourcing partner to another outsourcer or the reintegration of the formerly outsourced service during the transition phase.

TABLE 6.4 Divergent Goals for Cost Quantification

Goal	Implications
Budgeting	Providing guidelines of how much may be spent, categorization to provide internal comparability, orienting towards general controlling and accounting guidelines
Cost accounting	Usually, no special way of dealing with security, main goal is to meet compliance regarding financial aspects
Benchmarking	Comparability with other organizations, identification of differences, point out different strategies or starting points
Risk management	Preparation for controlling decisions, determine advantageousness of measure
Cost-benefit-analysis investment/projects	Economic assessment of certain measures/projects, return on investment (ROI) analyses, the overall costs of a measure or project need to be identified
Surveys/research	Identification of trends towards higher/lower security spending, determination of preferences (technical/organizational measures)

- Costs for the management of the outsourcing relationship.
- Costs in managing all of the supplier relationships, including gaining visibility into fourth parties and nth parties in the supply chain.

6.3.1.4 Difficulties in Finding the Right Scope and Baseline

Confusions exist around what falls under IT security, information security, cyber security, and their associated risk domains. This makes it challenging to reach consensus on the scope of the problem and the right baseline that needs to be applied for evaluation. For example, the nature of information security costs make it unlikely that this kind of costs can be seen as a subset of IT costs and, thus, be put in relation to be overall IT budget of a company, especially in industries with highly sensitive information, the importance of information security may not have been fully understood.

6.3.1.5 Lack of Resources and Clear Ownership to Implement Controls

This is often a reflection of a lack of senior management appreciation of a need for controls or, more specifically, for changes in controls occasioned by rapidly changing technologies, particularly if there has been no cost-justification for them. The responsibility for internal controls is also often not clearly defined or is placed with persons whose priorities are such that internal controls must be neglected (Courtney, 1982).

6.3.2 Challenges in Determining the Optimal Level of Investment in Security and Risk

Challenges for determining how much should be spent on cyber security and risk exist on entity, portfolio, and global levels are summarized in this section.

On the entity level:

- *Most organizations still treat spending on cyber security as a cost rather than an investment.* Many organizations still see cyber security as a cost of doing business, rather than an enabler that supports business and a value creator for the organization, its partners, as well as customers (Bojanc and Jerman-Blazic, 2008; Cavusoglu et al., 2004).
- *There is an inclination to define security-related problems too narrowly.* There is an inclination to define the scope of security-related problems no greater than is needed to encompass a specific instance which created the immediate concern. Suboptimization of controls as a consequence of too severe compartmentation of concerns means that controls which are applicable to a broad array of problems are justified only in their ability to contain several problems (Courtney, 1982). This results in suboptimization of investment in the most cost-effective controls.
- *Difficulties in quantifying benefits.* The most common benefits of investment in cyber security are the reduction of occurrence of the incidents and consequently the losses caused by the incidents. These benefits are often very difficult to be predicted very accurately. The biggest problem lays in the assessment of the cost savings related to potential security incidents that have not yet occurred. The more successful information security is, the harder it is to notice and calculate the benefits.
- *Lack of general models to aid decision-making.* There is a lack of general and reliable models that organizations could use in making decisions about how much is the optimal and most appropriate investment in security controls and systems (Bojanc and Jerman-Blazic, 2008). This also relates to the lack of pertinent education or experience in the persons charged with the selection or implementation of controls (Courtney, 1982).

On the portfolio level:

- *Lack of benchmark of what good looks like.* One of the underlying issues in determining the value of cyber security activity is the lack of a substantive benchmark for what "good" looks like. For example, the ISO 27001 series provide a purely qualitative guide for information security practices, with no hard measures for what constitutes best practice. In turn, this translates into a propensity for intuition-based risk management practice, as identified as a problem by expert panel member B, given the implied information asymmetry between information security professionals and business decision-makers (Walker, 2012). Some data does exist, but these datasets are not complete nor good enough to be practically useful. In particular, there is a lack of quality sector-based data that are tailored for sector-specific risk scenarios.

On the global level:

- *Current motivations favor self-protection over prevention for the good of the whole*. Anderson (2001) observes that current motivations favor self-protection over prevention for the good of the whole. On the Internet, this explains the trend toward proliferation of localized firewalls and spam filters rather than ISP-based controls (Mercuri, 2003).
- *Software market is a "market for lemons."* In a Nobel prize-winning work, economist George Akerlof examines how the quality of goods traded in a market can degrade in the presence of information asymmetry between buyers and sellers, leaving only "lemons" behind (Akerlof, 1970). His paper imagines a town in which 50 good used cars (worth $2000) are for sale, along with 50 "lemons" (worth $1000 each). The sellers know the difference but the buyers do not. What will be the market-clearing price? One might initially think $1500, but at that price no one with a good car will offer it for sale; so, the market price will quickly end up near $1000. Because buyers are unwilling to pay a premium for quality they cannot measure, only low-quality used vehicles are available for sale. The software market suffers from the same information asymmetry. Vendors may make claims about the security of their products, but buyers have no reason to trust them. In many cases, even the vendor does not know how secure its software is. So, buyers have no reason to pay more for more secure software, and vendors are disinclined to invest in protection (Anderson and Moore, 2006a).
- *Lack of statistically robust historical data*. To accurately measure benefits and costs of cyber security investment, it is critical to have information about the likelihood of cyber incidents as well as the impact of cyber risks, which can be caused by unsecure information systems. Since cyber security factors are continually changing because of rapidly developing technologies, it is difficult to acquire enough historical data to evaluate the likelihood and cost of cyber risk factors. Estimation of various indirect costs is highly complex. For example, implementing new controls for securing information may lead to potential productivity loss in an organization, which is impossible to estimate (GAO, 1999; Chaia et al., 2011)

6.3.3   General Limitations of Approaches: Game Theory in Security Investment

The game-theoretic aspect of cyber security was first noted by Jajodia and Millen (1993):

> *Computer security is a kind of game between two parties, the designer of a secure system, and a potential attacker (Cavusoglu et al., 2004).*

Tighter security technology employed by firms requires higher investment, but also makes hacking more difficult. Hackers do not select their targets randomly. They rationally make their choice based on how much effort will be required to succeed in hacking and the reward as a result. The strategic interaction between a firm's investment and hacking activity must be captured in the model used to determine investment levels. Because decision theory is designed to analyze decision making under uncertainty where "nature" is the only "opponent," it is fundamentally inadequate to deal with security investment decision-making where these behavioral effects occur. Hence, modeling the interaction between firm and hacker decisions requires game theory (Cavusoglu et al., 2004).

6.4   CURRENT MODELS FOR CYBER RISK COST OPTIMIZATION

6.4.1   Cost Models for Determining how much to Investment in Security and Risk

6.4.1.1   Benchmarking

Benchmarking is an effective tool that allows an organization to visualize its security posture relative to an ideal or peer group (e.g., industry vectors), and to view existing gaps in its cybersecurity posture. One approach involves a diagnostic toolkit that assesses a company along key dimensions and provides a score that can be compared against those of peer groups. Examples of key dimensions can include:

- *Business assets*. Understanding of "crown-jewel" business processes and data, common view of their criticality across the organization and awareness of their presence on the underlying infrastructure.
- *Threat perception*. Effectiveness of the organization in collecting, analyzing, and disseminating threat information.
- *Defense*. Evaluation of the various defenses across the processes, defense tools, people, and organizational skills, and along proactive defense, attack detection, and response management (Ramasubramanian and Hall, 2013).

TABLE 6.5 Steps for Quantitative Risk Assessment

Steps	Calculation
Step 1. Determining the single loss expectancy (SLE)	SLE is calculated as:
	Single loss expectancy = asset value × exposure factor
	Items to consider when calculating the SLE include the physical destruction or theft of assets, the loss of data, the theft of information, and threats that might cause a delay in processing. The exposure factor is represented in the impact of the risk over the asset, or percentage of asset lost. As an example, if the asset value is reduced two-thirds, the exposure factor value is 0.66. If the asset is completely lost, the exposure factor is 1.0.
Step 2. Determining the annual rate of occurrence (ARO)	This step involves conducting a threat analysis to determine the likelihood of an unwanted event. The goal is to estimate the ARO.
Step 3. Determining the annual loss expectancy (ALE)	This third and final step of the quantitative assessment seeks to combine the potential loss and rate per year to determine the magnitude of the risk. This is expressed as ALE. ALE is calculated as:
	Annual loss expectancy (ALE) = annual rate of occurrence (ARO) × single loss expectancy (SLE)

6.4.1.2 Cost-Benefit Analysis

As discussed in detail in Chapter 5, Economic Modeling and the Implementation of Effective Mitigating Controls, cost-benefit analysis (CBA) technique is one of the most popular metrics applied to cyber risk management (Mercuri, 2003). CBA is well established in microeconomic and management accounting theory and can be used to determine estimated levels of expenditures appropriate to the values of assets requiring protection. CBA is application independent, involves identification and measurement of all related costs and benefits, should include lost opportunity costs from diversion of resources, needs to account for shared costs and uses, and must consider and address risks, uncertainties, qualitative factors, and assumptions (Clark, 1995).

6.4.1.3 Quantitative Risk Assessment

Quantitative assessment deals with numbers and dollar amounts. It attempts to assign a cost (monetary value) to the elements of risk assessment and to the assets and threats of a risk analysis. To fully complete a quantitative risk assessment, all elements of the process (asset value, impact, threat frequency, safeguard effectiveness, safeguard costs, uncertainty, and probability) are quantified. Therein lies the problem with purely quantitative risk assessment: where it is difficult to assign dollar values to some elements, some qualitative measures must be applied. A quantitative assessment requires substantial time and personnel resources. Calculations should also include all associated costs, such as: (1) lost productivity; (2) cost of repair; (3) value of the damaged equipment or lost data; and (4) cost to replace the equipment or reload the data (Gregg, 2005). The quantitative assessment process involves the following three steps listed in Table 6.5.

6.4.1.4 Return on Security Investment

ROSI is a model based on ROI.

ROI is a popular accounting metric for comparison of business investments (Bojanc and Jerman-Blazic, 2008). ROI equals the present value of accumulated net benefits over a certain time period, divided by the initial costs of investment:

$$\text{ROI} = \frac{\text{Benefits} - \text{cost of investment}}{\text{cost of investment}}$$

If a new e-commerce web server costs €10,000 and is expected to bring in €50,000 income over the course of 4 years, the ROI for the 4-year period is 400%. ROI can help an organization to decide which of the possible options gives the most value for money invested. For example, a company might use ROI when deciding whether to invest in internal development of a new technology/solution or to purchase a commercial product/solution.

The cost of information security investments can be considered as a compound of the system configuration specific costs and the operating costs. System configuration specific costs are typically one-time spend costs for purchase (or development), testing and implementation of defense solution that protects information assets from possible threats. Operating costs are represented by annual maintenance (upgrades and patching of the defense solution), training users and network administrators, monitoring the solution (Mizzi, 2005). On the other hand, it is very difficult to define, assess, or measure the benefits. Firewalls, intrusion detection systems (IDS), antivirus software, and other security solutions do not generate revenue that can be measured. Therefore, the benefits of information security investment are measured as cost savings that result from preventing information security breaches (Gordon and Loeb, 2006). Benefits can, therefore, be represented as a difference between ALE without security investment and ALE with security investment.

Typically, the initial benefits will rapidly increase with investments and later the benefit growth is stabilized due to the reduction of the probability of security breaches. On the other hand, the cost of security investment could be initially low, but later it can increase due to the needs for higher levels of security infrastructure in the organization. The organizations should invest in security solutions up to the point where the net benefits (i.e., benefits minus costs) are at maximum. In the Gordon–Loeb model introduced later in this section, the optimal investments in information security are ranging from 0% to 36.8% of the potential loss due to a security breach (Gordon and Loeb, 2002). Later it was also found that in some special scenarios investments up to 50% (or even up to 100%) of the AntiVirus are allowed (Willemson, 2006). This model had also been successfully used in some empirical analysis (Tanaka et al., 2006, 2005). A simple equation for calculating the ROSI is as follows (Bojanc and Jerman-Blazic, 2008):

$$\text{ROSI} = \frac{\text{ALE}_{\text{without investment}} - \text{ALE}_{\text{with investment}} - \text{cost of investment}}{\text{cost of investment}}$$

The calculation of an example is illustrated as follows: the ALE of the threat of virus infection on a web server is €8750, and after the purchase and implementation of a €1600 worth antivirus safeguard the ALE is valued at €3400. The annual cost of maintenance and operation of the safeguard is €450, so the ROSI in the first year is:

$$\frac{(8750 - 3400 - 1600 - 450)}{(1600 + 450)} = 160\%$$

While ROI tells what percentage of return will be provided with the investment over a specified period of time, it does not tell anything about the magnitude of the project. So, while a 124% return may seem attractive initially, this approach does not support a comparison between having a 124% return on a €10,000 project and a 60% return on a €300,000 investment.

6.4.1.5 Net Present Value

In the case of long-term investments, the time attribute presents a problem in calculating the ROI. A index known as NPV are used along with ROI to justify expenditures. The NPV is a financial metric for comparing benefits and costs over different time periods. The methodology behind NPV is in discounting all anticipated benefits and costs to today's value, where all benefits and costs are expressed in a monetary unit (e.g., Euros) (Bojanc and Jerman-Blazic, 2008; Gordon and Loeb, 2006).

The essence of the NPV is to compare the discounted cash flows associated with the future benefits and costs to the initial cost of an investment. The NVP gives the value of the cash return that is expected and is calculated by summation of the present net value of the benefits for each year over expected lifetime periods and by subtracting the initial costs of the project. Suppose B_t is the present value of the net benefits of period t, C_t all costs and i the internal rate of discount. The NPV of the investment is calculated as follows:

$$\text{NPV} = \sum_{t=0}^{\infty} \left(\frac{B_t - C_t}{(1+i)^t} \right)$$

A positive NPV means that the project generates a profit, while a negative NPV means that the project generates a loss. The NPV is useful in cases when alternatives are being evaluated. For example, an organization chooses between two security solutions where one costs €15,000 in advance and the other costs yearly €5000 for 3 years. Both solutions cost €15,000, but the second solution is better because organization can invest the remaining money in other places for a defined time. Therefore, the real cost of the second solution is less than €15,000.

An important characteristic of NPV is that it provides cash value of the expected return and therefore indicates the magnitude of the project; the drawback is in the lack of information about when the expected return would occur (Bojanc and Jerman-Blazic, 2008).

6.4.1.6 Internal Rate of Return

Like the NPV, the internal rate of return (IRR) is often used to analyze long-term investments. The IRR equals the percentage discount rate that makes the NPV of the investment equal to zero (Bojanc and Jerman-Blazic, 2008):

$$\sum_{t=0}^{n} \frac{B_t - C_t}{(1+\text{IRR})^t} = 0$$

IRR is particularly useful when a multi-year investment is made with costs that change radically from 1 year to the next. But like ROI, IRR does not give any indication of the magnitude of the project involved (Bojanc and Jerman-Blazic, 2008).

6.4.1.7 Comparisons of Return on Investment, Net Present Value and Internal Rate of Return

Each of these financial measures above has its own strengths and weaknesses. The ROI is intended to be used for evaluating past investments, in contrast to the NPV and IRR, which are typically used to make decisions about potential new investments (Gordon and Loeb, 2006). ROI has the difficulty in defining what the magnitude of the investment is and, unlike the NPV or IRR, the ROI does not consider the time value of money. However, calculating ALE is more difficult for the NPV and IRR. In most cases, the NPV and IRR are better indicators than a simple ROI calculation (Gordon and Richardson, 2004). To get a clear and complete picture of a prospective investment, the standard approach should be based on all of these measures. Although ROI has a number of limitations, when compared with NPV and IRR, ROI is still by far the most popular metric used. According to the 2007 CSI Survey, 39% of organizations use ROI as a metric, 21% use NPV, and 17% use IRR (Bojanc and Jerman-Blazic, 2008).

For example, an organization with 500 computers is decided to reduce the security risk. It is estimated that the potential annual loss from security breach would cost the organization €1,000,000. The current implemented information security controls reduce the security risk by 80%, but this is not good enough. The organization's security goal is to reduce the probability of security breach to max 10%. The investment is intended for 4 years; after that period, the state of security in the organization will be evaluated again.

The organization wants to choose between three alternatives. The first alternative is a low-cost (LC) security solution. It reduces the probability of a security breach to 10%, which is just within the limits of security objectives. The purchase price of this solution is €60,000 plus an estimated €20,000 for yearly maintenance costs.

The second alternative is a professional solution (PRO). It reduces the probability of a security breach to just 1%. Its purchase price is €100,000, while the annual renewal price is €30,000. Because this is a more PRO, the technical staff needs training, which costs €30,000. However further yearly maintenance costs will be only €5000.

The third alternative is outsourcing (OUT). The company providing outsourcing service assures that a probability of security breach is no more than 7%. The company charges €150,000 for implementing security solution and €25,000 for annual maintenance and support. There is no need for extra in-house technical support.

Benefits for each alternative can be simply calculated by using the ALE and the promised reduction in probability of security breach:

Benefits$_{(LC)}$ = €1,000,000 × (90%−80%) = €100,000
Benefits$_{(PRO)}$ = €1,000,000 × (99%−80%) = €190,000
Benefits$_{(OUT)}$ = €1,000,000 × (93%−80%) = €130,000

In Table 6.6 the benefits are represented together with the costs for all alternatives. The first comparison is calculating the ROI. From ROI calculation we get the results:

ROI$_{(LC)}$ = 186%
ROI$_{(PRO)}$ = 176%
ROI$_{(OUT)}$ = 108%

So far it looks like the LC solution is the favorite. However, the ROI does not provide information on the actual magnitude. Furthermore, ROI does not consider the time value of money. In this case, the NPV calculation gives a different result:

NPV(LC) = €223,676
NPV(PRO) = €416,289
NPV(OUT) = €222,325

TABLE 6.6 Calculated Benefits and Costs for All Alternatives

Year	Rate	Alternative LC			Alternative PRO			Alternative OUT		
		A	B	C	A	B	C	A	B	C
0			60,000			100,000			150,000	
1	0.05	100,000		20,000	190,000	30,000	40,000	130,000	25,000	
2	0.05	100,000		20,000	190,000	30,000	5000	130,000	25,000	
3	0.05	100,000		20,000	190,000	30,000	5000	130,000	25,000	
4	0.05	100,000		20,000	190,000	30,000	5000	130,000	25,000	

A = benefits (€); B = purchase and upgrade costs (€); C = maintenance costs (€).

TABLE 6.7 The Comparison Between ROI, NPV, and IRR Calculation

Alternative	ROI (%)	NPV	IRR (%)
LC	186	€223,676	128
PRO	176	€416,289	130
OUT	108	€222,325	59

The final comparison is done with a calculation of the IRR. The IRR confirms the NPV results, and is in favor of PRO solution:

$$IRR_{(LC)} = 128\%$$
$$IRR_{(PRO)} = 130\%$$
$$IRR_{(OUT)} = 59\%$$

The presented example has some limitation, but it can provide an approximate qualitative estimation. The PRO alternative is most expensive, but it also seems the most appropriate choice because NPV and IRR rank it first. The LC alternative has the highest ROI, but this is mainly due to ROI limitations. The comparison between the three approaches is presented in Table 6.7.

6.4.1.8 Gordon and Loeb Model

The Gordon–Loeb model (Gordon and Loeb, 2002) specifically considers how the security vulnerabilities and associated loss affect the optimal level of resources that should be devoted to security. The analysis has shown that:

1. For a broad class of security breach probability functions, the optimal amount to spend on information security is an increasing function of the level of vulnerability of such information.
2. For a second broad class of security breach probability functions, the optimal amount to spend on information security does not always increase with the level of vulnerability of such information. For this second class, the optimal amount to spend on information security initially increases, but ultimately decreases with the level of vulnerability of such information. Thus, the second class of security breach probability functions also shows that managers allocating an information security budget should normally focus on information that falls into the midrange of vulnerability to security breaches.

Hence, a meaningful endeavor for managers may be to partition information sets into low, middle, and high levels of security breach vulnerability. Some information sets may be so difficult to protect to a very high level of security, that one may be best off defending them only at a moderate level.

They also presented an economic model to describe the optimal monetary investment to protect a given set of information assets. This model aims to determine the optimal amount for an enterprise investment toward protecting an asset, e.g., an information set, such as a customer database. This model is such that, for a given potential loss, the optimum amount to spend to protect an information asset does not always increase with an increase in an information set's vulnerability. In addition, the model shows that the amount a firm should spend to protect information assets should generally be only a small fraction of the expected loss.

6.4.1.9 Full Cost Accounting Model

Full cost accounting is a systematic approach for identifying, summing, and reporting the actual costs of an activity. It takes into account past and future outlays, overhead (oversight and support services) costs, and operating costs. In this respect, it can be seen to overcome the objection to ROSI that it is unrealistic to fixate on capital expenditure over revenue expenditure when considering information security expenditure (Walker, 2012).

Externalities can be defined as costs and benefits which are not naturally captured in the pricing of the activities to which they attach. This may also pertain where the costs and benefits of an activity are felt by different parties, resulting in a misalignment of incentives, as argued by Anderson and Moore (Anderson and Moore, 2006a). This results in the oversupply of goods and services where there are negative externalities, such as pollution, or undersupply, where there are positive externalities, as would be argued to be the case where information security is concerned.

It may, therefore, be useful to draw lessons, where possible, from innovative models used in other areas where externalities are a significant factor. One good example would be waste management which displays many commonalities with information security. For example:

- Neither is generally thought of as a revenue generating activity.
- Both are display classic characteristics of public goods, with free rider problems and undersupply unless provided by a centralized authority, e.g., municipal governments for waste management and driven by central government legislation for information security.
- In both cases, failure to supply has negative effects, but these are difficult to accurately quantify in advance.
- Comparative data exists on consequence but is incomplete and its applicability would be open to challenge. For example, ineffective sewerage resulted in cholera outbreaks in 19th century London, but the only way of modeling the probability and effect of a major sanitary failing in the 21st century would be theoretical.

The State of Florida uses a full cost accounting approach for its solid waste management. Full cost accounting is a systematic approach for identifying, summarizing, and reporting the actual costs of an activity. It takes into account past and future outlays, overhead (oversight and support services) costs, and operating costs. In this respect, it can be seen to overcome the objection to ROSI that it is unrealistic to fixate on capital expenditure over revenue expenditure when considering information security expenditure.

Bebbington and Thomson (1996) lay out a series of layers of cost to be considered in a full cost accounting model. These are laid out, in a form adapted for information security, in Table 6.8.

Working through the tiers systematically would enable an organization to produce a holistic picture of the costs and benefits of its information security expenditure.

TABLE 6.8 Layers of Costs to be Considered for a Full Cost Accounting Model for Information Security

Tier	Description	Content
0	Usual costs	Direct and indirect costs which would be associated with an activity using a conventional accounting approach, including both revenue and capital expenditure.
1	Hidden costs	Additional costs usually found in overheads/general accounts. These would include regulatory management systems, and monitoring costs, both revenue and capital in nature.
2	Liability costs	These costs can emerge dependent on other events, e.g., changes in legislation, and their likelihood can only be estimated. Examples might include fines and other regulatory costs.
3	Less tangible benefits	Costs and benefits that are likely to arise from improved security management. These costs and benefits could include the effect of goodwill arising from a project; changed attitudes of suppliers, etc.
4	Environmentally focused benefits	These values would be informed by estimates of the industry and social impacts and alternatives.

The number of steps for this model to be adapted for information security include (Bebbington et al., 2001):

- *Define the cost objective for a new project or process*, covering the end-to-end extent of an activity. The failure to do this would result in incomplete consideration of costs and benefits.
- *Specify the scope of analysis.* This serves to determine what subset of all possible externalities are to be considered. Moreover, this would be important in identifying the various layers of externality which might include, for example, regulatory impacts. It would not be useful to try to include all conceivable externalities (e.g., impact on competitors); rather, only those externalities which can be directly identified with a particular project or activity should be included.
- *Identify and measure external impact.* This requires an explicit link to be made between the cost objective and the externalities which arise from it. It requires the gathering of data on both the cost objective itself and the identified externalities. The first set can largely be drawn from boundary transactions, that is, where there is a consumption or movement of resources resulting in a monetary transaction. With regard to externalities, secondary data sets such as reported costs of incidents and historical fines under the Data Protection Act from the Information Commissioner's Office.
- *Cost external impact* (e.g., monetization of the externalities). In many respects, this is the most problematic stage and often dependent on a convincing scope that have been identified earlier in the process. This is often the area regarded as the most subjective and subject to challenge, as it will tend to be "story dependent."

The sum of costs from Tier 0 to Tier 4 in Table 7.8 then produces a theoretical model for a full cost analysis. However, estimation of probability as well as the relative balance between costs and benefits can still be problematic. One solution to this is to articulate clear assumptions about facts in the calculations. For example, the economic climate, which has an impact on the overall level of criminality, should be expressed in a flexible way, that is, "best case", "medium" and "worst case". This would allow conscious decisions about confidence levels and would provide a clear rationale for revisions if specific assumptions are proven incorrect. Furthermore, it would allow for improved confidence in decisions over time, both from a psychological perspective and by providing internal benchmarks which can be refined over time. This is something that ROSI does not do, as a specific application of it will only ever be "generally in line with events" or "not aligned". Turning this into a model for determining the return on a particular activity would therefore produce:

$$\text{Return} = \frac{(A + B + C) + (D + E + (F \times \text{probability of F}))}{(D + E + (F \times \text{probability of F}))}$$

Where:

- A is the direct benefit of the activity/project (as per Tier 0).
- B is fewer tangible benefits (as per Tier 3).
- C is positive network effects (as per Tier 4).
- D is Tier 0 costs.
- E is Tier 1 costs.
- F is the cost of contingent liabilities (as per Tier 2).

6.4.2   Cost Models for Projection

When determining investment options, decision-makers must consider not only the costs incurred today, but also the costs incurred as a consequence of their choices, or, in other words, this requires cost accounting and cost projections. Cost accounting methods assist in appropriately allocating observed costs based on actual resource consumption. Cost projection determines the upcoming costs as well as the time frame in which they will be incurred. Models in use for cost projection include Cyber VaR (as covered in Chapter 5, Economic Modeling and the Implementation of Effective Mitigating Controls), Monte Carlo Method (as covered in Chapter 5, Economic Modeling and the Implementation of Effective Mitigating Controls), and Delphi Method.[2]

---

2. Delphi method is a forecasting or decision-making technique for predictive analysis.

6.4.3   Risk Management Options and Associated Cost

6.4.3.1   Defense-in-Depth and Holistic Thinking

A systemic and holistic approach to data security requires a broad problem definition so that we can find controls which displace the greatest possible problem scope and, as consequence, are fully cost-justified. The objective is to select a fully complementary set of controls, or security measures, which displace the greatest scope for the least cost (Courtney, 1982). No single control guarantees security by itself. Every security control is imperfect, but at the same time, has its own unique place within a security architecture. This approach is called defense-in-depth or a layered system of defenses architecture. The problem with deployment of multiple controls was stated succinctly by Axelsson (2000):

> *The best effort is often achieved when several security measures are brought to bear together. How should intrusion detection collaborate with other security mechanisms to this synergy effect? How do we ensure that the combination of security measures provides at least the same level of security as each applied singly would provide, or that the combination does in fact lower the overall security of the protected system?*

These questions are important because firms commonly consider how much value a security control will add to security in isolation with other controls already in place. Failing to recognize the interaction between security technologies can lead to poor security architecture design decisions. Cavusoglu et al. (2004) showed that both complementary and substitution effects might exist between security technologies. By considering a security architecture that includes both a firewall and an intrusion detection system (IDS), they show that the firewall and the IDS may complement or substitute for one another depending on the firm's security cost structure and the detection rate of the IDS. For some firms, using both technologies may be worse than using only one of them.

6.5   COST OF SECURITY CONFIGURATIONS

Configuration management and performance evaluation of security controls is another dimension that is mostly overlooked in current practices towards economic modeling (Cavusoglu et al., 2004). Software Engineering Institute[3] (SEI)'s guidelines on installing intrusion detection systems (Allen et al., 2000) cautions firms against accepting the default settings automatically and advises appropriate configuration to balance security and operational requirements. This has an impact on the overall cost considerations of various security options. To understand the implications of security system configuration on the cost-benefit tradeoff, consider the following scenarios:

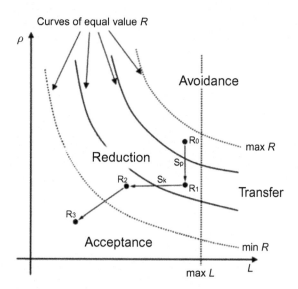

FIGURE 6.2   Risk minimizing strategies (Bojanc and Jerman-Blazic, 2008).

---

3. Carnegie Mellon University Software Engineering Institute: https://www.sei.cmu.edu/9.

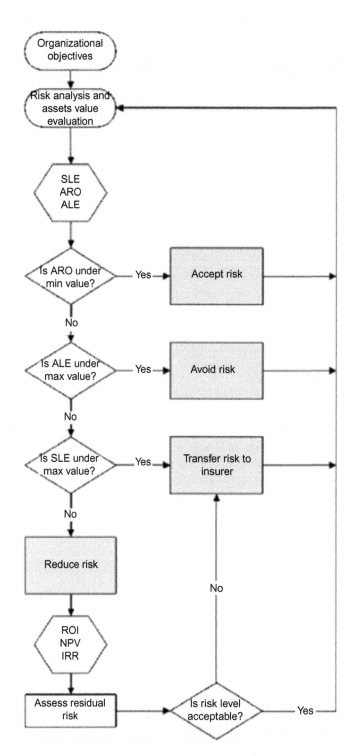

FIGURE 6.3 Decision tree for choosing the risk management option (Bojanc and Jerman-Blazic, 2008).

1. A firm sets up its authentication system to log-off a user if the user fails to enter their user identity and password correctly three times consecutively.
2. Another firm sets the limit to only one incorrect login attempt.

The first configuration will result in fewer improper rejections compared to second, but on the other hand the first firm will fail to recognize a higher number of unauthorized accesses compared to the second scenario because of higher chances of guessing true credentials in the first scenario. The costs associated with a configuration are false positive (Type-I) and false negative (Type-II) costs. These two types of costs can vary widely. Depending on the firm, the cost of a false positive can be much higher than the cost of false negative, or vice versa. Different costs associated with Type-I and Type-II errors require that a firm calibrates its security controls appropriately to balance them. If the cost associated with a false negative is extremely high, the firm may choose a higher level of false positive rate because the value of protected assets through the control is worth the added inconvenience of higher rate of false positives (Cavusoglu et al., 2004).

6.6 DECISION MODEL FOR OPTIMAL RISK MANAGEMENT STRATEGIES

Once residual risk of an entity is determined, a decision model is required for selecting from mainly four cyber risk management options (Bojanc and Jerman-Blazic, 2008):

1. *Risk avoidance*. Avoiding the threats and attacks by eliminating the source of risk or the asset's exposure to the risk. This is usually applied in cases when the severity of the impact of the risk outweighs the benefit that is gained from having or using particular asset, e.g., full open connectivity to the Internet.
2. *Risk mitigation/risk reduction*. Reducing the asset's exposure to the risk by implementing appropriate technologies and tools such as firewall and antivirus systems, etc., or adopting appropriate security policies like passwords, access control and port blocking, etc. Mitigation is the primary risk management strategy.
3. *Risk transfer*. Transferring the risk responsibility by partially shifting the risk to either outsourcing security service provision bodies or buying insurance. This way of transferring the risk is becoming, in the last period, an increasingly important strategy for applying security measures within the organization.
4. *Risk acceptance*. Accepting the security measures as a cost of doing business. Risk retention is a reasonable strategy for risk would be greater over time than the total loss sustained.

In Fig. 6.2, security risk assessments are divided into four regions, which are defined by three boundaries. The first boundary defines the minimum ARO value, under which the risk of threat can be accepted. For example, one could ignore risks with occurrence value less than once in 1000 years. The second boundary is the maximum SLE, above which the impact may have catastrophic consequences. For this type of threat, one possible solution is transferring the risk to insurance company or reducing the occurrence value under the boundary limit. The third boundary is the maximum ALE value, which defines threat avoidance. The remaining risks can be mitigated by security investments. The procedure and the steps in minimisation of security risks are illustrated in Fig. 6.3.

minimizes the risk of fire damage will affect the decisions of his neighbors; airlines may decide not to screen luggage transferred from other carriers who are believed to be careful with security; and people thinking of vaccinating their children against a contagious disease may choose to free-ride off the herd immunity instead. In each case, several widely varying Nash equilibrium outcomes are possible, from complete adoption to total refusal, depending on the levels of coordination between principals.

Katz and Shapiro (1985) famously noted how network externalities affected the adoption of technology. Network effects can also influence the deployment of security technology. The benefit a protection technology provides may depend on the number of users that adopt it. The cost may be greater than the benefit until a minimum number of players adopt. So each decision-maker might wait for others to go first, and the technology never gets deployed. Ozment and Schechter (2006) have analyzed different approaches for overcoming bootstrapping problems faced by those who would deploy security technologies. This challenge is particularly topical. A number of core internet protocols, such as domain name system (DNS) and routing, are considered insecure. More secure protocols exist; the challenge is to get them adopted. Two security protocols that have already been widely deployed, secure shell (SSH) and IPsec, both overcame the bootstrapping problem by providing significant intra-organizational benefits. In the successful cases, adoption could be done one organization at a time, rather than needing most organizations to move at once. The deployment of fax machines also occurred through this mechanism: companies initially bought fax machines to connect their own offices (Anderson and Moore, 2006a).

Taking these factors into account, as Nagaraja and Anderson (2006) point out, this may mean that, in scenarios where there are continual multi-round interactions between attack and defense, e.g., in the case of the protection of an organization's information assets against outside infiltration and attack, there are implications for defensive structures. Localized cliques are better able to align their incentives than larger structures based on concentric rings of defense. They point to examples of this in the real world where political revolutionary organizations set up "cell" structures as a defensive measure, and, in the IT world, the relative fragility of ring-architecture based peer-to-peer architectures (Walker, 2012).

Citing Akerlof's Nobel prize-winning work on the "market for lemons" (Akerlof, 1970), Anderson and Moore point out the significance of information asymmetry, or rather the absence of information, i.e., security investment are designed to an extent to protect against future events about which there exists limited information. This would tend to suggest that there will be investment decisions made on observable characteristics, e.g., price, rather than less readily observable characteristics, such as effectiveness. As a consequence, cheaper, less effective security measures may drive out more expensive, but more effective, ones.

Gordon and Loeb (2002) presented an economic model to determine the optimal amount for an enterprise investment towards protecting a digital asset. This model is such that, for a given potential loss, the optimum amount to spend to protect an information asset does not always increase with an increase in an information set's vulnerability. It indicates that, even within the range of justifiable investments in information security, the maximum amount a risk-neutral firm should spend is only a fraction of the expected loss due to security breaches. For two broad classes of security breach probability functions, this fraction never exceeds 37% of the expected loss. For most cases, however, this fraction is substantially below the 37% level (Gordon and Loeb, 2002). It is shown that for a given potential loss, a firm should not necessarily focus its investments on information sets with the highest vulnerability. Since extremely vulnerable information sets may be inordinately expensive to protect, a firm may be better off concentrating its efforts on information sets with midrange vulnerabilities.

6.2 CURRENT INFORMATION SECURITY/RISK MANAGEMENT BUDGET

According to a 2016 survey, about 40% of financial services in North America alone with more than $1 billion in revenue had budgeted $10 million or more for information security (Office of Financial Research, 2017). During a February 2017 survey, 14% of C-level respondents stated that cyber security accounted for more than 10% of their annual IT budget.[1] Tables 6.1 and 6.2 show more detailed figures on security spending. Table 6.3 shows the drivers and focus areas of money spent.

---

1. https://www.statista.com/statistics/811116/us-consumer-business-cyber-security-budget-percentage/.

- The cumulative effect of incomplete information and ineffective incentivization of security spending may lead to suboptimal investment decisions. Information security cannot be effectively accounted for without better data. To a certain extent this can be generated within organization, but more robust data sets would come from a sectoral or national view.
- The assessment of cost-effectiveness of security controls. Given a fixed budget, entities should be able to spend in the most cost-effective manner to reduce its information risks (Gordon and Loeb, 2002). The cost-effectiveness justification approach attempts to justify each security controls' costs and benefits to arrive at an optimal mix of security controls (Frosdick, 1997; Cerullo and Cerullo, 2005). This is covered in Chapter 5, Economic Modeling and the Implementation of Effective Mitigating Controls.

Anderson and Moore have flagged a number of key concepts in their work around the economic aspects of information security. Their 2008 paper is a summation of various earlier pieces of their work, and hence forms a useful reference point. There are two fundamental points that underlie much of their work. First of these is that economics and security (Walker, 2012; Anderson and Moore, 2008), historically, have been intimately linked, e.g., wealthy nations could afford larger (or, perhaps more accurately, more effective) armies and navies, and were thus more secure. Secondly, psychology has an immensely important role to play in the economics of information security, as it informs the context in which economic decisions are made, and is pertinent to some observable characteristics of information security.

In their 2006 science article (Anderson and Moore, 2006a), the authors point out that systems are particularly prone to failure when the person guarding them is not the person who bears the entire cost of the failure. This is particularly pertinent in large organizations where there is a clear distinction between the "guard" entity, and the "business" entity. The former is likely to be in the form of a discrete IT or information security function, while the latter is likely to have control over the financial resources required for information security-related investments. This creates misaligned incentives the business stakeholders in an investment will tend to see the investment as a "one off" activity, to be achieved at lowest cost since many benefits accrue to other players.

This underlines the significance of externalities in security investment, as effective protection often depends on the efforts of many actors. At the same time, the benefits of a secure business environment may accrue to many parties. Hence, information security economics displays both positive and negative externalities, and, importantly, network effects (Anderson and Moore, 2006a). A network externality is a network, or a community of software users, that is more valuable to its members the larger it is. This not only helps explain the rise and dominance of operating systems, from System/360 through Windows to Symbian, and of music platforms such as iTunes; it also helps explain the typical pattern of security flaws. Put simply, while platform vendors are building market dominance, they have to appeal to vendors of complementary products as well as to their direct customers; not only does this divert energy that might be spent on securing the platform, but security could get in the way by making life harder for the implementers. So, platform vendors commonly ignore security in the beginning, as they are building their market position; later, once they have captured a lucrative market, they add excessive security in order to lock their customers in tightly (Anderson and Moore, 2006a).

Another instance of externalities can be found when analyzing security investment, as protection often depends on the efforts of many principals. Budgets generally depend on the manner in which individual investment translates to outcomes, but this, in turn, depends not just on the investor's own decisions, but also on the decisions of others.

System reliability can depend on the sum of individual efforts, the minimum effort anyone makes, or the maximum effort any makes. Program correctness can depend on the weakest-link (the most careless programmer introducing a vulnerability) while software validation and vulnerability testing might depend on the sum of everyone's efforts. There can also be cases where the security depends on the best effort—the effort of an individual champion. A simple model by Varian provides interesting results when players choose their effort levels independently. For the total-effort case, system reliability depends on the agent with the highest benefit-cost ratio, and all other agents free-ride. In the weakest-link case, the agent with the lowest benefit-cost ratio dominates. As more agents are added, systems become increasingly reliable in the total-effort case but increasingly unreliable in the weakest-link case. One of the implications is that software companies should hire more software testers and fewer (but more competent) programmers.

Work such as this has inspired other researchers to consider *interdependent risk*. An influential model by Kunreuther and Heal (2003) notes that the security investments can be strategic complements: an individual taking protective measures creates positive externalities for others that in turn may discourage their own investment. This result has implications far beyond cyber security. The decision by one apartment owner to install a sprinkler system that

Chapter 7

Kilogram of Cyber Risk: Introducing Bitmort and Hekla

Chapter Outline

7.1 Risk Metrology	**117**	
7.1.1 History of Metrology	117	
7.1.2 Traceability and Calibration	119	
7.1.3 Uncertainty	119	
7.1.4 Metrology and Cyber Risk	120	
7.2 Micromort	**120**	
7.2.1 Willingness-to-Pay and Value of a Micromort	120	
7.2.2 Value of a Statistical Life	121	
7.2.3 Microlife	121	
7.3 Value-at-Risk	**122**	
7.4 Introducing Bitmort and Hekla	**123**	
7.5 Risk Calculations	**125**	
7.5.1 Measuring Strength of Controls for Digital Assets Using Bitmort	125	

7.5.2 Measuring Cost-Effectiveness of Controls for Digital Assets Using Bitmort — 125
7.5.3 Articulating an Entity's "Willingness-to-Pay" for Risk Reduction for Digital Assets Using Bitmort — 125
7.5.4 Articulating an Entity's Cyber Risk Limit Using *Hekla* — 125
7.5.5 Articulating an Entity's Cyber Risk Appetite Using *Hekla* — 125
7.5.6 Measuring an Entity's Cyber Risk Pricing Using *Hekla* — 125
7.5.7 Measuring an Entity's Cost of Risk Reduction Using *Hekla* — 125
7.5.8 Measuring an Entity's Cyber Risk Return on Investment Using *Hekla* — 126
7.5.9 Using Bitmort and *Hekla* on a Portfolio of Entities — 126

The heart of science is measurement.

— Erik Brynjolfsson

7.1 RISK METROLOGY

7.1.1 History of Metrology

Metrology is the science of measurement. It establishes a common understanding of units, crucial in linking human activities. The ability to measure alone is insufficient. Standardization is crucial for measurements to be meaningful. The first record of a permanent standard was in 2900 BC, when the royal Egyptian cubit was carved from black granite. The cubit was decreed to be the length of the Pharaoh's forearm plus the width of his hand, and replica standards were given to builders. The success of a standardized length for the building of the pyramids is indicated by the lengths of their bases differing by no more than 0.05%.

Modern metrology has its roots in the French Revolution's political motivation to standardize units in France, when a length standard taken from a natural source was proposed. This led to the creation of the decimal-based metric system in 1795, establishing a set of standards for other types of measurements. To ensure conformity between the countries, the Bureau International des Poids et Mesures (BIPM) was established by the meter convention. The metric system was modernized with the creation of the International System of Units (SI) as a result of a resolution at the 11th Conference Generale des Poids et Mesures (CGPM) in 1960.

Digital Asset Valuation and Cyber Risk Measurement. DOI: https://doi.org/10.1016/B978-0-12-812158-0.00007-7

Metrology is divided into three basic overlapping activities:

1. *The definition of units of measurement.* The SI defines seven base units: length, mass, time, electric current, thermodynamic temperature, amount of substance, and luminous intensity. By convention, each of these units are considered to be mutually independent. However, in reality, they are interdependent given some definitions contain other base SI units. All other SI units are derived from the seven base units as shown in Table 7.1.
2. *The realization of these units of measurement in practice.* Three possible methods of realization are defined in the International Vocabulary of Metrology (VIM):
   - A physical realisation of the unit from its definition, for example, meter.
   - A highly-reproducible measurement as a reproduction of the definition.
   - The use of a material object as the measurement standard, for example, until 20 May 2019, the kilogram remains defined by a platinum alloy cylinder, the International Prototype Kilogram, informally Le Grand K or IPK, manufactured in 1889, and carefully stored in Saint-Cloud, a suburb in Paris.
3. *Linking measurements made in practice to the reference standards.* A standard is an object, system, or experiment with a defined relationship to a unit of measurement of a physical quantity. Standards are the fundamental reference for a system of weights and measures by realizing, preserving, or reproducing a unit against which measuring devices can be compared. There are three levels of standards in the hierarchy of metrology:
   - *Primary standards* (the highest quality) do not reference any other standards.
   - *Secondary standards* are calibrated with reference to a primary standard.
   - *Working standards*, used to calibrate (or check) measuring instruments or other material measures, are calibrated with respect to secondary standards. The hierarchy preserves the quality of the higher standards.

These overlapping activities are used in varying degrees by three basic sub-fields of metrology:

4. *Scientific metrology* is concerned with the establishment of units of measurement, the development of new measurement methods, the realization of measurement standards, and the transfer of traceability from these standards to users in a society. This type of metrology is considered the top level of metrology which strives for the highest degree of accuracy. BIPM maintains a database of the metrological calibration and measurement capabilities of institutes around the world. These institutes, whose activities are peer-reviewed, provide the fundamental reference points for metrological traceability.
5. *Applied, technical, or industrial metrology* is concerned with the application of measurement to manufacturing and other processes and their use in society, ensuring the suitability of measurement instruments, their calibration and quality control. Producing good measurements is important in industry as it has an impact on the value and quality of the end product, and a 10%−15% impact on production costs. Recognition of the metrological competence in

TABLE 7.1 SI Units

Base Quantity	Name	Symbol	Definition
Length	meter	m	The length of the path traveled by light in a vacuum during a time interval of 1/299792458 of a second.
Mass	kilogram	kg	The mass of the international prototype kilogram (IPK).
Time	second	s	The duration of 9192631770 periods of the radiation corresponding to the transition between the two hyperfine levels of the ground state of the cesium-133 atom.
Electric current	ampere	A	A constant current which, if maintained in two straight parallel conductors of infinite length and negligible circular cross-section, placed 1 m apart in a vacuum, would produce a force equal to 2×10^{-7} newtons per meter.
Thermodynamic temperature	kelvin	K	The fraction 1/273.16 of the thermodynamic temperature of the triple point of water.
Amount of substance	mole	mol	The amount of substance of a system which contains as many elementary entities as there are atoms in 0.012 kg of carbon-12.
Luminous intensity	candela	cd	The luminous intensity, in a given direction, of a source emitting monochromatic radiation of a frequency of 540×1012 Hz with a radiant intensity in that direction of 1/683 Watt per steradian.

industry can be achieved through mutual recognition agreements, accreditation, or peer review. Industrial metrology is important to a country's economic and industrial development as well as the condition of a country's industrial-metrology program indicates its economic status.

6. *Legal metrology* concerns activities which result from statutory requirements and concern measurement, units of measurement, measuring instruments, and methods of measurement and are performed by competent bodies. Such statutory requirements may arise from the need for protection of health, public safety, the environment, enabling taxation, protection of consumers, and fair trade. The Western European Legal Metrology Cooperation (WELMEC) was established in 1990 to promote cooperation in the legal metrology in the European union. In the United States, legal metrology is under the authority of National Institute of Standards and Technology (NIST).

7.1.2 Traceability and Calibration

Metrological traceability is defined as the property of a measurement result whereby the result can be related to a reference through a documented, unbroken chain of calibrations, each contributing to the measurement of uncertainty. It permits the comparison of measurements, whether the result is compared to the previous result in the same laboratory, a measurement result from a year ago, or to the result of a measurement performed anywhere else in the world. The chain of traceability allows any measurement to be referenced to higher levels of measurements back to the original definition of the unit.

Traceability is most often obtained by calibration, establishing the relationship between an indication on a measuring instrument (or secondary standard) and the value of the standard. A calibration is an operation that establishes a relation between a measurement standard with a known measurement uncertainty and the device that is being evaluated. The process will determine the measurement value and uncertainty of the device that is being calibrated and create a traceability link to the measurement standard (JCGM, 2008). The four primary reasons for calibrations are: (1) to provide traceability; (2) to ensure that the instrument (or standard) is consistent with other measurements; (3) to determine accuracy; and (4) to establish reliability (French College of Metrology, 2006). Traceability works in a pyramid structure. At the top level there are the international standards, at the next level national metrology institutes calibrate the primary standards through realization of the units creating the traceability link from the primary standard and the unit definition (WMO, 2017). Through subsequent calibrations between national metrology institutes, calibration laboratories, and industry and testing laboratories the realization of the unit definition is propagated down through the pyramid (WMO, 2017). The traceability chain works upwards from the bottom of the pyramid, where measurements done by industry and testing laboratories can be directly related to the unit definition at the top through the traceability chain created by calibration (NPL, 2010).

7.1.3 Uncertainty

Measurement uncertainty is a value associated with a measurement which expresses the spread of possible values associated with the measurand—a quantitative expression of the doubt existing in the measurement (Eurolab, 2006). There are two components to the uncertainty of a measurement (NPL, 2010):

- *Uncertainty interval* is a range of values that the measurement value is expected to fall within.
- *Confidence level* is how likely the true value is to fall within the uncertainty interval.

Uncertainty is generally expressed as follows (Euramet, 2008):

$$Y = y \pm U$$
$$\text{Coverage factor:} \quad k = 2$$

Where y is the measurement value and U is the uncertainty value and k is the coverage factor,[1] which indicates the confidence interval. The upper and lower limit of the uncertainty interval can be determined by adding and subtracting the uncertainty value from the measurement value. The coverage factor of $k = 2$ generally indicates a 95% confidence that the measured value will fall inside the uncertainty interval (French College of Metrology, 2006). Other values of k can be used to indicate a greater or lower confidence on the interval. For example $k = 1$ and $k = 3$ generally indicate 66% and 99.7% confidence, respectively (NPL, 2010). The uncertainty value is determined through a combination of statistical analysis of the calibration and uncertainty contribution from other errors in the measurement process, which can be evaluated from sources such as the instrument history, manufacturer's specifications, or published information.

---

1. Equivalent to standard deviation if the uncertainty distribution is normal

7.1.4   Metrology and Cyber Risk

Two established systems of risk measures are introduced in this book. They are micromort in medicine and value-at-risk (VaR) in finance. They are both considered applied metrology. Cyber risk as an emerging risk has no known measures. The thinking behind micromort and VaR are applied to cyber in this book and a set of risk units, bitmort and hekla, are proposed as measures for cyber risk. This book is the first book that provides a comprehensive theory built around novel cyber risk measurement units.

7.2   MICROMORT

Micromort is a unit of microrisk.

1 micromort is defined as 1 in 1 million probability of death.

During the 1970s, risk assessment was a field of interest for statisticians and actuaries alike. These professionals set out to develop a mathematical model that would determine exactly how risky a particular activity might be. Ronald A. Howard, a professor at Stanford University, is the birth father of the term that came to be known as the micromort. Broken down, the creation is simple: "*micro*" meaning small and "*mort*" deriving from the Latin word for death, thus simply put, a micromort came to be the tiny measure of "potential deadliness." Howard created the risk unit to help inform patients about the risks of medical conditions or treatments and to consider those risks in making medical decisions (Howard, 1989) as he wrote: "It appears that many people consider probabilities less than one in 100 to be too small to worry about." The concept of the micromort was to provide a mathematical way to compare the risk of a variety of different activities. The purpose behind coining a term for those exceptionally small risks was to translate them into whole numbers that could be immediately compared.

This description of risk has helped to place various daily activities in perspective. For example, drinking only a couple glasses of wine would accrue a single micromort. An hour spent on canoeing would accrue ten micromorts. Taking a bite out of a juicy hamburger with all the savory additives would record one's lifeline at an extra 0.1 micromorts. People were exposed to 270 micromorts from riding motorbikes in the United States in 1989. Women are exposed to 120 micromorts from giving birth (vaginal). Babies are exposed to 430 micromorts on the day of birth from being born (Walker et al., 2014).

1 micromort roughly equals:

- Traveling 9.7 km by motorbike (accident) (Spiegelhalter, 2009).
- Traveling 27 km by walking (accident).
- Traveling 370 km by car (accident).
- Traveling 19,000 km by jet in the United States (terrorism).
- Drinking 0.5 L of wine (cirrhosis of the liver) (Howard, 1989).
- Smoking 1.4 cigarettes (cancer, heart disease) (Howard, 1989).
- Living 2 days in New York or Boston in 1979 (air pollution) (Howard, 1989).
- Drinking Miami water for 1 year (cancer from chloroform) (Howard, 1989).
- Eating 100 charcoal-broiled steaks (cancer) (Howard, 1989).
- Eating 40 tablespoons of peanut butter.

Micromorts are best used to measure the size of acute risks, i.e., immediate deaths. Risks from lifestyle, exposure to air pollution, and so on, are chronic risks in that they do not kill straight away, but reduce life expectancy. Howard (1989) included such risks in his original 1979 work. Some more applications of micromort are shown in Table 7.2.

7.2.1   Willingness-to-Pay and Value of a Micromort

Another application of the micromort framework is to measure people's "willingness-to-pay" to avoid them, e.g., how much they are willing to pay for safety features on cars:

The value of 1 micromort is defined as the amount of money a person is willing to pay to avoid 1 micromort.

This value is around $50 in 2009 (Howard, 1989; Russell and Norvig, 2009). This is the most interesting attribute of micromort. It means that it is both an objective and subjective measure. However, utility functions are often not linear, i.e., the more a person has already spent on their safety the less they are willing to spend to further increase their safety. Therefore, the $50 valuation should not be taken to mean that a human life (1 million micromorts) is valued at

TABLE 7.2 Applications of Micromort

Death From	Context	Time Period	N Death	N Population	MMs per Unit of Exposure	Reference
All causes	US	2010	2,468,435	308,500,000	22 per day, 8000 per year	Murphy et al. (2013)
All causes	Canada	2011	242,074	33,476,688	20 per day, 7200 per year	Statistics Canada (2015)
Non-natural cause	US	2010	180,000	308,500,500	1.6 per day, 580 per year	Murphy et al. (2013)
All causes— first year of life	US	2013			16.7 per day, 6100 per year	National Center for Health Statistics (2013), Blastland and Spiegelhalter (2014)
Scuba diving	US-insured members of DAN	2000–06	187	1,131,367 members	164 per year as member of DAN, 5 per dive	DAN (2014)
Skydiving	US	2000–16	413	48,600,000 jumps	8 per jump	USPA (2018)
Running marathon	US	1975–2004	26	3,300,000 runs	7 per run	Kipps et al. (2011)

$50,000,000. Furthermore, the local linearity of any utility curve means that the micromort is useful for small incremental risks and rewards, not necessarily for large risks (Russell and Norvig, 2009).

Of course, depending on risk appetite and financial affordability, different individuals can price the same risk differently. Today, micromort has also been used to measure cost-effectiveness of countermeasures. Governments around the world price the reduction of 1 micromort differently, e.g., the UK Department of Transport prices the reduction of 1 micromort at £1.60,[2] while the US Department of Transport prices the same at $6.20 (US Department of Transportation, 2011).

7.2.2 Value of a Statistical Life

Government agencies use a nominal value of a statistical life (VSL)—or value for preventing a fatality—to evaluate the cost-effectiveness of expenditure on safeguards. United States Environmental Protection Agency uses VSL to express the benefits of mortality risk reductions in monetary terms cost benefit analyses of its rules and regulations. In the UK the VSL stands at £1.6 million for road improvements.[3]

7.2.3 Microlife

A microlife is a unit of risk representing half an hour change of life expectancy (Spiegelhalter, 2012):

A daily loss or gain of 30 minutes can be termed a microlife, because 1 000 000 half hours (57 years) roughly corresponds to a lifetime of adult exposure.

Microlives are intended as a simple way of communicating the impact of a lifestyle or environmental risk factor, based on the associated daily proportional effect on expected length of life. Similar to the micromort, the microlife is intended for rough but fair comparisons between the sizes of chronic risks (Spiegelhalter, 2012). This is to avoid the biasing effects of describing risks in relative hazard ratios, converting them into somewhat tangible units. Similarly, they bring long-term future risks into the here-and-now as a gain or loss of time. The microlife exploits that for small hazard ratios the change in life expectancy is roughly linear (Haybittle, 1998). They are by necessity rough estimates, based on averages over population and lifetime. Effects of individual variability, short-term or changing habits, and causal factors are not taken into account. Some applications of microlife are shown in Table 7.3.

---

2. Department for Transport GMH, United Kingdom. TAG Unit 3.4: The Safety Objective. Retrieved from: http://www.dft.gov.uk/webtag/documents/expert/unit3.4.1.php

3. Department for Transport GMH, United Kingdom. Retrieved from: http://www.dft.gov.uk/webtag/documents/expert/unit3.4.1.php

TABLE 7.3 Application of Microlife

Risk Factor	Men	Women
Smoking		
Smoking 15–24 cigarettes	−10	−9
Alcohol intake		
First drink (of 10 g alcohol)	1	1
Each subsequent drink (up to 6)	−½	−1
Obesity		
Per 5 units above body mass index of 22.5 each day	−3	−3
Per 5 kg above optimum weight for average height each day	−1	−1
Sedentary behavior		
2 h watching television	−1	−1
Diet		
Red meat, 1 portion (85 g, 3 oz)	−1	−1
Fruit and vegetable intake, 5 servings (blood vitamin C > 50 nmol/L)	4	3
Coffee intake		
2–3 cups	1	1
Physical activity		
First 20 min of moderate exercise	2	2
Subsequent 40 min of moderate exercise	1	½
Statins		
Taking a statin	1	1
Air pollution		
Per day living in Mexico City versus London	−½	−½
Geography		
Per day being a resident of Russia versus Sweden	−21	−9
Era		
Per day living in 2010 versus 1910	15	15
Per day living in 2010 versus 1980	8	5

7.3 VALUE-AT-RISK

Value-at-risk (VaR) is a measure of the maximum potential change in value of a portfolio of financial instruments with a given probability over a pre-set horizon (RiskMetrics, 1995):

> *For a given portfolio, time horizon, and probability p, the p VaR is defined as threshold loss value, such that the probability that the loss on the portfolio over the given time horizon exceeds this value is p.*

There are three ways in which VaR can be measured:

1. *Covariance approach.* Assuming that the returns generated by exposure to multiple market risks are normally distributed, a variance–covariance matrix of all standardized instruments representing various market risks can be used to estimate the standard deviation in portfolio returns and compute the VaR from this standard deviation.
2. *Historical simulation.* VaR can be computed from running a portfolio through historical data, i.e., a historical simulation, and estimated from the probability that the losses exceed specified values.

3. *Monte Carlo simulation.* Assuming return distributions for each of the individual market risks, VaR can be computed from running a Monte Carlo simulation.

Each measure comes with its own pluses and minuses. The variance−covariance approach is simple to implement, but the normality assumption can be tough to sustain. Historical simulations assume that the past time periods used are representative of the future and Monte Carlo simulations are time and computation intensive. All three yield VaR measures that are estimates and subject to judgment.

VaR can be traced as far back as the capital requirements for the New York Stock Exchange imposed on member firms back in 1922, but blossomed into relevance with measuring market risk used in banks and other financial service firms in the 1990s (Holton, 2002). Its usage in these firms has been driven by the failure of the risk tracking systems used until the early 1990s to detect dangerous risk taking on the part of traders and it offered a key benefit: a measure of capital at risk under extreme conditions in trading portfolios that could be updated on a regular basis.

Origins of this development are not mathematical, Leavens (1945), who published this theory in 1945, offered a quantitative example which is questioned to be the first VaR ever to be published. Markowitz (1952) and Roy (1952) both published similar VaR measures in 1950s, working toward creating a means of selecting portfolios that would, in some cases, optimize reward for a given level of risk. Each publication proposed VaR measures that included covariances between risk factors that make it able to reflect hedging and diversification effects. Because of the limited availability of processing power, VaR measures from this period were largely theoretical, and were published primarily in the context of the emerging portfolio theory (Holton, 2002).

In 1989, J. P. Morgan introduced an analytical tool, RiskMetrics, to compute VaR (Guldimann, 2000) using data points established in the bank. In 1992, RiskMetrics was made freely available to all market participants and popularized the usage of VaR. Today, VaR is the standard measure of financial market risk it is commonly used by both financial and non-financial firms. It took the financial services industry 30 years to refine VaR to the point where it is useful and trustworthy.

However, VaR also has its limitations. Berkowitz and O'Brien (2001) found that forecasts showed difficulties in large-scale VaR models. Taking the global trading portfolios of large trading banks as an example, thousands of positions with thousands of market risk factors that relate to interest rates, exchange rates, equity and commodity prices, given a large number of positions and risk factors in addition to generating daily forecasts, it's a no wonder it is impossible for the structure of the models to accurately measure correlation between the many market risk factors with trading positions. Estimates that correlate with risk structure must be considered rough approximations. While the end result gives representation to a wide range of potential risks, the various compromises dampen any advantage in forecasting aggregated portfolio risk.

Following a proposal by World Economic Forum, the concept of VaR has been applied to the cyber context, called Cyber VaR. More on Cyber VaR is covered in Chapter 5, Economic Modeling and the Implementation of Effective Mitigating Controls, and Chapter 6, The Point of Diminishing Return on Cyber Risk Investment.

7.4 INTRODUCING BITMORT AND HEKLA

In this book, attributes of established risk measures VaR and micromort are applied to the definition of cyber risk units. In Table 7.4, a comparison is made between the needs for cyber risk measurement and the applications of micromort.

A Class D asset is any type of digital asset as listed in International Digital Asset Classification (IDAC), and it is one type of valuable asset in entity E's digital asset inventory.

TABLE 7.4 Comparing the Need of Cyber Risk Measurement With Application of Micromort

Needs of Cyber Risk Measurement	Applications of Micromort
To measure the effect of control factors on the probabilities of class D assets losing their value.	Micromort measures the effect of day-to-day activities (modifiable risk factors) on the probability of human death.
To articulate entity E's "willingness-to-pay" for the reduction of risk of class D assets.	The value of micromort reflects the "willingness-to-pay" for the reduction of risk.
To measure cost of controls to reduce risk exposure of class D assets.	The cost of reducing 1 micromort reflects the cost-effectiveness of countermeasures to reduce risk.

Based on this comparison, attributes of micromort can be borrowed to define a cyber risk measurement. However, differences between the nature of human mortality risk and "digital mortality" risk must be taken into consideration. Firstly, micromort was created on the basis that human death is a certain event with a probability of 1. It has been applied based on statistics of all causes (both natural and non-natural) to human death, including suicide. In comparison, the economic lifespan of digital assets can be eternal with the recent breakthrough in digital storage capability (The Daily Beast, 2016). This definition is used in this book:

"Digital death" is defined as a binary condition when a digital asset loses all of its economic value.

Currently, the majority of digital assets will eventually "die," either "naturally" through retirement or replacement, or "non-naturally" due to external threats, such as the compromise of its confidentiality, integrity, and availability. The impact of economic lifespan is further analyzed in Chapter 9, Principles of Cybernomics. In this book, cyber risk measures are defined based on the following assumption:

Assumption 1: All classes of digital assets will eventually reach a state of "digital death" and lose all of their economic value.

Secondly, different classes of digital assets are exposed to different inherent risks. So, each class of digital assets should have its own set of microrisks, similar to if we were to track microrisks for all organisms and not only humans. We have not yet tracked microrisks of any other organisms so we cannot draw any comparisons. Nevertheless, all digital assets are made of bits, just like all organisms are made of cells. How different fundamental inherent factors are for different classes of digital assets is left for further discussion in Chapter 9, Principles of Cybernomics. In this book, cyber risk measures are defined based on the following assumption:

Assumption 2: The inherent differences between different classes of digital assets are distinct enough for their risks to be monitored and analyzed separately.

Based on the two assumptions above, Bitmort$_D$ (BM$_D$) is defined as follows for class D assets:

Bitmort$_D$ (BM$_D$) for a given class D digital assets is 1 in a million probability of its digital death, i.e., a binary condition when the asset loses all of its economic value. The value of 1 BM$_D$ is the amount of money an entity is willing to pay to reduce 1 BM$_D$ for its class D assets.

The same scale of million is chosen for bitmort (BM) based on the following facts:

- There were 707,509,815 data records lost globally in 2015[4] out of an estimated population of 95,100,000,000 total records (3.17 billion Internet users in 2015[5] with an average of 30 online records per person[6]), which is roughly a probability of 0.0074.
- There were a total number of 499,331 recorded deaths in England and Wales in 2012 out of a population of 56,567,000,[7] which is a probability of 0.0088.

Because there is no way to decide what scale to use without substantial loss data collected for different types of digital assets, the scale of million is sufficient as a start. It can always be scaled up or down, similar to byte−megabyte−gigabyte and meter−centimeter−millimeter.

When residual risk measured in BM becomes statistically available for various types of digital assets, it is possible to aggregate them along with asset value to generate a Cyber VaR curve, representing the entity's residual cyber risk:

$$\text{VaR} = \sum_{i=1}^{n} V_i f_{D_i}$$

where VaR is value at risk for all digital assets of an entity E; entity E's digital asset inventory $D = \{D_1, D_2, \ldots, D_n\}$; the value of each asset $V = \{V_1, V_2, \ldots, V_n\}$; and f_{D_i} is the amount of residual risk D_i is exposed to be measured in BM$_{D_i}$s.

---

4. 2015 Data Breach Statistics − Breach Level Index Findings (2015). Retrieved from: http://www.safenet-inc.com/resources/data-protection/2015-data-breaches-infographic/
5. Number of Internet users worldwide from 2005 to 2015. Retrieved from: http://www.statista.com/statistics/273018/number-of-internet-users-worldwide/
6. Based on expert judgement.
7. Office for National Statistics Deaths, 2013. Registered in England and Wales (Series DR). Retrieved, June, 2014, from: https://www.ons.gov.uk/peoplepopulationandcommunity/birthsdeathsandmarriages/deaths/bulletins/deathsregisteredinenglandandwalesseriesdr/2013-10-22

To compute the Cyber VaR curve, historical simulation and Monte Carlo simulation can be used. Under historical simulation, BMs are extracted under a number of different historical time windows which are defined by the entity. While historical simulation measures risk by replicating one specific historical path of cyber risk ecosystem, Monte Carlo simulation attempts to generate a large number of paths using repeated random sampling to produce a probability distribution.

The risk measure *hekla* is defined as follows:

hekla is a probability, where a 12-month hekla VaR is the loss limit an entity can afford from cyber incidents. The value of hekla is the amount of money the entity is willing to pay to reduce its hekla by 1% for the same loss limit.

The time horizon of 12 months is chosen to reflect cyber risk exposure over one financial year, which should be considered in budget planning and integrated with enterprise risk management (ERM) frameworks.

7.5 RISK CALCULATIONS

Given Company A's digital asset inventory $D = \{D_1, D_2, \ldots, D_n\}$, D_1 being regulated PII. Section below demonstrates how BM and *hekla* are used for risk calculation.

7.5.1 Measuring Strength of Controls for Digital Assets Using Bitmort

In Company A, the implementation of firewall can reduce risk exposure of D_1 by f BM_{D_1}s, and not having appointed a CISO can increase the same by c BM_{D_1}s.

7.5.2 Measuring Cost-Effectiveness of Controls for Digital Assets Using Bitmort

It costs Company A $5000 using solution X and $10,000 using solution Z to reduce risk exposure of D_1 by 1 BM_{D_1}. Therefore, solution X is more cost-effective than solution Z.

7.5.3 Articulating an Entity's "Willingness-to-Pay" for Risk Reduction for Digital Assets Using Bitmort

Company A prices the reduction of 1 BM_{D_1} from the risk exposure of D_1 in the tens of cents per record.

7.5.4 Articulating an Entity's Cyber Risk Limit Using *Hekla*

The maximum loss amount Company A can tolerate from cyber incidents is a 12-month 7% VaR of $100 million (or 10% of its total revenue) from cyber loss. This means Company A's cyber loss limit is $100 million (or 10% of its total capital), with a *hekla* of 7%.

7.5.5 Articulating an Entity's Cyber Risk Appetite Using *Hekla*

Company A's cyber risk appetite is a *hekla* of maximum 4% where the 12-months *hekla* VaR is $100 million (its risk limit).

7.5.6 Measuring an Entity's Cyber Risk Pricing Using *Hekla*

If Company A is willing to spend $10 million to bring its *hekla* from 7% down to 6% with the same loss limit, it means Company A prices its own *hekla* at $10 million.

7.5.7 Measuring an Entity's Cost of Risk Reduction Using *Hekla*

If in practice, it takes Company A $15 million to reduce its *hekla* from 7% to 6% with the same loss limit, then the cost of the reducing *hekla* by 1% in Company A is $15 million.

7.5.8 Measuring an Entity's Cyber Risk Return on Investment Using *Hekla*

Company B's digital value composition is >95% similar to Company A's. Therefore, Company B has similar inherent cyber risk exposure as Company A, and it follows the same process to compute its *hekla*. Due to different ways of control implementation, the cost of reducing *hekla* by 1% in Company B is $5 million whereas it costs Company A $15 million to do the same. Thus, Company B is more cost-effective than Company A in managing its cyber risk. Cyber risk return on investment is essentially the reduction of *hekla* per every dollar spend.

7.5.9 Using Bitmort and *Hekla* on a Portfolio of Entities

BM and *hekla* are measures that can be "stacked" on the portfolio level. All applications of BM and *hekla* can be applied on a portfolio of entities and on the macroeconomic level.

Chapter 8

Three Views of Cybernomics: Entity View, Portfolio View, and Global View

Chapter Outline

8.1 Cybernomics 127
8.2 Portfolio Level 127
  8.2.1 Supplier Risk 127
  8.2.2 Systemic Risk 129
    8.2.2.1 Systemic Cyber Risk in Financial Services Sector 129
    8.2.2.2 Systemic Cyber Risk in Transportation Sector 130
    8.2.2.3 Systemic Cyber Risks in the Healthcare Sector 131
  8.2.3 National Digital Strategies and Policies 132
  8.2.4 Cyber Regulations 132
    8.2.4.1 General Data Protection Regulation 132
    8.2.4.2 NIS Directive 133
    8.2.4.3 Cybersecurity Act of 2015 133
    8.2.4.4 FISMA Reform 133
    8.2.4.5 Gramm–Leach–Bliley Act 134
    8.2.4.6 Health Insurance Portability and Accountability Act 134
8.3 Global Level 134
  8.3.1 Major Infrastructural Cyber Threats 134
    8.3.1.1 Major Worms 134
    8.3.1.2 Cyber Terrorism 136
    8.3.1.3 Mega Data Breaches 136
    8.3.1.4 Privacy Concerns of Technology Giants 137
  8.3.2 Risk Data Schemes and Data Sharing: Barriers and Solutions 137
  8.3.3 Cyber Infrastructure as a Public Good and the Privatization of the Internet 138
8.4 Three Views of Cybernomics 138
  8.4.1 Entity Level 138
  8.4.2 Portfolio Level 139
  8.4.3 Global Level 140

You must look within for value but must look beyond for perspective.

— Denis Waitley

8.1 CYBERNOMICS

Built around value, control, risk, return, and especially bitmort (BM) and hekla introduced in previous chapters, cybernomics is an area of study that integrates cyber risk management and economics to study the requirements of a databank in order to improve risk analytics solutions for: (1) the valuation of digital assets; (2) the measurement of risk exposure of digital assets; and (3) the capital optimization for managing residual cyber risk. Establishing adequate, holistic, and statistically robust data points on the entity, portfolio, and global levels for the development of a cybernomic databank is essential for the resilience of our shared digital future.

In previous chapters, cybernomic challenges and solutions on the entity level were discussed. This chapter discusses these issues on portfolio and global levels. In this book, entity ("micro") level includes any enterprises, establishment, organization, worker, household, or individual. Portfolio ("macro") level includes any industries, sectors, nation states, geo-regions, and supply chains.

8.2 PORTFOLIO LEVEL

8.2.1 Supplier Risk

The concept of supply chain came through business management and was first described by Michael Porter in 1985. A supply chain is the network of all the individuals, organizations, resources, activities, and technology involved in the creation and sale of a product, from the delivery of source materials from suppliers to the manufacturer, through to its eventual delivery to the end user. The supply chain segment involved with getting the finished product from the manufacturer to the consumer is known as the distribution channel. In sophisticated supply chain systems, used products may re-enter the supply chain at any point where residual value is recyclable. Supply chains link value chains. A value chain is a set of activities that a firm operating in a specific industry performs in order to deliver a valuable product or service for the market. In a supply chain, the closer to the end user a function or firm is, the further downstream it is said to be. For example, raw material extraction or production are elements of the supply chain considered to be upstream. Supply chain management is a crucial process because an optimized supply chain results in lower costs and a faster production cycle. As globalization continues, supply chain efficiencies are becoming more and more optimized.

Cyber security within the supply chain is a subset of supply chain security and is focused on the management of cyber security requirements for information technology systems, software, and networks through the entire supply chain. Typical supply chain cyber security activities for minimizing risks include buying only from trusted vendors, disconnecting critical machines from outside networks, and educating users on the threats and protective measures they can take. According to NIST (2015), current key cyber supplier risks include:

- Third party service providers or vendors, from janitorial services to software engineering, with physical or virtual access to information systems, software code, or Internet Protocol (IP).
- Poor information security practices by lower-tier suppliers.
- Compromised security vulnerabilities in supply chain management or supplier systems.
- Counterfeit hardware or hardware with embedded malware.
- Third-party data storage or data aggregators.

Some of the key challenges to cyber supplier risk management include (McKinsey, 2013) the following.

1 Lack of Comprehensive Inventory of Suppliers

Regulators now expect organizations to know their third parties, how each of them interacts with consumers, and what activities it performs. Many firms do not have this information readily available. Supplier databases can be incomplete, and some of the most sensitive risks can reside in relationships that are not found in them. Cobranded partnerships, joint ventures, sponsorships, and similar relationships can account for up to 80% of the spending that some business units assign to suppliers. But these relationships are often managed in ways that emphasize commercial goals, with only a secondary focus on risk. Furthermore, in some firms individual business units have different ways of tracking their suppliers, making it difficult to compare and collate them across an entire organization. An effective database of third parties should include any noncustomer entity with which an organization has a business relationship.

2 Lack of Comprehensive Catalogue of Supplier Risks

Many organization today do not have an essential process established to identify the true drivers of its supplier risks and guide its mitigation program. To monitor consumer risk successfully, organizations must develop a comprehensive catalogue of these risks, also known as breakpoints, which form the basis for scorecards, audit routines, and other monitoring activities. Consider one breakpoint for a third-party call centre: if there is a risk that agents will misrepresent product information to customers, a bank may investigate this specific problem by having calls monitored and may request regular reports on their quality and on customer-escalation metrics. Identifying the relevant breakpoints for each category of suppliers and determining the relative weight and importance of every breakpoint can be challenging. Building a master register of breakpoints and their associated risk weights for all of these categories can help. Although broadly relevant to most firms, the master register can be adapted to the particular circumstances of an individual organization and its unique third-party relationships.

3 Onerous and Resource Intensive Processes

Once a firm has a complete inventory of third-party suppliers and the risks they pose to customers, the suppliers need to be segmented by risk levels, for example, into high-, medium-, and low-risk categories. Most leading organizations have 200–300 high-risk relationships at a time irrespective of the total number of third parties with which they contract. Specific due-diligence activities are aligned with risk categories identified by the risk-based segmentation, hence a supplier in the high-risk category is subject to all due-diligence investigations which can be overly onerous and resource intensive. It is still challenging to come up with an effective segmentation that can help a firm determine how to utilize its resources strategically.

4   Lack of Integrated Governance and Management Processes

Currently, organizational alignment can be particularly challenging when decision-making rights are spread across a range of businesses and functions, such as procurement, compliance, and operational-risk management. For example, clear, actionable management reports and well-designed workflow systems are essential for accountability across the business units, compliance, and audit. To work well, these tools must track and monitor the relevant data. They also must aid the workflow within and across business units and give managers a clear picture of real-time risk, with action-able recommendations. Most organizations currently have tools that address one or two of these functional needs, but none has a single tool that performs all three.

8.2.2   Systemic Risk

Systemic risk is the risk that an event will trigger a loss of economic value or confidence in, and attendant increases in uncertainty about, a substantial portion of the financial system that is serious enough to quite probably have significant adverse effects on the real economy (European Parliament, 2009). It has already been recognized that cyber risk can be systemic (AIG, 2016). The World Economic Forum (WEF, 2016) published its working definition on systemic cyber risk as:

> *Systemic cyber risk is the risk that a cyber event/attack(s) of other adverse event(s) at an individual component of a critical infrastructure ecosystem will cause significant delay, denial, breakdown, disruption or loss, such that the services are impacted not only in the originating component but consequences also cascade into related (logically and/or geographically) ecosystem components, resulting in significant adverse effects to public health or safety, economic security, or national security. The adverse real economic, safety, and security effects from realized systemic risk are generally seen as arising from significant disruptions to the trust in, or certainty about, services and/or critical data (i.e., the integrity of data), the disruption of operations and, potentially, the incapacitation or destruction of physical assets.*

Our economy's reliance on highly connected and interconnected technology have given rise to the creation of single points of failures such as Society for Worldwide Interbank Financial Telecommunication (SWIFT) systems, as well as complex interdependence and sets of concentrated dependencies. For example, reliance on a diminishing number of large ports in the shipping industry, or as a large number of businesses have grown dependent on software or hardware solutions provided by a small number of outsourcing vendors, should there be a compromise in the confidentiality, integrity, or availability of the data stored by those vendors, ramifications would not only be felt by the customers of those vendors, but also the end users of every business affected.

These vulnerabilities in turn can lead to cascading consequences if the cyber risk is realized. Such cascading consequences can propagate:

- *Sequentially from one system to another.* This potential effect arises when the smooth functioning of one or more systems is conditional on that of another system. An upstream example is a cyber financial system dependent on the continuos availability of electricity.
- *Simultaneously to many systems.* This potential effect stems from many systems depending on other critical systems, or on key service providers, e.g., the financial services, transportation and healthcare sectors all depending on the uninterrupted functioning of position, navigation and timing systems.
- *Beyond systems and their participants to other markets and sectors.* For example, a systemic failure of the financial services sector can have catastrophic effects on economic and national security worldwide.

Three examples of systemic cyber risk on the portfolio level are given below, from the financial services sector, transportation sector and healthcare sector.

8.2.2.1   Systemic Cyber Risk in Financial Services Sector

Financial services represent one of the most connected components of the modern economy. Financial services entities are connected through networks of electronic systems with innumerable entry points. Financial systems are intercon-nected in a variety of ways. Tighter direct relationships between systems, stronger indirect relationships arising from the activities of large financial institutions in multiple systems, and broader commonalities, such as the use of common third-party service providers, e.g., SWIFT, RTGS (Real-Time Gross Settlement), have led to a complex web of inter-connections. While all financial transactions are exposed to a level and variety of risks, payment, clearing and settle-ment arrangements in particular are of fundamental importance for the functioning of the financial system and the

TABLE 8.1 Patterns and Impact of Potential Cyber Systemic Risk in Financial Services Sector

Potential Patterns of Attack	Potential Impact of Systemic Risk
• A number of simultaneous cyber attacks on systemically important institutions and critical/core financial infrastructures. • A large-scale cyber attack on the SWIFT network, potentially coming from a connected institution or directly impacting SWIFT, forcing SWIFT to discontinue the service or shutdown traffic. • A coordinated, simultaneous cyber attack on the RTGS or SWIFT network, resulting in a widespread disruption that could create short-term catastrophic results in a global economy. • A cyber attack on crossing systems or automated trading that could take advantage of trading complexity and capacity, increasing the risk of disorderly markets through the malfunction of algorithmic programs, and the risk of market misconduct, such as unsolicited information leakage and possible market manipulation of "dark pools" (private exchanges for trading securities).	• Failure of an institution's ability to meet its payment or settlement obligations, which could trigger a contagion effect where other financial institutions would not be able to meet their settlement obligations. • Failure or severe or prolonged disruption of a core payment and settlement system, which can be compromised at various endpoints, affecting multiple country and locations' securities markets. • The loss or compromise of the availability and integrity of key financial data. • Widespread loss of trust and confidence in the payment and settlement systems.

conduct of transactions between economic agents in the wider economy. Any significant or prolonged disruption impacting payment, clearing, and settlement arrangements could touch all major aspects of financial risk, such as:

- *Credit risk.* Defaults on obligations within the payment system, imposing direct unexpected loss on other participants.
- *Liquidity risk.* Insufficient liquidity to fulfill settlement obligations.
- *Market risk and business risk.* Other transactional risks, including loss of revenue arising from suspension of payment services due to disruption or insolvency.

Table 8.1 shows some potential patterns of attack and impact of systemic risk in financial services sector.

In a scenario of systemic risk, central banks may be forced to take exceptional measures, such as the injection of liquidity funds, repurchase agreements, guarantees to extend the settlement window, and reductions in the cost of intraday and overnight borrowing.

8.2.2.2 Systemic Cyber Risk in Transportation Sector

The transportation sector includes the systems, networks, assets, people, and vehicles of multiple transportation modes, including aviation, highway and motor carriers, maritime, mass transit and passenger rail, freight rail, and shipping, and can also include pipeline systems. The transportation sector today is a truly global endeavor that plays a key role in the movement of people and goods, underpinning international trade and commerce. Transportation systems also provide lifeline services to communities and are vital to response and recovery operations. For many decades, transportation and logistics companies have invested much of their time and money into ensuring the integrity and reliability of their physical infrastructure and assets. However, relatively less attention has been paid to the possibility of a cyber attack on their IT systems, which, depending on the source of the threat, could have consequences ranging from inconvenient to catastrophic. The risk is very real. IT problems and cyber risks are listed as the top two causes of supply chain disruption (BCI, 2015). Also, large-scale data breaches which could be precursors to disruptive events as attackers can use schematics or supply chain data to systemically disrupt trade and commerce are common in the sector (Verizon, 2013).

The interconnected nature of the transportation sector and its centrality to the efficient functioning of the global economy have meant that the actors in this sector are particularly at risk of systemic attacks that could have consequences that reach far beyond the entity immediately affected. It is clear that transportation systems are very interconnected and interdependent, and that the complex nature of these systems and processes makes it difficult to respond to and isolate issues in case of a coordinated cyber attack. These closer interdependencies have also created additional single points of failure and increased the potential for disruptions to spread quickly and widely across multiple transportation and supply chain networks. The consequences of a potential port closure due to a cyber attack are another example of the effects resulting from concentrated dependency or single point of failure. As shipping has become increasingly channeled through the ever-decreasing number of ports capable of loading and off-loading the largest container ships, single points of failure exist in both physical and online worlds. While an impact of a single cyber attack on an entity within the transportation system is difficult to estimate, given not only the myriad of different methods and objectives the attackers could have, but also the sheer diversity of the sector, it is clear that if an attack were to breach critical systems on which communication nodes for the sector depend, consequences could be catastrophic.

Examining the consequences of systemic cyber attacks in the aviation sector demonstrates the possibility for widespread and cascading consequences. Aircraft design is increasingly reliant on network connectivity and electronic data exchange for efficiency gains, making the industry ever more reliant on the transfer of real-time automated data from ground to aircraft. If the systems were compromised, consequences for the safety of the crew, passengers, and cargo could be disastrous. The same can be said for air traffic control systems or position, navigation and timing systems. In June 2015, the Polish national airline, LOT, announced that it canceled flights due to a cyber attack against the airline's ground computer systems at Warsaw's Okecie airport that left it unable to create flight plans (Security Affairs, 2015).

While malware does not discriminate, it can be developed to target a particular industry. "Zombie Zero" malware represents just such an example and it underscores the growing cyber security risks faced by shippers and their logistics and transportation partners in a wireless, mobile world where technology changes rapidly. Logistics firms use scanners to track shipments, as they are loaded and unloaded from ships, trucks, and airplanes. Zombie Zero targeted the scanners at shipping and logistics firms for over a year. Once an infected scanner was connected to the target's wireless network, it attacked the corporate network and the scanned information, including origin, destination, contents and value, and shipper and recipient information was compromised.

Some of the consequences from systemic cyber risks in the transportation sector could include:

- Increased pressure on other ports and associated infrastructure to cope with redirected throughput.
- Immediate cost and delays as a result of rerouted vessels.
- Subsequent construction project delays.
- Potential manufacturing holdups.
- Delays or even the nonarrival of essential food or health products.
- Financial repercussions at the port and throughout the port's supply chain at the micro and macro levels.

8.2.2.3 Systemic Cyber Risks in the Healthcare Sector

Similar to the transportation and financial industries, the healthcare sector faces a range of risks stemming from its production of critical information and reliance on key infrastructure. The targets are many. Cyber criminals can focus efforts not only on patients, but on healthcare providers, insurers, pharmaceutical manufacturers, and distributors as well. Cyber criminals can use multiple methods of entry, such as phishing, stealing laptops, capitalizing off human error, social engineering and more. According to the US Department of Health and Human Services, 1614 breaches of unsecured protected health information have been reported since 2009, affecting nearly 160 million individuals.[1]

While an increasing number of data breaches, ransomware attacks and individual cyber-related events have been reported by various healthcare-related entities, the healthcare sector's lack of comparative investment in cyber security has resulted in a widespread dearth of foundational security best practices to ensure the confidentiality, integrity and availability of critical and sensitive personal and health-related information. The integrity of medical records can be put into question, potentially resulting in incorrect diagnosis and/or treatment with severe, possibly deadly, consequences to the patient. Attacks on these inherent healthcare system vulnerabilities can emanate from anywhere in the world and can have a profound impact on how routine and emergency care is provided to patients.

Cyber attacks targeting healthcare monitoring devices (Medjacking) emerged in 2015. Security researchers discovered security flaws in the Hospira infusion pump that could remotely force multiple pumps to dose patients with potentially lethal amounts of drugs. In addition to insulin pumps, deadly vulnerabilities were found in dozens of devices, including X-ray systems, CT scanners, medical refrigerators and implantable defibrillators. After the researchers' discovery, the US Department of Homeland Security (DHS) and Federal Drug Administration began warning customers not to use the devices due to the vulnerability.

---

1. Office for Civil Rights, Breach Portal, "Breaches Affecting 500 or More Individuals," available at https://ocrportal.hhs.gov/ocr/breach/breach_report.jsf.

The danger is very real and could include:

- Widespread disruption of network-enabled medical devices like pacemakers or medicine delivery systems.
- Widespread tampering of personal medical information, which could result in patients not receiving needed medications or incorrect dosages resulting in illness or death.
- Altering of environmental controls in patient care facilities, causing patient distress or spoilage of medicines.
- Network disruptions resulting in the unavailability of patient data and history during crucial moments and large-scale medical responses (such as in a pandemic).

8.2.3   National Digital Strategies and Policies

A national cyber security strategy is a plan of actions designed to improve the security and resilience of national infrastructures and services. It is a high-level top—down approach to cyber security that establishes a range of national objectives and priorities that should be achieved in a specific timeframe. Currently, the majority of countries in the world have published their national cyber security strategies. The North Atlantic Treaty Organization (NATO) Cooperative Cyber Defence Centre of Excellence (CCDCOE) maintains a consolidated list of them. The European Union Agency for Network and Information Security (ENISA) also provides an interactive map of all National cyber strategies in Europe.[2]

National cyber security strategies are critical in addressing portfolio level challenges. However, many of the current security strategies are too disjointed and often unintentionally work against addressing the highly-advanced, rapidly evolving security challenges facing the increasingly cyber-dependent critical infrastructures.

8.2.4   Cyber Regulations

A cyber security regulation comprises directives that safeguard information technology and computer systems with the purpose of forcing companies and organizations to protect their systems and information from cyber attacks. Cyber regulations are enforced by governments, or industry regulators such as banking regulators.

Below are some of the current challenges when it comes to cyber regulations:

1. *Delay in the enactment of laws.* Various considerations determine the creation of laws in different countries, so their promulgation depends on a multiplicity of factors, such as political issues or other issues affecting local initiatives. As a result, the ratification of legislation is often postponed.
2. *Laws falling behind in context and time.* The development of standards may often fall far behind the rapid technological advances. Just as organizations continuously update their standards in response to evolving risks and new technologies, the law must be at the forefront when it comes to responding to present and emergent issues which may need to be regulated.
3. *Technical and legal heterogeneity.* Different countries adhere to international or regional conventions differently. Legal and technical disparities make it difficult to respond to, investigate, and rule on cybersecurity incidents, and inhibit international collaboration.
4. *Conflicts of laws and basic principles.* Legislation is generally quite effective when it comes to regulating behaviour. Based on the idea that the Internet is free and has no physical borders, there are cases where although legislation is applied on a national level, constitutional or legal conflicts arise, mainly concerning the meanings and conceptions of privacy and freedom of expression. In this case, the eternal debate between privacy and security may come into play.
5. *Limitations on the scope of application.* The absence of legislation or agreements on specific aspects of certain issues can undermine international collaboration, even within the same territory. Public and private sectors face a challenge when it comes to access to information for investigations, with implications for security, the right to privacy, and commercial interests, mainly of tech companies.

8.2.4.1   General Data Protection Regulation

The European data protection laws have long been regarded as a gold standard all over the world. In 2016 the European Union (EU) adopted the General Data Protection Regulation[3] (GDPR) as it replaces the 1995 Data Protection Directive. As of May 25, 2018, member states were required to ensure that the GDPR is fully implementable in their countries.

---

2. https://www.enisa.europa.eu/topics/national-cyber-security-strategies/ncss-map.
3. General Data Protection Regulation: https://eugdpr.org/.

Household Internet names (e.g., Facebook), health care providers, insurers, banks, *any* company that handles sensitive personal data are all required to be compliant with the new regulation. Below are the specifics regarding the law:

- A presence in an EU country.
- No presence in the EU, but it processes personal data of European residents.
- More than 250 employees.
- Fewer than 250 employees but its data-processing impacts the rights and freedoms of data subjects, is not occasional, or includes certain types of sensitive personal data. That effectively means almost all companies.
- A third-party processor not in compliance means your organization is not in compliance.
- The new regulation also has strict rules for reporting breaches that everyone in the chain must be able to comply with.
- Organizations must also inform customers of their rights under GDPR.

A company could face steep penalties of up to €20 million, or 4% of global annual turnover, whichever is higher, for noncompliance. The reformed regulation also requires companies to notify their users within 72 hours of a data breach. This requirement is strict for many companies. Take the Equifax breach that exposed personal information of nearly 150 million people as an example, the company spent weeks stopping the attack and then figuring out how to contain damage before ever informing the public.

Management consulting firm Oliver Wyman predicts that the EU could collect as much as $6 billion in fines and penalties in the first year. A Pricewaterhousecoopers (PwC) survey showed that 92% of US companies consider GDPR a top data protection priority (PwC, 2017).

8.2.4.2 NIS Directive

As part of the EU Cybersecurity strategy the European Commission proposed the EU Network and Information Security (NIS) Directive. The NIS Directive is the first piece of EU-wide cybersecurity legislation. The goal is to enhance cybersecurity across the EU. The NIS Directive was adopted in 2016 and subsequently, because it is an EU directive, every EU member state has started to adopt national legislation, which follows or "transpose" the directive. EU directives give EU countries some level of flexibility to take into account national circumstances, for example to reuse existing organizational structures or to align with existing national legislation. The NIS Directive has three parts:

1. *National capabilities:* EU member states must have certain national cybersecurity capabilities of the individual EU countries, e.g., they must have a national Computer Security Incident Response Team (CSIRT), perform cyber exercises, etc.
2. *Cross-border collaboration:* Cross-border collaboration between EU countries, e.g., the operational EU CSIRT network, the strategic NIS cooperation group, etc.
3. *National supervision of critical sectors:* EU member states have to supervise the cybersecurity of critical market operators in their country. This include ex-ante supervision critical sectors (energy, transport, water, health, and finance sector, etc.) and ex-post supervision for critical digital service providers (Internet exchange points, domain name systems, etc.)

8.2.4.3 Cybersecurity Act of 2015

At the end of 2015, the United States Congress approved what is known as the Cybersecurity Act of 2015 to protect the country from cyberattacks responsibly and promptly, through a framework promoting the exchange of information between the private sector and the government about computer threats. Under the act, information about a threat found on a system may be shared with the aim of preventing attacks or mitigating risks that may affect other companies, agencies, or users. Through the use of information gathering, security checks and other protective measures, organizations, and governments are able to coordinate intelligence and defensive actions.

8.2.4.4 FISMA Reform

FISMA Reform or FISMA 2014 replaced FISMA (Federal Information Security Management Act) of 2002. The act recognized the importance of information security to the economic and national security interests of the United States. The act requires each federal agency to develop, document, and implement an agency-wide program to provide information security for the information and information systems that support the operations and assets of the agency, including those provided or managed by another agency, contractor, or other source. FISMA explicitly emphasized a "risk-based policy for cost-effective security." FISMA requires agencies to conduct annual reviews of the agency's information security program and report the results to Office of Management and Budget (OMB). OMB uses this data to assist in its oversight responsibilities and to prepare annual report to Congress on agency compliance with the act.

8.2.4.5 Gramm–Leach–Bliley Act

The Gramm–Leach–Bliley Act (GLBA) is also known as the Financial Services Modernization Act of 1999. It removed barriers in the market among banking companies, securities companies, and insurance companies that prohibited any one institution from acting as any combination of an investment bank, a commercial bank, and an insurance company. Title V of GLBA has imposed requirements on the ways in which consumer data is handled by financial services companies. The primary focus of Title V, and the area that has received the most attention, is the sharing of personal data between organizations and their nonaffiliated business partners and agencies. Consumers must be given notice of the ways in which their data is used and must be given notice of their right to opt out of any data-sharing plan. Title V also requires financial services organizations to provide adequate security for systems that handle customer data. Security guidelines require the creation and documentation of detailed data security programs addressing both physical and logical access to data, risk assessment and mitigation programs, and employee training in the new security controls. Third-party contractors of financial services firms are also bound to comply with the GLBA regulations.

8.2.4.6 Health Insurance Portability and Accountability Act

The Health Insurance Portability and Accountability Act (HIPPA) was enacted by the United States Congress in 1996. It was created primarily to modernize the flow of healthcare information, stipulate how personally identifiable information maintained by the healthcare and healthcare insurance industries should be protected from fraud and theft, and address limitations on healthcare insurance coverage. The HIPAA Privacy Rule requires appropriate safeguards to protect the privacy of personal health information, and sets limits and conditions on the uses and disclosures that may be made of such information without patient authorization. The Act provides for substantial penalties for failures to certify or comply with the new standards and operating rules. Saving money by neglecting safety will eventually cost health care providers far more money than they would have spent originally.

8.3 GLOBAL LEVEL

The global, borderless nature of cyber infrastructure means that cyber risk is inherently a global challenge. Today cyber is also viewed by the wider risk community as the risk most likely to intensify in the years to come (Global Risks Report, 2017). Cyber threats can easily have cross-border impact which are difficult to tackle from national and regional levels without broad and effective international collaboration. Multinational technology providers also have great influence in the prevention and response to cyber threats, hence there is a growing concern in how they could be better regulated.

Awareness of the challenges in cyber risk as a global risk is increasing. However, it is still under-resourced in comparison to the potential scale of the threat, a view that is even more compelling when considered in the context of a more familiar issue—natural catastrophes. Analysis suggests that the takedown of a single cloud provider could cause $50−120 billion of economic damage−a loss somewhere between Hurricane Sandy and Hurricane Katrina. While it is not exactly apples to apples, the annual economic cost of cyber risk is now estimated at worth of $1 trillion, a multiple of 2017's record-year aggregate cost of approximately $300 billion from natural disasters (Global Risks Report, 2017).

8.3.1 Major Infrastructural Cyber Threats

8.3.1.1 Major Worms

The term "virus" was first coined by Frederick Cohen in describing self-replicating computer programs in 1984. He defined a virus as "a program that can infect other programs by modifying them to include a possibly evolved copy of itself (Cohen, 1984). A Trojan is a common type of virus. It is a piece of malware that is often disguised as legitimate software. Trojans can be employed by cyber thieves and hackers trying to gain access to users' systems. Users are typically tricked by some form of social engineering into loading and executing Trojans on their systems. Once activated, Trojans can enable cybercriminals to spy on you, steal your sensitive data, and gain backdoor access to your system. These actions can include deleting, blocking, modifying and copying data, as well as disrupting the performance of computers or computer networks. A computer worm is a standalone malware computer program that replicates itself in order to spread to other computers. Often, it uses a computer network to spread itself, relying on security failures on the target computer to access it. Worms almost always cause at least some harm to the network, even if only by consuming bandwidth, whereas viruses almost always corrupt or modify files on a targeted computer. Table 8.2 shows a list of major worms since then that have caused significant financial impact.

TABLE 8.2 Major Worms That Have Caused Significant Financial Impact

	Financial Impact ($)	Description
WannaCry ransomware attack (2017)	Four billion	WannaCry is a ransomware crypto worm which targeted computers by encrypting data and demanding ransom payments in the Bitcoin cryptocurrency.
Tiny Banker Trojan (2016)	Unknown figure	A spoofing worm that uses HTTP injection to force the user's computer to believe that it is on the bank's website. It infected more than two dozen major banking institutions in the United States.
Regin (2014)	Unknown figure	A sophisticated malware and hacking toolkit used by the US National Security Agency (NSA) and its British counterpart, the Government Communications Headquarters (GCHQ), targeting specific users of Microsoft Windows-based computers.
CryptoLocker (2013)	27 million	A ransomware attack using a trojan that encrypts certain types of files stored on local and mounted network drives using RSA public-key cryptography with the private key stored only on the malware's control servers.
Flame (2012)	Unknown figure	A modular computer virus related to Shamoon used for targeted espionage in Middle Eastern countries.
Shamoon (2012)	Unknown figure	A modular computer virus targeting recent 32-bit NT kernel versions of Microsoft Windows. The virus was intended for cyber warfare and was used against the national oil companies of Saudi Arabia. The virus is distinctive in nature due to the cost of attack and recovery.
Duqu (2011)	Unknown figure	A collection of computer malware thought to be related to the Stuxnet worm thought to have been created by Unit 8200.[a]
Stuxnet (2010)	Set back Iran's nuclear program by 2 years	A malicious computer worm targeting SCADA systems and caused substantial damage to Iran's nuclear program. It was believed to be a jointly built American/Israeli cyber weapon.
Daprosy (2009)	Unknown figure	A malicious computer program that spreads via local area network connections, spammed emails and USB mass storage devices.
Conficker (2008)	$9.1 billion	Once a computer was infected, this worm downloaded and installed malware from sites controlled by the hackers, including things like keystroke loggers and remote PC-control software.
MyDoom	38 billion	MyDoom slowed down global internet access by 10%, and caused some website access to be reduced by 50%. The worm contains the text message "andy; I'm just doing my job, nothing personal, sorry," leading many to believe that the worm's creator was paid.
Sobig.F (2003)	$37 billion	The virus stalled or completely crashed internet gateways and email servers, resulting in the merciless slowing down of global internet access. It harvested email addresses from various documents found in the infected computers. The virus then sent itself to these addresses.
ILOVEYOU (2000)	$15 billion	ILOVEYOU is a computer worm sent as an attachment to an email message with the text "ILOVEYOU" in the subject line, leading unsuspecting users to think it was a mere text file. Upon opening the attachment, the worm sent a copy of itself to everyone in the Windows Address Book and with the user's sender address. It also made a number of malicious changes to the user's system. The actual damage occurred during the removal of the infection from computers, as email servers and computer networks had to be shut down before the virus could be removed.
Morris Worm (1988)	Unknown figure	Widely considered the first internet worm and one of the first well-known programs exploiting buffer overflow vulnerabilities.

RSA, Rivest-Shamir-Adleman; *SCADA*, Supervisory Control and Data Acquisition.
[a]*Unit 8200 is an Israeli Intelligence Corps unit responsible for collecting signal intelligence (SIGINT) and code decryption.*

8.3.1.2 Cyber Terrorism

Cyber terrorism is a cyber attack using or exploiting computer or communication networks to cause sufficient destruction or disruption to generate fear or to intimidate a society into an ideological goal (NATO, 2008).

Experienced cyber terrorists who are very skilled in terms of hacking can cause massive damage to government systems, hospital records, and national security programs, which might leave a country, community, or organization in turmoil and in fear of further attacks (Laqueur et al., 2002).

The Baltic state of Estonia was the target of a massive denial-of-service attack that ultimately rendered the country offline and shut out from services dependent on Internet connectivity in April 2007. The infrastructure of Estonia including everything from online banking, mobile phone networks, government services, to access to health care information was disabled. The tech-dependent state experienced severe turmoil.

The cyber attack was a result of an Estonian-Russian dispute over the removal of a bronze statue depicting a World War II-era Soviet soldier from the center of the capital, Tallinn (Hower and Uradnik, 2011). In the midst of the armed conflict with Russia, Georgia likewise was subject to sustained and coordinated attacks on its electronic infrastructure in August 2008. In both of these cases, circumstantial evidence points to coordinated Russian attacks, but attribution of the attacks is difficult and the proof establishing legal culpability is lacking.

In 2008, directly as a result of the attacks, NATO opened a new center of excellence on cyber defense to conduct research and training on cyber warfare in Tallinn (Love, 2011).

The chaos resulting from the attacks in Estonia illustrated to the world the dependence countries had on information technology. This dependence then makes countries vulnerable to future cyber attacks and terrorism (Hower and Uradnik, 2011).

8.3.1.3 Mega Data Breaches

A data breach is a security incident in which sensitive, protected, or confidential data is copied, transmitted, viewed, stolen, or used by an individual unauthorized to do so. Data breaches may involve financial information such as credit card or bank details, personal health information (PHI), personally identifiable information (PII), trade secrets of corporations, or intellectual property. Most data breaches involve over-exposed and vulnerable unstructured data such as files, documents, and sensitive information.

The Yahoo breach disclosed in 2016 may be one of the most expensive today. It may lower the price of its acquisition by Verizon by $1 billion. Historical mega breaches are listed in Table 8.3. It is notoriously difficult to obtain information on direct and indirect value loss resulting from a data breach. A common approach to assess the impact of data breaches is to study the market reaction to such an incident as proxy for the economic consequences. This is typically

TABLE 8.3 Mega Data Breaches

Brand	Number of Accounts	Cause	Year
Yahoo	Three billion user accounts	Hacked	2016
Adult Friend Finder	More than 412.2 million user accounts	Hacked	2016
Massive American business hack (including 7-Eleven and Nasdaq)	160,000,000	Hacked	2012
Adobe Systems	152,000,000	Hacked	2013
Under Armour	150,000,000	Hacked	2018
eBay	145,000,000	Hacked	2014
Equifax	143,000,000	Poor security	2017
Heartland	130,000,000	Hacked	2009
Rambler.ru	98,167,935	Hacked	2009
TK/TJ Maxx	94,000,000	Hacked	2007
MyHeritage	92,283,889	Hacked	2018

conducted through the use of event studies where a measure of the vent's economic impact can be constructed by the security prices observed over a relatively short period of time.

8.3.1.4 *Privacy Concerns of Technology Giants*

The speed at which global technology giants changed the way people lead their lives without being concerned about any roadblocks was remarkable until 2018 when scandals surrounding Facebook started surfacing in such high frequencies that industry observers began questioning if the social media giant with over 2 billion users would be able to survive in the long term.

The Facebook−Cambridge Analytica data scandal involves the collection of personally identifiable information of 87 million Facebook users (Solon, 2018) and reportedly a much greater number more (Hern, 2018) that Cambridge Analytica began collecting in 2014. The data was allegedly used to attempt to influence voter opinion on behalf of politicians who hired them. Following the discovery, Facebook apologized amid public outcry and risen stock prices. The way that Cambridge Analytica collected the data was called "inappropriate" (BBC News, 2018).

In December 2015, The Guardian reported that United States Senator Ted Cruz was using data from this scandal and that the subjects of the data were unaware that companies were selling and politicians were buying their personal information (Davies, 2015). In March 2018, The New York Times, The Guardian, and Channel 4 News made more detailed reports on the data scandal with new information from former Cambridge Analytica employee Christopher Wylie, who provided clearer information about the size of the data collection, the nature of the personal information stolen, and communication among Facebook, Cambridge Analytica, and political representatives who hired Cambridge Analytica to use the data to influence voter opinion (Rosenberg et al., 2018; Graham-Harrison and Cadwalladr, 2018).

The scandal was significant for inciting public discussion on ethical standards for social media companies, political consulting organizations, and politicians. Consumer advocates called for greater consumer protection in online media and right to privacy as well as curbs on misinformation and propaganda.

Facebook shares fell more than 24% to a low set on March 26, 2018, losing roughly $134 billion in market value in the process. By May 10, it had recovered the entire $134 billion (CBS, 2018).

Internet giant Google also reported voluminous data leakage in 2018, including exposing up to 500,000 users of its social network Google Plus between 2015 and March 2018. This resulted in the shutdown of Google Plus as a service.

Apart from concerns over privacy best practices and the sales of users' data, privacy concerns of tech giants also include whether or not they inform users when the government requests data and if they take a stand against gag orders.

8.3.2 Risk Data Schemes and Data Sharing: Barriers and Solutions

It is widely recognized that effective two-way information sharing between the public and private sectors is required to protect critical cyber infrastructure. This is a daunting task because it involves coordinating, organizing, and analysinganalyzing millions of disparate information feeds. While there is a public interest in managing infrastructure risk, doing so is not purely a public responsibility. The vast majority of infrastructure facilities are owned and operated by private interests. As a result, infrastructure risk management requires cooperation between the public and private sector in developing risk data schemes and collaboration in risk data sharing.

Currently, some efforts and mechanisms have been established for sharing such information and some data sharing schemes do exist such as Joint Terrorism Task Forces (JTTFs)[4], Fusion Centers[5], Homeland Information Threat and Risk Analysis Center[6], InfraGard[7], Information Sharing and Analysis Centers[8], Terrorism Early Warning Groups Information-sharing Portals[9], etc. However, barriers remain that inhibit both the private and public partners from obtaining the information needed to protect infrastructure. Law enforcement agencies face challenges when sharing classified intelligence from the top-down and incident reports from the field-up. Our critical infrastructure is currently placed at significant risk as a result of limited progress to support learning and application of newly gained knowledge to protect or even respond to recover from advanced cyber threats. Overcoming these barriers requires new thinking about the intelligence generation process, the mechanisms and practices upon which the process relies, and the responsibilities of

---

4. https://www.fbi.gov/investigate/terrorism/joint-terrorism-task-forces.
5. https://www.dhs.gov/state-and-major-urban-area-fusion-centers.
6. https://www.dhs.gov/office-cyber-infrastructure-analysis.
7. https://www.infragard.org/.
8. https://www.nationalisacs.org/.
9. https://isportal.berec.europa.eu/.

those in the private sector who participate in it. For example, critical infrastructure asset owners and control system vendors should report industrial control system specific security incidents and government agencies should provide up-to-date information to asset owners and operators on observed adversary tactics and techniques, especially when investigations reveal attacker capabilities to side-step or exploit relied upon security technologies (Willis et al., 2009).

Currently in the private sector there are concerns toward risk data sharing over: (1) leaks of proprietary information to competitors; (2) losing customers or investors if company vulnerabilities become public; (3) liability they might incur in, for instance, reporting suspicious behavior to public authorities; and (4) the risk that voluntary disclosures will bring to bear regulatory procedures, for instance, over environment effects.

Notice that all of these concerns have as much, or more, to do with what happens to information once disclosed to some government body as to the simple fact that the government collected it. It is not as important that the government knows the information as it is *what* that government does with the information. That is, in all cases the concern is that information will be passed, or leaked, from its original recipient and purpose to others, perhaps unpredictably. As a result, all the information-sharing mechanisms discussed in the next section, and especially those intended to reach out to the private sector, grapple with the balance between using information and protecting it.

On the government side, procedures were developed, especially in intelligence but also in law enforcement, to protect information, not share it. The holy grail of intelligence is protecting "sources and methods." Thus, the balance in all intelligence procedures is tipped toward protecting information, not moving it quickly around. As a result, the crust of security procedures only deepens, and while the watchword in the government is "risk management," the actual practice is still better characterized as "risk avoidance."

8.3.3   Cyber Infrastructure as a Public Good and the Privatization of the Internet

Similar to energy, public transport, and water, our cyber infrastructure today should be considered a public good. In economics, a public good is a good that is both nonexcludable and nonrivalrous, in that individuals cannot be effectively excluded from use and where use by one individual does not reduce availability to others. An important question regarding public goods is whether they should be owned by the public or the private sector. As more and more enterprises migrate to public cloud infrastructure, there is a growing trend that the "Internet" as we know it, is going through a process of privatization. This means the private sector will be increasingly responsible for enforcing risk control and implementing fundamental security of the future of infrastructure.

8.4   THREE VIEWS OF CYBERNOMICS

In this section, the three views of cybernomics are introduced. Built around bitmort and hekla, the entity, portfolio, and global views of cybernomics provide an integral framework with the objective to address some of the fundamental risk data challenges discussed earlier in this chapter.

8.4.1   Entity Level

In the entity view of cybernomics as shown in Fig. 8.1, for entity E.

E's digital value is the sum of the aggregated value of its core value assets and aggregated value of its supportive value assets. E maintains a digital asset inventory with economic value assigned to each asset. Each asset listed in E's digital asset inventory follows standard classification in International Digital Asset Classification (IDAC). E maintains a microeconomic loss scenario inventory developed around its critical assets.

E uses microcybernomic databank and modeling to optimize its capital modeling for managing residual cyber risk. E monitors its cyber risk factors, which are categorized under Cyber Risk Quadrant as technological, nontechnological, inherent, and control factors. E reads measures of these risk factors from its entity-level interface with the cybernomic databank. It uses a combination of statistical modeling and scenario analysis to quantify cyber loss and uses scenario-based control assessment to optimize its investment on measures that are the most cost-effective for risk reduction. E also gets the most relevant entity-level simulation scenarios from the cybernomic databank. In return, E feeds its incident and microeconomic loss information back to the cybernomic databank.

For a given class of asset D in E's asset inventory, BM_D is defined as one in a million probability of its digital death. The value of 1 BM_D is the amount of money E is willing to pay to reduce 1 BM_D for D type of asset. Following this process, risk exposure of all assets in E's asset inventory, cost of risk reduction of each type of asset, and E's

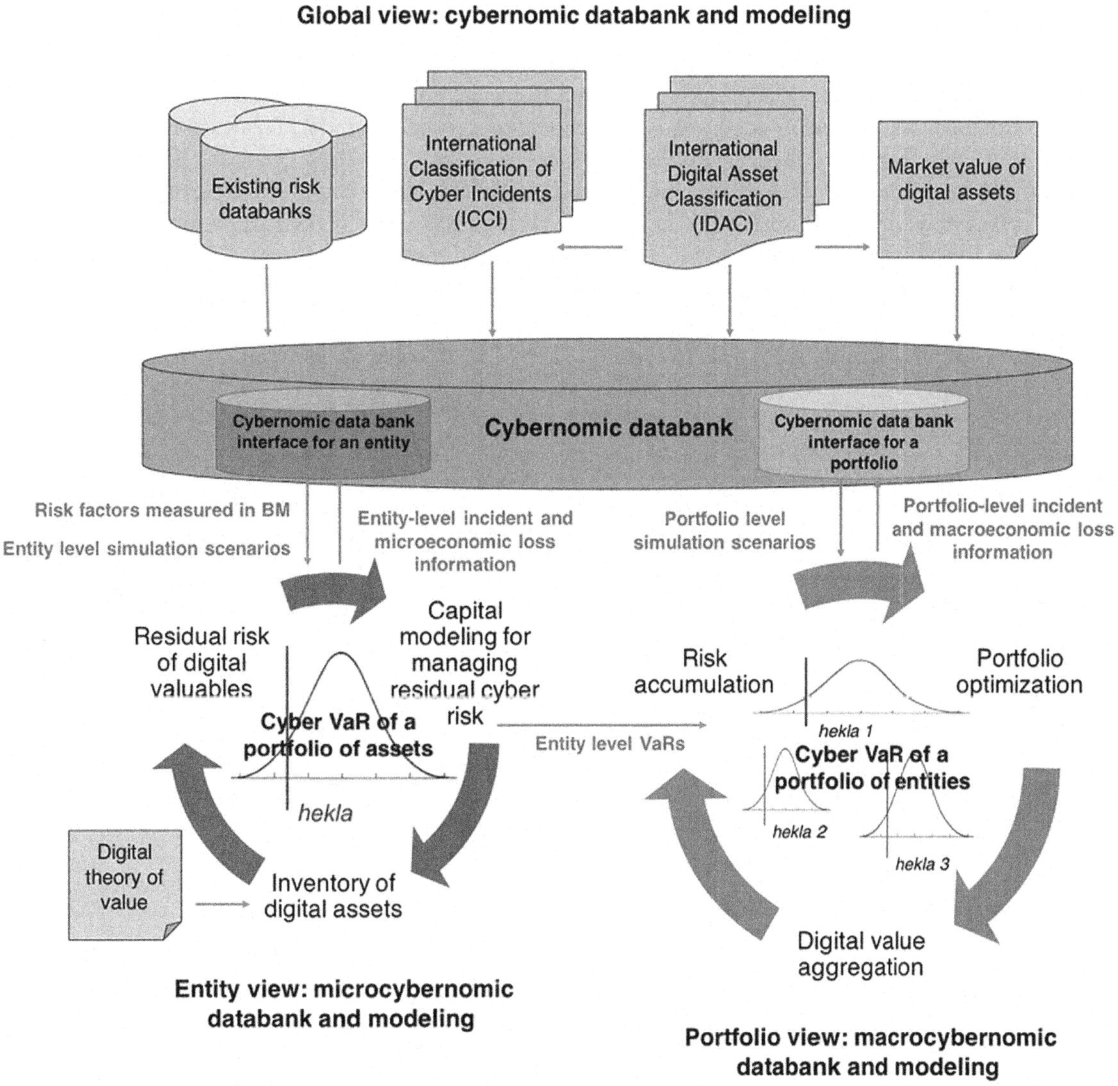

Global view: cybernomic databank and modeling

FIGURE 8.1 Three views of cybernomics.

"willingness-to-pay" to reduce their risk exposures can be measured and aggregated into a 12-month value at risk (VaR) curve.

Hekla is a probability, where a 12-month hekla VaR is the loss limit E can afford from cyber incidents. The value of hekla is the amount of money E is willing to pay to reduce its hekla by 1% for the same loss limit. Hekla can be used to articulate E's risk limit, risk appetite, and risk pricing.

Both BM and hekla are stackable on portfolio and global levels.

8.4.2 Portfolio Level

In the portfolio view of cybernomics as shown in Fig. 8.1, for multinational corporations, insurers, investors, or policy makers who manage a portfolio of entities P.

P uses macrocybernomic databank and modeling to optimize portfolio returns. P aggregates digital value from its portfolio of entities, calculates portfolio cyber VaR stacked from cyber VaRs of individual entities. Then, it determines portfolio level hekla and manages available capital accordingly. The portfolio view reads portfolio level simulation scenarios from its portfolio-level interface with the cybernomic databank. In return, P feeds its incident and macroeconomic loss information back to the cybernomic databank.

8.4.3 Global Level

In the global view of cybernomics as shown in Fig. 8.1, a databank and cybernomic model evolve around the classification schemes of assets IDAC and associated incidents listed in International Classification of Cyber Incident (ICCI). It integrates with existing risk databanks to cover socio-economic, geo-political risk factors. Market values of digital assets listed in IDAC are monitored. Risk factors are categorized under Cyber Risk Quadrant. Through public–private data partnership schemes, incident and loss data are collected from both entity and portfolio levels to support statistical modeling. The cybernomic model correlates risk factors and cyber loss to calculate risk exposures measured in BM and identify Key Cyber Risk Factors. The cybernomic databank feeds risk exposure information and simulation scenarios to entities. It also feeds portfolio-level simulation scenarios to portfolio risk managers based on historical incidents.

Chapter 9

Principles of Cybernomics

Chapter Outline

9.1 Unique Attributes of Digital Assets **142**
  9.1.1 Characteristic 1: Digital Value Creation Does Not Decrease, but Increases, Through Usage 142
  9.1.2 Characteristic 2: Duplication Does Not Increase Digital Value 142
  9.1.3 Characteristic 3: Digital Value Production and Distribution Entails Higher Fixed Costs and Lower Variable Costs 142
  9.1.4 Characteristic 4: Digital Value Can Be Distributed Via Multi-Sided Markets 143
  9.1.5 Characteristic 5: Digital Value Is Limitless 143
    9.1.5.1 Characteristic 5a: Digital Value Has Limitless Utility to the Owner 143
    9.1.5.2 Characteristic 5b: There Are Limitless Opportunities to Distribute and Consume Digital Value 144

9.2 Digital Value Matrix: Categorization of Digital Assets Based on Their Economic Functions **144**
9.3 Characteristics of the Fourth Industrial Revolution **145**
  9.3.1 Characteristic 1: Velocity 145
  9.3.2 Characteristic 2: Cross-Jurisdictional Economies of Scale Without Mass 145
  9.3.3 Characteristic 3: Heavy Reliance on Intangible Assets, Especially Intellectual Property 145
  9.3.4 Characteristic 4: The Importance of Data, User Participation, and Their Synergies With Intellectual Property 145
  9.3.5 Characteristic 5: Fusion of Technologies 146
  9.3.6 Characteristic 6: Consumption Externality 146
  9.3.7 Characteristic 7: Indirect Network Effects 146
  9.3.8 Characteristic 8: Lock-In Effects and Competition 146

9.4 Models for Digital Asset Valuation **146**
  9.4.1 Method 1: Intrinsic Value 146
    9.4.1.1 1a: Intrinsic Cost of Production 147
    9.4.1.2 1b: Direct Financial Conversion 147
  9.4.2 Method 2: Extrinsic Value 147
    9.4.2.1 2a: Market Value 147
    9.4.2.2 2b: Usage Value 147
  9.4.3 Method 3: Subjective Value 147
  9.4.4 Method 4: Opportunity Value 148
9.5 Measuring the Digital Economy **148**

9.6 Digital Theory of Value **148**
  9.6.1 Law of Machine Time 149
    9.6.1.1 Principle 1a: Progress of Digital Economy Should Be Measured Against Machine Time 149
    9.6.1.2 Principle 1b: Sensemaking Is a Universal Challenge and a Value Driver 149
    9.6.1.3 Principle 1c: Risk Management Is an Island of Stability in the Sea of Change 149
  9.6.2 Law of Recombination 149
    9.6.2.1 Principle 2: Recombination Is an Engine for Growth 149
  9.6.3 Law of Hyperconnectivity 150
    9.6.3.1 Principle 3a: Hyperconnectivity Is an Engine for Growth 150
    9.6.3.2 Principle 3b: The Gravity of Value Creation will be Increasingly in the Virtual Space Where Value Creation is Location Independent 150
    9.6.3.3 Principle 3c: Nontechnical Barriers, Such As Geopolitical, Regulations, Legal Frameworks, Are Limiting Factors 150
  9.6.4 Law of Subjectivity 150
    9.6.4.1 Principle 4: A Greater Component of Value Is Increasingly Subjective, Reflecting Only in an Entity's Willingness-to-Pay 150
  9.6.5 Law of Abundance 150
    9.6.5.1 Principle 5a: The Digitally Empowered Entity has Limitless Economic Potential 150
    9.6.5.2 Principle 5b: Consumer Reception and Power Supply are Limiting Factors 150
    9.6.5.3 Principle 5c: The Attention of a Consumer Is the New Scarce Resource 151
  9.6.6 Law of the New Division of Labor 151
    9.6.6.1 Principle 6a: The Digital Economy Is Creating a New Social Divide Based on the New Labor Value Chain 151
    9.6.6.2 Principle 6b: The Optimal Path to Intrinsic Value Creation Is a Combination of Human and Machine Intelligence 151

Digital Asset Valuation and Cyber Risk Measurement. DOI: https://doi.org/10.1016/B978-0-12-812158-0.00009-0

9.7 Cyber Risk Quadrant: Applying Medical Risk Measurement to Cyber **151**
   9.7.1 Applying Medical Risk Model for Measuring Cyber Risk 151
   9.7.2 Using Scenario Analysis for Control Assessment and Loss Quantification 152
9.8 Introducing Bitmort and Hekla **153**
9.9 Risk Calculations **155**
   9.9.1 Measuring Strength of Controls for Digital Assets Using Bitmort 155
   9.9.2 Measuring Cost-Effectiveness of Controls for Digital Assets Using Bitmort 155
   9.9.3 Articulating an Entity's "Willingness-to-Pay" for Risk Reduction for Digital Assets Using Bitmort 155
   9.9.4 Articulating an Entity's Cyber Risk Limit Using Hekla 155
   9.9.5 Articulating an Entity's Cyber Risk Appetite Using Hekla 155

   9.9.6 Measuring an Entity's Cyber Risk Pricing Using Hekla 155
   9.9.7 Measuring an Entity's Cost of Risk Reduction Using Hekla 155
   9.9.8 Measuring an Entity's Cyber Risk Return on Investment Using Hekla 156
   9.9.9 Using Bitmort and Hekla on a Portfolio of Entities 156
9.10 Three Views of Cybernomics **156**
   9.10.1 Entity View 157
   9.10.2 Portfolio View 157
   9.10.3 Global View 157
9.11 Discussions and Limitations **157**
   9.11.1 Accuracy 157
   9.11.2 Analytical Capabilities 158
   9.11.3 Testing and Validation 158
   9.11.4 Economic Lifespan of Digital Assets 158
   9.11.5 Fundamental Inherent Differences of Digital Assets 158

We cannot solve our problems with the same thinking we used when we created them.

— Albert Einstein

This chapter summarizes all the novel concepts introduced in this book, and also provides discussions and limitations.

9.1 UNIQUE ATTRIBUTES OF DIGITAL ASSETS

Five characteristics of digital assets introduced in cybernomics.

9.1.1 Characteristic 1: Digital Value Creation Does Not Decrease, but Increases, Through Usage

To the contrary of many traditional physical assets, sharing of intangible digital assets tends to increase its value. The more people who use it, the more economic benefits can be extracted from it (Moody and Walsh, 1999; Ikegami, 1992), e.g., Wikipedia, Instagram.

9.1.2 Characteristic 2: Duplication Does Not Increase Digital Value

Two copies of data assets have the same value as a single copy because no "new" information is created. Duplication of information does not add new value but additional cost (Moody and Walsh, 1999). Too many copies of the same corporate data, for example, can cause significant additional management overhead. It is important, however, to differentiate duplication from reproduction elaborated in Characteristic 3.

9.1.3 Characteristic 3: Digital Value Production and Distribution Entails Higher Fixed Costs and Lower Variable Costs

In many cases the production of digital goods and services entails relatively higher fixed costs and lower variable costs.[1] Software development, for instance, requires considerable investments in infrastructure and human labor; however, once the final program has been developed it can be maintained, sold, or distributed at very low marginal costs. While in many cases marginal costs will remain nonnegligible, there are also a range of nonrival consumption goods,

---

1. Variable cost changes in proportion with production volume.

such as software, e-books, or music, which can be reproduced at an effective marginal cost of zero (OECD, 2018). For example, WhatsApp has only 50 employees but was attracting more than 1 million new users per day at the time when it was acquired by Facebook for $19 billion.

9.1.4   Characteristic 4: Digital Value Can Be Distributed Via Multi-Sided Markets

The digital economy has given rise to "platform economy," rooted in multisided markets (OECD, 2018). In a traditional, single-sided market, sellers engage with only one specific set of customers, for example, a reader buying a book in a book shop. In multisided markets, there are more than one set of customers acquiring different products and services from a company, for example, Amazon retail and Uber. Multisided markets are defined by the joint presence of two characteristics:

1. *Indirect network externalities.* Indirect network effects occur when an increase in end-users on one side of the market increases the utility of end-users on another market side, e.g., Airbnb (OECD, 2018). The prevalence of positive indirect externalities of positive indirect externalities implies that the firm operating the platform can reap benefits over and above the marginal utility of end-users, allowing them to increase the number of users (for transactions) by charging more on one side of the market while reducing the price for end users on other sides.
2. *Nonneutral pricing strategies.* As a consequence of indirect network externalities, pricing structures are nonneutral in the sense that optimal prices can be below the marginal cost of provision on one market side while being above it on the other side(s); end users with lower price elasticities will typically be overcharged and vice versa. The result also implies that it may be optimal for platform operators, depending on the magnitude of the indirect network externalities as well as on price elasticities, to provide goods or services free of charge to end users on one (or potentially more) market sides. As a consequence, the so-called barter transaction may arise, implying that goods or services are effectively traded without monetary compensation against other valuable inputs such as user engagement, user data or user-generated content. Such a strategy is adopted by many social network platforms, email services and media providers. In these cases, end users often benefit from "free" access to a specific service. However, platform operators typically compensate for this by extracting data from users and transactions and then by selling services based on that data to the other side of the market. The primary example is the sale of customer-targeted advertisements to advertisers on the other side of the market (OECD, 2018). Many argue that Facebook did not "purchase" user registrations, but user data and user-generated data are the company's core asset which led to the largest technology Initial Public Offering (IPO) in history.

9.1.5   Characteristic 5: Digital Value Is Limitless

Economic value theories to date are based on scarcity of resources. It is one of the most fundamental assumptions of the discipline of economics. Today, some argue "limitless" computing has arrived,[2] making digital value theory inherently unique from past theories. Of course, nothing is limitless in absolute terms. In this book, "limitless" means that limitation of the resources no longer plays as a constraint in value creation and distribution. The limitless nature of digital value is twofold.

9.1.5.1   *Characteristic 5a: Digital Value Has Limitless Utility to the Owner*

Referring to Characteristic 1, intangible digital assets cannot be consumed by use, and its utility is maintained regardless of change of ownership. Because intangible digital assets do not only disappear but increases value through transfer and consumption, it represents a limitless utility to the owner. Thus, this contradicts with a basic premise of conventional theory which says that utility of a resource is limited for the owner (Ikegami, 1992). As to the value of credibility, it shows that utility value of a piece of information depends upon social credibility of the owner. The social credibility arises from the owner's capability to transmit useful information and to coordinate transfer. It presupposes that the owner has some kind of competence to create value (Ikegami, 1992).

---

2. Eric Brewer (VP Infrastructure, Google) spoke about the Future of the Cloud at UC Berkeley on May 12, 2016.

9.1.5.2 Characteristic 5b: There Are Limitless Opportunities to Distribute and Consume Digital Value

In the traditional study of economics, it is usual to set up a short-run as well as the pair of assumptions that: (1) the amount of resources available for a society is limited; and (2) the market exists as a measure of substitutability of those limited resources. To find an optimal distribution of resources by means of free competition under these assumptions has always been thought to be the fundamental purpose of economics (Andress, 2004). However, with the growth of cloud computing, especially in its third wave of "cloud native" services, both information storage and processing are reaching a state of "limitless." Prospects of quantum computing developments will further unleash the limitless nature of computing. There are limitless ways to distribute and consume digital value. Characteristic 4 is a mere use case of this attribute of digital value. This changes the fundamental assumptions of economics.

Considering the unique attributes of digital value discussed above, in this book intrinsic digital value and extrinsic digital value are defined as:

> **Intrinsic digital value** is the critical elements that make it possible for the digital asset to exist in the first place. **Extrinsic digital value** describes the limitless opportunities to distribute and consume the digital asset so that it is more useful to prospective users.

9.2   DIGITAL VALUE MATRIX: CATEGORIZATION OF DIGITAL ASSETS BASED ON THEIR ECONOMIC FUNCTIONS

In cybernomics, digital assets are categorized based on their economic functions using the Digital Value Matrix. The dimensions and categories are defined as:

> *First dimension: Core value assets (CA) versus supportive assets.* As a strategic resource, digital assets can be the sole value created by a business, serve as a basis for making critical decisions, or keeping and supporting business processes.
>
> *Category 1: CA ("What is").* When digital assets are, or are tied to, products and services that define the nature of the entity, what the entity profits from, or is about—i.e., what the entity "is" digitally. Under the business context, core value creation activities can include product and service development, research and development, marketing, sales, and contract management, etc.
>
> *Category 2: Supportive value assets (SA)[3] ("How it is run").* When digital assets support secondary activities, human needs, technology, organization, and technical infrastructure necessary for the creation, consumption, and distribution of goods and services—i.e., how the entity is "run" digitally. Under the business context, supportive activities can include procurement, logistics, human resource management, infrastructure, and operations, etc.
>
> *Second dimension: Digitized assets versus digital-native assets.* As a driver for economic growth, there is a difference between value digitized from traditional economics versus value created from intrinsic digital innovation.
>
> *Category 1: Digitized assets.* Conversion of traditional assets into digital form, e.g., email, electronic patent applications, digital storage, e-commerce. Digitization helps traditional assets benefit from leveraging limitless extrinsic digital value.
>
> *Category 2: Digital-native assets.[4]* Intrinsically digital assets that do not have an equivalent or alternative in the physical, analog world, e.g., software, blockchain, and multi-sided digital platforms.

Similar to the Nice Classification, an International Digital Asset Classification (IDAC) should be developed on the global level, using more categories that can reflect the economic functions of digital assets.

An entity E's digital composition can, thus, be described by the ratio of its CA to SA:

$$\text{CA:SA} = \{c_i, p_i\} : \{s_j, q_j\} \quad i = 1, 2, \ldots, N_c, \quad j = 1, 2, \ldots, N_o$$

where CA—E's core value assets in bytes; SA—E' supportive value assets in bytes; c—a type of asset listed in International Digital Asset Classification (IDAC) which is of core value to E; p—E's core digital asset c in bytes; s—a

---

3. Previously referred to as "operational assets" in Ruan (2017). The term supportive value is used instead because it encompasses a broader range of activities including operations.
4. Previously referred to as "Assets born digital" in Ruan (2017). The term digital-native is used instead because it is a better phrase which means the same.

type of asset listed in IDAC which is of supportive value to E; q—E's supportive value asset s in bytes; N_c—the number of core value assets in entity E; N_o—the number of supportive value assets in entity E.

Similarly, entity E's DA (digitized assets in bytes) to NA (digital-native assets in bytes) ratio can also be calculated. An entity's digital value composition describes its nature of innovation. For example, a global retail company selling traditional goods will have a high SA:CA ratio, while a software development company will have a high CA:SA ratio and a high NA:DA ratio.

Using the economic categorization of digital assets above, a list of examples of digital assets on individual, organizational, national, and global levels are provided in Chapter 1, Digital Assets as Economic Goods. A list of example attributes that contribute to the creation, distribution, and consumption of digital value is also provided in Chapter 1.

9.3 CHARACTERISTICS OF THE FOURTH INDUSTRIAL REVOLUTION

Eight characteristics of the Fourth Industrial Revolution are introduced in cybernomics.

9.3.1 Characteristic 1: Velocity

Digitization has led to an acceleration of economic activities. In the digital space, transactions between end users in different jurisdictions can be concluded without loss of time and digital content, and can be accessed immediately from any device connected to the Internet. As a result, digital products and services disseminate faster, markets clear faster, ideas circulate faster, and it becomes much easier for businesses to identify, engage, and develop their customer bases. This increase in the speed of economic activity implies that businesses can gain significant competitive advantages by being the first to move into, and potentially dominate, a new market.

9.3.2 Characteristic 2: Cross-Jurisdictional Economies of Scale Without Mass

The digital market provides any digital products and services the potential to reach a global spread. Production of digital value has much lower barrier to entry and can happen from anyone who has access to a device connected to the Internet (Ross, 2016). Economic activities occurring in digital markets break traditional jurisdictional boundaries, creating multifaceted challenges to global regulatory and legal frameworks. For example, a user contributes to value creation by sharing their preferences (e.g., liking a page) on a social media forum. This data will later be used and monetized for targeted advertising. The profits are not necessarily taxed in the country of the user (and viewer of the advert), but rather in the country where the advertising algorithms have been developed, for example. This means that the user contribution to the profits is not taken into account when the company is taxed (European Commission, 2018; OECD, 2018).

9.3.3 Characteristic 3: Heavy Reliance on Intangible Assets, Especially Intellectual Property

Digitized enterprises are characterized by the growing importance of investment in intangible, especially IP assets which could either be owned by the business or leased from a third party. For many digitalized enterprises, the intense use of IP assets, such as software and algorithms supporting their platforms, websites, and many other crucial functions, are central to their business models (OECD, 2018).

9.3.4 Characteristic 4: The Importance of Data, User Participation, and Their Synergies With Intellectual Property

Data, user participation, network effects, and the provision of user-generated content are commonly observed in the business models of more highly digitalized businesses. The benefits from data analysis are also likely to increase with the amount of collected information linked to a specific user or customer. The important role that user participation can play is seen in the case of social networks, where without data, network effects and user-generated content, the businesses would not exist as we know them today. In addition, the degree of user participation can be broadly divided into two categories: active and passive user participation. However, the degree of user participation does not necessarily correlate with the degree of digitalization: for example, cloud computing can be considered as a more highly digitalized business that involves only limited user participation (OECD, 2018).

9.3.5   Characteristic 5: Fusion of Technologies

The Fourth Industrial Revolution is characterized by its fusion of technologies that blurs the boundaries between digital, physical, and biological worlds; and the fusion is not limited to these three spheres. The majority of MIT Breakthrough Technologies from 2010 involve innovations spanning multiple disciplines. The majority of today's top issues require multidisciplinary inputs. The fusion is everywhere, and it is a main driver for economic growth.

9.3.6   Characteristic 6: Consumption Externality

In digital markets, utility from the consumption of a specific good or service is often dependent on the number of other end users consuming the same good or service. This effect is called a direct network externality, sometimes also referred to as a direct network effect or consumption externality; it is a positive externality in that the larger the network, the larger the end-user utility. Consumption externality is a prevalent force behind the rise of the platforms. The most obvious examples are social media and online messaging services. Both applications are practically useless to the user if he or she is the only person using them, however, their value increase as the number of other users increases. The effect is apparent, for instance, in the case of online gaming or operating systems (OECD, 2018).

9.3.7   Characteristic 7: Indirect Network Effects

In contrast to direct network effects, indirect network effects arise in the context of multi-sided markets, which occur when a specific group of end users (e.g., users of a social network) benefit from interacting with another group of end users (e.g., advertisers on a social network) via an online platform. Digitization has allowed the emergence of online platforms and networks, and we have seen an increasing number of platform-based businesses in many different sectors, such as accommodation rental, transportation, or peer-to-peer e-commerce (OECD, 2018).

9.3.8   Characteristic 8: Lock-In Effects and Competition

Digital transactions can be carried out on different electronic devices; however, end-user devices often rely on different operating systems. As a result, customers may be locked in to a particular operating system once they have acquired a specific device. This effect is due to psychological as well as monetary switching costs which end users have to incur in order to switch from one system to another—e.g., a change from a specific smartphone (including operating system) to another, implying a loss in access to previously accumulated applications and data (OECD, 2018). For a global corporation, a change from a primary cloud provider to another, could imply significant costs in re-architecting applications. Due to the ubiquitous and pervasive nature of many digital technologies and devices that people are exposed to on a daily basis, for example, iOS versus Android, how these systems dictate our everyday choices and options can be comparable to political systems.

In terms of competition, it may be more difficult for new firms to gain significant market shares if an incumbent firm already dominates the market (OECD, 2018). Once a critical mass of end users has switched to the new product, it becomes possible for the formerly dominant firm to lose its entire market share within a short time space. This has been the case, for instance, with search engines, web browsers, and social media platforms (OECD, 2018). As Alstyne et al. (2016) puts it, scale now trumps differentiation.

9.4   MODELS FOR DIGITAL ASSET VALUATION

Built on the Digital Value Matrix, four methods are outlined for digital asset valuation.

9.4.1   Method 1: Intrinsic Value

Intrinsic digital value *is the critical elements that make it possible for the digital asset to exist in the first place.* The intrinsic value of the digital asset is determined through fundamental analysis without reference to its market value. Intrinsic value can be measured using the following.

9.4.1.1   1a: Intrinsic Cost of Production

Replacement cost or cost to produce the critical elements that make it possible for the digital asset to exist, including labor, capital, infrastructure, and taxation, etc. For example, the value of a piece of software is the number of man-days, technology cost, intellectual property, and other costs that were put into the development of it.

9.4.1.2   1b: Direct Financial Conversion

Direct conversion of the financial value of the nondigital equivalent of the asset.

9.4.2   Method 2: Extrinsic Value

Extrinsic digital value *describes the limitless opportunities to distribute and consume the digital asset so that it is more useful to prospective users.* The extrinsic value of a digital asset is determined using its market price, or its usage value.

Table 9.1 shows core value activities and supportive value activities based on a generic business model. Digitization can automate, increase cost efficiency, productivity, extend shelf-life, or end-user empowerment of all the activities.

9.4.2.1   2a: Market Value

The extrinsic market value of the digital asset is the price at which the digital valuable would trade in a competitive market. For example, currently payment card numbers with CVV2 and date of birth are sold at $15 per record in the United States and at $30 per record in the United Kingdom, respectively. Payment card numbers with full personal information are sold at $30 per record in the United States and at $35 per record in the United Kingdom (Intel Security, 2015). Extrinsic market value can be measured using market-based, income-based, and options models.

9.4.2.2   2b: Usage Value

Usage value is a different concept from value-in-use. Extrinsic consumption from usage value considers the characteristics of digital assets that their value increases through usage. Digitization always makes it easier to share, reproduce, reuse, and increase the shelf-life of an asset, hence usage value is a multiplying factor. The valuation of mobile application start-ups, for example, is directly correlated with the size of its user base. The more a photo or a story is shared on a free social media platform such as Facebook, the more "valuable" it becomes, and this cannot be explained by classical economics.

9.4.3   Method 3: Subjective Value

The subjective value of the digital asset is determined by the importance the entity places on it; it is measured by how much an entity is willing to pay.

TABLE 9.1 Core Value Activities and Supportive Value Activities

Core Value Activities	Supportive Value Activities
Creation of a product or service	Procurement
Marking and sales	Human resources
Execution	Firm infrastructure (including technical infrastructure)
Distribution/transfer to the customer	Inbound and outbound logistics
Research and development (including problem-finding and acquisition, problem-solving, choice)	Operations

TABLE 9.2 Digital Valuation Model

	Digitized	Digital-Native
Core value	Direct financial conversion × extrinsic (usage)	*f* (intrinsic, extrinsic (market, usage), subjective)
Supportive value	Opportunity value	

9.4.4   Method 4: Opportunity Value

Opportunity value is a concept originated from opportunity cost. Opportunity cost is the value of the choice in terms of the best alternative while making a decision, for example, firm A chooses to digitize part of its business while firm B does not. Opportunity value of the digital asset is defined in this book as:

> The **opportunity value of digitized asset** is the value of using it comparing to using the nondigital alternative; the **opportunity value of digital-native asset** is the value of using it comparing to the nonexistent alternative, that is the alternative that such asset did not exist at all.

Business Impact Analysis (BIA) can be used to calculate OV when the digital option is unavailable, and the resulting nondigital or nonexistent alternative becoming the only option. Business Consequences (BC) can include financial, legal, reputation, and regulatory impact (ISF, 2000). For example, Amazon's 2013 service down time cost Amazon as a cloud service provider $66,240 per minute (Clay, 2013). Business impact can be measured using scenario analysis combined with defined loss categories.

Through BIA, the time and effort saved from having the digital option can be revealed from the difference between cost of the alternative and cost of the digital option required to produce the same result. For example, a study in 2010 has concluded that the average search time is 22 minutes offline comparing to 7 minutes online (Chen et al., 2010).

Based on the four methods introduced above, digital assets in economic categories introduced in Chapter 1 can be valued using the Digital Valuation Model in Table 9.2.

9.5   MEASURING THE DIGITAL ECONOMY

Based on the above analysis, in this book, the total output of digital economy should be measured from three components:

- Value created from digitalization of traditional industries, where digitization serves as the enabler and multiplier.
- Value created from digital-native industries, where digitization servers as the disrupter.
- Value created from the digital option. Opportunity value created from the mere existence of digital technologies comparing two scenarios: (1) the nondigital alternative and (2) the nonexistent alternative.

9.6   DIGITAL THEORY OF VALUE

This section introduces Digital Theory of Value with an attempt to summarize unique phenomena that cannot be explained by any traditional theories of values and principles that can help us understand various forces behind the formation of the future of value. In this book, the digital value of an entity is defined as:

> The sum of the aggregated value from its core value assets and the aggregated value from its supportive value assets.

Entity E's total digital value can be calculated as:

$$V = \sum_{i=1}^{N_c} cv_i + \sum_{j=1}^{N_o} sv_j$$

where V is the total digital value of entity E; cv is the value of core value asset c of entity E; sv is the value of supportive value asset o of entity E; N_c is the number of core value assets in entity E; and N_s is the number of supportive value assets in entity E.

9.6.1   Law of Machine Time

9.6.1.1   Principle 1a: Progress of Digital Economy Should Be Measured Against Machine Time

Currently, all of our economy measures are still based on traditional metrics against "human time" that we are most familiar with. The fact that machine time is different from human perception of time by its exponential nature means progress of the digital economy is measured using the wrong yardstick.

In digital theory of value, the relative machine time is calculated as:

$$\text{Number of years} = \frac{2^{\frac{2(\text{Current year}-1965)}{3}} - 2^{\frac{2(\text{Current year}-1966)}{3}}}{2^{\frac{2(\text{Base year}-1965)}{3}} - 2^{\frac{2(\text{Base year}-1966)}{3}}}$$

where current year is the year of calculation, base year is the relative year that the current year is compared to. For example, using this equation, the progress we experienced in 2018 is equivalent to 4096 years using the base year of 2000.

9.6.1.2   Principle 1b: Sensemaking Is a Universal Challenge and a Value Driver

Exponential progress makes it increasingly challenging to force old perceptions, old solutions, old mind-sets into the new problems that arise. For example, in problem-solving, almost all problems require a multidisciplinary approach. This is because the old disciplinary boundaries cannot accommodate the complexity of today's problems as they span multiple disciplines. The rising instability of the global systems as a result of the pace of change can cause significant fear, division, isolation, and instability (Guillen, 2015). The rapid disappearance of history and familiar frame of references means revolutionary megastructures are required to address the constant challenge of sensemaking, which will be an important driver for the future of value. This book is all about starting such efforts to build such new structures.

9.6.1.3   Principle 1c: Risk Management Is an Island of Stability in the Sea of Change

Exponential[5] progress toward a future that is harder to predict makes risk management an island of stability in the sea of change. With value comes risk. Risk management around the future of value requires highly adaptive models that can respond to more "Black Swan" events. As Charles Darwin put it, "it is not the strongest of the species that survives, nor the most intelligent. It is the one that is the most adaptive to change."

9.6.2   Law of Recombination

9.6.2.1   Principle 2: Recombination Is an Engine for Growth

Transdisciplinarity connotes a research strategy that crosses many disciplinary boundaries to create a holistic approach, such as research on effective information systems for biomedical research, i.e., bioinformatics, as well as concepts or methods that were originally developed by one discipline but are now used by several others, such as ethnography, a field research method originally developed in anthropology but now widely used by other disciplines. Steve Jobs famously said that "the musicians play their instruments. I play the orchestra," and acknowledged that the skill for "connecting the dots" will be high on the value chain.

In genetics, recombination is defined as the formation by the process of crossing-over and independent assortment of new combinations of genes in progeny that did not occur in the parents. Weitzman (1998) borrowed the term to describe an idea-based growth model, which shows that knowledge can build upon itself in a combinatoric feedback process that may have significant implication for economic growth. Referring to Characteristic 2 of digital assets in Chapter 1, Digital Assets as Economic Goods, digitization has made collaboration of ideas faster and easier than ever. Meaningful and divergent aggregation of quality data can fuel recombinant growth of ideas which can lead to powerful innovative breakthroughs. Recombination is the growth mindset and a multiplying factor in the digital economy.

---

5. The black swan theory or theory of black swan events is a metaphor that describes an event that comes as a surprise, has a major effect, and is often inappropriately rationalized after that fact with the benefit of hindsight.

9.6.3   Law of Hyperconnectivity

9.6.3.1   Principle 3a: Hyperconnectivity Is an Engine for Growth

The world is now "flat." As a main feature of the new era of globalization, hyperconnectivity has given rise to multi-sided markets where consumers are also participants of the creation of new products and services. It provides an instant global reach to any digitally empowered entity. In highly interdependent, hyperconnected societies, access to information is no longer the barrier, the challenge is to capture insight that generates economic value, and this is the new battle field of innovation and IP creation. This requires new mega global structures that can adapt to the explosion of complex economic information created from connecting the world population to a brand-new level.

9.6.3.2   Principle 3b: The Gravity of Value Creation will be Increasingly in the Virtual Space Where Value Creation is Location Independent

Digitization will continue to change our way of work, bringing greater flexibility. The future of work is mobility and location independent. With nearly 50% of millennial workers already freelancing, freelancers are predicted to become the US workforce majority within a decade. Its growth has outpaced overall US workforce growth by three times since 2014 (Upwork, 2017). This means that the traditional major city hubs for value creation in various sectors and industries—e.g., San Francisco for startups and London for finance—may gradually be replaced by virtual communities made of global nomads who are not bound to a fixed location of work (Ross, 2016). This is also the driver behind the emergence of co-working and co-living spaces around the world for millennials who combine work and play, without compromising on overall productivity.

9.6.3.3   Principle 3c: Nontechnical Barriers, Such As Geopolitical, Regulations, Legal Frameworks, Are Limiting Factors

While digital growth accelerates, the real limiting factors are nontechnical systems developed for problem-solving in the "old world" which are failing to adapt and catch up. This includes legal and regulatory frameworks currently used to govern digital issues such as cyber security, privacy, and financial reporting, which are by default pan-jurisdictional.

9.6.4   Law of Subjectivity

9.6.4.1   Principle 4: A Greater Component of Value Is Increasingly Subjective, Reflecting Only in an Entity's Willingness-to-Pay

Phenomena described here both contribute to the conclusion that a much greater component of value in digital economy will be subjective. It is up to the consumers how much attention, time, and money they are willing to spend on a product or service. There will also be a greater influence from the herd mentality, that is, people can be influenced by their peers to adopt certain behaviors on a largely emotional, rather than rational basis. It requires new systems of regulation and new tools for prediction.

9.6.5   Law of Abundance

9.6.5.1   Principle 5a: The Digitally Empowered Entity has Limitless Economic Potential

Comparing to traditional means of value creation where the business owner must employ thousands of people or spend a fortune upfront in its infrastructure (factory, computing infrastructures, manufacturing equipment, etc.), digital value creation and distribution often incur much lower reproduction cost. Digitization gives the digitally empowered entity access to more economic potential than ever before. Because digital value has unlimited utility to the owner with low marginal cost, and there is limitless ways to scale its value, the digitally empowered entity has limitless economic potential. The most important competitive edge then becomes creating intrinsic value in the first place.

9.6.5.2   Principle 5b: Consumer Reception and Power Supply are Limiting Factors

Given limitless potential for value creation, the only limiting factors are two:

1. Battery power. Our digital life today is still constrained by its battery life.

2. Human cognitive capability to consume as long as humans are targeted as consumers. As discussed in Chapter 1, Digital Assets as Economic Goods, value creation requires the capability to comprehend from the user's perspective. Studies show that humans are slow to comprehend exponential growth, and growth of digitization is constrained by how fast human consumers can adapt to it.

9.6.5.3 Principle 5c: The Attention of a Consumer Is the New Scarce Resource

The explosion of digital content, services, and products have led to the billion-dollar wellness industry, developing tools, trainings, meditative habits, and a culture for balance between the online and offline worlds. "Digital-detox" has become the latest trend for people who are constantly exposed to a hyperconnected world of distraction. In the digital economy, when consumers are also participants of value creation, their contribution is often paid by "paying attention," for example, by following a brand on social media, and every economic decision requires attention. A successful app often employs the smartest people and uses the smartest algorithms in order to monetize from how much attention and time its users are spending in it, even if it is a free app. As long as humans are still targeted as consumers of the digital economy, the competing demand for human attention makes it the new scarce resource in the economy of abundance.

9.6.6 Law of the New Division of Labor

9.6.6.1 Principle 6a: The Digital Economy Is Creating a New Social Divide Based on the New Labor Value Chain

Taking into consideration the power and limitations of automation, the following new labor value chain will create greater social divide based on skill sets that are important for the future of value creation (in the order from high value to low value):

1. Human labor that participates in job creation in the new economy.
2. Conventional human labor that is difficult to be replaced by automation.
3. Human labor that supports the operations of digital systems (the new blue collar).
4. People who will not be able to keep up or are below the barrier to entry.

Skills that will remain high on the labor value chain referring to point 2 above:

1. Cognitive skills that require high adaptivity, spontaneity without prior knowledge (out-of-the box thinking), e.g., from creative work and scientific research to performance arts and stand-up comedy.
2. Relationship skills used for intensive human interaction and communications in complex situations.
3. Physical skills that require high adaptivity.

9.6.6.2 Principle 6b: The Optimal Path to Intrinsic Value Creation Is a Combination of Human and Machine Intelligence

Given the limitations and constraints of both machine and human intelligence, the optimal path forward in intrinsic value creation, e.g., through building high performing teams, is by combining them. Such teams should leverage the processing speed, storage capacity, and analytical power from machines combined with the adaptivity, intuition, ability to imagine and build trusting relationships from billions of years of natural evolution. The labor force of the crowd is also a form of human participation in intrinsic value creation, which is inherently a highly efficient global labor force that is not limited by any geographical boundaries.

9.7 CYBER RISK QUADRANT: APPLYING MEDICAL RISK MEASUREMENT TO CYBER

9.7.1 Applying Medical Risk Model for Measuring Cyber Risk

In order to measure cyber risk, a cybernomic databank is required in order to identify Key Cyber Risk Factors (KCRF) correlated with an entity's risk profile. The cyber risk exposure of an entity is influenced by a wide range of dynamic technological and nontechnological profiling factors, internal vulnerabilities, and external threats. The motives of attackers, in particular, are largely determined by nontechnological factors (Huq and TrendLabs Research, 2015).

In medicine, modifiable risk factors are factors that can be treated or controlled, including lifestyle factors such as cigarette smoking, physical inactivity, and excessive alcohol use (Derby et al., 2000). Nonmodifiable risk factors refer to any risk factor for a particular condition which cannot be modified. Age, for example, is the most important nonmodifiable risk factor for stroke (Sacco, 1995). Borrowing this established risk categorization scheme, in cybernomics, cyber risk factors are categorized under the Cyber Risk Quadrant (CRQ) within four types of factors:

- *Technological factors*. Attributes that are related to the usage of technology.
- *Nontechnological factors*. Attributes that are not related to the usage of technology, including people, process, socio-economic, and geo-political factors.
- *Inherent factors*. Intrinsic attributes based on the nature of the business, industry, core operations, goods and services the entity provides, or macro trends and attributes that have pan-industry impact on entities in certain geo-regions, or even global impact. Inherent factors determine an entity's inherent cyber risk exposure and are factors the entity cannot easily change.
- *Control factors*. Attributes of the entity that are nonintrinsic and can be changed or improved. Control factors reflect an entity's control effectiveness against cyber loss and are the subject of investment when it comes to risk mitigation.

An entity's residual cyber risk is then calculated as:

$$\text{Residual cyber risk} = \text{inherent risk} \div \text{control effectiveness}$$

So, the cyber risk factor categorization scheme makes the calculation of an entity's residual cyber risk very straightforward. It can also help the entity holistically identify, monitor, and benchmark on both technological and nontechnological factors. Traditional threat and vulnerability analyses still apply. Vulnerabilities can fall under both the inherent factor (when they are inherent to the business and cannot be mitigated) and the control factor (when necessary security measures are not in place).

KCRF can be identified only with consistent monitoring and correlation of risk factors and cyber loss. In order to standardize incident data collection, an International Classification of Cyber Incidents (ICCI) also needs to be developed in conjunction with the International Digital Asset Classification (IDAC), similar to the International Classification of Disease (ICD).[5]

9.7.2 Using Scenario Analysis for Control Assessment and Loss Quantification

In order to identify controls that will be the most effective in reducing an entity's cyber risk exposure, scenario analysis[6] is used in cybernomics to assess the entity's controls against its most damaging cyber-loss events. Once the entity has identified its most valuable digital assets, a cyber loss scenario inventory can be developed around those assets. These are the loss events the entity's is "genetically" most exposed to. A basic example is shown in Table 9.3.

Then, microeconomic loss can be quantified using the loss categories listed in Table 9.4. Monetary loss estimation under each loss category can come from historical incidents, industry reports, forensic reports, expert judgments, external studies, and statistical databases, etc.

With increasing sophistication and interdependency of IT outsourcing, and the usage of cloud computing in particular, quantifying macroeconomic losses in IT supply chain has become a main obstacle for cyber insurers and reinsurers. Detailed process for macroeconomic loss quantification is out of scope for this book, but the Cambridge Center of Risk Studies has proposed two stress test scenarios for cyber catastrophes to quantify macroeconomic losses (Ruffel et al., 2014; Centre for Risk Studies, 2014).

Scenario analyses are currently recommended in all cases of cyber loss quantification to compensate for the lack of quality historical loss data. Going forward, both the statistical approach and scenario analysis should be used. The statistical approach involves forecasting an entity's cyber loss using probability and statistical models with the aid of the cyber risk databank. It should be used to monitor risks continuously. Scenario analysis, especially stress scenario analysis, does not necessarily require the use of a probability or statistical model. Instead, the conditions of a cyber incident can be arbitrarily chosen or based on major incidents in crisis situations. Scenario analysis should be used on a case-by-case basis to estimate risk in unique circumstances.

---

6. Scenario analysis is a process of analyzing possible future events by considering alternative possible outcomes. As a main method of projections, scenario analysis does not try to show one exact picture of the future.

TABLE 9.3 Digital Assets and Associated Cyber Loss Events

Digital Valuables		Cyber Loss Scenarios
Core value assets	IP of a critical product	IP theft, industrial espionage, etc.
	Regulated PII	Data breach, data leakage, etc.
	Sensitive financial data	Cyber fraud, data corruption, malfunction of trading algorithms, ransomware, etc.
Operational assets	Business critical IT services	System downtime due to technical malfunction, human error, etc.
	Payment website	Denial-of-Service (DoS) attack, insider attack, etc.

TABLE 9.4 Microeconomic Loss Quantification Method

Loss Category	Microeconomic Loss Quantification Method
Direct loss (financial loss, physical asset damage, death, and bodily injury)	Loss based on valuation of the digital valuable affected, direct losses on expenses, etc.
Incident investigation and response	Cost of paying internal forensic team and external consultants for investigation and response to the incident, including technical tools and applications required for purchase and installation.
Reputational damage (applicable after incident has gone public)	Estimated economic loss correlated to the size of the readership of the media the incident is publicized on, and through reputation rating agencies (e.g., BizRate[a]).
Legal liabilities	Liability (e.g., per record in case of PII breach) as defined in laws, regulations, contracts and agreements.
Regulatory penalties	Regulatory fines e.g., 5% of revenue.
Impact on share price	From implicit market value (estimates) and explicit market value (observed).

[a]*BizRate.com. (n.d.). Retrieved from http://www.bizrate.com.*

9.8 INTRODUCING BITMORT AND HEKLA

Cybernomics applies attributes of established risk measures Value-at-Risk (VaR) and micromort to the definition of cyber risk units. In Table 9.5 a comparison is made between the needs for cyber risk measurement and the applications of micromort.

A Class D asset is any type of digital asset as listed in IDAC, and it is one type of valuable asset in entity E's digital asset inventory.

Based on this comparison, attributes of micromort can be borrowed to define a cyber risk measurement. However, differences between the nature of human mortality risk and "digital mortality" risk must be taken into consideration. Firstly, micromort was created on the basis that human death is a certain event with a probability of 1. It has been applied based on statistics of all causes (both natural and non-natural) to human death, including suicide. In comparison, the economic lifespan of digital assets can be eternal with the recent breakthrough in digital storage capability (The Daily Beast, 2016). Definition below is used in cybernomics:

'Digital death' is defined as a binary condition when a digital asset loses all of its economic value.

Currently, the majority of digital assets will eventually "die" either "naturally" through retirement, or replacement, or "non-naturally" due to external threats such as the compromise of its confidentiality, integrity, and availability. Cyber risk measures are defined based on the following assumption:

*Assumption 1: all classes of digital assets will eventually reach a state of 'digital death' and lose **all** of their economic value.*

TABLE 9.5 Comparison Between Needs for Cyber Risk Measurement and Applications of Micromort

Needs of Cyber Risk Measurement	Applications of Micromort
To measure the effect of control factors on the probabilities of class D assets losing their value.	Micromort measures the effect of day-to-day activities (modifiable risk factors) on the probability of human death.
To articulate entity E's "willingness-to-pay" for the reduction of risk of class D assets.	The value of micromort reflects the "willingness-to-pay" for the reduction of risk.
To measure cost of controls to reduce risk exposure of class D assets.	The cost of reducing 1 micromort reflects the cost-effectiveness of countermeasures to reduce risk.

Secondly, different classes of digital assets are exposed to different inherent risks. So each class of digital assets should have its own set of microrisks, similar to if we were to track microrisks for all organisms and not only humans. We have not yet tracked the microrisks of any other organisms so we cannot draw any comparisons. Nevertheless, all digital assets are made of bits, just like all organisms are made of cells. In cybernomics, cyber risk measures are defined based on the following assumption:

Assumption 2: the inherent differences between different classes of digital assets are distinct enough for their risks to be monitored and analyzed separately.

Based on the two assumptions above, Bitmort$_D$ (BM$_D$) is defined as follows for class D assets:

Bitmort$_D$ (BM$_D$) for a given class D digital assets is 1 in a million probability of its digital death, i.e., a binary condition when the asset loses all of its economic value. The value of 1 BM$_D$ is the amount of money an entity is willing to pay to reduce 1 BM$_D$ for its class D assets.

The same scale of million is chosen for BM based on the following facts:

- There were 707,509,815 data records lost globally in 2015[7] out of an estimated population of 95,100,000,000 total records (3.17 billion internet users in 2015[8] with an average of 30 online records per person[9]), which is roughly a probability of 0.0074.
- There were a total number of 499,331 recorded deaths in England and Wales in 2012 out of a population of 56,567,000,[10] which is a probability of 0.0088.

Because there is no way to decide what scale to use without substantial loss data collected for different types of digital assets, the scale of million is sufficient as a start. It can always be scaled up or down, similar to byte−megabyte−gigabyte and meter−centimeter−millimeter.

When residual risk measured in BM becomes statistically available for various types of digital assets, it is possible to aggregate them along with asset value to generate a Cyber VaR curve, representing the entity's residual cyber risk:

$$\text{VaR} = \sum_{i=1}^{n} VifDi$$

where VaR is value at risk for all digital assets of an entity E; entity E's digital asset inventory $D = \{D_1, D_2, \ldots, D_n\}$; the value of each asset $V = \{V_1, V_2, \ldots, V_n\}$; and f_{Di} is the amount of residual risk D_i is exposed to be measured in BM$_{Di}$s.

To compute the Cyber VaR curve, historical simulation and Monte Carlo simulation can be used. Under historical simulation, BMs are extracted under a number of different historical time windows which are defined by the entity.

7. 2015 Data Breach Statistics — Breach Level Index Findings (2015). Retrieved from: http://www.safenet-inc.com/resources/data-protection/2015-data-breaches-infographic/.

8. Number of Internet users worldwide from 2005 to 2015. Retrieved from: http://www.statista.com/statistics/273018/number-of-internet-users-worldwide/.

9. Based on expert judgement.

10. Office for National Statistics Deaths, 2013. Registered in England and Wales (Series DR). Retrieved June 2014, from https://www.ons.gov.uk/peoplepopulationandcommunity/birthsdeathsandmarriages/deaths/bulletins/deathsregisteredinenglandandwalesseriesdr/2013-10-22.

While historical simulation measures risk by replicating one specific historical path of cyber risk ecosystem, Monte Carlo simulation attempts to generate a large number of paths using repeated random sampling to produce a probability distribution.

The risk measure hekla is defined as follows:

hekla is a probability, where a 12-month hekla VaR is the loss limit an entity can afford from cyber incidents. The value of hekla is the amount of money the entity is willing to pay to reduce its hekla by 1% for the same loss limit.

The time horizon of 12 months is chosen to reflect cyber risk exposure over one financial year, which should be considered in budget planning and integrated with enterprise risk management frameworks.

9.9   RISK CALCULATIONS

Given Company A's digital asset inventory $D = \{D_1, D_2, \ldots, D_n\}$, D_1 being regulated PII. Section below demonstrates how BM and hekla are used for risk calculation.

9.9.1   Measuring Strength of Controls for Digital Assets Using Bitmort

In Company A, the implementation of firewall can reduce risk exposure of D_1 by f BM_{D1}s, and not having appointed a Chief Information Security Officer can increase the same by c BM_{D1}s.

9.9.2   Measuring Cost-Effectiveness of Controls for Digital Assets Using Bitmort

It costs Company A $5000 using solution X and $10,000 using solution Z to reduce risk exposure of D_1 by 1 BM_{D1}. Therefore, solution X is more cost-effective than solution Z.

9.9.3   Articulating an Entity's "Willingness-to-Pay" for Risk Reduction for Digital Assets Using Bitmort

Company A prices the reduction of 1 BM_{D1} from the risk exposure of D_1 in the tens of cents per record.

9.9.4   Articulating an Entity's Cyber Risk Limit Using Hekla

The maximum loss amount Company A can tolerate from cyber incidents is a 12-month 7% *VaR* of $100 million (or 10% of its total revenue) from cyber loss. This means Company A's cyber loss limit is $100 million (or 10% of its total capital), with a hekla of 7%.

9.9.5   Articulating an Entity's Cyber Risk Appetite Using Hekla

Company A's cyber risk appetite is a hekla of maximum 4% where the 12-months hekla VaR is $100 million (its risk limit).

9.9.6   Measuring an Entity's Cyber Risk Pricing Using Hekla

If Company A is willing to spend $10 million to bring its hekla from 7% down to 6% with the same loss limit, it means company A prices its own hekla at $10 million.

9.9.7   Measuring an Entity's Cost of Risk Reduction Using Hekla

If in practice, it takes Company A $15 million to reduce its hekla from 7% to 6% with the same loss limit, then the cost of the reducing hekla by 1% in Company A is $15 million.

9.9.8 Measuring an Entity's Cyber Risk Return on Investment Using Hekla

Company B's digital value composition is >95% similar to Company A's, therefore Company B has similar inherent cyber risk exposure as Company A, and it follows the same process to compute its hekla. Due to different ways of control implementation, the cost of reducing hekla by 1% in Company B is $5 million whereas it costs Company A $15 million to do the same. Thus, Company B is more cost effective than Company A in managing its cyber risk. Cyber risk return on investment is essentially the reduction of hekla per every dollar spend.

9.9.9 Using Bitmort and Hekla on a Portfolio of Entities

BM and hekla are measures that can be "stacked" on the portfolio level. All applications of BM and hekla can be applied on a portfolio of entities and on the macroeconomic level.

9.10 THREE VIEWS OF CYBERNOMICS

There are three views of cybernomics: the entity view, portfolio view, and global view, as shown in Fig. 9.1.

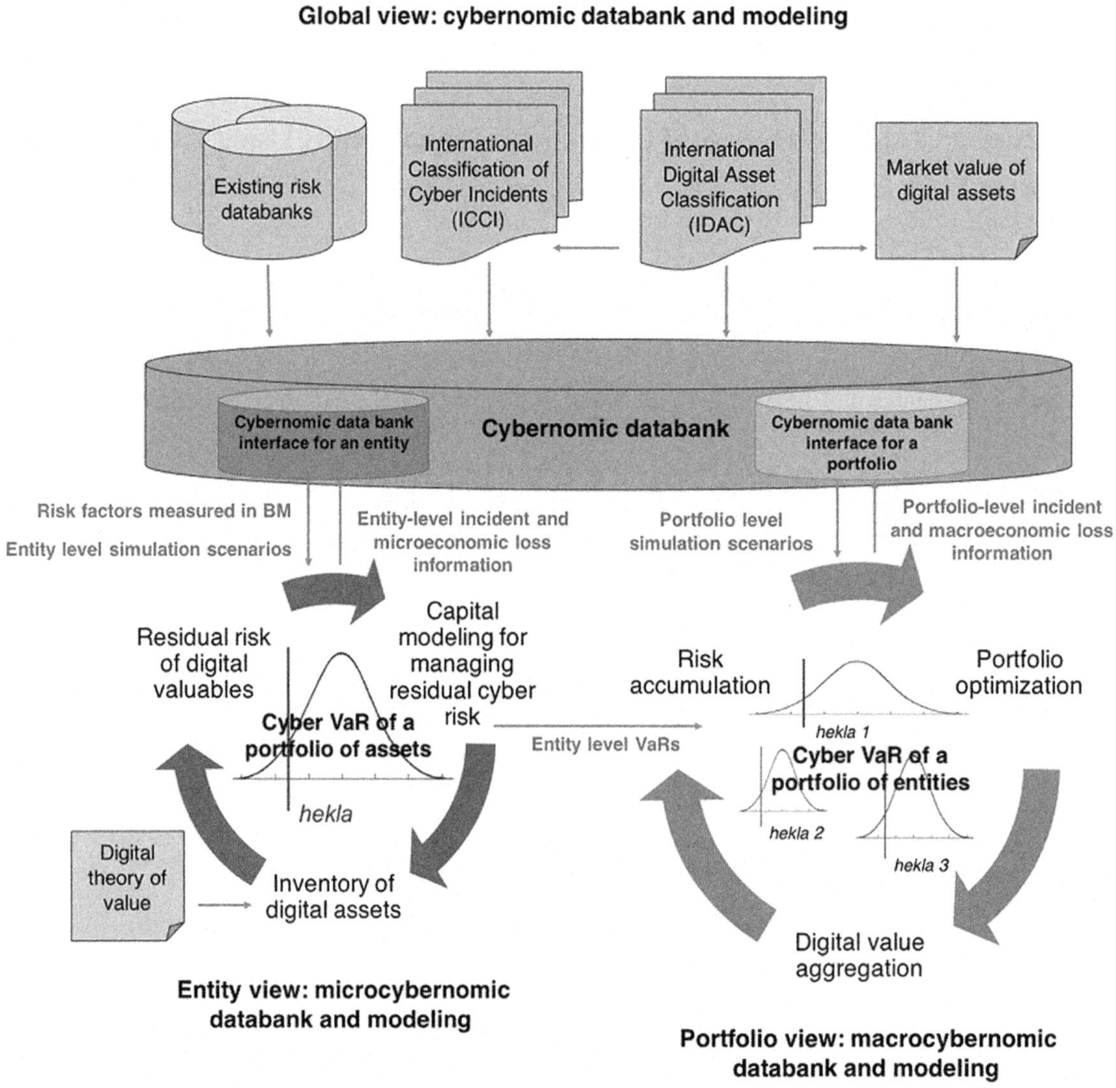

FIGURE 9.1 Three views of cybernomics.

9.10.1   Entity View

In the entity view of cybernomics as shown in Fig. 9.1, for entity E:

E's digital value is the sum of the aggregated value of its core value assets and aggregated value of its operational assets. E maintains a digital asset inventory with economic value assigned to each asset. Each asset listed in E's digital asset inventory follows standard classification in IDAC. E maintains a microeconomic loss scenario inventory developed around its critical assets.

E uses microcybernomic databank and modeling to optimize its capital modeling for managing residual cyber risk. E monitors its cyber risk factors, which are categorized under Cyber Risk Quadrant as technological, nontechnological, inherent and control factors. E reads measures of these risk factors from its entity-level interface with the cybernomic databank. It uses a combination of statistical modeling and scenario analysis to quantify cyber loss, and uses scenario-based control assessment to optimize its investment on measures that are the most cost-effective for risk reduction. E also gets the most relevant entity-level simulation scenarios from the cybernomic databank. In return, E feeds its incident and microeconomic loss information back to the cybernomic databank.

For a given class of asset D in E's asset inventory, BM_D is defined as one in a million probability of its digital death. The value of 1 BM_D is the amount of money E is willing to pay to reduce 1 BM_D for D type of asset. Following this process, risk exposure of all assets in E's asset inventory, cost of risk reduction of each type of asset, and E's "willingness-to-pay" to reduce their risk exposures can be measured and aggregated into a 12-month VaR curve.

Hekla is a probability, where a 12-month hekla VaR is the loss limit E can afford from cyber incidents. The value of hekla is the amount of money E is willing to pay to reduce its hekla by 1% for the same loss limit. Hekla can be used to articulate E's risk limit, risk appetite, and risk pricing.

Both bitmort and hekla are stackable on portfolio and global levels.

9.10.2   Portfolio View

In the portfolio view of cybernomics, as shown in Fig. 9.1, for multinational corporations, insurers, investors, or policy-makers who manage a portfolio of entities P:

P uses macrocybernomic databank and modeling to optimize portfolio returns. P aggregates digital value from its portfolio of entities, calculates portfolio cyber VaR stacked from cyber VaRs of individual entities. Then, it determines portfolio level hekla and manages available capital accordingly. The portfolio view reads portfolio level simulation scenarios from its portfolio-level interface with the cybernomic databank. In return, P feeds its incident and macroeconomic loss information back to the cybernomic databank.

9.10.3   Global View

In the global view of cybernomics as shown in Fig. 9.1, a databank and cybernomic model evolve around the classification schemes of assets (IDAC) and associated incidents (International Classification of Cyber Incident), and integrates with existing risk databanks to cover socio-economic, geo-political risk factors. Market values of digital assets listed in IDAC are monitored. Risk factors are categorized under Cyber Risk Quadrant. Through public—private data partnership schemes, incident, and loss data are collected from both entity and portfolio levels to support statistical modeling. The cybernomic model correlates risk factors and cyber loss to calculate risk exposures measured in bitmort and identify KCRF. The cybernomic databank feeds risk exposure information and simulation scenarios to entities. It also feeds portfolio-level simulation scenarios to portfolio risk managers based on historical incidents.

9.11   DISCUSSIONS AND LIMITATIONS

9.11.1   Accuracy

It is important to note that it is valuable for cyber risk managers to measure the difference between a $50 million exposure and a $10 million exposure, but it is irrelevant to measure the difference between $10 million and $11 million. It costs exponentially more to reach this level of accuracy that is likely to be counterproductive to improving cost-effectiveness.

9.11.2 Analytical Capabilities

The solution conceptualized in this chapter relies on advanced data analytics capabilities that are on a trajectory of exponential growth. Compared to the 1990s when J. P. Morgan built the first analytics tool to compute VaR, we enjoy a tremendous advantage in storing and processing large datasets. As a result, the major obstacle to advancement for this field is not the lack of technological capabilities to compute datasets, but to break down necessary nontechnological barriers and establish a wide range of data points under the three views of cybernomics.

9.11.3 Testing and Validation

This is the first of a series of publications introducing the discipline of cybernomics. Testing and validation using real-world data is a work in progress and will be published in separate papers. Nevertheless, it is impossible to validate the entire framework due to the lack of data points. Validation can only be made in parts. The purpose of publishing this book is also to invite testing and validation from the research community. It took years to validate VaR and decades to validate micromort due to the time required for data collection, yet it was important to put forward the definitions first so that data collection can take place in a structured manner.

9.11.4 Economic Lifespan of Digital Assets

It has already been proven technically feasible for digital assets to outlive humanity. In the meantime, we are suffering increasing "data pollution" in these early days of Big Data. The low-end tasks of selection, normalization, and cleansing of large datasets often cost more than analytics. This will eventually become an overhead that nobody is willing to pay. The alternative is to set a "self-deletion" date for certain classes of digital assets. Due to the uncertainty of which path will be taken in the future, definitions in this book are based on the assumption that there will be limited economic life-spans for all classes of digital assets.

9.11.5 Fundamental Inherent Differences of Digital Assets

Definitions in this book require microrisks of different classes of digital assets to be tracked separately based on the assumption that inherent differences of digital assets are distinct enough for their risks to be tracked in separate data-banks. However, it does not rule out the possibility of a more unified approach to the definition of this risk unit since all digital assets are fundamentally made of bits.

Chapter 10

Case Study: Insuring the Future of Everything

Chapter Outline

10.1 History and Context of Cyber Insurance 159
10.2 Current Offerings, Coverage, and Policy Limits 161
    10.2.1 Current Policy Coverage 161
    10.2.2 Types of Breaches That Lead to Claims 162
    10.2.3 Reputation Loss as Part of First-Party Loss 163
    10.2.4 Policy Limits 163
10.3 Underwriting and Assessment Process 164
    10.3.1 Conducting a Thorough Information Security Risk Audit 164
10.3.2 Assessing Current Coverage 164
10.3.3 Evaluating Available Policies 164
10.3.4 Selecting Appropriate Policies 164
10.4 Claim Study 165
10.5 Current Challenges in the Cyber Insurance Market 165
    10.5.1 Lack of Sufficient Quality Actuarial Data 166
    10.5.2 Asymmetric Information 167
10.6 Cybernomics and the Future Growth of the Cyber Insurance Market 167

It seems to be a law of nature, inflexible and inexorable, that those who will not risk cannot win.

— John Paul Jones.

10.1 HISTORY AND CONTEXT OF CYBER INSURANCE

Traditional approaches to security architecture and design have attempted to achieve the goal of the elimination of risk factors—the complete prevention of system compromise through technical and procedural means. Insurance-based solutions to risk long ago admitted that a complete elimination of risk is impossible and, instead, have focused more on reducing the impact of harm through financial avenues, providing policies that indemnify the policy holder in the event of harm. It is becoming increasingly clear that early models of computer security, which focused exclusively on the risk-elimination model, are not sufficient in the increasingly complex world of the Internet. There is simply no magic bullet computer security. No amount of time or money can create a perfectly hardened system (Sieglel et al., 2002).

Much of the potential risk from conducting business on the Internet is not fundamentally new. For example, a firm would incur liability risk of copyright infringement or defamation of character whether the information is distributed through the Internet or through television, radio, or magazines. Similarly, a firm would suffer a loss of business whether an interruption is caused by a fire, a flood, or by a hacker's denial-of-service (DoS) attack. Some of the overlapping coverage between cyber and traditional first-party and third-party insurance policies are as follows:

- First Party
  - Commercial property insurance.
  - Commercial crime policy and fidelity bonds.

- Third Party
  - Commercial General Liability (CGL) policies: (1) bodily injury or property damage; and (2) personal and advertising injury.
  - Directors and Officers (D&O) policies, Errors & Omissions (E&O) policies.

Digital Asset Valuation and Cyber Risk Measurement. DOI: https://doi.org/10.1016/B978-0-12-812158-0.00010-7

While the business risk of being connected to the Internet is analogous to many traditional business types of risk, some characteristics of internet-related cyber risk are unique, in terms of location, degree, and visibility. For example, a perpetrator of information theft or property damage may be thousands of miles away from the business location when committing crime via the Internet. The damages from a virus can go beyond the effects on the data and software of the targeted business, causing the initial targeted business to incur a liability. Additionally, since the commodity on the Internet is information, security breaches, such as the theft of the firm's strategically sensitive information, often go undetected. Thus, insurance companies, including American International Group, Chubb, Fidelity, and Deposit, Marsh, Lloyds of London, and J.S. Wurzler, introduced new policies covering varying aspects of cyberspace risk. In designing these new policies, insurance companies addressed issues related to pricing, adverse selection, and moral hazard (Gordon et al., 2003).

Before the late-1990s, little commercial demand existed for property or liability insurance specifically covering losses from network security breaches or other IT-related problems. However, the rapid growth of e-commerce, followed by distributed denial-of-service (DDoS) attacks that took down several leading commercial websites in February 2000, kindled significant interest in such coverage. The Y2K computer problem, although ultimately resulting in little direct damage or loss, brought further attention to cyber-risk issues and pointed out the limitations of existing insurance coverage for IT failures (Baer and Parkinson, 2007).

By 2002, in response to the legal uncertainties, insurers had written specific exclusionary language into their commercial property and liability policies to exclude coverage of "electronic data," "computer code," and similar terms as tangible property. Computer code is deemed to be intangible. Property and casualty policies were never written to assess these exposures and were never priced to include them. This was affirmed by two appeals in court in 2003.[1]

Potential liability from IT security breaches has increased as a result of such federal legislation as the Health Insurance Portability and Accountability Act (HIPPA) and the Graham-Leach-Bliley Act (GLBA), which mandate protection of sensitive personal medical and financial records. California also passed a Security Breach Information Act,[2] requiring prompt public disclosure of any breach that might have compromised computer-based personal information about a California resident. This California law, which went into effect in July 2003, essentially sets a national requirement for any business or other organization that maintains a database with identifiable individual records. Starting around 1998, a few insurance companies developed specialized policies covering losses from computer viruses or other malicious code, destruction or theft of data, business interruption, denial of service, and/or liability resulting from e-commerce or other networked IT failures. Coverage was spotty and limited, but premiums were high. Moreover, numerous legal disputes arose over whether such losses could come under general commercial property or liability policies that were written to cover direct physical damage to tangible assets (Baer, 2003; Kesan et al., 2004, 2005).

Over the next few years, the cyber insurance market has both broadened and differentiated. Underwriters include both large insurance companies and several smaller, more specialized firms. Most carriers now offer a combination of property, theft, and liability coverage (see Table 10.1). Increasingly, cyber insurance products are designed for specific markets—for example, American International Group (AIG) and Chubb have policies tailored for financial service organizations (Baer and Parkinson, 2007).

As of 2015, Lloyds Banking Group has introduced a separate code for cyber insurance. In addition to large insurance companies which provide cyber insurance offerings, there is also an emergence of InsureTech start-ups which are bringing higher risk awareness, efficiency and more innovative products (EIOPA, 2018).

A quality insurance policy, e.g., from a specialized insurance carrier of top financial strength and global reach, can also provide superior loss prevention and analysis recommendations. It often provides premium discounts for the purchase of certain security products and services from companies known to the insurer, which serve as a dovetail into a company's own risk assessment program. Initially, determining potential loss and business impact due to a security breach allows organizations to choose the right policy for their specific needs. The insurance component then complements the technical solutions and policy procedures. A vital step is choosing the right insurance carrier by seeking companies with specific underwriting and claims units with expertise in the area of information security, top financial ratings, and global reach. The right carrier should offer a suite of policies for companies to choose from which can provide adequate coverage to fulfill these four purposes (Sieglel, 2002):

---

1. Ward General Insurance Services Inc. *v* Employers Fire Insurance Company: https://caselaw.findlaw.com/ca-court-of-appeal/1445761.html. America Online Incorporated *v.* St. Paul Mercury Insurance Company: https://caselaw.findlaw.com/us-4th-circuit/1330432.html.
2. www.securitymanagement.com/library/SB1386_ca0203.pdf.

TABLE 10.1 Coverage Offered by Major Cyber Insurance Carriers

Coverage property and theft	ACE	AIG	Chubb	CNA	St. Paul Travelers	Zurich	Liberty Mutual
Maximum limit (US$ millions)	15	25	25	10	N/A	7.5	N/A
Destruction of data or software	Y	Y	Y	Y	Y	Y	Y
Recovery from viruses or other malicious code	N/A	Y	Y	Y	Y	Y	Y
Business interruption	Y	Y	Y	Y	Y	Y	Y
Denial of service	Y	Y	Y	Y	Y	Y	
Data theft	Y	Y	Y	Y	Y	Y	Y
Cyberextortion	Y	Y	Y	Y	Y	Y	Y
Losses due to terrorist acts	Y	Y	Y	Y	Y	Y	N/A
Liability							
Maximum limit (US$ millions)	50	25	50	10	25	7.5	N/A
Network security liability	Y	Y	Y	Y	Y	Y	Y
Content/electronic media injury	Y	Y	Y	Y	Y	Y	N/A
Privacy/breach of confidentiality liability	Y	Y	Y	Y	Y	Y	Y

In Table 10.1, the company: (A) will assist in placing higher limits up to US$75 million; (B) offers limits up to US$20 million on a highly selected basis; and (C) offers some first-party cyber coverage as part of traditional property policies, not as specialized polices.
Betterley (2017).

1. Assistance in the evaluation of the risk through products and services available from the insurer.
2. Transfer of the financial costs of a successful computer attack or threat to the carrier.
3. The provision of important post-incident support funds to reduce the potential reputation damage after an attack.
4. The additional purpose of insurance, when properly placed, is also to provide positive reinforcement for good behavior by adjusting the availability and affordability of insurance, depending on the insured's security program. It also helps condition the continuation of such insurance on the maintenance of that quality.

10.2   CURRENT OFFERINGS, COVERAGE, AND POLICY LIMITS

10.2.1   Current Policy Coverage

Current cyber insurance products tend to provide three basic types of coverage: liability arising from theft of data, remediation in response to the breach, and legal and regulatory fines and penalties (Sieglel, 2002; Betterly Risk Consultants, 2006). So-called internet insurance policies vary widely, with some providing relatively little real coverage. A properly crafted internet-risk program should contain multiple products within a suite concept, permitting a company to choose which risks to cover depending upon where it is in its Internet maturity curve (Sieglel, 2002). A suite should provide at least six coverages, with some examples of coverage from major insurers provided in Table 10.2:

1. *Web content liability* provides coverage for claims arising out of the content of your website, including the invisible meta-tags content, such as libel, slander, copyright, and trademark infringement.
2. *Internet professional liability* provides coverage for claims arising out of the performing of professional services. Coverage usually includes both web publishing activities as well as pure internet services such as being an ISP, host, or web designer. Any professional service conducted over the Internet can usually be added to the policy.
3. *Network security coverage* comes in two basic types:
   a. *First-party coverage* provides, upon a covered event, reimbursement for loss arising out of the altering, copying, misappropriating, corrupting, destroying, disrupting, deleting, damaging, or theft of information assets, whether

TABLE 10.2 Policy Offerings From Three Top Cyber Insurers[a]

Munich Re	Chubb	Hiscox
• Data breach response expenses • Identity recovery • Computer attack • Cyber extortion • Data breach liability • Network security liability • Electronic media liability	• Cyber incident response fund • Business interruption • Contingent business interruption • Digital data recovery • Network extortion • Cyber, privacy and network security liability • Payment card loss • Regulatory proceedings • Electronic, social, and printed media liability	• Data breach response • Cyber business interruption • Hacker damage • Cyber extortion • Privacy and security liability • Payment card loss • Regulatory liability • Contractual liability • Media liability

[a]https://cyberpolicy.com.

or not criminal. Typically, the policy will cover the cost of replacing, reproducing, recreating, restoring, or recollecting. In case of theft of a trade secret (a broadly defined term), the policy will either pay or be capped at the endorsed negotiated amount. First-party coverage also provides reimbursement for lost e-revenue as a result of a covered event. Here, the policy will provide coverage for the period of recovery plus an extended business interruption period. Some policies also provide coverage for dependent business interruption, meaning loss of e-revenue as a result of a computer attack on a third-party business (such as a supplier) upon which the insured's business depends.

   b. *Third-party coverage* provides liability coverage arising from a failure of the insured's security to prevent unauthorized use or access of its network. This important coverage would apply, subject to the policy's full terms, to claims arising from the transmission of a computer virus, theft of a customer's information (most notably including credit card information), and so-called denial-of-service liability.

4. *Cyber-extortion coverage* provides reimbursement of investigation costs, and sometimes the extortion demand itself, in the event of a covered cyber-extortion threat. Cyber extortion is the act of cyber-criminals demanding payment through the use of or threat of some form of malicious activity against a victim, such as data compromise or denial-of-service attack.

5. *Public relations or crisis-communication coverage* provides reimbursement up to $50,000 for use of public relations firms to rebuild an enterprise's reputation with customers, employees, and shareholders following a computer attack.

6. *Criminal reward funds coverage* provides reimbursement up to $50,000 for information leading to the arrest and conviction of a cyber-criminal. Given that many cyber-criminals hack into sites for "bragging rights," this unique insurance provision may create a most-welcomed chilling effect.

All carriers now offer coverage of losses due to foreign-based, government-certified acts of terrorism as per the Terrorism Risk Insurance Act (TRIA) of 2002,[3] and some provide additional endorsements for domestic-based and other noncertified terrorist acts (Baer and Parkinson, 2007).

10.2.2   Types of Breaches That Lead to Claims

There are mainly three types of breaches than lead to insurance claims:

1. *Symptomatic.* A breach is symptomatic when a firm is breached through exploitation of firm-specific vulnerabilities. Such compromises suggest questionable health of a firm's security program. Consequently, stakeholders downgrade their perception of the firm's security. An example of a symptomatic breach is the 2014 Sony hack. A hacker group called "Guardians of Peace" (GOP) leaked a release of confidential data from the film studio Sony Pictures. The leaked data included personal information of employees, their families, emails between employees, information

---

3. The TRIA was originally set to expire in 2005. It was extended to 2007, then again to 2014. On January 2015, the Terrorism Risk Insurance Program Reauthorization Act of 2015 extended the TRIA through the year 2020.

about executive salaries, copies of the then-unreleased Sony films, and other information. The perpetrators then employed a variant of the Shamoon wiper malware to erase Sony's computer infrastructure.

2. *Systemic*. A systemic breach occurs when the affected firm has no reasonable or even known way to defend itself against a new threat vector, especially when the threat is transmitted through the business networks. In this case, stakeholders do not alter their perception of a firm's IT security for systemic breaches, IT security programs plan only for known threats, and firms are all understood to be part of the internetworked global economy where such unknowns are always possible. In 2017, over 200,000 victims and more than 300,000 computers were infected by the WannaCry ransomware cryptoworm, which targeted computers running the Microsoft Windows operating system by encrypting data and demanding ransom payments in the Bitcoin cryptocurrency.

3. *Public*. A breach is public if it is publicly observed, such as a webpage being defaced, or an observable distributed denial-of-service attack disables a firm's e-commerce transactions or is disclosed through legal requirements or accounting norms. By this definition, breaches that are not made public are private (Bandyopadhyay, et al., 2009).

10.2.3   Reputation Loss as Part of First-Party Loss

Perhaps the most difficult, and yet one of the most important, risks to understand is the intangible risk of damage to the company's reputation. Will customers give a company their credit card numbers once they read in the paper that a company's database of credit card numbers was hacked into? Will top employees remain at a company so damaged? And, what will be the reaction of the company's shareholders? Again, the best way to analyze reputation risk is to attempt to quantify it. What is the expected loss of future business revenue? What is the expected loss of market capitalization? Can shareholder class or derivative actions be foreseen and, if so, what can the expected financial cost of those actions be in terms of lawyer fees and potential settlement amounts? (Sieglel et al., 2002) (Table 10.3).

10.2.4   Policy Limits

Since cyber-risk insurance is a new product, underwriters are generally reluctant to offer large policies comparing to traditional insurance. Lloyds offers limits for its cyber policy of $50,000,000 and gives custom quotes up to $200,000,000. As more experience is gained in this area, these limits are expected to be raised. Additionally, insurers may also offer alternate policies providing high limits in combination with substantially raised deductibles. Thus, firms will be able to secure higher total coverage by combining policies from multiple insurers, for example, having one policy cover the first $20,000,000 of losses and another policy cover losses over $20,000,000 (Sieglel et al., 2002).

TABLE 10.3 Standalone and Package Cyber Coverage Combined (Year-End 2015)

Rank	Company	Direct Written Premium ($)	Policies In-Force Claims Made
1	American International Group	215,563,000	16,418
2	Chubb Limited	121,132,000	5119
3	XL Group Ltd.	113,482,000	1310
4	AXIS Capital Holdings Ltd.	83,223,000	3067
5	Beazley Insurance Co.	68,954,000	13,324
6	Travelers Companies, Inc.	65,026,000	31,887
7	CNA Financial Corp.	57,637,000	24,981
8	Allied World Assurance Co.	29,938,000	1002
9	Berkshire Hathaway, Inc.	20,467,000	72,909
10	Ironshore Inc.	17,272,000	1615
	Industry	**998,298,000**	**577,375**

10.3   UNDERWRITING AND ASSESSMENT PROCESS

For the insureds on the entity level, there are four steps in its risk-management process to choose the right insurance policies (Gordon et al., 2003): (1) conducting a thorough audit, (2) assessing current coverage, (3) evaluating available policies, and (4) selecting appropriate policies.

10.3.1   Conducting a Thorough Information Security Risk Audit

The first step is to conduct a thorough audit of current information security risk. This audit should uncover the firm's information security risk exposure and if possible, place a dollar value on that exposure. The audit is part of loss prevention services that are usually paid by the applicant which can cost up to $50,000. Typically, these services include anything from a free online self-assessment program, to a full-fledged on-site security assessment, for example based on ISO 17799. Some insurers may also add other services, such as an internal or external network scan. For example, AIG underwriters will determine whether they require an onsite audit to bind coverage based on the results of self-assessments. The AIG self-assessment covers items such as:

- Standard configurations with security documentation for firewalls, routers, and operating systems.
- Information security policies, including password management, virus protection, encryption, and security training for employees.
- Vulnerability monitoring and patch management.
- Physical security and access controls, including remote access.
- Privacy and confidentiality policies.
- Backup and restoration provisions.
- Business continuity planning.
- Periodic testing of security controls.
- Outsourcing and other third-party security provisions.

Nearly all insurers also provide cyber-risk management services to help clients identify exposures, take loss prevention, as well as mitigation measures.

Although policy language about what is insured and what perils and risks are covered have become more standardized, cyber insurance policies are still largely written and priced to match individual client practices and exposures. Consequently, there are no published standard rates as state insurance regulators would require for standard products. Insurance rates continue to be set on a customer-by-customer basis and can vary considerably based on the results of security assessments and audits (Baer and Parkinson, 2007).

10.3.2   Assessing Current Coverage

The next step is to assess current coverage. Corporate executives should thoroughly review existing traditional insurance program, including its property insurance covering business interruption, comprehensive general liability (CGL) insurance, directors and officers insurance (often called D&O), professional liability insurance, and crime policies. This review should focus on gaps in relevant coverage in the current policies (Sieglel, et al., 2002).

10.3.3   Evaluating Available Policies

The third step is to examine and evaluate available insurance policies. Cyber insurance is a relatively new product and its policies differ widely in coverage and price. For example, does the firm require coverage for losses due to a crash of the firm's website, a denial-of-service attack, potential liabilities from third parties, or libellous statements appearing on the company's website? It is important to consider a firm's potential losses and the security measures in place when evaluating a policy. For example, firms that pose a low moral hazard threat should carefully analyze insurance policies that are cheaper for firms exhibiting this feature.

10.3.4   Selecting Appropriate Policies

The fourth step is to select the policy appropriate for the unique circumstances of a given company, and the firm's risk tolerance is a key determinant of the appropriateness of a particular insurance policy. A number of factors should

TABLE 10.4 Overall Number of Records Exposed and Associated Costs (Net Diligence, 2016)

	Median Number of Records Exposed	Overall Number of Records Exposed (Million)	Average Cost per Record ($)	Overall Costs (Million)
2011	45,000	1.7	1.36	2.43
2012	29,000	1.4	3.94	3.60
2013	1,000	2.4	307	0.95
2014	3,500	2.4	956	0.73
2015	2,300	3.2	964	0.674
2016	1,339	2.04	17,035	0.665

be considered in making a selection: (1) the policy should have the desired additional coverage at an acceptable price, (2) the trade-off between risk reduction and cost of insurance should be evaluated, and (3) the portion of financial risk the firm wants the insurer to cover and the residual portion the firm is willing to bear itself. Finally, since cyber insurance is a new product, there is often considerable room for negotiating prices with brokers and/or agents (Gordon et al., 2003).

10.4 CLAIM STUDY

Cyber insurance claims are the most valuable data source as they contain exact loss data with associated costs. Table 10.3 shows the overall number of records exposed and associated costs from 2011 to 2016 based on a 2016 study with 176 cyber claims submitted (Net Diligence, 2016), 163 out of the 176 claims involved the loss, exposure or misuse of some type of sensitive personal data. The remaining 13 incidents involved business interruption, lost hardware and DDoS attacks. 68% of the claims reported the number of records exposed. The number of records exposed in a data breach ranging from 1 to 78 million, the average number of records exposed was 2.04 million. The median number of records exposed over the years was much smaller. It is clear that more claims are being submitted for breaches with a relatively small number of records exposed. Because data breaches involve many types of data and many types of costs, costs can range anywhere from a few hundred dollars to millions. High per-record costs are possible regardless of breach size, the cost of 1 record can be as high as $1.5−2 million, 66% of the claims in the dataset reported both the number of records lost and the total breach cost. The minimum cost per record was $0.03 and the maximum cost per record was $1.6 million. The average cost per record was $17K, while the medium cost was $39.82.

10.5 CURRENT CHALLENGES IN THE CYBER INSURANCE MARKET

Cyber insurance can, in principle, be an important risk management tool for strengthening IT security and reliability for both entities and society at large (Baer and Parkinson, 2007). As with fire insurance, the prospective benefits of well-functioning markets for cyber insurance should accrue to stakeholders both individually and collectively, including:

- A focus on market-based risk management for information security, with a mechanism for spreading risk among participating stakeholders.
- Greater incentives for private investments in information security that reduce risk not only for the investing organization but also for the network as a whole.
- Better alignment of private and public benefits from security investments.
- Better quantitative tools and metrics for assessing security.
- Data aggregation and promulgation of best practices.
- Development of a robust institutional infrastructure that supports information security management.

As cyber insurance continue to mature, the remaining challenges are summarized in this section.

10.5.1 Lack of Sufficient Quality Actuarial Data

Pricing of insurance products traditionally relies on actuarial tables constructed from voluminous historical records. Since the Internet is relatively new, there is a lack of quality actuarial data, which is manifested in the following specific challenges:

1. **Pricing of Premium**

   Extensive histories of cybercrimes and related losses do not exist. The repositories of information security breaches that do exist cover up to only 10 years and suffer from the fact that firms often do not reveal details concerning a security breach. Hence, it is challenging to insurer and reinsurer to figure out the right premium for exposure.

2. **Risk Correlation**

   To face a steady claim stream and avoid large spikes in pay-outs, insurers must maintain a sufficiently large policyholder base and insure risks that are relatively independent and uncorrelated. However, in the case of cyber insurance, risks might be correlated and interdependent. A monoculture in installed systems can make most systems vulnerable to the same event. For various reasons, digital markets often see fewer than five dominant players, and monoculture is not uncommon. Furthermore, risk can be interdependent: risks in one compromised system can propagate to other systems. Both characteristics are apparent in the case of worm attacks, which exploit vulnerabilities in widely installed software (e.g., Microsoft Windows or Microsoft Outlook) and propagate from compromised systems. Worms can infect a significant number of systems within a short period of time. For example, the Mydoom worm infected more than one million computers within six days of being identified, and at its peak was responsible for 20 to 30 percent of worldwide email traffic. Events that are likely to result in concurrent claims from a substantial proportion of policyholders impose a high "probability of ruin" on a cyber insurer, such as virus, worm attacks, and coordinated cyberattacks. Therefore obtaining reliable estimates of loss correlation is key to our understanding of the future of cyber insurance market (Baer and Parkinson, 2007).

3. **Limited Reinsurance Capacity**

   In other insurance markets, insurers also face events that prompt many claims at once, such as large natural disasters. In these situations, primary underwriters can limit their total exposure while still writing large individual policies and insuring many parties that might be affected by the same event by passing some of their risk to well capitalized reinsurers. Reinsurance is essentially insurance purchased by insurance companies. Global reinsurance capacity is estimated at US$400 billion. Reinsurance covered nearly half of the US$83 billion in insured property losses in 2005 including US$38 billion from Hurrican Katrina alone (Carpenter, 2006). Reinsurers use loss data spanning several years to set premiums and diversify risks geographically as well as by peril so that they can survive even major catastrophes like Katrina. Geographically diversifying or even quantifying cyber risks seems more problematic, however, because cyberattacks might be globally correlated and interdependent. The paucity of prior claims data coupled with the plausibility of simultaneous attacks worldwide make reinsurers reluctant to provide catastrophe protection for business interruption or related cyber losses that some think could reach US$100 billion (Oellrich, 2003).

   Insurers and reinsurers have spent a tremendous amount of time and resources over the past decade in an effort to quantify, through the use of sophisticated probabilistic and deterministic modeling, the actual expected losses to any existing or theoretical portfolio of risks, and in just about any real or hypothetical loss scenario be it an earthquake, windstorm, or other physical peril. Having convinced themselves that they can, thus, construct a portfolio of business from which they can expect an acceptable exposure to catastrophic loss from any one of these natural perils, along come these new cyber exposures. The Internet is very unique in that on the surface at least, it does not look to be able to be modeled in this way. Whereas natural peril losses occur in a specific geographical location, the Internet is both everywhere and nowhere at the same time, while the perils to be protected are still being fully identified and defined.

   Reinsurers are also securitizing risks from low-frequency, high-impact events such as hurricanes and earthquakes by selling special-purpose catastrophe bonds to investors that can be traded on securities markets. Catastrophe bonds pay high rates of interest, but the investor stands to lose interest payments and sometimes principal if insurance losses from the disaster exceed a specified amount. Catastrophe bonds represent a growing part of the reinsurance market and are being issued to cover perils beyond natural disasters, but they haven't yet been used to reinsure cyber risks (Baer and Parkinson, 2007).

4. Low Insurance Limits

The practical consequences of correlated and interdependent risks are seen in limited reinsurance capacity, which makes it difficult for large firms to obtain cyber insurance policy limits big enough for the policy to be attractive enough for large firms. greater than those set out in. For Fortune 500 companies, an underwriter's $25 million limit for coverage of direct, first-party losses simply isn't enough to make cyber insurance an important factor in managing IT security (Baer and Parkinson, 2007).

10.5.2   Asymmetric Information

Asymmetric information in insurance refers to a market situation in which one party in a transaction has insufficient information about the other party which leads to market failure. The problem of asymmetric information is common to all insurance markets. However, most markets function adequately given the range of tactics used by insurance companies to overcome these information asymmetries. Many of these remedies have developed over time in response to experience and result in the well-functioning insurance markets we see today.

1. Adverse Selection

Adverse selection refers to the problem that arises because a firm (or person) choosing to insure against a particular loss is likely to have private information not available to the insurance company at the time of contracting. For example, a person who does not feel well would be more prone to purchase health or life insurance than an average person shown in actuarial tables. To deal with the adverse selection problem for health and life insurance, underwriters require physical examinations, discriminated by lifestyle characteristics (such as smokers versus nonsmokers) and require a period of time to pass before the policy is effective.

For cyber insurance, the adverse selection problem manifests itself in terms of the likelihood of a security breach. To protect themselves from the adverse selection problem when offering cyber-risk policies, insurance firms typically require an information security audit before issuing a policy. Another response to the adverse selection problem is for insurance firms to identify high-risk users and differentiate the premium for such users. For example, J.S. Wurzler, an insurance firm offering a policy to cover loss from hackers, adds a surcharge to firms using Microsoft's NT software (Schneier, 2002). ThusWurzler treats the use of NT software as a precondition, much like a life insurance policy treats smoking or high blood pressure. To address this challenge, cyber insurers often team up with cyber security professional services to carry out security readiness assessment during underwriting process. For example, Travelers Cyber Advantage policy offers Cyber Resilience Readiness Assessment tool supported by Symantec cyber security consulting.

2. Moral Hazard

While adverse selection deals with the insured's private information prior to contracting for the insurance, the moral hazard problem deals with the lack of incentives by the insured to take actions that reduce the probability of a loss subsequent to purchasing the insurance. For example, a firm with fire insurance may be less inclined to take fire safety steps than a firm without such insurance. One way insurance policies can address the moral hazard problem is through the use of deductibles. By using deductibles, the insured will suffer some loss should the occurrence be realized. Thus, the deductible provides a monetary incentive for the insured to take actions that reduce the likelihood of the loss actually occurring (Gordon et al., 2003).

10.6   CYBERNOMICS AND THE FUTURE GROWTH OF THE CYBER INSURANCE MARKET

There are a number of ways the theory and framework of cybernomics introduced in this book can contribute to the future growth of the cyber insurance market.

On the entity level and with access to the microeconomic databank, the insured can use bitmort and hekla to model its risk limit, articulate its risk appetite and risk pricing, and hence determine how much of its residual risk should be transferred to cyber insurers.

On the portfolio level and with access to the macroeconomic databank, cyber insurers and reinsurers can have better risk data source to model KCRFs that have impact on portfolio level incidents, therefore better visibility into risk concentration.

On the global level and with access to risk data collected using data scheme built around IDAC and ICCI, pricing of premium can be more accurate and policy limit can also increase.

References

Allen, J., Kossakowski, K.P., Ford, G., Konda, S., and Simmel, D. (2000). Securing network servers. Retrieved April 15, 2019, from https://resources. sei.cmu.edu/asset_files/SecurityImprovementModule/2000_006_001_13634.pdf.

Allianz, 2016. Top business risks 2016. Allianz Risk Barometer.

AIG, 2016. Is Cyber Risk Systemic? AIG, New York.

Agarwal, A., et al., 2016. VAST Methodology: Visual, Agile, and Simple Threat Modeling. Various Interviews. Transformational Opportunities, Prescott Valley, AZ.

Akerlof, G.A., 1970. The market for "Lemons": quality uncertainty and the market mechanism. Q. J. Econ. 84 (3), 488–500.

Alberts, C.J., Dorofee, A.J., 2003. Managing Information Security Risks: The OCTAVE Approach. Addison-Wesley, Reading, MA.

Alstyne, M.W.V, Parker, G.G, Choudary, S.P., 2016. Pipelines, Platforms, and the New Rules of Strategy. Harvard Business Review, Brighton, MA.

Anderson, J., 1972. Computer Security Technology Planning Study. US Air Force Electronic Systems Division Tech, Bedford, MA.

Anderson, R., 2001. Why information security is hard—an economic perspective. Presented at Proceedings of 17th Annual Computer Security Applications Conference, 2001. IEEE, New Orleans, LA.

Anderson, R., Moore, T., 2006a. The economics of information security. Science 314, 610–614.

Anderson, R., Moore, T., 2006b. The economics of information security. Science 314 (5799), 610–613.

Andress, A., 2004. Surviving Security: How to Integrate People, Process and Technology, second ed CRC Press LLC, Boca Raton, FL.

Anderson, R., Moore, T., 2008. Information security: where computer science, economics and psychology meet. Philos. T. Roy. Soc. A. Available from: http://doi.org/10.1098/rsta.2009.0027.

Aon and Ponemon Institute, 2017. 2017 Global Cyber Risk Transfer Comparison Report. Ponemon Institute, North Traverse City, MI.

Aristotle (350BC). Politics.

Arthur, W.B., 2015. Complexity and the Economy. Oxford Economic Press, Oxford, UK.

Augment (2015). Virtual reality vs. augmented reality. Retrieved from https://www.augment.com/blog/virtual-reality-vs-augmented-reality/.

Axelsson, S., 2000. The base-rate fallacy and the difficulty of intrusion detection. ACM Trans. Inform. Syst. Secur. 3 (3), 186–205.

Baer, W.S., 2003. Rewarding IT security in the marketplace. Presented the 31st Research Conference on Communication, Information, and Internet Policy, 2003. TPRC, Washington, DC.

Baer, W.S., Parkinson, A., 2007. Cyberinsurance in IT security management. IEEE Secur. Privacy 5 (3), 50–56.

Bandyopadhyay, T.S., Mookerjee, V.J., Rao, R.C., 2009. Why IT managers don't go for cyber-insurance products. Commun. ACM 52 (11), 68–73.

Barkley, R.J., 1999. On the complexities of complex economic dynamics. J. Econ. Perspect. 13 (4), 169–192.

BBC News, 2018. Facebook scandal hit 87 million users. Retrieved from: <https://www.bbc.com/news/technology-43649018>.

Beattie, R., Butzmann, H.P., 2002. Convergence Structures and Applications to Functional Analysis. Springer Science & Business Media, Berlin, Germany.

Bebbington, J., Thomson, I., 1996. Business Conceptions of Sustainability and the Implications for Accountancy. Association of Chartered Certified Accountants, London, UK.

Bebbington, J., Gray, R., Hibbitt, C., Kirk, E., 2001. Full cost accounting: an agenda for action.

Beinhocker, E.D., 2006. The Origin of Wealth: Evolution, Complexity, and the Radical Remaking of Economics. Harvard Business School Press., Boston, MA.

Bell, G., Justice, C., Buffomante, T., Dunbar, K., 2017. AI adds a new layer to cyber risk. Retrieved June 16, 2017, from: <https://hbr.org/2017/04/ai-adds-a-new-layer-to-cyber-risk>.

Bennett, S.P., Kailay, M.P., 1992. An application of qualitative risk analysis to computer security for the commercial sector. Presented at Computer Security Applications Conference, Eighth Annual, 1992. IEEE, San Antonio, TX.

Bergeron, P., 1996. Information resources management. ARIST 31, 263–300.

Berkowitz, J., O'Brien, J., 2001. How accurate are value-at-risk models at commercial banks? Retrieved from Jeremy, B., James, O., 2001. How accurate are value-at-risk models at commercial banks? Retrieved from: <https://www.bis.org/bcbs/events/oslo/berkowitz.pdf>.

Betterly Risk Consultants, 2006. CyberRisk market survey 2006. Retrieved June 2006 from: <www.betterley.com/products.html>.

Betterley, R.S., 2017. The Betterley Report, Cyber/Privacy Insurance Market Survey.

Blastland, M., Spiegelhalter, D., 2014. The Norm Chronicles: Stories and Numbers About Danger and Death, first ed Basic Books, New York, NY, 9780465085705. p. 14.

Bloomberg, 2014. KKR adds cyber risk score to its assessment of companies. Retrieved from: <http://www.bloomberg.com/news/articles/2014-04-11/kkr-adds-cyber-risk-score-to-its-assessment-of-companies>.

Bloomberg, 2018. Digital economy has been growing at triple the pace of U.S. GDP. Retrieved from: <https://www.bloomberg.com/news/articles/2018-03-15/digital-economy-has-been-growing-at-triple-the-pace-of-u-s-gdp>.

Bob, S.W., 2003. Computer science. Retrieved December 2, 2003, from: <http://encarta.msn.com/text_761563863_1/Computer_Science.Html>.

Bodin, L.D., Gordon, L.A., Loeb, M.P., 2008. Information security and risk management. Commun. ACM 51 (4), 64–68.

Bojanc, R., Jerman-Blazic, B., 2008. An economic modelling approach to information security risk management. Int. J. Inform. Manage. 28 (2008), 413–422.

Bojanc, R., Jerman-Blažič, B., 2012. A quantitative model for information-security risk management. Eng. Manag 25 (2), 25–37.

Bostrom, N., 2014. Superintelligence: Paths, Dangers, Strategies. Oxford University Press., Oxford, UK.

Brecht, M., Nowey, T., 2012. A closer look at information security costs. Econ. Inform. Secur. Privacy 3–24. Available from: https://doi.org/10.1007/978-3-642-39498-0_1.

Brynjolfsson, E., McAfee, A., 2014. The Second Machine Age: Work, Progress, and Prosperity in a Time of Brilliant Technologies. W.W. Norton & Company, Inc, New York.

BSI, 1999. Preparing for BS 7799 Certification. BSI, London, UK.

Burnie, D., 2003. Science. Retrieved December 2, 2003, from: <http://encarta.msn.com/text_761557105_1/Science.html>.

Buzzard, K., 1999. Computer security—what should you spend your money on. Comput. Secur. 18 (4), 322–334.

Canetti, D., Gross, M., Waiseml-Manor, I., Levanon, A., Cohen, H., 2017. How cyberattacks terrorize: cortisol and personal insecurity jump in the wake of cyberattacks. Cyberpsychol. Behavior Social Netw. 20 (2), 72–77. Available from: https://doi.org/10.1089/cyber.2016.0338.

Carpenter, G., 2006. The world catastrophe reinsurance market. Retrieved August 2006 from: <www.guycarp.com/portal/extranet/insights/reports.html?vid = 22>.

Carpenter, M.G., Wyman, O., 2016. MMC Cyber Handbook 2016: Increasing Resilience in the Digital Economy. Marsh & McLennan Companies, New York.

Cavusoglu, H., Mishra, B.K., Raghunathan, S., 2004. The effect of Internet security breach announcements on market value of breached firms and internet security developers. Int. J. Electron. Commerce 9 (1), 69–104.

CBS, 2018. Facebook stock price recovers all 134 billion lost in after Cambridge analytics data scandal. Retrieved March 3, 2018, from: <https://www.cbsnews.com/news/facebook-stock-price-recovers-all-134-billion-lost-in-after-cambridge-analytica-datascandal/cambridge analytica datascandal>.

Centre for Risk Studies, 2014. Business Blackout: The Insurance Implications of a Cyber Attack on the U.S. Power Grid. University of Cambridge, Cambridge, UK.

Centre for Risk Studies and Risk Modelling Solutions, 2016. Managing cyber insurance accumulation risk.

Cerullo, M.J., Cerullo, V., 2005. Threat assessment and security measures justification for advanced IT networks. Inform. Syst. Control J. 1, 1–9.

Chai, S., Kim, M., Rao, H.R., 2011. Firms' information security investment decisions: Stock market evidence of investors' behaviour. Decis. Support Syst. 50 (4), 651–661.

Chen, L., Babar, M.A., Nuseibeh, B., 2013. Characterizing architecturally significant requirements. IEEE Softw. 30 (2), 38–45.

Chen, Y., Joen, G.Y., Kim, Y., 2010. A Day Without a Search Engine: An Experimental Study of Online and Offline Search.

Clarke, R., 1995. Computer matching by government agencies: The failure of cost/benefit analysis as a control mechanism. Inform. Infrastruct. Pol. 4 (1).

Clay, K. (2013). Amazon.com goes down, loses $66,240 per minute. Retrieved from: http://www.forbes.com/sites/kellyclay/2013/08/19/amazon-com-goes-down-loses-66240-per-minute/#405e458a3c2a

Cohen, F., 1984. Computer virus—theory and experiments. Retrieved from: < http://all.net/books/virus/index.html >.

Collège français de métrologie [French College of Metrology], 2006. Placko, Dominique, ed. Metrology in Industry—The Key for Quality, London, UK: ISTE. ISBN: 978-1-905209-51-4.

Courtney, R.H., 1982. A systematic approach to data security. Comput. Secur. 1 (2), 99–112.

Cullen, W., 1780. Synopsis Nosologiae Methodicae, vol. 2 Edinburgh, Scotland.

Daniels, D., Spafford, G., 1999. Identification of Host Audit Data to Detect Attacks on Low-Level IP. Purdue University, West Lafayette, IN.

Davenport, T., Patil, D.J. (2012) Data scientist: the sexiest job of the 21st Century. Retrieved from: https://hbr.org/2012/10/data-scientist-the-sexiest-job-of-the-21st-century.

Davies, H., 2015. Ted Cruz campaign using firm that harvested data on millions of unwitting Facebook users. Retrieved from: <https://www.theguardian.com/us-news/2015/dec/11/senator-ted-cruz-president-campaign-facebook-user-data>.

Dean, A., 2015. Japan's humanities chop sends shivers down academic spines, September 26, 2015, The Guardian. Retrieved from: < https://www.theguardian.com/higher-education-network/2015/sep/25/japans-humanities-chop-sends-shivers-down-academic-spines >.

Deloitte, L., 2016. The benefits and limits of cyber value-at-risk. Retrieved from: <https://www2.deloitte.com/lu/en/pages/risk/articles/benefits-limits-cyber-value-at-risk.html>.

Denning, D., Branstad, D., 1996. A taxonomy of key escrow encryption systems. Commun. ACM 39 (3), 34–40.

Department of Homeland Security, 2009. National Infrastructure Protection Plan. Department of Homeland Security, Washington, DC.

Derby, C.A., Mohr, B.A., Goldstein, I., Feldman, H.A., Johannes, C.B., McKinlay, J.B., 2000. Modifiable risk factors and erectile dysfunction: can lifestyle changes modify risk? Urology 56 (2), 302–306.

Dittrich, D.A., 2002. Developing an effective incident cost analysis mechanism. Retrieved from: <https://www.symantec.com/connect/articles/developing-effective-incident-cost-analysis-mechanism>.

Divers Alert Network (DAN), 2014. Fatalities_Proceedings. pdf. Durham, NC: Divers Alert Network.

Dorothy, E., Denning, 2000. Cyberterrorism. Georgetown University, Washington, DC.

Eddington, M., Brenda, L., Eleanor, S., 2005. Trike v.1 methodology document. Retrieved from: <http://www.octotrike.org/papers/Trike_v1_Methodology_Document-draft.pdf>.

Euramet, 2008. Metrology—In Short, third ed., DFM Denmark, NPL United Kingdom, PTB Germany.

European Commission, 2018. Proposal for a Council Directive Laying Down Rules Relating to the Corporate Taxation of a Significant Digital Presence. European Commission, Brussels, Belgium.

European Data Protection Supervisor, n.d. Retrieved from: <https://edps.europa.eu/data-protection/data-protection/legislation/history-general-data-protection-regulation_en>.

European Federation of National Associations of Measurement, Testing and Analytical Laboratories (Eurolab), 2006. Guide to the Evaluation of Measurement Uncertainty for Quantitative Test Results, Paris, France, Eurolab.

European Parliament, 2009. Defining and Measuring Systemic Risk, Strasbourg, France: European Parliament.

Fama, E.F., Fisher, L., Jensen, M.C., Roll, R., 1969. The adjustment of stock prices to new information. Int. Econ. Rev. 10 (1), 1−21.

Farahmand, F., Navathe, S., Sharp, G., Enslow, P., 2003. Managing vulnerabilities of information systems to security incidents. In: Proceedings of the ACM 2nd International Conference on Entertainment Computing, pp. 348−354.

Finne, T., 1998. A conceptual framework for information security management. Comput. Secur. 17 (4), 303−307.

FIPS, 2004. Standards for Security Categorization of Federal Information and Information Systems. NIST, Gaithersburg, MD.

Fogarty, M., 1996. A history of value theory. Retrieved from: <https://www.tcd.ie/Economics/assets/pdf/SER/1996/Martin_Fogarty.html>.

Frincke, D., 2000. Balancing cooperation and risk in intrusion detection. ACM Trans. Inform. Syst. Secur. 3 (1), 1−29.

Frosdick, S., 1997. The techniques of risk analysis are insufficient in themselves. Disaster Prevent. Manage. 6 (3), 165.

Forbes, 2016. 9 figure deals lift cybersecurity investment to an all time high. Retrieved from: <http://www.forbes.com/sites/stevemorgan/2016/02/08/9-figure-deals-lift-cybersecurity-investments-to-an-all-time-high/#2a7995a82aed>.

GAO, 1999. GAO Accountability Report 1999. Government Accountability Office, Washington DC.

Gartner, 2011. Gartner IT Key Metrics Data 2011: Summary Report (G00208297). Gartner, Stamford, CT.

Gartner, 2017. Calculating and comparing data center and public cloud IaaS costs. Retrieved from: <https://www.gartner.com/document/3815365?ref=unauthreader&srcId=1-4730952011>.

Geer, D., Hoo, K., Jaquith, A., 2003. Information security: why the future belongs to the quants. IEEE Secur. Privacy 1 (4), 24−32.

Geer, D.E., 2004. Security of Information When Economics Matters. Verdasys, Waltham, MA.

George, T., 2015. Coming into focus: cyber security operational risk. Retrieved from: <http://www.securityweek.com/coming-focus-cyber-security-operational-risk>.

Gerber, M., von Solms, R., 2005. Management of risk in the information age. Comput. Secur. 24, 16−30.

Global Risks Report, 2017. World Economic Forum Opinion Survey 2017.

Godfrey, J., Hodgson, A., Holmes, S., Kam, V., 1997. Financial Accounting Theory, third ed. Hoboken, NJ: John Wiley & Sons.

Gordon, A.L., Loeb, M.P., Sohail, T., 2003. A framework for using insurance for cyber-risk management. Retrieved from: <http://citeseerx.ist.psu.edu/viewdoc/download?doi=10.1.1.705.9851&rep=rep1&type=pdf>.

Gordon, L.A., Loeb, M.P., 2002. The economics of information security investment. ACM Trans. Inform. Syst. Security (TISSEC) 5 (4), 438−457.

Gordon, L.A., Loeb, M.P., 2006. Managing Cybersecurity Resources: A Cost−Benefit Analysis. McGraw Hill, New York.

Gordon, L., Richardson, R., 2004. The new economics of information security. Inform. Week 982, 53−57.

Graham-Harrison, E., Cadwalladr, C., 2018. Revealed: 50 million Facebook profiles harvested for Cambridge Analytica in major data breach. Retrieved from: <https://www.theguardian.com/news/2018/mar/17/cambridge-analytica-facebook-influence-us-election>.

Gregg, M., 2005. CISSP security-management practices. Retrieved July 7, 2017, from: <http://www.pearsonitcertification.com/articles/article.aspx?p=418007&seqNum=4>.

Gregory, M., 2008. Enterprise Risk Management: A Methodology for Achieving Strategic Objectives. John Wiley & Sons., Hoboken, NJ.

Guillen, M., 2015. The Architecture of Collapse: The Global System in the 21st Century. Oxford University Press., Oxford, UK.

Guldimann, T.M., 2000. The story of RiskMetrics. Risk 13 (1), 56−58.

Hackett, S.C., 2010. Environmental and Natural Resources Economics: Theory, Policy, and the Sustainable Society. ME Sharpe, Armonk, NY.

Hagiu, A., Rothman, S., 2016. Network Effects Aren't Enough. Harvard Business Review, Brighton, MA.

Hanson, J.M., Beard, B.B., 2010. Marshall Space Flight Center, Applying Monte Carlo Simulation to Launch Vehicle Design and Requirements Analysis.

Halliday, S., Badenhorst, K., von Solms, R., 1996. A business approach to effective information technology risk analysis and management. Inform. Manage. Comput. Secur. 4 (1), 19.

Harris, S., 2005. CISP All-in-One Exam Guide. McGraw-Hill, New York.

Harrison, D.M., 2017. Three years ago this equation predicted $2400 bitcoin for 2017. In 2020, it says bitcoin will be $30,000−CoinSpeaker.

Haybittle, J.L., 1998. The use of the Gompertz function to relate changes in life expectancy to the standardized mortality ratio. Int. J. Epidemiol. 27, 885−889.

Hectus, J., 2016. Cybersecurity beyond traditional risk management. Retrieved June 16, 2017, from: <http://www.lawjournalnewsletters.com/sites/lawjournalnewsletters/2016/09/01/cybersecurity-beyond-traditional-risk-management/>.

Henderson, S., Peirson, G., 1998. Issues in Financial Accounting, sixth ed. Longman Cheshire, Melbourne, Australia.

Hern, A., 2018. Far more than 87m Facebook users had data compromised, MPs told. Retrieved from: <https://www.theguardian.com/uk-news/2018/apr/17/facebook-users-data-compromised-far-more-than-87m-mps-told-cambridge-analytica>.

Herrera, M., 2017. Four types of risk mitigation and BCM governance, risk and compliance. Retrieved June 15, 2017, from: <https://www.mha-it.com/2013/05/four-types-of-risk-mitigation/>.

Holton, G.A., 2002. History of value-at-risk: 1922–1998. Retrieved from: <http://citeseerx.ist.psu.edu/viewdoc/download?doi=10.1.1.161.7403&rep=rep1&type=pdf>.

Hoo, K.S., 2000. How much is enough? A risk management approach to computer security. Retrieved October 25, 2006, from: <http://iis-db.stanford.edu/pubs/11900/soohoo.pdf>.

Howard, R.A., 1989. Microrisks for medical decision analysis. Int. J. Technol. Assess. Health Care 5, 357–370. Available from: https://doi.org/10.1017/S026646230000742X.

Hower, S., Uradnik, K., 2011. Cyberterrorism, first ed. Greenwood, Santa Barbara, CA.

Humberto, M., Peláez, S. 2010. Measuring effectiveness information security controls. Retrieved from https://www.sans.org/reading-room/whitepapers/basics/paper/33398

Humphreys, E.J., Moses, R.H., Plate, A.E., 1998. Guide to Risk Assessment and Risk Management. British Standards Institution, London, UK.

Huq, N., TrendLabs Research, 2015. Follow the Data: Dissecting Data Breaches and Debunking Myths: Trend Micro Analysis of Privacy Rights Clearinghouse 2005–2015 Data Breach Records. Trend Micro, Tokyo, Japan.

IDG Research and Getronics, 2002. The CIO Agenda: Taking Care of Business. CxO Media, Framingham, MA.

IMF (International Monetary Fund), 2018. Measuring the Digital Economy. IMF., Washington, DC.

Information Security Forum (2018). Threat horizon 2018. Retrieved April 15, 2019, from https://media.scmagazine.com/documents/217/isf_threat_horizon_2018_execut_54175.pdf.

Inmon, W.H., 1992. Building the Data Warehouse. John Wiley & Sons, Inc, New York, NY.

Insurance Business, 2015. Warren Buffet enters the cybersecurity insurance market. Retrieved from: <http://www.ibamag.com/news/warren-buffett-enters-the-cybersecurity-insurance-market-25540.aspx>.

ISF (2000). ISF methods for risk assessment and risk management. (n.d.) Retrieved from: https://www.enisa.europa.eu/topics/threat-risk-management/risk-management/current-risk/risk-management-inventory/rm-ra-methods/m_isf_methods.html.

ISF, 2017. Information security forum forecasts 2018 global security threat outlook. Retrieved from: <https://www.securityforum.org/news/information-secuy-threat-outlook/>.

ISO Survey, 2014. The ISO Survey of Management System Standard Certifications. ISO, Geneva, Switzerland.

Ikegami, J., 1992. The economics of intrinsic value. Kyoto Univ. Econ. Rev. 132 (1), 1–17.

Indian Council of World Affairs, 1986. India Quar: J. Int. Aff. vols. 42–43. New Delhi, India: Indian Council of World Affairs.

Information Security Forum, 2000. Simplified Process for Risk Identification (SPRINT) User Guide. Ensia, St. Paul, MN.

Institute of Standards and Technology, 2006. Microsoft Solutions for Security and Compliance and Microsoft Security Center of Excellence: The Security Risk Management Guide. Microsoft Corporation, Redmond, WA.

Intel Security, 2015. The Hidden Data Economy: The Market Place for Stolen Digital Information. McAfee., Santa Clara, CA.

Jajodia, S., Millen, J., 1993. Editor's preface. J. Comput. Secur. 1 (2–3), 85.

Jajodia, S., Miller, J., 2003. Editor's preface. J. Comput. Secur. 2 (2–3), 85.

Jevons, W., 1871. Theory of Political Economy, London, UK: Macmillan and Co.

Joint Committee on Guides for Metrology (JCGM), 2008. International Vocabulary of Metrology—Basic and General Concepts and Associated Terms, third ed, Sèvres Cedex, France: BIPM.

Jones, A., 1997. Penetration testing and system audit. Comput. Secur. 16, 595–602.

Jung, C., Han, I., Suh, B., 1999. Risk analysis for electronic commerce using case-based reasoning. Int. J. Intell. Syst. Account. Finan. Manage. 8, 62.

Kaplan, S., Garrick, B.J., 1981. On the quantitative definition of risk. Risk Anal. 1 (1), 11–27.

Katz, M.L., Shapiro, C., 1985. Network externalities, competition, and compatibility. Am. Econ. Rev. 75 (3), 424–440.

Keeney, M., Kowalski, E., Cappelli, D., Moore, A., Shimeall, T., Rogers, S. (2005). Insider Threat Study: Computer System Sabotage in Critical Infrastructure Sectors. National Threat Assessment Center United States Secret Service and Software Engineering Institute Carnegie Mellon University, Retrieved from 2019 April, 19, from https://resources.sei.cmu.edu/asset_files/SpecialReport/2005_003_001_51946.pdf.

Kenny, M., Zysman, J., 2016. The rise of platform economy, issues in science and technology. Retrieved from: <http://issues.org/32-3/the-rise-of-the-platform-economy/>.

Kesan, J., et al., 2004. The Economic Case for Cyberinsurance. University of Illinois Law and Economics., Urbana, IL.

Kesan, J., et al., 2005. Cyber-insurance as a market-based solution to the problem of cybersecurity. Presented at Workshop on the Economics of Information Security. Harvard University, Cambridge, MA.

King, J.E., McLure, M., 2014. History of the Concept of Value. University of Western Australia, Crawley, WA.

Kipps, C., Sanjay, S., Dan, T.P., 2011. The incidence of exercise-associated hyponatraemia in the London marathon. Br. J. Sports Med. 45 (1), 14–19. Available from: https://doi.org/10.1136/bjsm.2009.059535.

Kirkwood, A.S., 1994. Why do we worry when scientists say there is no risk? Disaster Prevent. Manage. 3 (2), 15.

Kissel, R., 2013. Glossary of key information security terms. Retrieved June 10, 2017, from <http://nvlpubs.nist.gov/nistpubs/ir/2013/NIST.IR.7298r2.pdf>.

Knibbs, G.H., 1929. The international classification of disease and causes of death and its revision. Med. J. Aust. 1, 2−12.

Kosub, T., 2015. Components and Challenges of Integrated Cyber Risk Management. Alexander Department of Insurance Economics and Risk Management Friedrich-Alexander University Erlangen-Nürnberg, Erlangen, Germany.

Kunreuther, H., Heal, G., 2003. Interdependent security. J. Risk Uncertain. 26 (2-3), 231−249.

Laney, D., 2017. Infonomics: How to Monetize, Manage, and Measure Information as an Asset for Competitive Advantage, first ed. Routledge, Abington, UK.

Laqueur, W., Smith, C., Spector, M., 2002. Cyberterrorism. Facts on File, New York.

Larsen, A., 1999. Global security survey: virus attack. Retrieved from: <http://www.informationweek.com/743/security.htm>.

Laskowski, N., 2014. Treat data as the asset it is. Retrieved June 5, 2017, from: <http://docs.media.bitpipe.com/io_11x/io_116803/item_934667/CIO%20Decisions%20eZine_June%202014.pdf>.

Leavens, D.H., 1945. Diversification of investments. Trusts Estates 80 (5), 469−473.

Liu, S., Kuhn, R., Rossman, H., 2009. Understanding insecure IT: practical risk assessment. IT Profess. 11 (3), 57−59.

Loch, K.D., Carr, H.H., Warkentin, M.E., 1992. Threats to information systems: today's reality, yesterday's understanding. MIS Quar. 17 (2), 173−186.

Love, M.C., 2011. Beyond Sovereignty: Issues for a Global Agenda. Cengage Learning, Independence, KY.

Luotonen, O., 1993. Risk Management and Insurances. Rovaniemen Painatuskeskus Oy, Helsinki, Finland.

Malwarebytes, 2016. State of Ransomware Report, Santa Clara, CA: Malwarebytes.

Marsh, 2015. UK cyber security: the role of insurance in managing and mitigating the risk.

Marcus, G., 2017. Deep Learning: A Critical Appraisal. New York University, New York.

Markowitz, H.M., 1952. Portfolio selection. J. Finan. 7 (1), 77−91.

Marshall, A., 1890. Principles of Economics. London, UK: Macmillan and Co., Ltd.

Marx, K., 1867. Capital. A Critique of Political Economy, Vol. 1. Progress Publishers, Moscow, Russia.

Masnick, M., 2008. Understanding the difference between price and value; product and benefit. Retrieved from: <https://www.techdirt.com/articles/20080819/0314402026.shtml>.

Matsuura, J.H., 2004. An overview of intellectual property and intangible asset valuation model. Res. Manage. Rev. 14 (1), 1−10.

Mayo, D., Hollander, R., 1991. Introduction to Part II—uncertain evidence in risk management. Acceptable Evidence: Science and Values in Risk Management. Oxford University Press, Oxford, UK, pp. 93−98.

McAlone, N. (2016) People became even more addicted to Netflix in 2015, according to Goldman Sachs. Retrieved April 14, 2019, from https://www.businessinsider.com/subscribers-spent-more-time-per-person-watching-netflix-in-2015-2016-1.

McCumber, J., 2005. Assessing and Managing Security Risk in IT Systems. CRC Press LLC., Boca Raton, FL.

McKinsey, 2013. Managing when vendor and supplier risk becomes your own. Retrieved from: <https://www.mckinsey.com/business-functions/risk/our-insights/managing-when-vendor-and-supplier-risk-becomes-your-own>.

McKinsey Global Institute (MGI) (2015). Digital America: A Tale of the Haves and Have-Mores. Retrieved April 14, 2019, from: https://www.mckinsey.com/industries/high-tech/our-insights/digital-america-a-tale-of-the-haves-and-have-mores.

McKnight, L., et al., 1997. Information security of Internet commerce. In: McKnight, L., Bailey, J. (Eds.), Internet Economics. MIT Press, Cambridge, MA, pp. 435−452.

Meadows, C., 2001. A cost-based framework for analysis of denial of service in networks. J. Comput. Secur. 9 (1/2), 143−164.

Menger, C., 1871. Principles of Economics. Braumüller, Austria: Wilhelm Braumüller.

Mercuri, R., 2003. Analyzing security costs. Commun. ACM 46, 15−18.

Microsoft, 2004. The security risk management guide. Retrieved October 25, 2006, from <http://www.microsoft.com/technet/security/topics/complianceandpolicies/secrisk/default.mspx>.

Millen, J., 1992. A resource allocation model for denial of service presented at Proceedings of the IEEE Symposium on Security and Privacy, 1992. IEEE Computer Society Press, Los Alamitos, CA. Washington DC.

Mizzi,A., 2005. Return on Information Security Investment (MBA dissertation). University of Malta, Msida, Malta.

Moody, D., Walsh, P., 1999. Measuring the value of information: an asset valuation approach. Presented at Seventh European Conference on Information Systems (ECIS'99). Copenhagen Business School., Copenhagen, Denmark.

Moscovici, P., 2018. Keynote speech by commissioner Moscovici. Presented at the Masters of Digital 2018 Event, 2018. European Commission, Brussels, Belgium.

Muradlidhar, K., Batra, D., Kirs, P., 1995. Accessibility, security, and accuracy in statistical databases: the case for the multiplicative fixed data perturbation approach. Manag. Sci. 41 (9), 1549−1564.

Murphy, S.L., Xu, J., Kochanek, K.D., 2013. Deaths: Final Data for 2010. Centers for Disease Control and Prevention, Bethesda MD.

Nagaraja, S., Anderson, R., 2006. The topology of covert conflict. Presented at Fifth Workshop on the Economics of Information Security, 2006. University of Cambridge, Cambridge, England.

NATO, 2008. Centre of Excellence—Defence Against Terrorism. IOS Press, Amsterdam, Holland.

National Center for Health Statistics, 2013. Life Tables. Centers for Disease Control and Prevention., Hyattsville, MD.

National Physical Laboratory (NPL), 2010. Good Practice Guide No. 18, a Beginner's Guide to Measurement. Teddington, UK: National Physical Laboratory.

Net Diligence, 2016. Cyber Claims Study. Gladwyne, PA: NetDiligence.

Neubauer, T., Klemen, M., Biffl, S., 2006. Secure business process management: a roadmap. First International Conference on Availability, Reliability and Security (ARES'06). IEEE, Piscataway, NJ, 8 pp.

Newton, C., 2017. How a Typo Took Down S3, the Backbone of the Internet, Washington, DC, The Verge. Retrieved 2019 May, 7, from https://www.theverge.com/2017/3/2/14792442/amazon-s3-outage-cause-typo-internet-server.

Ng, I.C.L., Ho, S.Y., 2014. Creating New Markets in the Digital Economy: Value and Worth. Cambridge University Press, Cambridge, UK.

NIST, 1975. FIPS 65, Guidelines for Automatic Data Processing Risk Analysis. National Institute of Standards and Technology, Gaithersburg, MD.

NIST, 2008. NIST Special Publication 800-60 Volume I rev1: Guide for Mapping Types of Information and Information Systems to Security Categories. National Institute of Standards and Technology, US Department of Commerce, Gaithersburg, MD.

NIST, 2012. NIST Special Publication 800-30 Rev 1: Guide for Conducting Risk Assessments. US Department of Commerce., Washington, DC.

NIST, 2013. NIST Special Publication 800-53 Rev 1: Security and Privacy Controls for Federal Information Systems and Organizations. National Institute of Standards and Technology, Gaithersburg, MD.

OECD, 2014. Measuring the Digital Economy: A New Perspective. OECD Publishing, Paris, France.

NIST, 2015. NIST Special Publication 800-161, Supply Chain Risk Management Practices for Federal Information Systems and Organizations.

OECD, 2018. Tax Challenges Arising from Digitalisation—Interim Report 2018. OECD Publishing, Paris, France.

Oellrich, H., 2003. Cyber insurance update. Retrieved from: <http://cipp.gmu.edu/archive/cip_report_2.6>.

Office of Financial Research (2017). *2017 Financial Stability Report*. Retrieved April 15, 2019, from https://www.financialresearch.gov/financial-stability-reports/2017-financial-stability-report/.

Oppenheim, C., Stenson, J., Wilson, R.M.S., 2001. The attributes of information as an asset. New Library World 102 (11/12), 458−464. Available from: https://doi.org/10.1108/03074800110696979.

Osborn, S., Sandhu, R., Munawer, Q., 2000. Configuring role-based access control to enforce mandatory and discretionary access control policies. ACM Trans. Inform. Syst. Secur. 3 (2), 85−106.

Ozment, A., Schechter, S.E., 2006. Proceedings of the Fifth Workshop on the Economics of Information Security, 2006. University of Cambridge, Cambridge, England.

Penman, S., 2016. Valuation: state of the art. Schmalenbach Bus. Rev. 17, 3−23. Available from: https://doi.org/10.1007/s41464-016-0002-y.

Peyravian, M., Roginsky, A., Zunic, N., 1999. Hash-based encryption. Comput. Secur. 18 (4), 345−350.

Pfleeger, C., 1997. Security in Computing, 2nd ed. Prentice-Hall, Englewood Cliffs, NJ.

Ponemon Institute, 2013. Managing Cyber Security as a Business Risk: Cyber Insurance in the Digital Age. Ponemon Institute, North Traverse City, MI.

Ponemon Institute, 2016. 2016 Cost of Data Breach Study. Ponemon Institute, North Traverse City, MI.

Porter, M., 1985. Competitive Advantage: Creating and Sustaining Superior Performance. The Free Press, New York.

Power, R., 2001. 2001 CSI/FBI computer crime and security survey. Comput. Secur. 17 (2), 29−51.

PriceWaterhouseCoopers (PWC), 2010. Information Security Breach Survey 010. Inforsecurity Europe, London.

PwC, 2017. GDPR Preparedness Pulse Survey.

Ramasubramanian G., Hall, K. (2013). How do you measure cyber risk? Retrieved July 07, 2017, from https://www.weforum.org/agenda/2013/11/how-to-measure-cyber-risk/.

Ricardo, D., 1817. On the Principles of Political Economy and Taxation, London, UK: John Murray.

Risk Acceptance, 2016. Retrieved June 15, 2017, from: <https://www.enisa.europa.eu/topics/threat-risk-management/risk-management/current-risk/risk-management-inventory/rm-process/risk-acceptance>.

RiskMetrics, 1995. RiskMetrics - Technical document. Morgan Guaranty Trust Company, New York, NY.

Rosenberg, M., Confessore, N., Cadwalladr, C., 2018. How Trump consultants exploited the Facebook data of millions. Retrieved from: <https://www.nytimes.com/2018/03/17/us/politics/cambridge-analytica-trump-campaign.html>.

Ross, A., 2016. The Industries of the Future. Simon & Schuster., New York.

Ross, R., 2007. Managing enterprise risk in today's world of sophisticated threats: a framework for developing broad-based, cost-effective information security programs. EDPACS: EDP Audit Control Secur. Newsl. 35 (2), 1−10.

Roy, A.D., 1952. Safety first and the holding of assets. Econometrica 20 (3), 431−449.

Royal Society, 1992. Risk: Analysis, Perception and Management, Report of a Royal Society Study Group. The Royal Society, London, UK.

Ruan, K., 2017. Introducing cybernomics: a unifying economic framework for measuring cyber risk. Computer & Security 65, 77−89.

Ruffle, S.J., et al., 2014. Stress Test Scenario: Sybil Logic Bomb Cyber Catastrophe. Centre for Risk Studies, University of Cambridge., Cambridge, UK.

Ruskin, J., 1871. Munera Pulveris, Six Essays on the Elements of Political Economy. Greenwood Press, New York.

Russell, S., Norvig, P., 2009. Artificial Intelligence, 3rd ed. Prentice Hall, Engle Wood Cliffs, NJ.

Saaty, T.L., 1990. The Analytic Hierarchy Process. RWS Publications, Pittsburgh, PA.

Sacco, R.L., 1995. Risk factors and outcomes for ischemic stroke. Neurology 45 (2 Suppl. 1), S10−S14.

Sajko, M., Bača, M., Rabuzin, K., 2006. How to calculate information value for effective security risk assessment. J. Inform. Organ. Sci. 30 (2), 263−278.

SANS, 2016. SANS Security Report. SANS Institute, North Bethesda, MD.

Sandhu, R.S., Coyne, E.J., Feinstein, H.L., Youman, C.E., 1996. Role-based access control models. IEEE Comput. Soc. 29 (2), 38−47.

Scarff, F., Carty, A., Charette, R., 1993. Introduction to the Management of Risk. HMSO, Norwich, UK.

Schneier, B., 1996. Applied Cryptography, 2nd ed Wiley, New York, NY.

Schechter, S., 2002. Quantitively differentiating system security, presented at Workshop on Economics and Information Security, 2002. University of California, Berkeley, Berkeley, CA.

Schneier, B., 2002. Computer security: it's the economics, stupid. Presented at the Workshop on the Economics of Information Security. University of California Berkeley, Berkeley, CA.

Security Affairs, 2015. Hackers targeted the Polish airline LOT, grounded 1,400 passengers, 22 June 2015, available at: <http://securityaffairs.co/wordpress/37997/cybercrime/hacked-airline-lot.html>.

Shameli-Sendi, A., Aghababaei-Barzegar, R., Cherie, M., 2016. Taxonomy of information security risk assessment (ISRA). Comput. Secur. 57, 14−30.

Shannon, C.E., 1948. A Mathematical Theory of Communication. Bell Syst. Tech. J. 27 (3), 379−423. Available from: https://doi.org/10.1002/j.1538-7305.

Shen, Y., Guo, B., Shen, Y., Duan, X., Dong, X., Zhang, H., 2016. A pricing model for big personal data. Tsinghua Sci. Technol 21 (5), 482−490.

Sieglel, C.A., Sagalow, T.R., Serritella, P., 2002. Cyber-risk management: technical and insurance controls for enterprise-level security. Inform. Syst. Secur. 11 (4), 33−49.

Simmons, G., 1994. Cryptanalysis and protocol failures. Commun. ACM 37 (11), 56−64.

Smith, A., 1776. The Wealth of Nations, Edinburgh, Scotland: William Strahan, Thomas Cadell.

Smith, D., 2010. Hype Cycle for Cloud Computing (Rep. No. G00201557). Gartner, Stamford, CT.

Solon, O., 2018. Facebook says Cambridge Analytica may have gained 37 m more users' data. Retrieved April 6, 2018, from: <https://www.theguardian.com/technology/2018/apr/04/facebook-cambridge-analytica-user-data-latest-more-than-thought>.

Spears, J.L., 2005. A holistic risk analysis method for identifying information security risks. Security Management, Integrity, and Internal Control in Information Systems. Springer, Fairfax, VA, pp. 185−202.

Spiegelhalter, D., 2009. 230 miles in a car equates to one micromort: the agony andecstasy of risk-taking. The Times.

Spiegelhalter, D., 2012. Using speed of ageing and "microlives" to communicate the effects of lifetime habits and environment. BMJ. Available from: https://doi.org/10.1136/bmj.e8223.

Staff, E.R., 2006. Enterprise risk management: frameworks, elements, and integration. Retrieved July 21, 2017, from: <https://erm.ncsu.edu/library/article/frameworks-elements-integration/>.

Stanford, 2016. Artificial Intelligence and Life in 2030. Stanford University., Stanford, CA.

Stanford Encyclopedia of Philosophy, 2014. Intrinsic v.s. extrinsic value. Retrieved from: <https://plato.stanford.edu/entries/value-intrinsic-extrinsic/>.

Statistics Canada, 2015. Leading causes of death, by sex (both sexes). Ottawa, Canada: Statistics Canada.

Stigler, G., 1950. The development of utility theory. J. Polit. Econ. 58, 307−327.

Stoneburner, G., Goguen, A., Feringa, A., 2002. Risk Management Guide for Information Technology Systems. National Institute of Standards and Technology, Gaithersburg, MD.

Strang, R., 2001. Recognizing and meeting Title III concerns in computer investigations. Comput. Crimes Intellect. Prop. 49 (2), 8−13.

Straub, D.W., Welke, R.J., 1998. Coping with systems risk: security planning models for management decision making. MIS Quar. 23 (4), 441−469.

Strutt, J., 1993. Risk Assessment and Management: The Engineering Approach. Centre for Industrial Safety and Reliability, Cranfield University, Bedford, UK.

Suh, B., Han, L., 2003. The IS risk analysis based on a business model. Inform. Manag. 41 (2), 149−158.

Suojanen, T., 2000. Technical Communication Research: Dissemination, Reception, Utilization (unpublished master's thesis). University of Tampere, Finland.

Susskind, R., Susskind, D., 2016. The Future of Professions: How Technology Will Transform the Work of Human Experts. Oxford University Press, Oxford, UK.

Syamsuddin, I., Hwang, J., 2010. The use of AHP in security policy decision making: an open office calc application. J. Softw. 5 (10). Available from: https://doi.org/10.4304/jsw.5.10.1162-1169.

Symantec, 2018. 2018 Internet security threat report. Retrieved from: <https://www.symantec.com/security-center/threat-report>.

Tanaka, H., Liu, W., Matsuura, K., Sudoh, O., 2005. Vulnerability and information security investment: an empirical analysis of e-local government in Japan. J. Account. Public Pol. 24, 37−59.

Tanaka, H., Liu, W., Matsuura, K., 2006. An empirical analysis of security investment in countermeasures based on an enterprise survey in Japan. In: The Fifth Workshop on the Economics of Information Security. Presented at The Fifth Workshop on the Economics of Information Security. University of Cambridge, Cambridge, England.

Tapscott, D., 1994. The Digital Economy—Promise and Peril in the Age of Networked Intelligence. McGraw-Hill., New York.

Taylor, K.S. (1996). Human society and the global economy. Retrieved June 10, 2017, from: https: //www.d.umn.edu/cla/faculty/jhamlin/4111/2111-home/value.htm#summary.

The Daily Beast, 2016. The data that can outlive humanity. Retrieved from: <http://www.thedailybeast.com/articles/2016/04/12/the-data-that-can-outlive-humanity.html>.

The Economist, 2012. The Third Industrial Revolution. The Economist, London, UK.

Towards Data Science (2018). Top AI and machine learning trends in media and entertainment. Retrieved April 14, 2019, from https://towardsdatascience.com/top-ai-and-machine-learning-trends-in-media-and-entertainment-823f7efea928.

U.K. National Crime Agency, 2015. Cyber-attack suspects' average age down to 18. Retrieved from: <http://gadgets.ndtv.com/internet/news/cyber-attack-suspects-average-age-down-to-17-uk-agency-775908>.

US Department of Transportation, 2011. Treatment of the economic value of a statistical life in departmental analyses—2011 interim adjustment. Retrieved from: <http://www.dot.gov/policy/transportation-policy/treatment-economic-value-statistical-life>.

Ucedavélez, T., Marco, M.M., 2015. Risk Centric Threat Modeling: Process for Attack Simulation and Threat Analysis. John Wiley & Sons, Hoboken, NJ.

United States Parachute Association (USPA), 2018. Skydiving Safety, United States Parachute Association: Fredericksburg, VA.

Upwork (2017) Freelancing in America, 2017. Edelman intelligence. Retrieved from: <https://www.upwork.com/i/freelancing-in-america/2017/>.

Verizon, 2013. 2013 Data Breach Investigations Report. New York, NY: Verizon.

Vigna, G., Kemmerer, R.A., 1999. NetSTAT: a network-based intrusion detection system. J. Comput. Secur. 7 (1), 37−71.

Volz, D., 2015. Cyber attacks loom as growing corporation credit risk: Moody's. Retrieved from: <http://www.reuters.com/article/us-cybersecurity-moody-s-idUSKBN0TC2CP20151123>.

Vorster, A., Labuschagne, L., 2005. A framework for comparing different information security risk analysis methodologies. In: Proceedings of the ACM Annual Research Conference of the South African Institute of Computer Scientists and Information Technologists. White River, South Africa, pp. 95−103.

Walker, S., 2012. Economics and the cyber challenge. Inform. Secur. Technol. Rep 17 (1-2), 9−18.

Walker, K.F., Cohen, A.L., Walker, S.H., Allen, K.M., Baines, D.L., Thornton, J.G., 2014. The dangers of birth day. BJOG 1 (6), 714−718. Available from: https://doi.org/10.1111/1471-0528.12544.

WEF (World Economic Forum), 2015. Risk and Responsibility in a Hyperconnected World: Pathways to Global Cyber Resilience. WEF, Cologny, Switzerland.

Walras, M., 1874. Elements of Pure Economics, London, UK: Routledge.

Weitzman, M.L., 1998. Recombinant growth. Quar. J. Econ. 113 (2), 331−360.

Wells, A., 2013. Concerns over cyber security risks outweigh traditional risks. Retrieved June 16, 2017, from: <http://www.insurancejournal.com/magazines/features/2013/08/19/301657.htm>.

Wheeler, E., 2011. Security Risk Management: Building an Information Security Risk Management Program From the Ground Up. Syngress, Waltham, MA.

Willemson, J., 2006. On the Gordon & Loeb model for information security investment. Presented at The Fifth Workshop on the Economics of Information Security. University of Cambridge, Cambridge, England.

Willis, H.H., Lester, G., Treverton, G.F., 2009. Information sharing for infrastructure risk management: barriers and solutions. Intell. Natl. Secur. 24 (3), 339−365.

Wiseman, S., 1986. A secure capability computer system. Proceedings of the IEEE Symposium on Security and Privacy 86−94.

World Economic Forum, 2016. The fourth industrial revolution, Retrieved from: <https://www.weforum.org/about/the-fourth-industrial-revolution-by-klaus-schwab>.

World Economic Forum (WEF), 2016. Understanding Systemic Cyber Risk, Global Agenda Council on Risk & Resilience, Geneva Switzerland, World Economic Forum.

World Meteorological Organization Commission for Instruments and Methods of Observation (WMO), 2017. Metrological Traceability for Meteorology. World Meterological Organization: Geneva, Switzerland.

Yazar, Z., 2002. A Qualitative Risk Analysis and Management Tool—CRAMM. SANS Institute Reading Room, Fredericksburg, VA.

Zurich and Business Continuity Institute (BCI), 2015. Supply Chain Resilience Report 2015, November 2015. Berkshire, UK: BCI.

Further Reading

Badenhausen, K., 2018. The world's most valuable brands 2018: by the numbers. Retrieved from: <https://www.forbes.com/sites/kurtbadenhausen/2018/05/23/the-worlds-most-valuable-brands-2018-by-the-numbers>.

Barefoot, K., Curtis, D., Jolliff, W., Nicholson, J.R., Omohundro, R., 2018. Defining and Measuring the Digital Economy. BEA, Silver Spring, MD.

Biener, C., Eling, M., Wirfs, J.H., 2015. Insurability of cyber risk: an empirical analysis. Geneva Papers Risk Insurance 40 (1), 131−158. Palgrave MacMillan, London, UK.

Cundy, C., 2016. Cyber risk: cat modelling's biggest challenge yet. Retrieved July 5, 2017, from <https://www.insuranceerm.com/analysis/cyber-risk-cat-modellings-biggest-challenge-yet.html>.

Danielsson, J., Fouche, M., Macral, R., 2016. Cyber risk as systemic risk. Retrieved from: <https://voxeu.org/article/cyber-risk-systemic-risk>.

Denning, D., 1987. An intrusion-detection model. IEEE Trans. Softw. Eng. 13 (2), 222−226.

Dethlefs, R., 2015. How cyber attacks become more profitable than the drug trade. Retrieved May 1, 2015, from <http://fortune.com/2015/05/01/how-cyber-attacks-became-more-profitable-than-the-drug-trade/>.

Evans, S., 2017. WannaCry could be a catalyst for a new approach to cyber risks: Sciemus-Reinsurance News. Retrieved July 5, 2017, from: <https://www.reinsurancene.ws/wannacry-catalyst-new-approach-cyber-risks-sciemus/>.

Exposure, 2017. Exposure magazine snapshots: a new way of learning. Retrieved July 05, 2017, from: <http://www.rms.com/blog/2017/04/07/exposure-magazine-snapshots-a-new-way-of-learning/>.

Guha, R., Ken, H., 2013. How do you measure cyber risk? Retrieved July 7, 2017, from: <https://www.weforum.org/agenda/2013/11/how-to-measure-cyber-risk/>.

ISF, 2016. ISF forecasts 2017 global security threat outlook. Retrieved from: <http://www.securitymagazine.com/articles/87639-information-security-forum-forecasts-2017-global-security-threat-outlook>.

Justin, J., Laura, H., 2018. What the GDPR means for Facebook, the EU and you. Retrieved from: <https://www.cnet.com/how-to/what-gdpr-means-for-facebook-google-the-eu-us-and-you/>.

Kit, T.S., 1996. Human society and the global economy. Retrieved June 10, 2017, from: <http://www.d.umn.edu/cla/faculty/jhamlin/4111/2111-home/value.htm#summary>.

Linsmeier, T.J., Pearson, N.D., 2000. Value at risk. Financ. Anal. J. Available from: https://doi.org/10.2469/faj.v56.n2.2343.

Manyika, J., et al., 2015. Digital America: A Tale of the Haves and Have-Mores. McKinsey & Company, New York.

Marsh, 2016. MMC Cyber Handbook 2016 increasing resilience in the digital economy. Retrieved from: <https://www.marsh.com/us/insights/research/mmc-cyber-risk-handbook-2016.html>.

Miami-Dade Community College, 2003. Social science department: disciplines. Retrieved November 25, 2003, from: <http://www.mdcc.edu/kendall/social/disciplines.htm>.

Michael, N., 2018. General Data Protection Regulation (GDPR) requirements, deadlines, and facts. Retrieved from: <https://www.csoonline.com/article/3202771/data-protection/general-data-protection-regulation-gdpr-requirements-deadlines-and-facts.html?page = 2>.

Pelaez, M.H.S., 2010. Measuring Effectiveness in Information Security Controls. SANS Institute, North Bethesda, MD.

Richard, S., Raj, B., Claus, H., 2016. Evolving changes in cyber risk management. Retrieved from: <https://www.mmc.com/content/dam/mmc-web/Global-Risk-Center/Files/MMC-GRC-Evolving-challenges-in-cyber-risk-management-2016.pdf>.

Risk Control, n.d. Retrieved June 20, 2017, from: <https://www.irmi.com/online/insurance-glossary/terms/r/risk-control.aspx>.

Silvius, A.J.G., 2006. Does ROI matter? Insights into the true business value of IT. Electron. J. Inform. Syst. Eval. 9 (2), 93−104.

Starner, T., 2015. Cyber risk models remain elusive. Retrieved July 5, 2017, from: <http://riskandinsurance.com/cyber-risk-models-remain-elusive/>.

Index

Note: Page numbers followed by "*f*" and "*t*" refer to figures and tables, respectively.

A

AAA. *See* American Accounting Association (AAA)
Abundance law
  attention of human consumer, 46
  digitally empowered entity, 46
  humans' comprehension and power supply, 46
  intrinsic digital value, 46
Acceptable risk, 51–52, 68
Access control, broken, 66
Accessibility, 20, 20*t*
Accuracy, 157
ACID. *See* Atomicity, consistency, isolation, and durability (ACID)
Affordable Care Act (2010), 134
Agility, 19
AHP. *See* Analytic Hierarchy Process (AHP)
AI. *See* Artificial intelligence (AI)
AICPA. *See* American Institute of Certified Public Accountants (AICPA)
ALE. *See* Annual Loss Expectancy (ALE)
American Accounting Association (AAA), 91
American Institute of Certified Public Accountants (AICPA), 91
Analytic Hierarchy Process (AHP), 80
Analytical capabilities, 158
Annual Loss Expectancy (ALE), 79
Application Programing Interfaces (APIs), 64–65
AR. *See* Augmented reality (AR)
Artificial intelligence (AI), 8, 31–32, 47
Asset(s), 5
  asset-centric, 62
  data, 8
  digitally enabled devices, 8
  hardware, 7
  information, 6
  intangible, 32, 145
  intangible digital, 6, 11
  metadata, 8
  (networked) system assets, 7
  robotic, 8
  service, 7–8
  software, 7
  supportive, 144
  valuation methods, 5
Atomicity, consistency, isolation, and durability (ACID), 19
Attack simulation, 63

Attacker-centric, 62
Augmented reality (AR), 45
Authentication, broken, 65

B

B2B. *See* Business-to-business (B2B)
Balance sheet-oriented approach, 94
Barter transactions, 143
Baseline controls, 92
Basic CIS controls, 92*t*
Benchmark selection, difficulty in, 96
Benchmarking, 106
BIPM. *See* Bureau International des Poids et Mesures (BIPM)
Bit rot, 16
Bitmort (BM), 123–125, 127, 153–155
  digital assets
    articulating entity's "willingness-to-pay" for risk reduction for, 125, 155
    measuring cost-effectiveness of controls for, 125, 155
    measuring strength of controls for, 125, 155
  using on portfolio of entities, 126, 156
Bitmort$_D$ (BM$_D$), 124
Black swan theory, 42–43
BM. *See* Bitmort (BM)
Book value. *See* Historical cost
Breakpoints, 128
Bureau International des Poids et Mesures (BIPM), 117
Business Impact Analysis (BIA), 35, 148
Business risk, 130
  cyber risk as critical, 75–76
Business value, 24–25
Business-to-business (B2B), 30–31

C

Cancer Care Group (2015), 134
CBA. *See* Cost-benefit analysis (CBA)
CCDCOE. *See* Cooperative Cyber Defence Centre of Excellence (CCDCOE)
Centers for Medicare and Medicaid Services (CMS), 134
Central Intelligence Agency triad (CIA triad), 60, 87
CGPM. *See* Conference Generale des Poids et Mesures (CGPM)

Chief Information Security Officer (CISO), 81
CIA triad. *See* Central Intelligence Agency triad (CIA triad)
CIS Critical Security Controls, 92, 92*t*
CISO. *See* Chief Information Security Officer (CISO)
Clear ownership to implement controls, 105
CMS. *See* Centers for Medicare and Medicaid Services (CMS)
COBIT. *See* Control Objectives for Information and Related Technology (COBIT)
Committee of Sponsoring Organizations of the Treadway Commission (COSO), 53, 54*f*, 89, 91
Commodity, 4
Common Vulnerability Scoring System (CVSS), 63–64, 83
Complexity economics, new era of, 44
Compliance goals, 96
Comprehensive general liability (CGL), 164
Computer code, 160
Computer science/engineering, risk in, 50–51
Conference Generale des Poids et Mesures (CGPM), 117
Confidence level, 119
Consumption externality. *See* Direct network externality
Continual service improvement, 91
Continuous monitoring, 70
Control Objectives for Information and Related Technology (COBIT), 89–90
Control(s)
  compensating, 88
  cost-effective controls, 93–94
  definition, 87–88
  factors, 84, 152
  measuring benefits, 95–98
  measuring cost, 94–95
  objectives for information and related technology, 89
  scenario analysis for control assessment, 85–86
  score metrics, 95*t*
  selection and implementation, 92–93
  types, 88–91
Cooperative Cyber Defence Centre of Excellence (CCDCOE), 132
CORAS method, 83
Core value activities and supportive value activities, 34*t*

Core value assets (CVs), 12, 144
Corrective controls, 88
COSO. *See* Committee of Sponsoring Organizations of the Treadway Commission (COSO)
Cost, 3
  accounting methods, 112
  in anticipation, 80*t*
  quantification, 104, 104*t*
  in response, 80*t*
Cost models
  expected loss, 79–82
  expected severe loss, 79
  for incidents and losses, 78–82
    cost of cybercrime, 78–79
    loss categories, 79
  for investment
    benchmarking, 106
    CBA, 107
    comparisons of ROI, NPV and IRR, 109–110, 110*t*
    full cost accounting model, 111–112
    Gordon and Loeb model, 110–111
    IRR, 109
    NPV, 108
    quantitative risk assessment, 107, 107*t*
    ROSI, 107–108
  market value, loss in, 82
  perceived composite risk, 80–82
  for projection, 112
  standard deviation of loss, 79
Cost to break (CTB), 95
Cost-based models, 25–26
  TCO, 26
Cost-based valuation, 5*t*
Cost-benefit analysis (CBA), 69, 107
Cost-effective controls, 93–94
Covariance approach, 122
Credit risk, 53*t*, 130
Criminal reward funds coverage, 162
Cross-divisional nature, 104
Cross-jurisdictional economies of scale without mass, 32, 145
Cross-Site Scripting (XSS), 66
CTB. *See* Cost to break (CTB)
Customization, demand for, 46
CVs. *See* Core value assets (CVs)
CVSS. *See* Common Vulnerability Scoring System (CVSS)
Cyber attacks, 131
Cyber criminals, 131
Cyber-extortion coverage, 162
Cyber incident cost categories, 80*t*
Cyber infrastructure as public good and privatization of Internet, 138
Cyber insurance
  asymmetric information, 167
    adverse selection, 167
    moral hazard, 167
  claim study, 165
  claims, 165
  coverage offered by, 161*t*
  current policy coverage, 161–162
  cybernomics and future growth of, 167

history and context of, 159–161
  first party, 159
  third party, 159
lack of sufficient quality actuarial data, 166–167
  limited reinsurance capacity, 166
  low insurance limits, 167
  pricing of premium, 166
  risk correlation, 166
overall number of records exposed and associated costs, 165*t*
policy limits, 163
policy offerings from top cyber insurers, 162*t*
reputation loss as part of first-party loss, 163
standalone and package cyber coverage combined (year-end 2015), 163*t*
types of breaches leads to claims, 162–163
underwriting and assessment process, 164
  assessing current coverage, 164
  conducting thorough information security risk audit, 164
  evaluating available policies, 164
  selecting appropriate policies, 164–165
Cyber regulations
  Cybersecurity Act of 2015, 133
  FISMA Reform, 133
  General Data Protection Regulation (GDPR), 132–133
  Gramm–Leach–Bliley Act (GLBA), 134
  Health Insurance Portability and Accountability Act (HIPPA), 134
  NIS Directive, 134
Cyber risk
  Bitmort and Hekla, 123–125
  as critical business risk, 75–76
  determination, 106–112
  micromort, 120–121
  quadrant, 84–86, 85*t*, 151–152
  risk calculations, 125–126
  risk metrology, 117–120
  VaR, 122–123
Cyber risk cost optimization, models for
  cost models
    for investment, 106–112
    for projection, 112
  risk management options and associated cost, 113
Cyber-risk insurance, 163
Cyber risk investment, point of diminishing return on
  challenges for cyber risk management cost optimization, 104–106
  cost of security configurations, 113–115
  economics of information security, 99–102
  information security/risk management budget, 102–103
  median budget and percentage allocating to security, 103*t*
  models for cyber risk cost optimization, 106–113
Cyber risk management, 53–55, 55*f*, 57–70
  cost optimization challenges, 104–106
  limitations of approaches, 106

in quantifying optimal level of investment, 105–106
  in quantifying security costs, 104–105
ERM, 52–55, 53*t*
history and definitions of risk, 49–52
options, 115
risk analysis, 55–56
risk models, 70–72
Cyber risk measurement
  comparison with applications, 154*t*
  cost models for incidents and losses, 78–82
  methods for, 82–84
    CORAS method, 83
    CVSS, 83
    cyber value at risk, 83
    FAIR, 84
    Monte Carlo simulation, 83
    stochastic modeling, 82
  need and current challenges, 77–78
    accurate estimates requiring access to data and knowledge, 78
    current methods focus on technology, 77–78
    domain-based risk assessment, 78
    lack of common point of reference, 78
    PCR, 79
  uniqueness of cyber risk, 76–77
    scale, 77
    transdisciplinarity, 77
    velocity, 77
Cyber security, 95, 104–105
  controls, 87
  drivers and focus areas of cyber security spending, 103*t*
Cyber terrorism, 136
Cyber value at risk, 83
Cyber VaR, 83, 123
Cyber-insurance, 54
Cyberattack, 62
Cybercrime cost, 78–79
Cybernomics, 127, 153
  Bitmort and Hekla, 153–155
  characteristics of fourth industrial revolution, 145–146
  cyber risk quadrant, 151–152
  databank, 140, 151
  digital theory of value, 148–151
  digital value matrix, 144–145
  global level, 134–138
  limitations
    accuracy, 157
    analytical capabilities, 158
    economic lifespan of digital assets, 158
    fundamental inherent differences of digital assets, 158
    testing and validation, 158
  measuring digital economy, 148
  models for digital asset valuation, 146–148
  portfolio level, 128–134
  risk calculations, 155–156
  scenario analysis for control assessment and loss quantification, 152
  unique attributes of digital assets, 142–144
  views, 105, 139*f*, 156–157, 156*f*

entity level, 138–139, 157
  global level, 140, 157
  portfolio level, 139, 157
Cybersecurity Act of 2015, 133

D

DAM. *See* Digital assets management (DAM)
DAs. *See* Digitized assets (DAs)
Data. *See also* Information
  assets, 8
  about data, 8
  decay, 16
  degradation, 16
  format, 21, 21*t*
  with IP, 32
  quality, 14, 14*t*
  rot, 16
  science, 43
  sharing, 137–138
  volume, 18, 18*t*
Data flow diagram (DFD), 60–61
Data Protection Act, 112
DDoS. *See* Distributed Denial of Service (DDoS)
Decision model for optimal risk management strategies, 115
Decision theory, 51–52
  difference between frequency and probability, 52*t*
  differences between risk concepts, 52*t*
Deductive approach, 55
Deep learning, 47
Defense-in-depth approach, 113
Delivery cadence, 22, 22*t*
Denial of service, 62, 162
Dependability, 19
Deserialization, insecure, 66
Detective controls, 89*t*
Deterrent controls, 88
DFD. *See* Data flow diagram (DFD)
Digital access, 38
Digital asset valuation
  current methods, 23–28
    business performance value, 24–25
    cost-based models, 25–26
    direct conversion of financial value, 24
    income-based models, 27
    intrinsic value, 24
    market-based models, 26–27
    option models, 27–28
  as economic goods, 14–22
  examples, 36*t*
  existing challenges, 23
    inherent challenges, 23
    market challenges, 23
    regulatory and standardization challenges, 23
    taxation challenges, 23
  models, 33–35, 146–148
    extrinsic value, 34, 147
    intrinsic value, 33, 146–147

opportunity value, 35, 147–148
  subjective value, 35, 147
Digital assets, 6–9, 7*f*, 31
  articulating entity's "willingness-to-pay" for risk reduction, 125, 155
  and associated cyber loss events, 86*t*, 153*t*
  categorization, 7–8
    (networked) system assets, 7
    data assets, 8
    digitally enabled devices, 8
    hardware assets, 7
    metadata assets, 8
    robotic assets, 8
    service assets, 7–8
    software assets, 7
  categorization based on economic functions, 144–145
  economic good, 4–5
  economic lifespan, 158
  examples as economic goods, 9*t*
  fundamental inherent differences, 158
  managing digital assets in organization, 8–9
    DAM, 9
    IRM, 8–9
  measuring cost-effectiveness of controls for, 125, 155
  measuring strength of controls for, 125, 155
  origins and philosophical concepts of value, 2–4
Digital assets management (DAM), 9
Digital contracts, 38
Digital economy, 30–31, 46, 48, 151
  measurement, 35–40, 148
    digital-native industries, 38–40
    invisible economy, 40
    rate of digitalization of traditional industries, 35–38, 38*f*
  progress, 42
    measuring against machine time, 149
Digital markets, 30–31
Digital media, 31
Digital revenue, 37
Digital revolution, 31
Digital sector, 30–31
Digital theory of value, 40–48, 148–151
  fourth industrial revolution, 31–33
  law of abundance, 46, 150–151
  law of hyperconnectivity, 43–45, 150
  law of machine time, 40–43, 149
  law of new division of labor, 47–48, 151
  law of recombination, 43, 149
  law of subjectivity, 45–46, 150
  measuring digital economy, 35–40
  models for digital asset valuation, 33–35
Digital valuation model, 148*t*
Digital value, 143
  creation
    increasing through usage, 10, 142
    location-independent, 45, 150
  distributed via multi-sided markets, 10
  distributing multi-sided markets, 143
  duplication increasing, 142
  duplication not increasing, 10

limitless, 11
  opportunities to distributing and consuming, 11, 144
  utility to owner, 11, 143
  matrix, 11–14, 12*t*, 144–145
    global level, digital asset on, 14, 14*t*
    individual level, digital asset on, 13, 13*t*
    national level, digital asset on, 14, 14*t*
    organizational level, digital asset on, 13, 13*t*
  production and distribution, 10, 142–143
"Digital-detox", 151
Digital-enabling infrastructure, 30
Digital-native assets (NAs), 12, 144
Digital-native industries measurement, 38–40
  most valued start-ups, 39*t*
  platform revolution, 38–40, 39*t*
Digitalization, 30
  of traditional industries, 35–38, 38*f*
Digitally empowered entity, 46
Digitally enabled devices, 8
Digitization, 30–31, 33
Digitized assets (DAs), 12, 144
Direct cost, 80*t*
Direct financial conversion, 33, 147
Direct network effect. *See* Direct network externality
Direct network externality, 32–33, 146
Disruption, 38
Distributed Denial of Service (DDoS), 76, 160
Distribution channel, 128
DNS, 102
Domain-based risk assessment, 78
Duplication not increasing digital value, 10

E

E-commerce, 30–31
  platform-enabled, 30–31
Economic functions
  categorization of digital assets based on, 11–14
  digital assets categorization based on, 144–145
Economic good, 4–5
  digital assets valuation as, 14–22
    attributes of digital assets contributing to extrinsic digital value creation, 19–22
    attributes of digital assets contributing to intrinsic digital value creation, 14–19
Economic lifespan of digital assets, 158
Economics, 100
  of information security, 99–102
  of scale, 21, 21*t*
EF. *See* Exposure factor (EF)
Effectiveness assessment, 70
Electronic data, 160
Elevation of privilege (EoP), 62
Engine for growth
  hyperconnectivity, 150
  recombination, 149
Enterprise control environment, 87–88
  value and risk drivers for, 87–88, 88*t*

Enterprise risk management (ERM), 52–55, 53*t*, 87–88, 125
  cyber risk management, 53–55, 55*f*
Enterprise/information security architectures, 63
Entity (E)
  cost of risk reduction, 125, 155
  cyber risk
    appetite, 125, 155
    limit, 125, 155
    pricing, 125, 155
    return on investment, 126, 156
  digital value, 138
  level, 105, 138–139
  view, 157
  willingness-to-pay, 150
    for risk reduction, 125, 155
EoP. *See* Elevation of privilege (EoP)
EPO. *See* European Patent Office (EPO)
Equilibrium, 3
ERM. *See* Enterprise risk management (ERM)
Ethnography, 149
European Patent Office (EPO), 8
Exclusivity, 19, 20*t*
Expected loss, 79–82
Expected severe loss, 79
Expensive manual data collection, 97
"Expert judgement", 55
Exponential function, 40–41
  exponential growth represented in logarithmic graph, 42*f*
Exposure factor (EF), 79
Extrinsic consumption from usage value, 147
Extrinsic digital value, 11, 46, 144. *See also* Intrinsic digital value
  accessibility, 20, 20*t*
  data format, 21, 21*t*
  delivery cadence, 22, 22*t*
  economies of scale, 21, 21*t*
  exclusivity, 19, 20*t*
  level of structure, 22, 22*t*
  network connectivity, 20, 20*t*
  power supplies, 22, 22*t*
  reproduction cost, 21, 21*t*
Extrinsic market value, 147
Extrinsic value, 4, 34, 147
  generic business model, 34*f*
  market value, 34
  usage value, 34

F

Facebook–Cambridge Analytica data scandal, 137
Factor Analysis of Information Risk (FAIR), 84
Financial audit, 87–88
Financial Executives International (FEI), 91
Financial impact, worms causing significant, 135*t*
Financial risk, 129–130
Financial Services Modernization Act of 1999. *See* Gramm–Leach–Bliley Act (GLBA)

Financial services sector, systemic cyber risk in, 129–130, 130*t*
Financial value, direct conversion of, 24
FIPS 199 Impact Levels, 90*t*
First Industrial Revolution, 31
First-party coverage, 161–162
First-party insurance policy, 159, 167
First-party loss scenarios, 80*t*
FISMA Reform, 133
Formal standards, 54
Foundational CIS controls, 92*t*
Fourth Industrial Revolution, 31–33, 43, 145–146
  consumption externality, 32–33, 146
  cross-jurisdictional economies of scale without mass, 32, 145
  digitization of everything, 30–31
  heavy reliance on intangible assets, 32, 145
  importance of data, user participation, and synergies, 32, 145
  indirect network effects, 33, 146
  lock-in effects and competition, 33, 146
  velocity, 32, 145
"Free goods", 4–5
Fuel for innovative breakthroughs, 43
Full cost accounting model, 111–112
  layers of costs considering for, 111*t*
Functionality, usability, reliability, performance, and supportability (FURPS), 19
Fusion of technologies, 32, 43, 146

G

Game theory in security investment, 106
General Data Protection Regulation (GDPR), 132–133
Geopolitical, 45
GLBA. *See* Gramm–Leach–Bliley Act (GLBA)
Global positioning system (GPS), 7–8
Global view of cybernomics, 106, 140, 157
  cyber infrastructure as public good and privatization of internet, 138
  infrastructural cyber threats, 134–137
  risk data schemes and data sharing, 137–138
Globalized societies, new era of, 43–44
Gordon and Loeb model, 110–111
GPS. *See* Global positioning system (GPS)
Graham–Leach–Bliley Act, 160
Gramm–Leach–Bliley Act (GLBA), 134
Guardians of Peace (GOP), 162–163

H

Hardware, 94
  assets, 7
Health Insurance Portability and Accountability Act (HIPAA), 134, 160
Healthcare sector, systemic cyber risks in, 131–132
Heat map, 68, 70
Heavy reliance on intangible assets, 145
Hekla, 123–125, 139, 153–155

articulating entity's cyber risk
  appetite, 125, 155
  limit, 125, 155
  measuring entity's cost of risk reduction, 125, 155
  measuring entity's cyber risk
  pricing, 125, 155
  return on investment, 126, 156
  using on portfolio of entities, 126, 156
Higher fixed costs, digital value production and distribution entails, 142–143
HIPAA. *See* Health Insurance Portability and Accountability Act (HIPAA)
Historical cost, 5
Holistic thinking, 113
Human consumer attention, 46, 151
Human's comprehension, 46, 150–151
Hyperconnectivity, 45
  digital value creation, 45
  new era of complexity economics, 44
  new era of globalized societies, 43–44
  nontechnical barriers, 45

I

IBRD. *See* International Bank for Reconstruction and Development (IBRD)
ICCI. *See* International Classification of Cyber Incidents (ICCI)
ICD. *See* International Classification of Disease (ICD)
ICT. *See* Information and communications technologies (ICT)
IDAC. *See* International Digital Asset Classification (IDAC)
IDS. *See* Intrusion detection systems (IDS)
IIA. *See* Institute of Internal Auditors (IIA)
IMA. *See* Institute of Management Accountants (IMA)
IMF. *See* International Monetary Fund (IMF)
Income-based models, 27
Incomplete output, 96–97
Indirect cost, 80*t*
Indirect network
  effects, 33, 146
  externalities, 143
Inductive approach, 55
Information. *See also* Data
  asset, 6
  disclosure, 62
  literacy, 9
  set, 110–111
Information and communications technologies (ICT), 30–31
Information resource management (IRM), 8–9
Information security, 104, 112
  budget, 102–103
  economics, 99–102
  management system, 93
  risk, 50–51
Information Systems Audit and Control Association (ISACA), 89–90
Information technology (IT), 6, 31, 57

security management, 99–100
security process-oriented approach, 95
    cost associated with IT security activities,
        95t
threats and consequences, 58t
value grid, 25
Information Technology Infrastructure Library
    (ITIL), 89, 91
Infrastructural cyber threats
    cyber terrorism, 136
    major worms, 134–135
    mega data breaches, 136–137, 136t
    technology giants, privacy concerns of, 137
Inherent challenges for digital asset valuation,
    23
Inherent factors, 84, 152
Injection flaws, 65
Institute of Internal Auditors (IIA), 91
Institute of Management Accountants (IMA),
    91
Insurers, 166
Intangible assets, heavy reliance on, 32, 145
Intangible cost, 80t
Intangible digital assets, 6, 11
Intellectual property (IP), 8, 32
    heavy reliance on intangible assets, 145
    importance of data, user participation, and
        synergies, 145
    importance of data, user participation, and
        synergies with, 32
Internal audit, 87–88, 97–98
Internal rate of return (IRR), 109
    comparisons with ROI and NPV, 109–110,
        110t
International Accounting Standards Board, 5
International Bank for Reconstruction and
    Development (IBRD), 32
International Classification of Cyber Incidents
    (ICCI), 84–85
International Classification of Disease (ICD),
    84–85
International Digital Asset Classification
    (IDAC), 138, 144–145
International Monetary Fund (IMF), 32
International System (SI), 117, 118t
International Vocabulary of Metrology (VIM),
    118
Internet of Things (IoT), 30, 77
Internet privatization, cyber infrastructure as,
    138
Internet professional liability, 161
Internet Protocol (IP), 128
Intrinsic cost of production, 147
Intrinsic digital value, 11, 46, 144, 150.
    See also Extrinsic digital value
    age, 15–17
    aging attributes and measurements, 18t
    data quality, 14, 14t
    data volume, 18, 18t
    production cost, 19
    risk exposure, 15, 16t
    system quality, 19, 19t
Intrinsic value, 4, 24, 33, 146–147
    direct financial conversion, 33
    intrinsic cost of production, 33

Intrusion detection systems (IDS), 107–108
Intuitive approach, 55
Investment, cost models for, 106–112
Invisible economy measurement, 40
IoT. See Internet of Things (IoT)
IP. See Intellectual property (IP); Internet
    Protocol (IP)
IRM. See Information resource management
    (IRM)
IRR. See Internal rate of return (IRR)
ISACA. See Information Systems Audit and
    Control Association (ISACA)
ISO/IEC 27001 standard, 93
ISO/IEC 27002 control, 91, 91t
ISO/IEC 27004 standard, 96
IT. See Information technology (IT)
IT Governance Institute (ITGI), 89–90
ITIL. See Information Technology
    Infrastructure Library (ITIL)

K

Key Cyber Risk Factors (KCRF), 84–85, 151
Key performance indicators (KPIs), 24

L

Labor
    law of new division of, 47–48
        accuracy, 48
        deep learning and machine intelligence,
            47
        digital economy, 48
        labor increasingly less important factor in
            value production, 47
        optimal path to value creation, 48
        social necessities and barrier to
            entry, 47
    theory of value, 2
Law
    of abundance, 150–151
    of hyperconnectivity, 150
    of machine time, 150
    of new division of labor, 151
    of recombination, 149
    of subjectivity, 150
Layered system of defenses architecture, 113
LC security solution. See Low-cost security
    solution (LC security solution)
Legal controls, 88
Legal frameworks, 45
Legal metrology, 119
Likelihood determination, 66–67
Line of Defense (LoD), 97–98, 97t
Liquidity risk, 130
Lloyds Banking Group, 160
Lock-in effects and competition, 33, 146
LoD. See Line of Defense (LoD)
Logging and monitoring, insufficient, 66
Long-term cost, 80t
Loss quantification, scenario analysis for,
    85–86
Low-cost security solution (LC security
    solution), 109
Lower variable costs, 142–143

M

Machine intelligence. See Artificial intelligence
    (AI)
Machine time
    digital economy progress measuring against,
        149
    progress of digital economy, 42
    risk management, 42–43
    sensemaking increasingly universal
        challenge and value driver, 42
    underlying exponential function, 40–41
Macroeconomics, 3
    risks, 53t
Managed security services (MSS), 96
Marginal benefit, 3
Marginal cost, 3
Marginal utility, principle of diminishing, 3
Market challenges for digital asset valuation, 23
Market risk, 53t, 130
Market-based models, 26–27
    market for personal data, 27
Market-based valuation, 6t
Market value, loss in, 82
Maturity models/frameworks, 54
Measurement, 96
    benefits of controls, 95–98
    cost of controls, 94–95
    uncertainty, 119
Medical risk measurement to cyber, 84–86,
    151–152
    using scenario analysis for control
        assessment and loss quantification,
        85–86
Mega data breaches, 136–137, 136t
"Mere guesses", 55
Metadata assets, 8
Metric, 96
Metrological traceability, 119
Metrology, 117–119
Microeconomic(s), 3
    loss quantification method, 153t
    risks, 53t
Microlife, 121, 122t
Micromort, 120–121, 121t
    comparing of cyber risk measurement with
        application, 123t
    microlife, 121, 122t
    VSL, 121
    willingness-to-pay and value, 120–121
Misleading metrics, 96
Mission/business processes, 63
Modifiable risk factors, 84
Money, 3
Monte Carlo simulation, 83, 123
Moore's law, 17, 17f
MSS. See Managed security services (MSS)
Multi-sided markets, digital value distribution
    via, 10, 143
Multidimensional concept, risk as, 50
Multiplying factor, 147

N

NAs. See Digital-native assets (NAs)
National cyber security strategy, 132

National digital strategies and policies, 132
National Institute of Standards and
    Technologies (NIST), 79, 89, 92, 119,
    128
    life cycle approach, 93*f*
Natural science, 50
NCL. *See* NICE Classification (NCL)
Negligible risk, 68
Net present value (NPV), 100, 108
    comparisons with ROI and IRR, 109−110,
    110*t*
Network connectivity, 20, 20*t*
Network externality, 101
Network security coverage, 161−162
(Networked) system assets, 7
New York Stock Exchange, 123
NICE Classification (NCL), 11
NIS Directive, 134
NIST. *See* National Institute of Standards and
    Technologies (NIST)
NIST SP 800−53 control, 90, 90*t*
Non-modifiable risk factors, 84
Non-neutral pricing strategies, 10, 143
Non-technological factors, 84, 85*t*, 152
Nontechnical barriers, 45, 150
Nontechnical controls, 88, 89*t*
Nontechnological factors, 84
NPV. *See* Net present value (NPV)

O
OASIS, 7−8
Open Web Application Security Project
    (OWASP), 64−66
    evolution of vulnerabilities, 65*t*
    Top 10, 64−65
Operational risk, 53*t*
Operational statistics, 96
Opportunity cost, 3
Opportunity value, 35, 40, 147−148
    Business Impact Analysis (BIA), 35
    digital valuation model, 35*t*
Option models, 27−28
Organizations, 67
    CIS controls, 92*t*
    control environment, 87−88
    governance structures, 63
Outsourcing, 94, 104−105
OWASP. *See* Open Web Application Security
    Project (OWASP)

P
P2P. *See* Peer-to-peer (P2P)
PaaS. *See* Platform-as-a-Service (PaaS)
PASTA. *See* Process for Attack Simulation and
    Threat Analysis (PASTA)
PCR. *See* Perceived composite risk
    (PCR)
PDCA cycle. *See* Plan, Do, Check, Act cycle
    (PDCA cycle)
Peer-to-peer (P2P), 30−31
Penetration testing, 97
Perceived composite risk (PCR), 79

probability of losses under four cyber
    proposals, 81*t*
    value of three individual risk measures, 81*t*
Performance
    measures, 96
Permanent cost, 80*t*
Personal costs, 94
Personal data, market for, 27
PFD. *See* Process flow diagram (PFD)
Physical controls, 88
Plan, Do, Check, Act cycle (PDCA cycle), 93
Platform revolution, 38−40, 39*t*
Platform-as-a-Service (PaaS), 7−8
Portfolio of entities, using Bitmort and Hekla
    on, 126, 156
Portfolio view of cybernomics, 105−106, 139,
    157
    cyber regulations, 132−134
    national digital strategies and policies, 132
    supplier risk, 128−129
    systemic risk, 129−132
Power
    supply, 22, 22*t*, 46, 150−151
Predisposing condition, 67
Preventive controls, 88, 89*t*
Price, 3
Pricing of insurance products, 166−167
Process flow diagram (PFD), 62−63
Process for Attack Simulation and Threat
    Analysis (PASTA), 62−63
Production cost, 19
Projection, cost models for, 112
Public breach, 163
Public relations/crisis-communication
    coverage, 162
Pure private goods, 4−5

Q
Qualitative and quantitative approaches,
    comparison between, 71*t*
Qualitative and quantitative risk management
    methodologies, 71*t*
Qualitative assessment, 71
Qualitative models, 70
Quality data, 43
Quantitative assessment, 70
Quantitative models, 70
Quantitative risk assessment, 107, 107*t*
Quantity, 3

R
RAMS. *See* Reliability, availability,
    maintainability, and safety (RAMS)
RASR. *See* Reliability, availability, scalability,
    and recoverability (RASR)
RASUI. *See* Reliability, availability,
    serviceability, usability, and
    installability (RASUI)
Recombination, 43
    fusion of technologies, 43
    quality data, 43
Recovery controls, 88

Regulations, 45
Regulatory and compliance risk, 53*t*
Regulatory and standardization challenges for
    digital asset valuation, 23
Regulatory requirements, 54
Reinsurers, 166
Reliability, availability, maintainability, and
    safety (RAMS), 19
Reliability, availability, scalability, and
    recoverability (RASR), 19
Reliability, availability, serviceability,
    usability, and installability (RASUI), 19
Reliance on subjective judgments, 97
Reproduction cost, 21, 21*t*
Repudiation, 62
Residual risk, 69−70
    analysis, 63
Resource valuation, 72
Return on investment (ROI), 107
    comparisons with NPV and IRR, 109−110,
    110*t*
Return on security investment (ROSI),
    99−100, 107−108
Risk, 49, 50*t*
    acceptance, 69
    analysis, 55−56
    event tree example, 56*f*
    assessment, 56
    averse, 52
    avoidance, 69
    in computer science/engineering, 50−51
    control, 87, 88*t*
    data schemes, 137−138
    decision theory and acceptable risk, 51−52
    drivers, 87−88
    exposure, 15, 16*t*
    identification tools, 55
    lack of integrated governance and
        management processes, 129
    limitation/reduction, 69
    as multidimensional concept, 50
    in natural sciences and social sciences, 51*t*
    neutral, 52
    onerous and resource intensive processes,
        128−129
    only being relatively objective, 51, 51*f*
    optimal level of investment in, 105−106
    retention, 115
    scale example, 68*t*
    seeking, 52
    transfer, 69
Risk calculations, 125−126, 155−156
    articulating entity's cyber risk
        appetite, 125, 155
        limit, 125, 155
    using Bitmort and Hekla on portfolio of
        entities, 126, 156
    digital assets
        articulating entity's "willingness-to-pay"
            for risk reduction, 125, 155
        measuring cost-effectiveness of controls
            for, 125, 155
        measuring strength of controls for, 125,
            155

measuring entity's cost of risk reduction, 125, 155
measuring entity's cyber risk
　pricing, 125, 155
　return on investment, 126, 156
Risk management, 42–43, 57–70, 104, 149
　continuous monitoring, 70
　effectiveness assessment, 70
　options and associated cost, 113
　risk assessment, 57–68
　　impact analysis, 67
　　likelihood determination, 66–67
　　process, 57
　　risk classification, 57, 58*t*
　　risk determination, 67–68
　　system characterization, 57
　　threat identification, 57–63
　　vulnerability assessment, 63–66, 64*t*
　risk mitigation, 68–70
Risk management budget, 102–103
Risk metrology
　metrology, 117–119
　traceability and calibration, 119
　uncertainty, 119
Risk models
　advantages and disadvantages, 72*t*
　models, 71–72
　　perspective, 72
　　resource valuation, 72
　　risk measurement, 72
　qualitative and quantitative models, 70
　qualitative assessment, 71
　quantitative assessment, 70
Robotic assets, 8
ROI. *See* Return on investment (ROI)
ROSI. *See* Return on security investment (ROSI)
Routing, 102
Royal Society, 54–55

S
SAs. *See* Supportive value assets (SAs)
Scientific method, 50
Scientific metrology, 118
Second Industrial Revolution, 31
Security. *See also* Threat(s)
　configuration cost, 113–115
　　decision model for optimal risk management strategies, 115
　firms, 97
　game theory in security investment, 106
　measure life-cycle approach, 94
　misconfiguration, 66
　optimal level of investment in, 105–106
　performance metrics, 96–97
　security-centric, 62
Security Breach Information Act, 160
Security costs, challenges in quantifying, 104–105
　cyber security and risk management, 104
　difficulties in finding right scope and baseline, 105
　divergent goals exist for cost quantification, 104

lack of resources and clear ownership to implement controls, 105
lack of transparency on hidden costs, 104–105
SEI. *See* Software Engineering Institute (SEI)
Semi-private goods, 4–5
Sensemaking increasing universal challenge and value driver, 149
Sensitive data exposure, 65
Service
　assets, 7–8
　design, 91
　operation, 91
　strategy, 91
　transition, 91
Short-term cost, 80*t*
SI. *See* International System (SI)
Single loss expectancy (SLE), 79
Social necessities and barrier to entry, 47
Social science, 50
Socio-economic risk factors, 77–78
Software, 94
　assets, 7
　market, 106
Software Engineering Institute (SEI), 113–114
Software/architecture-centric, 62
Spoofing, 62
Spoofing, Tampering, Repudiation, Information disclosure, Denial of service, EoP (STRIDE), 62
Standard deviation of loss, 79
Statistical life value, 121
Stochastic modeling for cyber risk measurement, 82
Strategic risk, 53*t*
STRIDE. *See* Spoofing, Tampering, Repudiation, Information disclosure, Denial of service, EoP (STRIDE)
Subjective value, 35, 147
Subjectivity, 45–46
　demand for customization, 46
　greater component of value, 46
Supplier risk, 128–129
　comprehensive catalogue of third-party risks, 128
　comprehensive inventory of third parties, 128
Supply and demand, 3
Supply chain, 128
　management, 128
Supportive assets, 144
Supportive value assets (SAs), 12, 144
Symptomatic breach, 162–163
System characterization, 57
Systemic breach, 163
System quality, 19, 19*t*
Systemic cyber risk, 129
Systemic risk, 53*t*, 129–132
　systemic cyber risk
　　in financial services sector, 129–130, 130*t*
　　in healthcare sector, 131–132
　　in transportation sector, 130–131

T
Tampering, 62
Tangible cost, 80*t*
Tangible digital ach, 6
Taxation challenges for digital asset valuation, 23
TCO. *See* Total cost of ownership (TCO)
Technical controls, 88, 89*t*
Technological factors, 84, 85*t*, 152
Technology giants, privacy concerns of, 137
Terrorism Risk Insurance Act (TRIA), 162
Theory of value, 2
Third Industrial Revolution, 31
Third parties comprehensive inventory, 128
Third-party coverage, 162
Third-party insurance policy, 159, 167
Third-party loss scenarios, 80*t*
Third-party risks, comprehensive catalogue of, 128
Threat(s), 51
　analysis, 63
　　based on CIA, 61*t*
　　using CIA, 61*t*
　identification, 57–63
　　PASTA, 62–63
　　STRIDE, 62
　　Trike model, 63
　　underlying principle of VAST, 63
　modeling, 60–62
　threat-vulnerability pairing, 66–67
　and vulnerability models, 54
Total cost of ownership (TCO), 26, 94
　cost categories of IT, 26
Total Value of Ownership (TVO), 26
Traceability and calibration, 119
Trading, 3
Transdisciplinarity, 77
Transitory cost, 80*t*
Transportation sector, systemic cyber risk in, 130–131
Trike model, 63

U
Unacceptable risk, 68
Uncertainty, 119
　interval, 119
US Department of Health and Human Services, 131
Usage value, extrinsic consumption from, 147
User participation with IP, 32
Utility-based valuation, 6*t*

V
Value
　chain, 128
　drivers, 87–88, 88*t*
　　of intangible assets, 24*t*
　greater component of, 46
　labor increasingly less important factor in value production, 47
　optimal path to value creation, 48, 151
　origins and philosophical concepts, 2–4, 3*t*
　　intrinsic value *vs.* extrinsic value, 4

Value (*Continued*)
  subjective view *vs.* objective view, 2–3
Value of statistical life (VSL), 121
Value-at-risk (VaR), 122–123, 138–139, 153
VAST principle. *See* Visual, agile, and simple threat principle (VAST principle)
Velocity, 32, 77, 145
Vendor, 7–8
VIM. *See* International Vocabulary of Metrology (VIM)
Virtual reality (VR), 30, 45
"Virus", 134
Visual, agile, and simple threat principle (VAST principle), 63

VR. *See* Virtual reality (VR)
VSL. *See* Value of statistical life (VSL)
Vulnerability, 51
  assessment, 63–66, 64*t*, 97
    CVSS, 63–64
    OWASP (2017), 65–66
    OWASP Top 10, 64–65
  identification, 63

W
Web content liability, 161
Western European Legal Metrology Cooperation (WELMEC), 119

WhatsApp, 10, 142–143
World Bank Group, 32
World Economic Forum's Partnering for Cyber Resilience initiative, 83
Worms, 134–135

X
XML External Entities (XXE), 66
XSS. *See* Cross-Site Scripting (XSS)

Z
"Zombie Zero" malware, 131

Printed in the United States
By Bookmasters